The Olympics
and the Cold War,
1948–1968

D1453063

The Olympics
and the Cold War,
1948–1968

*Sport as Battleground
in the U.S.–Soviet Rivalry*

ERIN ELIZABETH REDIHAN

McFarland & Company, Inc., Publishers
Jefferson, North Carolina

ISBN (print) 978-1-4766-6788-1
ISBN (ebook) 978-1-4766-2728-1

LIBRARY OF CONGRESS CATALOGUING DATA ARE AVAILABLE

British Library cataloguing data are available

Front cover: Olympic Stadium in Rome during the XVII
Olympiad's opening ceremonies on August 25, 1960
(photograph by Harold Egeberg)

Printed in the United States of America

*McFarland & Company, Inc., Publishers
Box 611, Jefferson, North Carolina 28640
www.mcfarlandpub.com*

For Anna Scullin

Acknowledgments

It's been said that writing is a solitary pursuit, but I have been extremely fortunate in never having felt lonely along the way. The process was a lengthy one and I am eternally grateful to have had so many family, friends, and colleagues offering help, support, and valuable editing tips. I extend my sincerest gratitude to all who read drafts, offered critique, helped sharpen the focus of this project, and gave endless encouragement, but I would be remiss if I did not thank a few by name for their Olympic-sized contributions.

To Dr. Doug Little, my academic adviser at Clark University, for his critical eye and excellent writing advice throughout the process of completing my doctoral dissertation, on which this work is based.

To the Clark University reference librarians for their gracious assistance in tracking down countless books and articles from across the country.

To the librarians at the LA84 Foundation in Los Angeles—Shirley Ito, Michael Salmon, and Wayne Wilson—for all their knowledge and answers to my questions both throughout multiple visits to the Foundation's library and remotely.

To the librarians at the Olympic Studies Centre in Lausanne, Switzerland, for all of their help during my time at their archive and thorough answers to my questions afterwards.

To Al and Lynda Scullin for their guestroom, many interesting drives to Los Angeles, lots of stories, and even more laughs.

To John, for always being there and for never ceasing to believe, especially when I did.

And above all, to Mom and Dad, thanks for everything.

Table of Contents

Acknowledgments   vi

Introduction   1

Chapter 1. Sport in American Society   25

Chapter 2. Sport in Soviet Society   49

Chapter 3. 1948: The Austerity Games   74

Chapter 4. 1952: The Soviet Debut   95

Chapter 5. 1956: Blood in the Water   116

Chapter 6. 1960: The Games in Transition   140

Chapter 7. 1964: Politics Take Center Stage   165

Chapter 8. 1968: Politics as Main Event   189

Chapter 9. Post–1968 Experience and Conclusion   213

Chapter Notes   229

Bibliography   250

Index   259

Introduction

"I see the athletes of the future taking the oath before the Games, each upon the flag of their own country, and in the presence of the flags of other lands solemnly affirming that they have always been loyal and honorable in sport, and that it is in a spirit of loyalty and honor they approach the Olympic contests."
　　　　　　　　　　　—Baron Pierre de Coubertin, founder of the Modern
　　　　　　　　　　　　　　　　　　　　　　　Olympic Movement[1]

When U.S. Olympic basketball coach Pete Newell told his team in 1960, "They think they're going to beat us.... Guys, this is more than just a game. We're talking about a way of life," before the Americans' sold-out game against the Soviet Union, the stakes were obvious.[2] The superpowers' Olympic matchup during the Rome Games was neither merely a matchup to determine who would advance to the tourney semi-finals nor simply the most highly anticipated event of the Games.[3] Rather, this was a contest of east versus west, Moscow versus Washington, communism versus capitalism. The winner would earn precious Cold War bragging rights—along with a subtle sense that any subsequent win, even in the gold medal game, would be anticlimactic. Meanwhile, the loser would slink off the court fearing the diplomatic implications of its defeat. In this game, it was a jubilant American squad coasting to the 81–57 victory and eventually its fifth straight Olympic gold. However, by 1960, the Soviets were more often than not the ones reaping the Cold War bragging rights that accompanied all victories over their capitalist peers.[4] Newell's pep talk and the political implications attached to this basketball game were among the countless examples of how closely entwined Cold War politics were with the Olympic Games.

While the old adage goes that sports are only a game, the endless parallels between athletics and other facets of life, including politics, belie the simplicity of this statement. Though most associate sports with fitness or entertainment,

1

they are significant in many other ways. Beginning first in Britain in the eighteenth century before spreading throughout the European continent and later overseas, athletics have become much more relevant to global society since 1900. Perhaps nowhere is this more evident than in the United States, where throughout the course of the twentieth century—and especially after World War II—sports became almost a national religion as well as a multi-billion dollar industry. Sports are a great unifier, rallying a diverse population in support of favorite teams or in awe of great physical feats. Not only does the American public deify sports stars and treat important games as sacred, but sports have become a gauge for measuring national worth, at home and abroad. Sports are critical to the American psyche because they serve as a sort of national barometer. When American athletes perform well in international competition, their achievements represent victory for the United States in general, just as a Russian win brings bragging rights for all Russians. The same reasoning also applies to losses, in that a defeat becomes a cause for concern and introspection, as when the favored Soviet hockey team lost to the United States during the 1960 Winter Games. The sheer volume of print and media coverage of major sporting events like the Olympics and the wide public interest in such an event is proof of this correlation between sporting prowess and national image.

The growing emphasis on athletics took an understandably different trajectory in the Soviet Union, given the country's more recent origins and substantial upheaval throughout the first quarter of the twentieth century. Czarist Russia competed in the early Olympics but won few medals. Sports were less prevalent there than in the United States until the 1917 Revolution. The 1920s witnessed a growing emphasis on sport and so by the time Soviet athletes had caught up, relatively speaking, to their American rivals by World War II, sports had assumed many of the same roles in the Soviet Union as they had by 1900 in the United States. International athletic competition became a means of unifying a disparate population otherwise held together artificially by a common government. Encouraging mass participation in sport was a means to creating a more active population ready to meet any potential military challenge that might arise. Excellence in sport became a way to demonstrate Moscow's supremacy on the world stage and bettering its international image.

Additionally, sports assumed another important role behind the Iron Curtain: they became a channel through which the Soviet regime could gain a sense of international legitimacy and respect. While the United States was already a well-regarded nation and growing world power by the early twentieth century—with a reputation that only improved following its contribution to the two world wars—the Soviet Union was still a relatively new country with a political system that was unknown and unwelcome to many when it joined the International Olympic Committee (IOC) in 1951. Winning Olympic medals was a way of reminding the west that not only had the Soviet Union played a definitive role in the defeat of Germany in World War II, but that it was a legitimate nation that merited international recognition. From his country's initial forays into Olympic sport, Soviet General Secretary Joseph Stalin intended to use the Games to show that his country could challenge the United States on the world stage in terms of both ideological and athletic supremacy.

Because the superpowers held athletics in such high regard, both began to place heightened importance on Olympic achievement after World War II. This led to the evolution of the Games to a proxy Cold War battleground with unexpected and dramatic results. The years of the early Cold War witnessed a number of thrilling showdowns between Moscow and Washington on the field, in the press, and behind the scenes at IOC sessions, all of which affected the course of the Games. The purpose of this work is three-fold. First, it will provide an analysis of how sport factored into each superpower's Cold War tactical effort. Doing so will demonstrate how sport grew in priority, earning growing amounts of resources and attention from both Moscow and Washington. From there, it will look at the individual Olympiads within a twenty-year time frame, from 1948 to 1968, focusing on how diplomatic events shaped IOC discussions and the course of the Games themselves. It will finish with a brief analysis of the post–1968 Cold War-era Games to show how the politics evolved after Mexico City and following the retirement of IOC president Avery Brundage in 1972.

This study ends with 1968 because both the Games and the Cold War changed dramatically after this point. The onset of détente at a time when the superpowers simultaneously faced the greatest challenges to their respective hegemonies since 1945 forced Washington and Moscow to turn away from sport to focus on regaining control. Concurrently, the Olympics themselves changed in two fundamental ways. Politics continued to be driving force both on the field and behind the scenes, but the political incursions of the 1970s differed because they were not directly relevant to the Cold War. Instead tensions centered more on the rise of third world nations as medal contenders and the escalating costs of hosting an Olympics. And second, Brundage, an American Olympian and construction mogul who became IOC president in 1952, retired at age eighty-four. After serving on the United States Olympic Committee, which was called the United States Olympic Association (USOA) prior to 1961, for more than twenty years and working as IOC vice president for six, Brundage inherited control of the Olympic Movement in 1952 at a time when the Games were growing and changing rapidly. A capable and dedicated leader, Brundage directed the Olympic Movement through a time of great change and challenges. He strove to keep politics out of the Games, an ultimately fruitless campaign. Instead his efforts often inadvertently magnified diplomatic tensions within the Olympic Movement. A staunch anti-communist, Brundage was reluctant to grant the Soviet Union IOC membership because he feared the political ramifications. Nonetheless, Moscow did join and the nascent Cold War soon permeated the Olympic Movement, confirming Brundage's fears regarding politics and the Games. Despite his best efforts to the contrary, politics remained a constant consideration throughout his tenure.

Despite the best of intentions, Brundage never seemed to understand that issues of nationalism and diplomacy had played a role in the Games since the revival of the Olympic Movement more than fifty years earlier. The 1936 "Nazi" Olympics in Berlin serve as a prime example. The difference now was that the Games were caught in battle of conflicting ideologies, at times souring them, but more often adding a level of intrigue and interest that helped expand their appeal and audience throughout the early Cold War. As politics at times seemed to become an Olympic event in itself, the following chapters will demonstrate how the superpowers aided this development by treating the Games as part of the wider Cold War struggle.

The United States has been an influential member of the Olympic Movement since the revival of the Games at the end of the nineteenth century. It was one of the first countries that modern founder Baron Pierre de Coubertin approached in his search for supporters and participants, as he understood how important sports were to American society by the mid–1890s. The Games' utility as a gauge of international legitimacy increased proportionally as the Olympics themselves grew in size and global appeal. Obtaining the privilege of IOC membership, followed by success at the Games, is an acknowledged means by which a country can gain international recognition and global validity. As there is no greater athletic world stage than the Games, they became increasingly critical to demonstrating national prowess as the twentieth century progressed.

Perhaps this was never so true as during the early years of the Cold War when both superpowers struggled to assert their supremacy through any means possible. The Olympics drew much of their relevance from 1948 to 1968, from their intermingling with Cold War politics. This book will show that as both sides began to treat the Games as proxy Cold War battlegrounds, the Olympics themselves became more internationally important and appealing. While this undeniable politicization of the Games added to their legitimacy as a global movement, there were some who lamented this development because it detracted attention from the sports and the athletes themselves. But just as all competitive sporting events have their winners and losers, those who tried to eliminate politics lost. Efforts to extricate the diplomatic aspects played a critical role in the course of events and more often than not only served to intensify the political undertones of the Games, as will be discussed in reference to individual Olympiads. By examining contemporary current events, International Olympic Committee decisions, press coverage of the political aspects of the Olympics, and events at the Games themselves, this project will explore how the politicization of the Games became especially prevalent during the early years of the Cold War to the benefit of both the Olympic Movement and the superpowers. While the Olympics offered Washington and Moscow a relatively low-stakes environment in which to wage their battles for cultural and ideological supremacy, the Games themselves gained a greater sense of relevance and a larger audience from their association with this all-consuming conflict. However, while this type of political entanglement is perhaps most commonly associated with the Cold War-era events, it is important to realize that the mingling of diplomacy and the Olympics is as old as the Games themselves.

Historiography

The field of Olympic history is still under development. Scholarship on the 1936 Nazi Games and the boycotted Olympiads of the 1980s is quite prolific, but there is comparatively little that looks at the political aspects of the other less controversial Games. Scholars generally agree that the Games were political long before the Soviet Union competed in its first Olympics in 1952. However, there is still much to debate regarding the degree of this politicization and just how deeply it affected national sports infrastructures, IOC proceedings, and the Games themselves. The events between 1948 and 1968 prove that the convergence of the Cold War and the Olympic Movement brought political tensions to new heights, at times overshadowing the events on the field.

This work looks to fill the void of works that look closely at the early Cold War Olympics and treat a number of consecutive Games systematically. There are few texts that examine and compare several successive Olympiads in terms of political, and specifically Cold War, issues. While the Cold War itself was historically unprecedented, Barbara Keys has shown that the mixing of politics and sport was an established practice before 1945, particularly for the Olympic Movement as well as FIFA, the world soccer governing body. In her work *Globalizing Sport: National Rivalry and International Community in the 1930s*, Keys proves that the Olympics have always been political. She argues that the 1936 Summer Games set the standard for using the Olympics for diplomatic and nationalistic ends when Adolf Hitler tried to manipulate the Games to serve Nazi propaganda interests.[5] Throughout the 1930s, she writes, "international sport acted as a forum for nationalist rivalry, but nationalist impulses increased the internationalist power of sport."[6] Therefore, global sport and sporting diplomacy developed hand-in-hand. This work will argue that the Cold War represented the pinnacle of this confluence. The Games obtained global visibility and interest because the superpowers treated them so seriously, while Moscow and Washington gained a low-risk arena in which to wage their cultural clashes.

As such, neither the Cold War nor the Olympics would have developed in the same manner without the other's influence. Just as the United States and the Soviet Union competed for allies, economic dominance, and global supremacy, they also battled for superiority on cultural, technological, and sporting grounds. The heightened importance each placed on the medal count and the growing attention devoted to national fitness programs in turn made the Olympics matter more within each country's sphere of influence, be it NATO or the Warsaw Pact. At the same time, using the Olympics as an outlet for nationalist impulses gave the superpowers a safer venue in which to display their prowess, though this brought some unintended consequences. As Keys argued, "the growth of nationalist rivalry and international community in sport proceeded in tandem, each reinforcing the other."[7] The politicization of sport was nothing new, but the superpowers' shared focus on the Olympics and other international athletic events took this amalgamation to new heights throughout the 1950s and 1960s, drawing increased media and fan interest along the way.

As the Olympics became increasingly visible, they grew into a global phenomenon beyond Brundage's control, perhaps briefly achieving Baron Pierre de Coubertin's vision of the Games serving as an alternative to war. A sense of community formed among many of the athletes, transcending the national and ideological bounds to which their home countries so strictly adhered. There are also numerous examples of athletes from different countries falling in love at the Games and of spectators rallying behind a particularly endearing athlete, defying bitter national rivalries. Such storylines, made possible and more dramatic by the intrusion of outside political events, only added to the Games' global appeal. Even if a spectator's home country did not have an athlete challenging for the gold, there were always other compelling reasons to follow the action.

Most of the secondary literature available at this time looking at the Cold War-era Olympics focuses on the later years of the struggle, particularly the boycotts of the 1980s, and looks at individual Olympiads rather than taking a comparative approach. Nonetheless, these are valuable contributions to a growing body of sports history literature and the relevance of athletics to the international relations realm. This project strives to further the progress made by texts like David Maraniss's *Rome 1960,* which devotes some discussion to how Cold War tensions played into that Olympiad.[8] Maraniss's study of a single Games clearly demonstrates how politics, both American domestic issues and the ongoing chess match between Moscow and Washington heightened the drama in Rome, increasing their relevance to current events. He examines the Games through a number of lenses, highlighting both the ongoing civil rights struggle and the east-west tug of war over Berlin as backdrop for the drama in Rome. In doing so, Maraniss clearly demonstrates how politics compounded the Games' appeal for athletes and spectators alike, thereby casting politics as a positive force overall.

In looking at the Olympics and postwar politics, Janie Hampton's *The Austerity Olympics,* a study of the 1948 London Games, introduces the period at hand as well as the pressures developing out of the early Iron Curtain rhetoric, Berlin airlift, and other early Cold War skirmishes. Hampton demonstrates that the Games changed noticeably after World War II even before the Soviets took the field for the first time, as the precarious political balance created by the postwar settlement intensified the relationship between diplomacy and sportsmanship. The United States Olympic Association made clear that American athletes should not show up their less fortunate and perhaps unprepared competitors, as these Games occurred while Europe was still mired in its postwar recovery. This sense of chivalry and sportsmanship would all but evaporate four years later, a direct casualty of the Soviet debut in 1952. Hampton addresses the political aspect by showing how Games organizers and the nations involved largely tried to evade these overtones, with mixed success. Even without an official Soviet presence, Moscow remained on the minds on many at the Games.

Alfred Senn's *Power, Politics, and the Games* offers a sweeping look at how international relations influenced the Games from the 1890s through the 1998 Winter Olympics in Nagano, Japan. Senn argues that while some consider politics to be "an unwelcome intruder," these diplomatic tangents are critical to the Games' global appeal.[9] "The political dimensions of the Games are diverse and complicated…. Governments have tried to exploit the Games for their own ends, and at times the IOC has itself put pressure on governments. It is no surprise then that the Games have served as a focus for national rivalries and ideological rivalries between states."[10] It is the extent to which the Games became a focal point for Moscow and Washington that this project explores, as well as the instances in which the IOC invoked politics for its own ends. If nothing else, the fifteen-year debate over how to treat the two Germanys that emerged from World War II proves how complex IOC politics were during the Cold War.

Richard Espy's *The Politics of the Olympic Games* examines how the tangential nations found themselves drawn into the Cold War as it traces the German and Chinese issues from their roots in the 1950s up through 1980. Espy argues that governments have used the Games as a foreign policy tool because of its "essential neutrality.... Sport exhibits the state's relative sense of political and economic strength through its prowess as a competitor on the playing field."[11] Competing at the Games or behind the scenes at the IOC allowed nations to show off their strength without the same dangerous political stakes that accompanied military or nuclear strikes. Espy clearly dissents from Senn's contention that politics add a layer of intrigue to the Games, as he focuses almost entirely on their negative effects rather than the role of positive nationalism or patriotism created by this intense competition on and off the field.

In *Dropping the Torch*, Nicholas Sarantakes offers a comprehensive study of how Cold War politics affected—and some might argue—ruined one particular Olympiad when American president Jimmy Carter tried to use the 1980 Summer Games in Moscow as a bargaining chip to force the Soviets from Afghanistan.[12] If Brundage strove to use sport to overcome politics, Sarantakes provides a cautionary tale of what can happen when politics win. His incorporation of contemporary politics, news coverage, IOC proceedings, and some insight from the athletes, the real losers in 1980, provide the example for the structure of this work, albeit with some necessary modifications.

The current study will treat several consecutive Olympiads with similar breadth but less depth than Sarantakes provides on the Moscow Games. This text will add to the growing body of Olympic studies literature by establishing how the Olympics and the superpowers mutually benefitted from the impact of politics on the Games. It will build on the foundation provided by Senn and Espy to look more closely at how governmental involvement shaped the Games during a brief, specific window of time. Furthermore, it will demonstrate how the Games created an arena in which the superpowers could wage their Cold War battles without the same high stakes consequences that a military or diplomatic showdown would bring. At the same time, the Olympics profited from the added hype and intrigue that accompanied all superpower showdowns.

Viewed from this angle, the Olympics were as integral to Cold War sport as the space race was to Cold War technology. Walter McDougall has argued successfully in *The Heavens and the Earth* that the Dwight Eisenhower and John F. Kennedy administrations consciously used the space race as relatively low-risk means of exhibiting supremacy.[13] In the aftermath of several diplomatic standoffs and near collisions with Moscow, the White House increasingly looked for points of comparison outside the overt political realm to gauge their

Cold War progress. Similar cases have been made that the Fulbright and other exchange programs were alternate means of spreading American culture while exhibiting the superiority of the capitalist system.[14] As the Cold War intensified during the early 1950s, these seemingly non-political programs gained increased public scrutiny and garnered growing White House attention, resources, and critique.[15] The Games were no stranger to this new governmental involvement and surveillance, particularly during the Eisenhower and Kennedy administrations.

The Olympics served as perhaps the most accessible vehicle to the general public for ideological competition during the period at hand. They proved more entertaining on both sides of the Iron Curtain than programs like the space race or the use of third-world proxies as Cold War battlegrounds. Sports involved less fear of leaking sensitive information than did the space race and the common man understood more about sports than the principles of rocketry. The Olympics were a means of coupling patriotism with the spirit of competition fostered by watching games or participating in one of many 1950s sporting exhibition tours. As the Cold War began to escalate, both Washington and the American public followed the Olympics with increasing seriousness, looking for means of winning at any cost. Succeeding at the Games was one method of reassuring an uncertain public that the United States was as strong as Moscow. Though just a game, the fear of falling behind in the medal count became a source of anxiety. Losing ground in one aspect of the Cold War, like the Games, was perceived as just the beginning of a total loss to the other superpower in the same way that losing a key battle in a military struggle could lead to a loss in the wider war.

The use of the Games as a Cold War battleground did not happen overnight. But as the superpowers realized the propaganda potential that Olympic glory brought, both Moscow and Washington focused more closely on the Olympic Movement. This developed in stages parallel to the Cold War itself. It manifested itself via initiatives in both countries to increase the fitness of the population at large while more closely scrutinizing the efforts of the elite who showed Olympic potential. Though the nature of the Soviet government led to a more centralized endeavor in Moscow, the White House kept a close eye on American athletic development and increasingly intervened to ensure that United States Olympic Committee (USOC) was doing its part to win the Cold War. This mutual fixation on the Games intensified through the mid–1960s, until more pressing concerns simultaneously forced the White House and the Kremlin to turn their attention elsewhere. The onset of détente beginning with the global upheaval that characterized 1968 makes the Mexico City Summer Olympics a natural ending point for this study. Neither side approached the

1972 Games with the same fervor while the politics exhibited in Munich were of an entirely different and much more tragic vein.

At times when the Cold War political tensions were not running as high, as in the early 1970s under presidents Richard Nixon and Gerald Ford, the Olympics were not used in the same manner to promote this clash of cultures. Jeremi Suri argued in *Power and Protest* that détente was a global reaction to the various 1968 uprisings. At this time, Nixon and Soviet premier Leonid Brezhnev chose to collaborate in order to protect their authority in the face of these protests rather than challenge each other and risk further domestic resistance and uprisings.[16] This philosophy extended to the Olympics, where following the 1968 Games, the IOC witnessed a temporary calming of the continuous bickering between the American and the Soviet delegations. While the 1972 Olympics were highly contentious, it was the Palestinian Liberation Organization (PLO) who politicized the Munich Games, not Moscow or Washington. Following the signing of the Basic Treaty between Bonn and Berlin, relations between the two nations, and their sporting bodies, improved. East German athletes were welcomed at the Munich Games. After 1972, Brundage's successor as IOC president, Lord Michael Morris Killanin, proved to be a very different type of leader who some have argued was more in touch with contemporary global politics.[17] As such, he dealt with ongoing tensions in a more direct manner than Brundage, expediting the handling of certain issues, because he recognized that politics were part of the Games.

IOC Leadership: The Major Players

In setting the scene for discussing the individual Olympiads between 1948 and 1968, it is important first to identify the most influential figures whose ideals and decisions shaped the Olympic Movement through this period. While there were numerous transient personalities who affected the course of events at IOC meetings or the Games, including IOC representatives from member nations, the press, particularly sportswriters and columnists, impacted the Games, particularly during the period under study here when the IOC president wielded more individual power than today. Therefore, it is necessary to provide short biographical sketches of the first four leaders before analyzing the Games themselves.

Baron Pierre de Coubertin, a French nobleman and education theorist, was the founder of the modern Olympic movement. Following France's defeat at the hands of the Germans in the 1870 Franco-Prussian War, de Coubertin sought a means through which his home country could regain its sense of national pride. He believed that a multinational athletic contest, based loosely on the concept of the ancient Greek Olympics, would be the best, or perhaps the most accessible means through which France could redeem herself.[18] He reached out to colleagues in several western countries to help revive the Games. Because international sporting matches were increasingly popular by the late 1880s, de Coubertin's vision was fairly well-received. Plans for the first modern Games planned for Athens in 1896 were well underway by the early 1890s.[19]

De Coubertin was a prolific writer with a clear vision for the modern Games. However, neither he nor Brundage seemed to realize just how large the Olympic Movement would become or how quickly it would grow. Though politics played a role in the first Games, as their *raison d'être* was to improve France's national pride and international image, de Coubertin did not realize that other political forces would soon emerge. The ideologies of the twentieth century, including socialism and fascism, proved much more volatile and therefore too difficult to contain as the Games themselves continued to expand.[20] His personal conception of the Games was rather fixed, based on how he had interpreted the Ancient Olympics and his own theories on the importance of physical fitness and national pride.[21] This theoretical vision left little room for the Olympics to evolve or for the inevitable human factor to affect the Games.[22]

From his youth during the Third Republic, de Coubertin was a proud French patriot. His desirable social position created opportunities for him that largely remained out of reach for the average Frenchman during his lifetime. He capitalized on chances to travel and further his education, making connections that shaped both his worldview and the Olympic Movement. He enrolled in the military academy at St. Cyr in 1880, only to resign shortly after finishing his schooling. Though remaining a staunch nationalist, he looked for other means to express his love and loyalty to his homeland in place of military service.[23] His search for self-improvement and France's redemption led him to spend much of the 1880s traveling, writing, and later scheming on how to bring back the Olympics to achieve this latter purpose.

An independently wealthy man, de Coubertin had the means to finance the Games and thus shape them to his liking. He admired the English amateur system and structured the Olympics in a similar fashion—a decision with consequences that would far outlive de Coubertin himself. Under the British system, amateurs received no payment for their athletic feats—or for coaching—including prize money, making the Olympics the pursuit of the wealthy who could afford to train sufficiently for the competition and then pay their way to the Games. While this was not an issue during the first few Olympiads, it became problematic by the 1920s when there were fewer elite athletes able to finance this lifestyle.

Following an 1883 visit to Britain, de Coubertin looked for ways to bring British-style athletics to France.[24] He admired this fairly regimented and regulated system of competition through which amateur athletes could demonstrate their strength and skill. He attributed this program, which was spreading contemporarily from the Royal Navy to the public schools and universities, as one of the main reasons as to why Britain had been able to create and maintain her vast empire. He expounded upon the importance of sport in an 1887 speech in Paris.

> [Sport is] the most noteworthy aspect of English education: I mean the role that sports play in that education. This role is physical, moral, and social, all at the same time.... Sports mean movement and the influence of movement on bodies is something that has been evident from time immemorial. Strength and agility have been deeply appreciated among savage and civilized people alike. Both are achieved through exercise and practice: happy balance in the moral order.[25]

With sports rapidly gaining popularity across Europe and the United States— and steadily filtering into the various Asian and African colonies as well— global athletics events could be a means of demonstrating strength without incurring the threat of war. It was this vision and sense of purpose that led de Coubertin to search tirelessly for backers even in a time when the popularity of sport was still rather limited.

In addition to his desire to revive French patriotism, de Coubertin's faith in the unifying power of sport motivated the Games' revival. In an era when tensions were escalating palpably among the great powers, de Coubertin envisioned the Olympics as a venue where athletes could come together and compete peacefully, while also developing a sense of international camaraderie. Sport could transcend cultural and political barriers because the goodwill it fostered superseded these boundaries. While there was no official diplomatic role ascribed to the athletes competing in Athens, and the White House would not buy into the concept of athletic diplomacy until the Cold War, those who attended the 1896 Athens Games tacitly understood the political implications at stake.[26] There is little evidence that de Coubertin believed in or saw the need to enforce the strict division between politics and sport that Brundage later ascribed to him. Rather de Coubertin understood that politics were a natural component of international sport and sought to harness these tensions and direct them toward ends less damaging than war.[27]

De Coubertin believed that sport played a key role in daily and diplomatic life, though he did not foresee just how large a role politics would come to play within his movement. His goal in reviving the Games was to tap into sport's potential in a time when few others held athletics in the same high esteem. During the latter half of the nineteenth century, the common consensus was that sports were only the pursuit of the elite, those who had time to waste.[28] Despite a lack of widespread support, de Coubertin cultivated the interest of sporting leaders in other countries, including the United States, to bring what he once described as "a chimera" to fruition.[29]

From the mid–1880s until his death in 1937, de Coubertin remained an advocate for the Olympics and the importance of sport more generally, even after resigning as IOC president in 1924. By this time, his vision for the Games at times clashed with the wider IOC Executive Committee's, easing his transition to elder statesman. Though the Games could not prevent the outbreak of two world wars, the Olympics have proven time and again just how well they serve as a unifying force because sports have an ability to transcend the nationalist friction that can often paralyze traditional diplomatic channels. In this sense, de Coubertin was accurate in trumpeting the belief that sports have always been more just a game, at least when applied to the Olympics.

When de Coubertin stepped down as IOC president, the Belgian Count Henri de Baillet-Latour succeeded him, continuing the precedent of keeping IOC leadership in the hands of the nobility.[30] Baillet-Latour presided over the IOC until his death in 1942. His tenure spanned the controversial 1936 Summer Olympics in Berlin, still remembered nearly eighty years later as the Nazi Games for Hitler's infamous displays of German nationalism and memorable aesthetics. Baillet-Latour also decided to invite Germany to the 1928 Summer Games in Amsterdam, signaling forgiveness for Berlin's role in causing World War I. Despite his relatively permissive attitude toward Germany in 1936, Baillet-Latour's legacy is generally positive because he organized the successful 1920 Summer Games in Antwerp.[31] These Olympics occurred less than two years after Belguim's decimation during World War I had ended and these Games fulfilled their intended purpose of offering consolation to the Belgian people for their wartime suffering.[32] Baillet-Latour passed away during the Second World War, but the war's upheaval and disruption to the Olympic Movement led the IOC to postpone naming a new leader until 1946.

The IOC's third president, Sigfrid Edstrom, served from 1946 to 1952, a period of transition for the Olympic Movement following the Nazi Games and the twelve-year hiatus caused by World War II.[33] Edstrom is credited with helping to stage a postwar Games in London in 1948 that were both appropriately austere but also conducive to the postwar rebuilding and healing process in that city and around the world. Also, during his tenure, the Soviet Union made its Olympic debut, much to the chagrin of the many IOC members who loathed communism and had tried to block Soviet entry.

Brundage, the first and only American to serve as IOC president to date, took control in 1952 with the goal of ensuring that the Olympic Movement stayed true to its founder's conception. He fought to keep politics out the Games at all costs, an increasingly unreasonable expectation given the growing Cold War dynamic. However, Brundage's interpretation of de Coubertin's vision was often controversial. Brundage, a former Olympian himself, served as president of the American Olympic Association and as acting IOC president during World War II before succeeding Edstrom to become president in his own right in 1952. Throughout his twenty-year tenure, Brundage made more than his share of enemies through his, at times, blind adherence to his interpretation of the Olympic rules. Despite his efforts toward keeping the Movement true to de Coubertin's founding vision, the global athletic hierarchy and sporting press showered hostility on Brundage both during and in the aftermath of his tenure at the IOC helm.

Brundage's resume certainly qualified him to lead the Olympic Movement. He had competed in the 1912 Stockholm Games, finishing sixth in the pentathlon. After his track and field career ended, he quickly amassed a small fortune in the construction industry before embracing sports administration and real estate investment as his chief occupations. By the mid–1920s, he was climbing the ranks toward becoming president of the American Olympic Committee while also working for the Amateur Athletic Union (AAU). During the 1930s, he chaired the American Olympic Committee while also serving on the IOC. It was during the debate over a potential American boycott of the 1936 Summer Olympics in Berlin, sparked by Hitler's vow to exclude Jewish and other non–Aryan people from the Games, that Brundage first enunciated his firm belief that politics should never interfere with sport, especially the Olympics. As support for a boycott gained traction at home and in Britain, Brundage penned letters to several important Olympic leaders, rejecting the soundness of such of a move on the grounds that it was undeserved punishment for the athletes who had trained for the Games.[34] Evidence from correspondence between them—among other sources—showed that Brundage Edstrom, another future IOC president, were both relatively anti–Semitic, though fairly mild by contemporary standards. For both, the Games were always more important than individual concerns.[35]

Brundage made his feelings clear in a 1935 *New York Times* story. "The Olympic Games belong to the athletes and not the politicians.... [The American Olympic Committee] will never allow our athletes to be made martyrs to a cause not their own."[36] Following a divisive vote by the American Olympic Committee, the United States sent a delegation to Germany in 1936 to compete in a Games still remembered for their ugly displays of nationalism, but also for Jesse Owens' triumphs on the track. While Brundage shared this stance with many powerful allies, his perceived insensitivity toward Jewish athletes haunted him throughout his IOC career.[37]

Brundage's actions in the months leading up to the Berlin Games set the tone from his IOC presidency, which spanned from 1952 until 1972. During this time, he held firm to the belief that sport and politics, particularly the Olympics and issues of nationalism, were mutually exclusive. At times, his obdurate loyalty to this tenet gave the impression that he lacked any sense of cultural consideration. He also maintained that the Games should remain purely amateur and therefore true to their original conception, despite the changing times. Though the demands for a more modern and realistic approach to the Games intensified during his twenty-year tenure, Brundage refused to waver, even when his stance detracted more attention from the athletes than perhaps a concession to the political reality might have. While Brundage strove to achieve an apolitical sports showcase, his meddling often produced the reverse: a political spectacle couched in an athletic façade. American presidential and state department correspondence from this era at times referenced the tacit role athletes assumed as ambassadors making the Olympics always more than just a game.[38]

Brundage himself was always somewhat of a controversial figure. Though he was largely a self-made millionaire, he never understood and consequently never expressed any sympathy for the financial constraints that American and other amateur athletes faced. Instead of advocating for these athletes, he continued to harangue American Olympians for any perceived infractions of the amateur rules while turning a blind eye to Moscow's willful disregard for the same regulations. He remained loyal to a certain specific concept of amateurism despite the general sense of acknowledgment among his peers that it had become an outdated and unrealistic standard by the 1940s. And yet, the Soviets managed to evade the Olympics' strict amateur rules throughout the 1950s and 1960s, which many cited as the chief reason for their great success at the Games.

It is important to note that despite his best efforts to the contrary, Brundage lost his decades-long struggle to free the Games from extraneous forces. It is impossible to completely divorce international sport from international politics. Whenever nations compete, there is bound to be something more at stake than simply points on the playing field, especially during tense eras like the Cold War. As Keys has argued, the nationalist tensions and impulses that accompanied international sporting events added to the global intrigue and the international relevance of sport more generally.[39] Sports offer a means of comparison on a highly regulated plane by employing universal standards to gauge achievements. Nonetheless, there is no way to completely remove the outside added elements that politics inject. Many would argue that there is no need to do so because of the interest and added bragging rights that accompany these nationalistic concerns. As this project will show, even Brundage himself was not immune to the power of politics. Though he strove to remain above the fray, there were junctures at which he capitulated. And even at times when he refused to concede, these political forces were simply too much to overcome. By the 1968 Mexico City Games, a case can be made that the athletic feats on the playing field had become little more than a sideshow to the constant political spectacle. Coupled with the growing commercialism of the Olympic Movement, politics had changed the Games to something unrecognizable to the initial contests in Athens more than seventy years earlier.

For all his efforts to keep the Games true to what was perhaps a misinterpretation of de Coubertin's founding vision, Brundage soon became a reviled figure, both in the press and throughout the athletic world. His staunch adherence to what many believed even by the late 1940s to be an archaic concept of the Games won him few friends and many critics. Instead, the majority opinion of him closely mirrors this less than flattering February 1956 *Sports Illustrated* description. "Avery Brundage, the intractable, uncompromising, often tactless and undiplomatic Chicagoan ... the most powerful man in sport."[40] While the death of a public figure tends to bring about at least reconsideration if not outright of revision of one's legacy, Brundage has yet to receive this revaluation. Rather, *SI* eulogized him as "a bigot, a womanizer, and a monumental hypocrite."[41] In the weeks before the 1956 Summer Games in Melbourne, *The New Yorker* described him as "a zealous worker for the Olympic cause, is also a man who can be tactless on a heroic scale. With a few grating remarks he united all Australia in hatred of himself."[42] Four years later, the magazine devoted several pages to an in-depth profile of the controversial leader. Even this piece, which took a rather neutral tone overall, referenced his bouts of pretentiousness, even reprinting some of the more creative barbs from other publications. This included Red Smith's remark dubbing Brundage "the greatest practicing pansy, or sitting duck, of this century."[43] These epithets only intensified in critique and frequency with Brundage's increasingly stubborn insistence that his rules be followed.

The International Olympic Committee

In becoming IOC president, Brundage was part of a relatively exclusive circle, as only eight men to date have presided over the Olympic Movement. These men share the goal of holding the Games to a certain standard of excellence. This ideal tends to vary based on the current president's personal construction of the Movement. Yet while the position of IOC president brings with it a considerable amount of power and influence over the Olympic Movement, Brundage and the other seven presidents are not omnipotent. They must work with and preside over the International Olympic Committee to ensure that the Games stay true to their ideals. De Coubertin established the IOC to administer the Games from planning stages through the closing ceremonies, with its executive board serving as the highest authority in all related matters. The International Olympic Committee is a unique body that calls itself an "international non-governmental, non-profit organization."[44] It self-selects members to sit on an executive committee comprised of roughly 115 members headed by a president with limited veto power. The men and—since 1983— women who serve on the IOC are athletes, athletic officials, and other individuals invited by sitting members of the committee. In addition to membership in the IOC, each country that participates in the Games must have its own National Olympic Committee (NOC), which coordinates its country's Olympic effort and ensures that the IOC's rules are followed within its domain.[45]

As Brundage phrased it, "The reason for the success of the Olympic Movement is the way the IOC is constituted. The conception of [modern Olympic founder Pierre] de Coubertin was the soundest and wisest idea he ever had.... [T]he IOC-members do not represent their own country. They are considered as the ambassadors of the IOC in their respective countries."[46] The motive behind this configuration was to prevent politics and national interests from superseding the wellbeing of the Olympic Movement, though this is sometimes lost during the debates over various issues. Many of the heated discussions over the life of the IOC have initiated from this clause, as it is so difficult for members to totally discard their home country's concerns, particularly when it is clear that other members are pursuing their own political agendas.

While roughly ninety-two percent of the IOC's revenue today comes from media licensing and broadcast rights, this was not true before 1964 when television stations broadcast few Olympic events.[47] In the period under study, wealthy entrepreneurs and sports enthusiasts like Brundage provided almost all of the Games' funding, with national governments offering little monetary contribution, aside from autocracies like the Soviet Union who often financed their teams' training and travel expenses. The rationale behind this financial freedom was that it would permit the IOC to operate fairly autonomously from political concerns since it was not dependent on outside revenue sources. However, the political atmosphere surrounding the events of the 1936 so-called Nazi Games challenged this notion of separation before the Cold War destroyed it altogether. As IOC president and one of the chief financial contributors to the Olympics, Brundage wielded an unprecedented amount of power during his tenure, forcing participating nations to either appease him grudgingly or remain on the sidelines. Over time, however, his control lessened as political and commercial forces grew too strong even for him to defeat entirely.

Reviving the Games

While the Cold War ushered in a new level of political interference to the Olympic Movement, the Games have always been political, despite best intentions to the contrary. From the initial discussions regarding their resumption in the early 1890s, after a 1500-year hiatus, the Games and diplomacy have been inseparable. Aside from his interest in restoring French national self-worth, de Coubertin hoped that resurrecting this spectacle would provide an outlet for the growing tensions among the European great powers and prevent the outbreak of war. He believed the Olympics could provide a means through which European countries and the United States could channel their competitive urges and burgeoning nationalism rather than engaging in a military struggle.

After several years of discussion and planning, Athens, Greece hosted the first modern Olympic Games in April 1896. Only thirteen European nations and the United States competed in these inaugural contests. Fourteen men, most of whom were college athletes from Harvard and Princeton and all of whom funded their own voyages to Athens, represented the United States. Their experience in Greece was a positive one overall and organizers deemed the Games themselves a success. According to Jim Reisler in *Igniting the Flame: America's First Olympic Team,* by the closing ceremonies, "the Americans had become the world's newest diplomats, basking in the continued good cheer of their Greek hosts with whom a genuine warmth had arisen."[48] Even in the first modern Games, the competitors' behavior both on and off the field was perceived as representative of their countries. All possessed a tacit understanding that making a poor impression in Athens would have negative implications for how the rest of the world viewed the United States off the playing fields. Fortunately for Washington, there was no need for concern over how its athletes conducted themselves. The American Olympic team left behind many admirers when it returned home, including the Greek royal family.

Although de Coubertin and the Athens organizers were quite pleased with how athletes and spectators enjoyed the Games, the same could not be said regarding the subsequent contests in Paris in 1900, St. Louis in 1904, and London in 1908. Problems with organization and with a manageable time frame for the contests—the Paris Games spanned more than six months, with events held intermittently throughout the summer—hindered the expansion of and public interest in the Games.[49] The London contests witnessed the first charges of officials favoring the host country, as several seemingly biased decisions made throughout the course of the Games repulsed many spectators and non–British athletes alike. At the same time, exaggerated displays of nationalism by the British team disgusted many of the fans.[50] Gaudy displays of national pride have become all too common in the century since the first London Olympiad, showing that though the Games themselves have grown and changed dramatically, nationalism and politics are a constant in international competition. Stockholm hosted the 1912 Olympics, a relatively uncontroversial and generally well-regarded event. Brundage competed in the pentathlon and decathlon events, returning home without a medal.[51]

After World War I forced the cancellation of the 1916 Games, which Berlin would have hosted, political considerations became more prevalent during the interwar period. The International Olympic Committee decided against inviting the defeated Central powers to the 1920 Antwerp Games. It consciously chose Antwerp as host city to boost Belgian nationalism and offer consolation following the war's destruction in that country.[52] The popularity and political importance of the Olympics and sport more generally grew exponentially during the interwar period. By this time, sport was becoming an internationally recognized means of displaying national strength while promoting amity among nations in a time when traditional measures, including alliance systems like the League of Nations, were failing.[53]

The Olympic Movement expanded in 1924 when St. Moritz, Switzerland, hosted the first Winter Olympics. Though much smaller than the summer contests with a competitors' field comprised mainly of western European and American athletes, this foray into snow sports signified that the Games had become stable enough to weather substantial growth and change. The 1928 Summer Games in Amsterdam, another successful Olympiad, were noteworthy for their size. Not only were there more athletes present than at any previous spectacle, but the number of fans dwarfed previous contests, underscoring the exponential growth of spectator sport worldwide throughout the 1920s.[54] The 1932 Games in Los Angeles are identified today as the first truly international Olympics, as their location outside Europe encouraged Asian and American competitors to participate, while the glamor of being close to Hollywood and the allure of the city of LA attracted many who perhaps would not have otherwise traveled to the Games, given the Great Depression.[55] The White House did not capitalize on the Olympic presence, something that seems quite odd today. While it was precedent for the president of the host country to be present at the Opening Ceremony, Herbert Hoover decided to stay home, citing the ongoing struggles the Great Depression posed to his administration and the impending presidential election. Instead, Republicans and the media portrayed Franklin Roosevelt, then governor of New York, as an opportunist for appearing at that year's Winter Games in Lake Placid and for offering to appear in LA as Hoover's emissary.[56] It was not until the Cold War that the White House began to employ the Games to their full utility as a diplomatic tool.

Other world leaders proved far less hesitant to mix politics and the Olympics. The 1936 Berlin Games offered a prime example of the growing entanglement of sports and diplomacy as several nations, including the United States and Britain, debated at length whether or not to boycott the event in protest of Adolf Hitler's treatment of Germany's Jewish population.[57] In the end, neither decided to protest, to the effect that the Games offered an ugly lesson in how they could showcase not only great feats on the playing field but also controversial displays of overt nationalism and prejudice.[58] The Berlin Games remain the most controversial, given Hitler's attempts to manipulate them into a show of Aryan superiority, and other nations' subsequent debates regarding potential boycotts. The Olympics took an unplanned twelve-year hiatus during World War II with even stronger political undertones taking root when they resumed. The onset of the Cold War and the problems caused by a new set of vanquished nations fueled the ongoing diplomatic fire.

From the 1948 Games through the fall of the Berlin Wall in 1989, the clash between communism and capitalism, or more simply, east versus west, played a key role in the perception and shaping of the Games as well as in the motivation for nations to participate. As the Olympics evolved from a small-scale competition focused primarily on Europe to a truly global spectacle by 1968, several countries—with the United States and the Soviet Union in particular—acted deliberately to manipulate the International Olympic Committee and the countries involved in the Games to best suit their own interests. Brundage strove to counteract these efforts at every turn, with little success. Though he managed to force the two Germanys to collaborate on a single team for several olympiads and ensured that American athletes remained amateur, he could not claim victory in the larger war on politics. And many would argue, then and today, that this was for the best, as it served to heighten the world's interest in and therefore the relevance of the Games.

Some have argued that the United States' superpower status, coupled with having the advantage of Brundage, an American, serving as IOC president, put it in a unique position to influence the course of IOC politics. Though Brundage repeatedly portrayed himself and the Games as being above politics, there were clear points at which the IOC made decisions that catered to "national pride and arrogance."[59] At the same time, the United States actively sought to expand this influence and promote its own interests through the Olympic Movement. Both American and Soviet attitudes toward sport changed rapidly after World War II as athletics became increasingly important to both cultures. Olympic glory grew in importance to diplomatic ends beginning with the 1948 Games, the last without a Soviet team until Moscow's 1984 boycott. Several Cold War diplomatic incidents coincided with Olympic seasons. The Games became pawns in several international relations firestorms unique to this conflict, heightening their importance while simultaneously thwarting Brundage's hope of keeping the events free of political overtones. Because both Washington and Moscow held the Games in such high esteem and treated success in them as crucial, the Cold War accelerated the expansion of the Olympics to the professional showcase that they are today. As both the Soviets and the Americans devoted increasing amounts of funding and resources to increase their medal chances, other countries soon followed suit, bringing more prestige and larger audiences to the Games.[60]

In hindsight, Brundage's remark following Moscow's brutal 1968 crackdown in Czechoslovakia regarding the growing politicization of the Games, that, "if participation in sport is to be stopped every time the politicians violate the laws of humanity, there will never be any international contests," perhaps seems more pertinent now than it was then.[61] Although current global politics are less black and white than ever, the questions regarding future Olympic Games focus more on where rather than if they will occur. There are fewer headlines referencing current IOC president Thomas Bach than there were on Brundage in any given year of his tenure as IOC president, particularly in conjunction with international affairs. Now both the summer and winter Olympics are bigger than ever and transpire with arguably less political drama and interference than at any other point in their modern history despite the volatile international relations climate.

Yet as the following chapters will show, this has not always been the case. Soviet participation beginning in 1952 and propaganda campaigns by both superpowers to improve performance bequeathed the Games with heightened political and cultural importance and fueled their dramatic post–World War II expansion. Global interest in the Games has withstood the end of the Cold War and lasted into the twenty-first century.[62] Despite the best intentions of the purists like Brundage, sport and politics have proven inseparable, particularly in the battles of communism vs. capitalism. Perhaps former University of California Athletic Director Pete Newell said it best when he told the *Oakland Tribune* in 1961, "we must now accept the fact that athletics now form part of the total image we are presenting to the rest of the world."[63] Because international sport became so important in the twentieth century, it tends to provide ample media fodder contemporarily and later become the domain of scholars. As such, there is no shortage of works studying the political consequences of the Olympics. Though there have been prior studies on the Cold War and the Olympics, this project uses material from the IOC archives along with information from Brundage's personal papers and contemporary news sources to create a panoramic view of how the superpowers and those connected to the Olympic Movement benefitted from this meshing of diplomacy and sport from 1948 through 1968.

The Cold War on the Playing Fields

After first examining how sport developed in each superpower before and during the Cold War, this work will examine each individual Olympiad from 1948 to 1968. It will show how the Cold War affected Moscow's and Washington's respective approaches to the Olympics, press coverage, IOC proceedings, and events at the Games themselves. In doing so, it will trace four key themes. These themes help to explain why Cold War politics became such a major force within the Olympic Movement. The first factor is the contradictory approaches the superpowers took to sport. As the Soviet Union was highly centralized, Moscow was heavily involved in Soviet athletics than the White House was in American athletics from start to finish. The Soviet sporting administration provided employment for elite athletes that offered them ample training time and funding, while ensuring that they wanted for little in terms of material goods. The price for this was freedom, as these athletes were expected to toe the party line and subjugate their own needs and interests to those of the national team. Outside the Iron Curtain, the United States lacked a national sporting establishment and its athletes struggled to balance work, training time, and support for their families. Conversely, American sports stars were much freer to pursue their individual goals and faced considerably less pressure from Washington to mind strict political boundaries. These inherent contrasts lent themselves to sharply critical yet also entertaining wars of words that grew in their intensity as the Olympics became more important as an ideological battleground.

Moscow's and Washington's shared tendency to treat the Olympics as Cold War cannon fodder accelerated their growing politicization. Once the Soviets began competing in 1952, both superpowers quickly realized that the Games offered a highly visible yet low stakes stage on which they could prove their superiority. As the cultural Cold War heated up throughout the 1950s and into the first half of the 1960s, both intensified their efforts to dominate the Games, both behind the scenes at the IOC and on the playing field. The hotly contested medal count was a matter of great interest for the press and the spectators on both sides of the Iron Curtain, much to Brundage's chagrin. The IOC president reminded both sides on numerous occasions that "the Olympic Games are contests between individuals and not between nations," though this admonishment largely fell on deaf ears.[64] Each instance of direct competition between the superpowers became intense battles that sold out arenas and earned extensive press analysis. Victories were causes for grand celebration while losses fueled waves of panic. While Brundage maintained that politics and sport were separate, the athletes, media, and politicians on both sides of the Iron Curtain took great pride in disproving him, partly because of the Cold War bragging rights at stake. In the end, Brundage lost in the sense that politics are integral to the Games, yet the Olympic Movement won because this element heightened the stakes of the competition and increased the Games' visibility.

Tangential to these differing approaches and the rapid politicization of the Olympic Movement was the IOC's insistence that the Games were for amateur athletes only. Brundage was particularly hesitant to offer the Soviets IOC membership because he assumed its athletes were paid professionals, which many of them likely were. Nonetheless, Moscow joined the Olympic Movement officially in 1951 and the IOC largely turned a blind eye when the Iron Curtain countries flaunted this rule. However, not all member nations received this preferential treatment. Brundage came down particularly hard on the United States and the German Democratic Republic, holding these two countries to a higher amateur standard, while drawing the wrath of sporting officials in both countries for this uneven enforcement. There were many calls to level the playing field by admitting professional athletes from all nations or allowing some state funding during these years, to no avail. Brundage took great pride in the fact that American athletes did not take government handouts.

Just as Brundage was adamant that the Olympic Movement remain an amateur event, he was stubbornly opposed to the growing commercialization of the Games. As the Olympics gained grew in size and global visibility and as television satellite technology advanced, the marketing opportunities of the Games increased. Brundage was opposed to televising the events or allowing any type of commercial sponsorship for athletes because he felt that doing so ran contrary to de Coubertin's founding vision of a simple athletics competition among amateurs. Nonetheless, he proved unable to prevent television from influencing the course of the Games by the 1960s. Perhaps the moment that best demonstrated this failure was the Black Power salute by American track medalists John Carlos and Tommie Smith during the 1968 Summer Olympics in Mexico City. While this gesture might have passed without too much fanfare had it occurred twenty years earlier, television ensured that audiences around the world witnessed this clear sign of American racial unrest and obvious repudiation of Brundage's claim that the Games were apolitical.

In the end, Brundage lost on a number of counts. Paradoxically, instead of keeping politics out of the Olympics, he unwittingly played a role in the cultural Cold War. His efforts to force the two German states to collaborate on a unified team and use sport "to show the way for the diplomats" backfired.[65] While he liked to imagine himself and the Games as being above politics, he was unable to resist campaigning for a stronger American sporting infrastructure after a 1954 visit to the Soviet Union convinced him that Moscow was about to eclipse the United States as the global sporting leader. His refusal to sanction the Soviets for their brutal oppression of both the Hungarian and the Czechoslovakian revolts earned him the ire and ridicule of the press as well as several IOC member nations. His adherence to what many believed were outdated tenets on sport made him vulnerable to frequent biting criticism and yet he largely managed to impose his will on the Olympic Movement for two decades. Athletes and officials found themselves submitting to his authority because they realized that he had the power to exclude them from the Games should they stray. Though some of this power had eroded by the end of his tenure and his overall legacy is open to debate, there is no denying that the Olympic Movement would not have been the same without Brundage.

The discernible difference in how Moscow and Washington treated their respective Olympic efforts after 1968 and changes in the Cold War more generally create a twenty-year window in which to study the effects of the Cold War on the Olympics and vice versa. It is a compelling period marked by several high-stakes confrontations between the superpowers. Many would agree that much of the drama that permeated the Games made for more intriguing contests and only added to the Olympic appeal during the years under scrutiny. While the purists argue that something is lost when politics invade the Olympics, the reality is that diplomacy is an inherent aspect of all international sport. The Games would not be the same without these heightened stakes. Revere or revile them, politics are as much a part of the Games as the sports themselves.

CHAPTER 1

Sport in American Society

"We want to make sure that as our life becomes more sophisticated, as we become more urbanized, that we don't lose this very valuable facet of our national character: physical vitality, which is tied into qualities of character, which is tied into qualities of intellectual vigor and vitality"
—President John F. Kennedy, 1961[1]

In 1964, Attorney General Robert F. Kennedy took to the pages of *Sports Illustrated* magazine to discuss the importance of a strong finish by the United States Olympic team at the Summer Olympics in Tokyo. In a detailed article discussing the ways in which the American team could improve its medal chances, Kennedy drew a clear correlation between Olympic performance and international image.

> No nation officially "wins" the Olympics, but inevitably a country's showing is totaled unofficially and comparisons are made of those totals. So, though a nation's standing in international athletics is not the chief factor in its prestige, it does affect the reputation of its society and culture. During a military or nuclear stalemate such as the world is now experiencing athletics can become an increasingly important factor in international relations.[2]

In this same piece, the Attorney General expressed concern that the United States had experienced a decline in its medal total since 1948 and described an eight-point plan for improvement. While it might seem odd today for a Cabinet member to agonize over Olympic results, Kennedy's appeal was not out of context, given the contemporary circumstances. By 1964, the United States and the Soviet Union were at roughly high tide in the cultural Cold War, heightening the significance of the Olympic Games and other events outside the clear political realm like the space race and the Fulbright program.

For Kennedy and many other Washington leaders, beating Moscow on the playing field was critical to beating Moscow in the wider Cold War. This type of rhetoric encouraging American athletes and tying the Olympics to international prestige was quite typical of its time. Though the Cold War was less than two decades old when Kennedy penned this article, the history of athletics as an integral piece of American society and culture was much longer. Sports have enjoyed a rich history in the United States. They became part of the national identity more quickly than in Europe because athletics functioned as a common bond among the rapidly diversifying American population. One need not speak perfect English to cheer on the local baseball or soccer team. Amateur and college sports descended from English gentlemen's games, while the first American professional leagues, most notably baseball, and their accompanying hordes of spectators date back to the mid–1800s.[3] Two major developments encouraged the growth of American sport in the twentieth century. The eight-hour work day gave the average worker more leisure time to pursue sports while the growth of newspaper coverage and radio broadcasts of sporting events allowed spectators who could not be physically present at the games to follow their favorite teams more consistently. These gains in fan interest and press attention gradually encompassed the Olympics in the 1920s and 1930s, as the Games made newspaper headlines across the country and became items of national interest.

Warren Susman and Barbara Keys have argued that sports asserted themselves as an integral facet of American culture by the mid–1930s because they served both as a unifying force as well as an impetus for modernization. Sports provided a point of convergence for a nation with an increasingly diverse population, as well as a means of transcending linguistic barriers. Athletics were a modernizing influence in that individual sports gradually adopted standardized rules and complex hierarchies to preside over their leagues, mimicking the increasing professionalization of the twentieth century American federal government and business models.[4] Sports were also modern in the sense that they allowed comparison between athletes across local and national boundaries. Athletic achievement is largely measured in statistics because numbers provide an objective basis for determining the best sportsman. Doing so became increasingly important to American society by the 1930s because it mirrored the growing importance of numbers in other aspects of daily life. This emphasis on quantifiable results was part of the reason why baseball fans lauded Babe Ruth and still marvel at his playing statistics today.[5] Not only was he impressive to watch, but his stats clearly distinguished him from his competitors.

American sports became even more important during the Cold War because they offered a means of competing with Moscow outside the defined political realm. Sports' use of statistics and other quantifiable markers of achievement, including Olympic medals, made athletics quite conducive to the cultural Cold War that had developed by the mid–1950s. While the Soviet

Union shared this focus on sport as Cold War cannon fodder, the two nations diverged in their efforts to become the global sporting leader. Their differing approaches were largely a reflection of the inherent disparities in their general political ideologies. The Moscow government largely controlled the Soviet sporting infrastructure; yet, its American counterpart remained privatized. The White House and associated government agencies made several attempts to better coordinate American athletics, but there was never a single governing body comparable to the Soviets' All-Union Committee for Physical Culture & Sports Activities, known as the Sports Ministry. The USOC remained separate from the National Collegiate Athletics Association (NCAA) and the Amateur Athletic Union (AAU), although they sometimes worked toward the same goal and they frequently bickered over jurisdiction until Congress delegated authority to the USOC in 1978. While there were times when the lack of coordination among these entities hindered efforts to put its best team on the field, the system that produced a number of Olympic and world champions in a wide variety of sports was inherently American.

Tangential to this essential difference in approach was the national attitude toward team sports. The Soviet Union, as urged by the Kremlin, glorified team sports over individual contests, mirroring the collective aspect of communism. The Moscow government was so focused on the collective mindset that it frowned upon the use of the word "star" in conjunction with its athletes.[6] On the contrary, American fans and sportswriters alike tended to glorify individual sportsmen and their feats rather than the whole team. The relatively solo pursuits of golf, tennis, swimming, and baseball, the most individual of the team sports, all became popular spectator and recreational sports in the United States, while soccer never caught on to the same extent. Despite these differences, any event which pitted American athletes against the Soviet Union tended to attract a good deal of press and spectator attention.

By the early 1950s, Washington had begun to learn that organized sport provided a means through which the United States could battle in this unprecedented conflict on a level that was accessible to the general public.[7] While there was little that could be done to reassure the American people that the Soviets would never use their newly developed atomic weaponry or that they would stop annexing pieces of Eastern Europe, sports became a means through which the United States could demonstrate that it was the dominant power in the aftermath of World War II. Following a war layoff during which many professional athletes paused their training to enlist in the armed forces, American sport returned bigger and more integral to society than ever before. Additionally, the federal government began to learn what Stalin had realized more than a decade earlier regarding the propaganda potential of athletics. The White

House took a heightened interest in sporting developments, similar to its growing involvement with the space program, as rocketry also provided a Cold War achievement barometer. At first, Washington only offered counsel and encouraged better fitness among the American public; however, Soviet success at the 1952 Olympics motivated the White House to become more involved.[8] Nonetheless, Washington never undertook the same level of centralized, state-run programs that Moscow did, despite calls from athletes and fans alike for more aid and involvement.[9]

Regardless of the ongoing political tensions, athletic interactions between the superpowers enjoyed something of a golden age in the period from 1948 to 1968. Whenever the two sides faced off, a heightened sense of competition and public attention ensued, regardless of the sport, making for spirited matches that both sides treated as dress rehearsals for the Olympics. What made these games so engaging was that both the Soviets and the Americans bought into the importance of these matches. The interest and attention granted to these matchups was relatively equal, adding to the intensity and seriousness with which the athletes and the media alike approached these events. While American athletes visited and competed against many other countries during this period, no other matchups enjoyed the same public attention or enthusiasm as those against the Iron Curtain.[10]

The press perceived this growing public interest in the Cold War rivalry and took it to new heights. While sportswriting had begun to come into its own during the interwar period, its heyday was the 1950s and 1960s. As few sporting events were televised before the 1960s, newspapers and magazines were the main vehicles through which fans kept up with their favorite athletes or teams. The launching of *Sports Illustrated* magazine in 1954 offered readers a new avenue for in-depth features on college, professional, and international sporting events that went beyond the scope of the largely local coverage found in one's hometown daily paper. The sports column, which combined sideline analysis with editorial, became a common feature in newspapers across the country. Current events like the Cold War, which pervaded sport as it did nearly all facets of daily life, often found their way into these essays. While the American free press system largely allowed writers to either laud or lambast athletes, teams, or even the sports governance bodies as they saw fit, the absence of independent media outlets prevented this same type of writing from developing behind the Iron Curtain. As Soviet publications were usually subject to Kremlin approval, there were clear limits on what passed the censors. Therefore, self-critical pieces were extremely rare while those denouncing the American way were quite common on both sides. It was highly unusual for a writer in either country to let an opportunity to criticize the other pass without at least a pointed remark. Though hyperbolic at points, this prose helped fuel the Cold War sports rivalry among their readers.[11]

Both superpowers quickly embraced sport as a means to exhibit Cold War dominance, yet they did so in contrasting fashions, reflecting the intrinsic contradictions of their respective political systems. As such, American and Soviet audiences did not always follow the same sports.[12] By the 1930s, baseball and its growing pantheon of individual stars were widely accepted as the American past time; however, the game never achieved the same status behind the Iron Curtain. Instead, Stalin's masses flocked to soccer and hockey games and competed in track meets with thousands of other runners. While hockey attracted a solid following in the United States—particularly the Olympic superpower matchups beginning with the 1960 Winter Games—it never achieved the same cult status that it held in Europe. This difference in approach to sport manifested itself in the means through which each side looked to achieve their shared goal of athletic dominance. Each country's national government was active in sporting development, though in different ways. The Soviet Union realized the propaganda power of sport by the end of the 1920s and Stalin moved to channel this power much earlier than Washington, which took little interest in American sports after World War II.[13] Instead of direct involvement, the White House tended toward vocal support for American Olympians and encouragement of the general population to improve its fitness.

The United States and the First Modern Games

Long before the Cold War overtly politicized sport, the United States was one of the first countries involved in reviving the Olympic Games. America had already established itself as a sporting nation by the late 1880s. One of the first people that Baron Pierre de Coubertin approached regarding the Olympics was Princeton professor Edward Sloane because de Coubertin recognized that American sports already enjoyed a strong spectator foothold and he felt this interest might extend to international competition.[14] By this time, the AAU and the NCAA were nationally recognizable organizations with significant political sway. de Coubertin realized that selling the concept of the Games to the leadership of said groups was perhaps the best means of gaining support and attracting some of the best American athletes to Athens.

While a number of factors doomed de Coubertin's mission to garner broad American political support, fourteen American athletes competed in Athens. They returned home with a very favorable impression of Greece along with fond memories of the Games themselves. Though the opening days of competition received little American press attention, a few early successes set reporters from several daily publications sailing to Greece. James Connolly, a Harvard student who dropped out of school when the university refused his request for a leave of absence to compete, won the triple jump on 6 April, justifying his decision while simultaneously pushing the Olympics into the headlines back home. Connolly's was the first gold medal awarded at the Games.[15] Once news of his feat appeared in the *New York Herald* and other publications, American Olympic fever began to spread rapidly.[16]

While there were few world records threatened in Athens and the competition was far from global given the small number of nations represented, the crowds and the athletes alike seemed enamored with the prospect of renewing the spectacle every four years. In a cable report appearing in the *Boston Globe* during the midst of the Games on 12 April 1896, Princeton student Herbert Jamison confirmed as much. "I think the Olympics will be of very great value. They will arouse interest in athletics, gather nations together in friendly competition on lines of peace and exert a broadening influence on all competitors."[17] This statement showed that not only did Jamison enjoy his experience in Athens, but that he understood the diplomatic function of the Games as de Coubertin had envisioned them. While governments did not ascribe official ambassadorial roles to their participants, athletes and other visitors were always perceived as emissaries of their home countries. A poor showing on the field or an embarrassing incident off it would have reflected poorly on the transgressor's homeland. Luckily, the American delegation presented itself well, giving Washington no reason to fear for its global image.

Over the course of the ten-day event, the American team amassed twenty medals and captured eleven gold medals, the most top finishes of any competing nation.[18] While Greece more than doubled the American medal total with forty-five, the United States made a decidedly favorable impression on their hosts. They demonstrated to the rest of the field that the United States was a sporting power to watch in future Olympics and other international competitions.[19] The American athletes benefitted from a strong showing of support and admiration back home as well. A crowd of more than a thousand friends and admirers met the Princeton contingent when it arrived back in New Jersey, while the Boston area feted its new local heroes for weeks on end with a series of parties and celebrations in their honor.[20] The long-term effects of the American team's success were manifold. Several of the American representatives in Athens were one-time competitors; however, they left a lasting impression on their country. Beginning with the 1900 Olympics in Paris, there were always more athletes willing and eager to compete in the Olympics than there were spots on the American squad. Though the notion of Olympic trials for specific sports was still a ways in the future, more young men were competing in college sports by the turn of the century than had been the case a decade earlier. Many of these athletes eagerly sought a chance to represent their country on the growing world stage.

Pre–Cold War American Sport

Sports took on a much greater role in American society, both on the international/professional and on the grassroots levels in the twentieth century. Local newspapers had begun to include sports pages that reported daily on the home team's achievements in a number of events, with baseball as the most prevalent. In addition to providing a means of exercise and recreation, the cultural importance of sport as a unifying factor grew quickly after 1900. More than ever, the United States was a nation of immigrants, with newcomers arriving from all over the world. While there seemed to be at times many more barriers between ethnic groups than points of intersection, sports, for both participants and spectators, proved a means of bridging the gaps among these diverse groups of settlers.[21]

At the same time, wider changes in American society in these early decades facilitated the expansion of spectator sports and participation in amateur and professional leagues. Standardization of the eight-hour workday gave Americans more time to pursue sport, regardless of whether one preferred watching or playing. Newspapers began to devote more page space to covering athletics while the advent of commercial radio after World War I made it easier for fans to follow sports consistently.[22] Spectator sport was a major form of American entertainment by the 1920s, with baseball and collegiate football drawing the largest audiences. Basketball, a relative newcomer in terms of established sporting leagues, began to gain traction as well, though nothing could compete with the World Series each fall in terms of national attention and newspaper coverage.[23]

Although watching sports quickly became an integral part of American society, there was little attempt made either to regulate or commercialize athletics on a large scale basis, even after the infamous Black Sox scandal tainted the 1919 World Series and alienated many fans. Throughout the 1920s, intercollegiate athletics became the most prominent and regulated form of spectator sports. For example, universities soon realized how popular football was. They began to offer scholarships to promising players and built large stadiums to house thousands of fans, though these early efforts paled in comparison to today's investments of time and capital. After a period of fairly steady increase in interest from the 1890s through the 1920s, sports participation waned slightly during the Depression when an overall drop in disposable income forced many to curb their spending on leisure activity like attending baseball games.[24] While the Olympics received more attention overall after World War I than they had before the war, these sports garnered little spectator attention in the years between Games.

Even as the 1920s and 1930s witnessed a flourishing in popular interest in sports, the American government maintained a rather firm hands-off approach to athletics. Even during the discussions regarding whether or not the United States Olympic team should boycott Berlin four years later, the White House did not influence the USOC's decision to compete. The situation was quite different in 1980 when President Jimmy Carter decided almost singlehandedly that the United States would skip the Moscow Games to protest ongoing Soviet interference in Afghanistan. Franklin Roosevelt showed more interest in the Olympic Movement than Hoover, attending the 1932 Winter Games in Lake Placid, New York, in an official capacity as the Empire State's governor, but he was understandably preoccupied by the Great Depression and later World War II once he moved into the Oval Office. His administration refused to enter the discussions regarding a possible Berlin boycott, as the Olympics were deemed a private matter.[25]

Like the Games themselves, American sports in general largely went on hiatus during World War II. Major League Baseball continued to field teams each year, but many star players took a leave of absence from the game to defend their country. Sports became bigger than ever after the war, from new instructional leagues for children right up through the professional level. However, the onset of the Cold War added a layer of intrigue in American life that had not existed before World War II and gave sports a more strategic and prominent role in society. Americans had been skeptical of the Soviet Union since its creation and were reluctant to collaborate with Joseph Stalin to defeat the Germans. This aversion to communism and all things pertaining to Moscow only grew after the war, with Truman leading the way. The new commander in chief was much more suspicious of Stalin's motives and desire for expansion than Roosevelt had been. This flourishing antipathy for communism manifested itself in a sense of competition with the Soviets across the board.[26]

The rift between the superpowers soon seeped out from the military and political realms to encroach upon all aspects of daily life, including sports. Any and all points of contact between Americans and Soviets became competitions. Throughout the 1950s and especially the 1960s, international meets and tournaments in a variety of sports allowed American and Soviet athletes to compete on a more frequent basis. The Olympics proved particularly conducive to perpetuating this sense of rivalry because they occurred regularly and offered multiple opportunities for head-to-head competition within a two-week span. As such, both governments sought ways to improve on Olympic performance through all possible means. American governmental involvement in the Olympic Movement and in sporting pursuits more generally increased steadily with each presidential administration from the Truman years and into the early days of Lyndon Johnson's tenure until domestic protests and Vietnam concerns eclipsed this unwavering focus on the Cold War rivalry.[27] From the late 1940s through the mid–1960s, Washington gradually increased the attention and resources expended on athletics and physical fitness, both on the recreation and professional levels, to ensure that the United States remained competitive and dominant on the world stage.

The Truman Years: A Return to Sporting Normalcy

After World War II, American professional sports leagues experienced unprecedented growth. The advent of commercial television and national broadcasts brought baseball into homes across the United States, even those distant from the eastern cities that fielded teams. The 1950s saw the number of teams grow and drift as far west as California. The National Football League, though it had existed since 1920, really flourished during the late 1940s and 1950s. While there was some concern that Americans had grown too soft and lazy, the national appetite for watching others compete on the playing field and showcase their athletic prowess was stronger than ever. The idolatry of the modern athlete first witnessed in the 1920s reached new heights during the Cold War. College and professional athletes shared a growing national spotlight and ever increasing monetary rewards for their feats.[28]

The American public's quick return to sports spectatorship after World War II showed how important athletics were to society and national culture. As such, sports became an effective conduit for the increasingly hostile Cold War rhetoric emanating from Washington. The Kremlin had begun using sports, particularly soccer, as a means of forging ties with other countries and encouraging fitness among its constituency during the interwar period, once Stalin perceived the utility of sport as diplomatic tool. However, Moscow created highly centralized government programs to oversee the administration of sport behind the Iron Curtain. The three major amateur sporting bodies in the United States in 1946—the AAU, the NCAA, and the American Olympic Committee—were all privately funded. While subject to federal regulation, they were administered by private citizens rather than government employees.[29]

The White House began to take an interest in the athletic progress of the nation, but Truman had little direct authority over American sport. He could create groups like the President's Advisory Commission on Universal Training, but this body did not control the Olympic Movement or the other pre-established sporting organizations.[30]

Along with a growing admiration for sports stars, the early years of the Cold War witnessed a fear that the American public was falling behind the rest of the world, particularly the Soviet Union, in terms of physical fitness. Ensuring the continuation or improvement of the vigor of the American people was important to Truman. Almost immediately after the war ended, the president announced that thirty percent of the young men drafted for World War II had been deemed physically unfit for military service. His response was to campaign for Universal Military Training as a means of ensuring that the United States would be ready should another war break out.[31] He made a series of speeches emphasizing the importance of rectifying the "widespread physical and mental incapacity among the young people of our nation," as he termed it in November 1945, and tied better fitness to national security.[32] During a December 1946 meeting of the newly created President's Advisory Commission on Universal Training, Truman used strong rhetoric to emphasize the need for a fit population. "I have been somewhat of a student of history, and I have discovered that great republics of the past always passed out when their peoples became prosperous and fat and lazy, and were not willing to assume their responsibilities."[33] Here, Truman essentially warned that without a greater emphasis on physical fitness, the United States could soon fall into decline as the ancient Greek and Roman civilizations had, especially with an adversary like the Soviet Union looming overseas.

General Maxwell Taylor, the superintendent of West Point, echoed these calls for improved fitness within the general population—and criticized the president for not stressing this issue enough—during a summit on the topic in April 1948. According to Taylor, "the Grecian ideal of the importance of the whole man tends to disappear too easily in this age where technology and specialization count for so much."[34] This perceived need for a well-rounded citizenry soon became common Cold War rhetoric, reflecting the growing emphasis on the ideological divide between the superpowers.

Events in the sporting world and the accompanying press coverage reflected the growing rift between Moscow and Washington. In addition to a shared sense of relief that the Soviets decided not to compete in the 1948 Olympics, western sporting bodies proved reluctant to expose their athletes to communist influences. In 1949, *Washington Post* columnist Shirley Povich took a humorous tone when discussing the World Tennis Association's troubles with the Iron Curtain. The WTA faced pressure to "sever relations with the Russian satellite countries 'whose players are expected to act as Soviet agents.' If they're not content to stay behind the Iron Curtain, the viscount hopes it drops on their heads."[35] This quotation alluding to Viscount Templeton of London demonstrated how diplomacy was affecting sport, shedding light on the growing inextricability of sport and international relations. Povich declared in the same piece, "In the present state of world affairs, the democratic peoples would probably be willing to settle for the Soviet capture of international lawn tennis if the spread of communism could thus be contained…. If the Commies would leave us alone otherwise, they can have our tennis, I'd say."[36] This seemingly minor dig at the Soviet Union was just the beginning of the vicious verbal sparring that became synonymous with Cold War sport. Even a relatively low-profile game like lawn tennis was swept up in these growing Cold War tensions. If a concession in the sporting world was what it would take to keep the Iron Curtain from creeping west, many Americans—though maybe not tennis players—would have considered the matter.

Eisenhower and the Presidential Fitness Challenge

The Eisenhower years brought new crusades, both within the government and the private sector, to better prepare Americans to beat the Soviets and their Warsaw Pact allies. While Truman had verbally encouraged American fitness, his successors went further in undertaking more definitive action. A growing fear of Moscow led to a number of federal government initiatives during the Eisenhower and Kennedy administrations that sought to make Americans more formidable opponents on the playing field. Though they never fully realized the lofty goals that their creators set, many of these programs, like mandatory physical education classes in schools, remain in effect today.[37]

Though his policies and ideology were quite different from Truman's, Eisenhower also stressed the correlation between a physically fit nation and one best able to defend itself in the face of great challenges. The fear of a showdown with Moscow loomed large when he entered office in 1953. Like Truman, Eisenhower understood the importance of keeping up with the Soviets. As the Kremlin sought to expand its influence abroad through all viable means, including sport, Washington took steps to counter these efforts. In 1954, Eisenhower successfully urged Congress to divert over $5 million of the Emergency Fund for International Affairs toward athletic endeavors. This money financed international tours of elite athletes who performed and showcased the best of the American way of life in developing and third world countries. The response to these tours was overwhelmingly positive, according to American embassy personnel.[38] This venture was just one example of how seriously the White House approached international competition, especially the Olympics. When Washington and the American press usually depicted the Soviet athlete as an instrument of the state, they juxtaposed this negative image with one of the American athlete, particularly the Olympian, as a self-made champion. They were the best that society had to offer, updated examples of the American dream. Nonetheless, the increasingly pervasive "us vs. them" mentality embraced on both sides made simply participating insufficient. Gold medals became the ultimate end because they offered material proof of ideological superiority.[39]

Eisenhower focused on American youth as the best hope for improved fitness. A key administration goal was for the nation's youth to meet selective service requirements at a higher rate than their parents had during World War II. In a 1956 address to the Conference on the Fitness of American Youth, Eisenhower argued that "national policies will be no more than words if our people are not healthy of body, as well as of mind, putting dynamism and leadership into the carrying out of major decisions. Our young people must be physically as well as mentally and spiritually prepared for American citizenship."[40] The contemporary audience would have interpreted these "major decisions" as clear Cold War allusions. "American citizenship," as he and Truman defined it, included being prepared to defend or represent the United States to the best of one's physical and mental ability in all types of challenges. During the same speech, Eisenhower announced the creation of a President's Citizens Advisory Committee on the Fitness of American Youth, which was subsequently established via executive order on 16 July 1956.[41] This concern for physical fitness extended beyond national security issues and transcended administrations. Kennedy embraced this same crusade in the early 1960s. Throughout the first two decades of the Cold War, American losses in sports where they traditionally dominated often led to calls for increased physical fitness and criticism of the comfortable American way of life. These critiques were especially pointed whenever the Soviets or another Warsaw Pact nation emerged victorious, even at times drawing Brundage into the Cold War frenzy.

This increased emphasis on a fitter American public went beyond the White House and manifested itself in different ways. While international sporting news items had made for mostly minor headlines in the immediate postwar period, the 1950s saw a dramatic increase in the dissemination of athletic news in the United States and abroad. At home, the most important development in this sense was the launch of *Sports Illustrated* by Henry Luce, publisher of Time, Inc. Luce had established himself as an eager advocate for a stronger

American presence on the international stage before World War II. He argued in a widely read essay titled "The American Century" appearing in the 17 February 1941 issue of *Life* magazine that the United States had thus far "failed to play its part as a world power" and now needed to take a leading role as a benevolent influence abroad.[42] He contended that Americans should "accept wholeheartedly our duty and our opportunity as the most powerful and vital nation in the world and in consequence to exert upon the world the full impact of out influence."[43] Though written nearly five years before the start of the Cold War, Luce's vision was easily transferable to this era. In this new conflict of ideologies, the lines between black and white were very clearly drawn. The United States needed to establish itself as the benign foil to Stalin and the Soviet Union.

These sentiments on the importance of a strong American presence on the world stage also applied to sports. *Sports Illustrated* was not the first periodical devoted exclusively to national sports coverage, but it soon became both the most prestigious and one that has best stood the test of time. Luce, a staunch conservative, believed that "Americans were living under a cloud of mortal danger, but they were also assuming that 'peace was possible' ... [while] sports reflected 'the hopes of the American people in a very simple human way—in a way universally understood and richly appreciated.'"[44] Sports offered a means of escape for Americans, as they were a venue for optimism and a showcase for national pride. Sports offered a common ground where Americans and Soviets could compete at fairly low stakes but still gain a sense of national pride. Luce reasoned that everyone could appreciate and admire the skills of both amateur and professional athletes despite the linguistic and ideological barriers that separated the world's elite sportsmen. His personal belief that the United States needed to be aggressive in containing communism was downplayed in *Sports Illustrated* more than in the other branches of Time, Inc., but it continued to surface occasionally.[45]

While Eisenhower pressed public fitness initiatives, his administration pursued more covert means of increasing American sporting prowess and Cold War fitness. There was a growing fear by the 1950s that the Soviets' strong showing on the playing fields would soon threaten the United States' global propaganda initiatives, which played a critical role in their Cold War strategy.[46] The blank check that Eisenhower gave to Central Intelligence Agency (CIA) Director Allen Dulles and Secretary of State John Foster Dulles to roll back communism also applied to the realm of athletics where the CIA collaborated with various American sporting bodies to ensure that only the most positive images of the United States and its athletes were shared with the world. The objective was to foster an association between America and the values of peace and freedom—and athletic prowess—not solely behind the Iron Curtain but in Western Europe and the developing world also.[47] The cooperation between the AAU, USOA, and government agencies like the United States Information Agency, the CIA, and the Office of Policy Coordination was far more extensive than most realized contemporarily. Beginning with the International Cultural Exchange and Trade Fair Act of 1956, the federal government allocated $222,000 annually to send American athletes on international tours and exchanges.[48] The late 1950s also witnessed the creation of private AAU fundraising groups to try and keep up with the Soviets' growing dominance in global sport. These efforts culminated in the People to People Sports Committee, which fostered positive American images abroad but without the same emphasis on competition and domination.[49]

Sportswriters played a critical role in bringing spectators into the Cold War. In an age before most major athletic events were televised, Americans relied on sports journalism, both local newspapers and bigger magazines, to keep track of their favorite athletes and teams. *Sports Illustrated* quickly became a key source because the strength of its writers and the breadth of its coverage surpassed most of its competition. Its combination of features, game stories, and commentary took what local writers like Arthur Daley and Shirley Povich did and broadcast it to a national readership. Because it was a weekly rather than a daily publication and because its staff covered a wide range of events, it could provide more comprehensive of both American professional sports as well as frequent perspective on the international athletics scene. Because the Soviet Union was increasingly prevalent on the global sporting radar and because the Cold War was turning hot by the mid–1950s, Luce's venture outside the news-specific periodical soon paid off.

In comparison to the coverage that it received from many American daily newspapers, *Sports Illustrated* treated the Soviet Union relatively objectively. Though there were blatant instances of clear pro–American bias—as could be expected given the politics of its conservative publisher and the biases of its reading audience—the periodical proved to be a fairly reliable source for more balanced sports news and analysis. Its coverage of the Olympics, both in preview and retrospect, gradually became one of the event's most comprehensive sources, as its reporters profiled athletes around the world rather than focusing solely on the American team. Additionally, the magazine made a name for itself just two years into its existence through its well-publicized mission to aid the Hungarian defectors during the 1956 Melbourne Games.[50]

In addition to extensive coverage of collegiate and professional sports, *Sports Illustrated* ran stories throughout the 1950s focused on the ongoing national fitness campaign. One such article from 1957 detailed the calisthenics program at West Point as a model for the country. The author Dorothy Stull wrote, "like other schools, both military and civilian, West Point has felt the devastating effects of the increasing inactivity of American youth. Each year it is faced with the dismaying spectacle of the progressively worsening physical condition of the candidates for the academy. Lately, approximately half the candidates have been failing their physical entrance test because of overweight."[51] Stull lamented that the lack of physical fitness among West Point recruits was becoming a national security concern, particularly after World War II, when many army enlistees had failed mandatory fitness tests. "The job of making cadets physically fit gets harder and the time margin of safety smaller each year."[52] To counter this problem, West Point emphasized a program to turn all of its students into lifelong athletes as a means of improving the fitness of the general population. According to one colonel interviewed for the report, "'We're not just building muscle or ordering cadets to be fit,' says Colonel [Frank J.] Kobes. 'We have to sell the program. If we haven't taught cadets to like being active, they won't be active after they graduate.'"[53] This story was just one example of how private corporations and media outlets like *Sports Illustrated* became involved in the Cold War fitness crusade.

As the Cold War attained a sense of permanency and athletics became a recognized means of demonstrating strength on and off the field, the number of head-to-head competitions between the superpowers increased. Athletes relished these new opportunities to compete against relative unknowns and to showcase their athletic superiority. The sport that generated the most spectator interest was track and field. At one time considered an American-dominated sport, Soviet athletes made great strides toward leveling the playing field during the 1950s, making these meets highly competitive and entertaining. These events remained relatively friendly even in the face of increasing superpower tensions off the field. The athletes tended to use the meets, which were annual from 1958 to 1966, as practice runs for their biggest stage: the Olympics.[54] *Sports Illustrated* ran a preview in anticipation of the first American-Soviet track meet where it anticipated the highly competitive nature of the event while keeping an eye on Cold War politics. "In a rare moment of pessimism last week, John Foster Dulles conceded that the U.S. might well 'lose its shirt' in a diplomatic contest with Russia on Russian terms at the summit. No such pessimism clouds the determination of the potential diplomats who grace this page."[55] Following the precedent set at the first Olympics, the role that athletes naturally assumed as unofficial diplomats was tacitly understood by the 1950s. Dulles' "lose its shirt" comment in March 1958 was a reference to a proposed superpower summit to be held at the Kremlin and focused on lessening international tensions. At the time, Dulles announced that the United States had nothing to gain from going to Moscow to meet on Russian terms and would only end up making unfortunate concessions by attending.[56] Luckily for American athletes, the anticipated outcome on the track was more promising.

What soon became an annual tradition attracted many fans and promoted a healthy rivalry between Soviet and American runners. *Sports Illustrated* offered ample coverage of the annual event, terming it "the most important track meet the U.S. takes part in except for the Olympic Games."[57] American and Soviet track stars alike eagerly anticipated these opportunities to sharpen their skills and compete against their biggest rivals. Despite a number of ugly near confrontations between Moscow and Washington, the officials, athletes, and spectators at these events exhibited little of the hostility that poisoned international relations. It was not until the United States stepped up its involvement in Vietnam during the Johnson administration that tensions precluded these meets. The Soviets canceled the 1966 competition in protest of Washington's escalation in Southeast Asia while also distracted by their own increasing troubles with China.[58] Both sides took the results of these meets quite seriously, particularly once the competition was established as an annual event. *SI* dubbed the 1961 contest, held at Moscow's Lenin Stadium, "a struggle worthy of the nations and athletes involved," as the American men and Russian women triumphed.[59] Just two years later, another story in *Sports Illustrated* lamented the relative decline of American female runners in comparison to their European, primarily Soviet, peers. "Our girls golf, swim, ski, skate, and perform in most other sports, but they dodge track and field as though it were a combined course in weight lifting and wrestling…. Outclassed, outloved and out of fashion, our girls may have lost heart."[60] Concerns about lackluster results continued into the 1960s, bringing with them a sense of inferiority in comparison to Soviet female harriers alongside appeals for improvement.

Though track was perhaps the most visible Cold War rivalry, the superpowers' competition extended beyond the fieldhouse. Though it never received as much attention or as large a following as track, another solid rivalry developed between the superpowers' volleyball teams. Moscow dominated their first matchup at the 1964 Olympics as well as their meeting at the international men's volleyball championships in 1965. The American team finally beat the Soviets for the first time at the 1968 Olympics.[61] Basketball was another hotly contested sport, with the Soviets threatening the traditional American monopoly on the sport by the late 1950s.

Cold War politics and related visa problems prevented the same type of healthy rivalry from developing in ice hockey. In 1957, the United States boycotted the world championships in Moscow in protest of Moscow's actions during the Hungarian Revolution in 1956. Several nations had requested that the championships be moved to neutral Sweden, to no avail.[62] While the Americans shocked the world by beating the Soviets in the gold medal game at the 1960 Olympics in Squaw Valley, diplomatic issues had derailed a number of anticipated matchups between the superpowers throughout the previous decade. Problems between the superpowers arose again in 1962 when the U.S. State Department denied entry visas to the East German team for the world championships in Colorado because NATO did not recognize the German Democratic Republic. Moscow protested in vain.[63] In addition to preventing what could have been some great matchups, these problems disproved the IOC's belief that politics and sports were mutually exclusive.

Kennedy and the President's Council on Fitness

One could make the case that the American president who has most often been depicted as the picture of vigor and athleticism—if only in terms of his public persona—was John F. Kennedy. His staff took great care to depict the oft-ailing Kennedy as youthful and active. Improving American fitness was an important goal for his administration; Kennedy even intervened in the long-running dispute between the NCAA and the AAU as a means of preventing any detrimental disruption to American athletic training. Like Eisenhower, Kennedy addressed the annual Youth Fitness Conference, linking the nation's vitality to the physical wellbeing of its citizens.

> We do not want in the United States a nation of spectators. We want a nation of participants in the vigorous life…. I want to do better. And I think you want to do better. We want to make sure that as our life becomes more sophisticated, as we become more urbanized, that we don't lose this very valuable facet of our national character: physical vitality, which is tied into qualities of character, which is tied into qualities of intellectual vigor and vitality.[64]

In this speech from February 1961, Kennedy warned against the same national slovenliness over which Truman and Eisenhower had agonized before him. The ongoing White House fixation with national wellness showed that it was a persistent concern, even when not the chief priority.

Kennedy went further than either Truman or Eisenhower in backing his fitness rhetoric with definitive action. In July 1961, the president spoke again on the need for a more athletic American youth as part of a campaign for school-centered physical educational programs. In this address, he linked the strength of American democracy to the physical vitality of its citizens, using the Cold War rhetoric for which he was quite well-known. "This country is going to move through difficult days, difficult years. The responsibilities upon us are heavy, as the leader of the free world. We carry worldwide commitments. People look to us with hope, and if we fail they look to those who are our adversaries."[65] The connection between the position of the United States as the leader of the western world and its physical prowess was obvious. A few lines later, Kennedy elaborated upon this link further:

> We should make every effort to see that the intellectual talents of every boy and girl are developed to the maximum. And that also their physical fitness, their willingness to participate in physical exercise, their willingness to participate in physical contests, in athletic contests—all these, I think, will do a good deal to strengthen this country, and also to contribute to a greater enjoyment of life in the years to come. This is a responsibility which is upon all of us.[66]

This speech demonstrated the president's belief that fitness should be a priority for all Americans for both personal enrichment and for improved national strength. To this end, he created the Interagency Committee on International Athletics in 1963 to keep the White House informed on matters pertaining to American sporting endeavors.[67] The language of Executive Order 11117, its founding document, drew a clear link between sport and diplomacy. This order declared that "international amateur athletic competitions and related activities conducted by private individuals and organizations free from government sponsorship, interference, or control frequently make significant contributions to international good will and elevate standards of physical welfare throughout the world."[68] As such, Kennedy authorized the committee, comprised of individuals from a number of government departments and representatives from the various amateur sporting bodies, to gather information on amateur athletic events and coordinate with the State Department to maximize American good will opportunities. Though a powerful endorsement of the athlete's role as diplomat, the Committee made few contributions either to American sport or the State Department.

Perhaps the clearest parallel that Kennedy made between American diplomatic prowess and a fit population came in an August 1963 address entitled "Progress Report from the President on Physical Fitness." These remarks, coming on the heels of a goodwill tour to Europe, again betrayed Kennedy's concern that Americans were not as fit as their European peers. He drew a direct correlation between the United States' ability to lead both in war and in peacetime with the physical acuity of the nation at large:

> We have seen in World War II, in Korea and in the jungles of Southeast Asia that any weapon, no matter how brilliantly conceived, must depend for its effectiveness on the fighting trim of the soldier who uses it. And what is true for the weapons of war is also true for the instruments of peace. Whether it is the astronaut exploring the boundaries of space, or the overworked civil servant laboring into the night to keep a Government

President John F. Kennedy signs Detroit's bid to host the 1968 Summer Olympics in September 1963 with Michigan senator Philip A. Hart and representatives Martha W. Griffiths, Neil Staebler, and Harold M. Ryan looking on (Abbie Rowe. White House Photographs. John F. Kennedy Presidential Library and Museum. Boston).

program going, the effectiveness and creativity of the individual must rest, in large measure, on his physical fitness and vitality.[69]

While the World War II reference was a familiar example to all, the more contemporary allusions to Korea and "the jungles of Southeast Asia," namely Vietnam, add an unmistakable Cold War tone to this address. By 1963, the United States had begun to escalate its efforts in Vietnam, much to Moscow's consternation. It was notable that Kennedy also mentioned the space race, another intensifying Cold War battleground. Both Washington and Moscow emphasized the importance of putting the first man on the moon, pulling rocketry into the Cold War.[70] While the overarching message of this speech was that physical fitness is important for all aspects of life, the pervasive Cold War overtones regarding a more well-rounded population, first expressed during the Truman administration, are obvious even today.

Kennedy also modified the Council on Youth Fitness, a product of the

Eisenhower administration, to become the Council on Physical Fitness. The name change reflected the importance that his administration placed on fitness at all levels rather than exclusively on children. Eisenhower had created the Council on Youth Fitness in June 1956 to address the growing concern with the physical state of American youth, particularly those who might someday join the armed forces. Perhaps the most notable product of this committee was the President's Challenge, still administered in physical education classes across the country at the beginning of each school year.[71] Kennedy's extension of the program to encompass all Americans stressed the importance of physical fitness at all ages.

Writing again for *Sports Illustrated* in 1962, the president tied the strength of the United States to the physical health and vigor of its citizens. As such, all Americans had an obligation to devote themselves to improved fitness and increased athleticism.[72] These responsibilities were part of a larger commitment to maintaining the nation's wellbeing on all fronts. He cautioned against growing soft physically while fighting the Cold War in other ways. Kennedy feared that focusing too much on sedentary activities, though critical to national progress and to keeping pace with the Soviets, was creating an unfit American people. "It is paradoxical that the very economic progress, the technological advance and scientific breakthroughs which have, in part, been the result of our national vigor have also contributed to the draining of that vigor.... We cannot permit the loss of that physical vigor which has helped to nourish our growth and which is essential if we are to carry forward the complex and demanding tasks which are vital to our strength and progress."[73]

For Kennedy, athletics were a vital aspect of the Cold War. Physical strength was a means of maintaining "our capacity to undertake the enormous efforts of mind and courage and will which are the price of maintaining the peace and insuring the continued flourishing of our civilization."[74] Like Eisenhower, Kennedy did not hesitate to combine his appeals for better fitness with a jab at communism, writing that Americans, in contrast to their Soviet peers controlled by state athletic systems, enjoyed "liberation of the individual to pursue his own ends, subject only to the loose restraints of a free society, which is the ultimate meaning of our civilization."[75] This ongoing juxtaposition of communism and capitalism rationalized the American people's obligation to their society. Kennedy reminded his readers that the Soviet public was pursuing many of the same objectives only without the same freedoms.

In addition to rousing speeches and written appeals, Kennedy involved himself with matters of national fitness as an arbitrator. When the feud that had been brewing between the AAU and other amateur athletic groups, including the NCAA, reached a boiling point in December 1962, the president dispatched

World War II hero General Douglas MacArthur to serve as mediator. While this might seem an odd place for the president to intervene, Kennedy used a weekly news conference to justify his involvement, citing the consequences that could result should this dispute continue. "Their continued bickering is grossly unfair. There is no winner, but there are many losers—thousands of American amateur athletes, the American athletic community, and the traditions of American sportsmanship. On behalf of the country and on behalf of sport, I call on these organizations to submit their differences to an arbitration panel immediately. If we do not, we will not have an Olympic team in 1964."[76] While the United States went on to compete in the Olympics without this issue noticeably hindering its performance, the bickering between the AAU and other associations continued intermittently until the 1970s. That the president felt a need to intervene in such a quarrel, which might in other times be considered petty and beneath the concerns of his office underscored the contemporary importance of athletics by the early 1960s. Sports in general, and the Olympics in particular, were vital, low-stakes Cold War proving grounds. While a loss to the Soviets on the playing field was traumatic and inevitably triggered calls for improved American fitness, its results and consequences were less disastrous than the costs that a military skirmish would have incurred. Sports seemed to be matters of life and death at times, but most agreed that a fleeting loss of face on the playing field was always preferable to the consequences of a military or nuclear scuffle.

Johnson and the Shift in Focus

Lyndon Johnson also tied athletic performance to the Cold War when he assumed office after Kennedy's death, though he did not maintain the same level of commitment or personal involvement. In a speech to the President's Council on Fitness in July 1964, he reinforced the clear link that Kennedy had forged between physical fitness and America's ability to fight the Cold War. "The fitness of our Nation for the tasks of our times can never be greater than the general physical fitness of our citizens. A people proud of their collective heritage will take pride in their individual health, because we cannot stay strong as a country if we go soft as citizens."[77] The "tasks of our times" remark alluded to the Cold War and Vietnam, a growing concern for his administration. In the same speech, Johnson warned that not increasing the fitness of Americans carry a "tangible and measurable price."[78] This concern was particularly effective in Olympic years like 1964, because the United States was in search of redemption, having "lost" the medal counts at both the 1956 and 1960 Summer Games to the Soviets. Despite Johnson's warnings, however, the United States again finished a disappointing second in the Tokyo contests.

The president took this blatant Cold War rhetoric a step further in a May 1965 speech to the winners of the Physical Fitness Leadership Awards Program. Despite the young audience, Johnson did not shy away from linking physical fitness with Cold War prowess. "A strong nation must be a fit nation, and for these times in this 30th century in which we live we must all do everything we can to be physically fit at all times. But we must also be fit mentally and psychologically. The enemies of freedom are always quick and unerring in their exploitation of flabbiness and fat and any weaknesses that they may find either in our bodies or in our minds."[79] The imagery here was at once striking and foreboding, playing on the standard "us vs. them" mentality and depicting the Soviets as the enemies of freedom. Johnson drew parallels between the contemporary situation and other times of war, heightening the militaristic tone of this speech. "All through this century in which we live, the adversaries of our free society have mistakenly assumed that peoples that enjoy the abundance that we enjoy inevitably become unwilling and unable to bear the burdens as well as the challenges of modern times. This assumption, as you know, has always proved wrong. It was wrong in 1917, it was wrong in 1941, it is wrong now."[80]

However, Johnson presided over a changing Cold War. Soon more pressing concerns forced him to turn his attention away from athletics to growing challenges at home and abroad. The ongoing civil rights struggle turned violent beginning in 1964, with riots erupting in cities across the country. At the same time, Vietnam had become a public relations disaster. Under his watch, the war that he had inherited from Kennedy drained the administration's resources as well as a huge liability in terms of his public credibility. By the time he decided not to seek reelection in early 1968, it seemed that Johnson could do nothing right to save his public image or to regain his constituency's trust. As such, he was essentially a shadow of his former self, limiting his public appearances and worrying less about American fitness.[81]

American sports were changing by the late 1960s as well. The growing commercialism of college and professional sports left little room for the type of White House involvement that characterized the Kennedy years. The USOC was growing more powerful as the AAU saw its influence dwindle. Consequently, there was less bickering between these groups and the NCAA, decreasing the need for White House involvement in moderating disputes for a brief time. The changing tone in the wider Cold War decreased pressure to develop a well-rounded citizenry prepared for a clash of ideologies. The draft was in effect for Vietnam, yet there was less fear of an imminent conflict with Moscow because the Soviet Union faced its own share of struggles. Soviet premier Leonid Brezhnev faced anti–Moscow uprisings behind the Iron Curtain and a period of general domestic decline. As such, neither Johnson nor Brezhnev had the energy or the resources to continue fighting the Cold War at the same high-tension levels as their predecessors. While sports, and especially the Olympics, remained quite important in both countries, Moscow and Washington deemphasized the propaganda aspect of athletics. Nixon's administration would continue this trend following his election in November 1968.

Conclusion

American interest in sport skyrocketed after World War II. Professional and collegiate sports became bigger than ever. Millions of spectators flocked to games across the country and followed their favorite teams via radio, newspaper, and later television. With the dawn of the Cold War, Washington began to take an increased interest in sport as well for two key reasons. First, there was a growing concern that the United States general population was growing complacent in its physical fitness. This anxiety was rooted in a concern that the draft may soon face a numbers crunch, as so many young men had failed the mandatory fitness exams during World War II. Beginning under Truman and lasting into Johnson's tenure, the White House urged Americans to improve their physical prowess through a number of initiatives. This crusade placed a special emphasis on American youth, establishing programs that still exist today. The second piece of the Oval Office's heightened interest in sport was overtly political and closely linked to the Olympics. With the onset of the Cold War, victories on the international playing field became conflated with national worth and global image. While the Olympics provided the most visible and therefore most important stage for these matchups, all competition between the superpowers brought high stakes, consequently meriting close White House attention.

To this end, Washington piloted a number of initiatives to make the United States the dominant global sporting power during the first two decades of the Cold War. Many of these originated directly from the Oval Office. From the Eisenhower-era President's Fitness Challenge to Kennedy's appeals in *Sports Illustrated*, the Cold War sharpened the focus on the nation's health. As a result, the lines between sport for sports sake and sport for political gain were often blurred and sometimes crossed, whether intentionally or not. While a more fit population was important for a traditional war, international sports competitions, and especially the Olympics, were critical battles in the growing cultural Cold War. In this all-consuming ideological struggle, beating Moscow by all means possible was the ultimate end. Never was this truer than during the Kennedy years. With the tactical Cold War at a virtual stalemate after the 1962 Cuban Missile Crisis, winning on the playing field, or in the space race, was a means of pulling ahead in what he had famously termed the "long twilight struggle" during his inaugural address.[82]

At the same time, this rhetoric was effective only because sport was already a critical component of American society at the dawn of the Cold War. These words and initiatives would have been empty without a population that enjoyed sport and embraced athletes as cultural icons. Washington's plans for a fitter America were directed at a public that attended college and professional games in large numbers, who read the local sports pages, and followed the Olympics fairly closely for two weeks every four years. As such, the public was receptive to appeals for improved performance at all levels. By the late 1950s and early 1960s, there were signs that Americans were more active and were passing fitness tests with greater regularity than the World War II generation.

A parallel growth in Olympic interest among spectators and sportswriters on both sides of the Iron Curtain allowed the government to tie achievement in the Games to the wider Cold War. There was enough public interest that Soviet-American track meets were televised and that sporting publications ran previews and forecasted the outcome of such events. Sportswriters eagerly dissected all interactions between east and west, offering both news and critiques. At the top, the White House treated their various initiatives to improve American performance quite seriously throughout the first two decades of the Cold War. From presidential speeches and initiatives to the private citizens who wrote in to *Sports Illustrated* concerned with how the United States was handling its Olympic pursuits, it is evident that sport and the Games were key pieces of American society throughout the Cold War, particularly from 1948 to 1968.

CHAPTER 2

Sport in Soviet Society

"We consider our sportsmen to be among the world's best; they would be wonderful ambassadors for Russia."[1]
—Soviet soccer official, 1945

Sports assumed critical social and political roles in the Soviet Union during the Cold War, adopting many of the same functions as in the United States. Like Washington, Moscow used athletics, and especially the Olympics, to gain Cold War prestige and to demonstrate ideological supremacy. However, sport and its functions evolved differently there from the United States. While spectator sport was a major form of entertainment in the United States by the late nineteenth century, it took a bit longer for Soviet sport to achieve this same sense of cultural significance, due to the changes wrought by the revolution. However, when Moscow caught up with the west early into Joseph Stalin's tenure as General Secretary, it begun to promote sport among fellow communist countries for both cultural and diplomatic ends.[2]

Soviet sport assumed diplomatic functions as early as the 1920s. First, Moscow used athletics to prove cultural superiority, but sport had a second and perhaps more critical purpose: to help the Soviet Union establish itself as a legitimate entity on the world stage. Later, when the Soviet Union moved into a period of relative stagnation in the waning days of Khrushchev's power, achieving Olympic and athletic glory more generally became a strategy to deflect attention from the country's political misadventures and other disheartening domestic problems. This proved a viable distraction for only a few brief years before these problems became too critical to ignore.[3] However important sport was to American society and politics during the Cold War, it was even more so behind the Iron Curtain because it fulfilled so many purposes.

The Soviets shared the emphasis placed on the Olympics and international athletic competition more broadly that characterized American sport during the Cold War. Like the United States, Moscow began to view Olympic achievement as a means of demonstrating political supremacy after World War II. This increased emphasis on athletic glory for diplomatic means peaked during the early 1960s following the Bay of Pigs invasion and the Cuban Missile Crisis, which when taken together, served as a reminder to all that neither country was really winning the tactical Cold War. The Soviet Union also used sport to demonstrate the superiority of the communist way of life to its satellites in order to deter revolts, especially in the German Democratic Republic, which was the Kremlin's strongest and most important ally. The development of sport behind the Iron Curtain transpired within four distinct phases, which correspond roughly to the stages of Soviet diplomacy: isolation during the early years following the Russian Revolution, limited re-entry to the world stage during the 1930s through World War II, full international integration during the early Cold War until Stalin's death, and co-dominance with the United States during the Khrushchev and Brezhnev years. These latter two stages were fairly continuous, as the athletics system that Stalin had developed proved self-sustaining. While the focus of this chapter will be on the latter two periods, it is necessary to look briefly at the pre–Cold War years in order to provide context for Soviet behavior during the Cold War.

Post-Russian Revolution: Upheaval and Isolation

Imperial Russian participation in the Olympic Games prior to 1917 had been sporadic. Their intermittent appearances resulted mostly from the political upheaval that plagued the country throughout the first quarter of the twentieth century. Czarist Russia had not competed in the augural Athens contests, instead making its Olympic debut in Paris in 1900. Five Russian athletes competed in France, but none brought home a medal.[4] The Russo-Japanese War and the obstacles it presented to overseas travel kept the athletes away from St. Louis. They competed in the first London Games in 1908, capturing the Russian Empire's first three Olympic medals.[5] Russia competed for a final time while under czarist rule in 1912 and won five medals.[6] The Russians seemed to take their Olympic entries seriously for the first time in the Stockholm Games, as 159 athletes comprised the team that traveled to Sweden, a dramatic increase from the six who had competed in London.[7]

After the Revolution, the newly formed Soviet Union did not compete in another Olympics until the 1952 Summer Games. The country was still in the throes of revolution during the 1920 Antwerp Games, though the new Soviet Union did receive an invitation to participate, unlike Germany. Once Stalin consolidated his power in 1923, his administration focused almost entirely on increasing worker productivity and fomenting an international socialist revolution to the exclusion of other pursuits.[8] The Olympics were not part of his plans. Sport was important to the new Soviet Union, but only sport among the communists. Stalin withdrew his people from all international athletic competition that was not strictly among socialist parties or nations in the mid–1920s, including soccer, which was becoming both a national favorite and a global phenomenon. Part of the rationale for this retreat was a deep-seated reluctance to accept the international sport governing bodies' rules.[9] This hesitation resurfaced when the Soviets debated joining the IOC following World War II. Moscow was wary of joining international federations where Stalin would not be the decision maker. It often refused to play by anyone else's rules, because it equated doing so with participating in bourgeois politics.[10]

Despite this aversion to joining sporting bodies, the 1920s proved to be a critical period for Soviet athletic development. A sense of failure following the 1912 Games and their embarrassing legacy for czarist Russia left a lasting impact that withstood the transition to communism. While the new Soviet leaders had no interest in joining the Olympic Movement, there was a perceived need to demonstrate the superiority of communist sport over the established world sporting federations like the IOC and FIFA, soccer's international governing body. When the IOC held the first Winter Games in 1924, the Soviets countered with their own version of winter contests.[11] Additionally, Moscow recognized sport's utility as an effective foreign policy tool more than twenty years before Washington did. Stalin felt that sports development was too important to diplomacy to be left to private control. This proved to be one of the key differences in how the growth of sport manifested itself in the United States versus within the Soviet Union. While Washington generally left the administration and progress of its elite athletes in the hands of private interests, both individual coaches and larger bodies like the USOC, Stalin maintained that Soviet sport was a state matter.

The Kremlin created two agencies to oversee sport and ensure that this modernization process was taken seriously: the International Association of Red Sports and Gymnastics Association, also known as the Sportintern, and the State Committee for Physical Culture and Sport. These bureaus, which lasted into the 1930s, oversaw athletics at all levels.[12] The Kremlin's primary objective became improving the fitness of young Soviet men to better prepare them to serve in the armed forces. As discussed in the previous chapter, the United States used athletics for this same end following the Second World War. One of the many differences between post–World War II American initiatives and the earlier Sportintern was that the latter soon became an international body that recruited workers from around the world. The American programs were purely domestic. The United States only later looked to provide an example for developing countries, but never formed an umbrella organization. On the contrary, an executive council with representatives from several European countries with active communist parties governed the Sportintern, though the Soviet Union was always the dominant voice and Stalin always had the final say. The Sportintern held three international conferences during the 1920s and aligned itself closely with the German workers' movement, which dated back to the 1890s.[13] It moved under the Comintern umbrella in 1924 and soon found itself under almost total Kremlin control. The Comintern was the common name for the Communist International, a Moscow based political organization founded by Vladimir Lenin, whose stated intent was to foment world revolution and to overthrow the bourgeoisie. Under its jurisdiction were a number of socialist organizations like the Red Sport International and the Communist Youth International.[14]

A second rationale for the creation of the Sportintern was to compete with the IOC and rival European sports governing bodies for prestige on an international level to prove the supremacy of communist sports over capitalist. It held a number of international sporting competitions throughout its short lifetime to provide an alternative to the Olympics that did not force athletes to submit to the "bourgeois" nationalism of de Coubertin and the IOC. While Moscow dismissed the Olympics as elitist because the IOC required that athletes compete under national flags rather than celebrating individual glory and because of their strict rules regarding amateurism, the Sportintern-sponsored Workers' Olympics prided themselves on their openness to all workers and on their intent of creating international camaraderie in lieu of rivalries.[15] The Kremlin elected to dissolve the Sportintern in 1937, as Moscow had changed its views on direct competition with the west and on joining western federations.[16] With the realization that head-to-head match ups with non-communists were the only means of proving Soviet supremacy on the field, the worker sports movement fell out of favor in Moscow.[17] Simultaneously, the Sportintern had lost its luster throughout Europe because worker sports in other countries had slowly diminished in significance in favor of increased contact with non-communist teams.

Seemingly incessant upheaval and bureaucratic reorganization impaired the efficacy of the State Committee for Physical Culture and Sport and its ability to make any lasting changes to Soviet athletics. Part of the problem was that Stalin held sport as so important to foreign policy that the Kremlin kept the agency under a much closer eye than other bureaus. This limited its ability act without official approval, which took time to obtain. Additionally, the Committee, like all Soviet bureaus, was subject to numerous restructurings according to five-year plans over its short lifespan. The Committee, along with the Sportintern, fell prey to Stalin's constant bureaucratic reconfiguring by the late 1930s.[18]

While opportunities for international competition were sporadic at best throughout the 1920s outside the Workers Olympics, Moscow encouraged the public to remain active by joining the teams and clubs that their cities or workplaces sponsored.[19] This push for a fitter population continued into the 1930s, where the growth of spectator sports mirrored that in the United States. But these publics embraced different games. Americans focused on and embraced individual sports while Moscow encouraged team events, reflecting the inherent dichotomy in their national governments and mindsets. While baseball became the great American pastime, soccer, ice hockey, and track prevailed as the Soviet favorites. National and local leagues sprang up across the country and training centers dotted the countryside, each with the hopes of developing the best new talent.[20] Throughout the 1930s, these athletes competed primarily against teams from either within the Soviet Union or other communist-friendly nations, many of which became Soviet satellites or Soviet Socialist Republics following World War II.

Early Reintegration: 1930s–1940s

The 1930s saw the Kremlin begin to retract its aversion to non-socialist international sporting bodies, as Moscow began to rely more heavily on the global propaganda value of sport, setting the stage for the Cold War. Because there was little serious communist competition to be had (the low level of competition offered limited opportunity for the Soviets to sharpen their skills) and because Stalin felt that Soviet Union was secure enough to begin aggressively recruiting new prospective communist countries, the Kremlin started scheduling matches with western nations.[21] The Physical Culture Council, which by the 1930s largely controlled sport in the Soviet Union, looked into first allowing soccer games with noncommunist teams in 1933, having decided that the benefits of playing western teams outranked potential drawbacks. These matches improved the quality of Soviet soccer while boosting morale. They also gave Moscow opportunities to demonstrate the supremacy of communist sport over the capitalist model a decade before Washington began to consider the Soviets their chief competition in all things.[22]

However, this plan to use sport to demonstrate global political supremacy did not go quite as smoothly as the Council had envisioned. Western FIFA members, though wary of the communists, were not unanimously opposed to playing against the Soviets. However, they were reluctant to do so without Moscow joining FIFA and consenting to play by its regulations. The Soviets were unwilling to concede this point without a fight because they disliked the emphasis that FIFA placed on national associations.[23] While the 1920s Worker Olympics had been competitions among individuals rather than nations, FIFA was comprised of member nations whose national soccer teams played each other. There was no room for transnational teams or for matches against non-member nations. FIFA was willing to bend the rules for Moscow throughout the mid–1930s because several of its members had expressed an interest in facing off against the Soviets. It extended an invitation for provisional status, which would permit matches between its members and the Soviets, though this brought the expectation that Moscow would soon seek full membership. In making this exception, FIFA acknowledged that the Soviets would ignore some of its rules, but Moscow showed little interest in full membership. Like Stalin's later demands to restructure the IOC to better fit Soviet interests in 1951, the Kremlin tried—and failed—to mold FIFA to its liking. When this faltered and the Soviets continued to resist membership, they saw their opportunities to play western nations diminish rapidly. Most FIFA members were increasingly unwilling to jeopardize their own membership by playing the Soviets. Accordingly, there were few matches between the Soviets and FIFA teams throughout the latter half of the 1930s or during the World War II years when international sport all but disappeared.[24]

While Moscow tried to use FIFA to move to the forefront of global sport, it simultaneously undertook a conscious effort to improve its international prestige by building up its own image as a sporting power. Though this program began in the early 1930s, it did not include sending a team to the Berlin Games. The daily newspaper *Sovetsky Sport*, first published in 1924 and still in print today more than twenty years after the Soviet Union's dissolution, aimed to increase its international circulation during the 1930s to improve the publication of Soviet athletic feats.[25] Some of this effort was devoted to improving relations between the Kremlin and its communist peers in other countries like the French Popular Front and its Albanian counterpart, though this strategy netted few gains.[26] A concentrated endeavor toward a rapprochement with the western sports powers began in 1934 under the tagline "catch up to and overtake bourgeois records in sport."[27]

As part of this goal, the Physical Culture Council closely monitored western athletic activity and looked to emulate these training programs. Simultaneously, it promoted Soviet sport accomplishment by all means available to draw attention to the country's growing athletic prowess. A soccer match scheduled against the Czechs in 1934 received remarkable amounts of Kremlin and press attention because beating a recognized soccer power like Czechoslovakia was perceived as the gateway to games against other skilled teams. Playing other accomplished teams would then improve the Soviets' reputation and skill level in soccer.[28] Moscow did manage to schedule games with other western teams and its teams were relatively successful in the matches they did play; however, Stalin's continued refusal to join FIFA severely limited Soviet opportunities by the end of the decade. The only real exception to this growing isolation was an athletic exchange between the Soviets and Nazi Germany following the signing of the Molotov-Ribbentrop Pact in 1939. Over the subsequent year, more than 400 athletes from the two countries faced off in a variety of sports including soccer, track, tennis, and gymnastics, until Operation Barbarossa commenced in June 1941.[29]

As in the United States, World War II pushed sports to the back burner temporarily, but they grew bigger and more culturally important than ever once the Axis powers had fallen. An emphasis on true international competition quickly replaced the prewar focus on competing primarily against other communist-friendly societies. Even though they offered the same sports as the Olympics, or perhaps because of this overlap, the Worker Olympics and other communist-only events never received the same media and spectator attention as the Olympics or FIFA, thereby limiting their utility as a propaganda tool.[30] Part of the rationale for the switch was a heightened emphasis on sport to showcase Soviet supremacy. Opening up the competition created more opportunities for this.

From this point, the development of American and Soviet sport began to converge, as both looked for ways to capitalize on the propaganda power of international athletics. Yet while the American sports hierarchy remained mostly private, the Kremlin looked toward state-sponsored initiatives to accomplish its sporting agenda.[31] One of the first steps in doing so involved increasing the number of interactions with sporting teams outside the Soviet Union to improve foreign impressions of Soviet prowess.

The armistice gave the Soviets their first chance to show off their soccer prowess via a series of games in Britain in late 1945. The first meaningful foray into noncommunist sport came when the Moscow Dynamo soccer team accepted an invitation to play a series of friendly matches against British teams. This trip occurred in the short window of amity between the end of the war in the Pacific and the descent of the Iron Curtain, as Winston Churchill would term it in March 1946. Soviet troops stationed in western Europe after the European armistice had played several informal matches in September and October with military teams from France and Britain, but this visit was much more scripted and treated quite seriously in both countries. This was Moscow's and London's chance to reinforce the friendship that the war had spawned between Britain and Soviet Union.[32]

In terms of sport, it was a moment of great pride for the Soviet athletes to be invited to play in London, given Britain's rich soccer history and place at the center of FIFA, which the Soviets finally joined in 1946.[33] The matches were highly publicized and quite popular in Britain, as many were curious about Moscow's soccer program and the Soviet Union in general. The Soviets performed admirably while abroad and made the most of the tourism opportunities as well.[34] Not only did they outscore Britain's Arsenal Football Club nineteen goals to nine, making for a strong showing on the pitch, but the Soviet Union began to realize fully the foreign policy powers of sport and soon started planning other goodwill trips intended to showcase their talent while also boosting their international popularity. The *New York Times* quoted an unnamed Soviet team official in November 1945 as saying, "We consider our sportsmen to be among the world's best; they would be wonderful ambassadors for Russia."[35] Despite the relative success of the Dynamo visit and the Soviet Union's subsequent FIFA membership, Soviet athletes found themselves largely shut out of this type of international competition over the next decade because of the growing sense of distrust and lack of communication on both sides of the Iron Curtain. Until the Helsinki Olympics and then not again until the 1956 Melbourne Games, the Soviet teams faced only opponents from fellow eastern European teams who frankly did not offer the same level of challenge nor did they garner the same sense of public interest as had the British tour.[36] In this sense, the tour was a relative failure in terms of its diplomatic objectives for both countries involved. Britain largely failed in its mission to use soccer as a means of maintaining its position as one of the Big Three, as it soon found itself on the outside looking in terms of global control, as the superpowers became the sole movers in terms of international power dynamics while the Soviets failed to break into the western sporting ranks.[37]

From Onlookers to Olympians: The Early Cold War

The advent of the Cold War and the sense of competition it bred between Stalin and Truman further elevated sport's place in Soviet society. Despite Moscow's undeniable contributions to the Allied war effort, its unsavory political system won it few friends outside Eastern Europe. Stalin recognized this and the role that sport could play in demonstrating the superiority of the communist way of life. As such, the Kremlin stressed athletic achievement not only as a means of creating a fit population ready to fight the Cold War but also sport as political tool. This search for acceptance soon included IOC membership because the Olympics had become the most publicized and globally visible international sports venue. Sport was a means of finding common ground with the west and demonstrating that the Soviet Union was a legitimate nation, much like those who already belonged to the IOC.

In order to facilitate this transition to full involvement in the western sports world and to enable its athletes to compete at the highest level, the Soviet government dedicated itself to improving its athletic organization at all levels. As discussed, the Soviets already had a strong centralized athletics system in place before World War II that overshadowed anything that existed in the United States. While Brundage and the IOC were adamant that politics and sport should not mix, the two were inextricable in the Soviet Union because it was a centralized state. Soviet assertions to the contrary did nothing to allay these suspicions. The All-Union Committee for Physical Culture and Sports Activities, which oversaw all organized athletics after World War II, was answerable directly to the Central Committee of the Communist Party.[38] Under the Sports Ministry, as it was commonly termed, was a comprehensive network of sporting clubs and administrations that tiered down to the local level, encompassing all age groups and ability levels. The fact that the Sports Ministry answered to the Kremlin made the following statement, taken from a promotional brochure published in advance of the Tokyo Olympics relatively absurd. "The physical culture movement in the USSR is being conducted on an entirely autonomous basis. The movement is led not by any State organ but by an elected social organization—the Union of Sports Associations and Organizations of the USSR."[39] Nonetheless, the Soviets maintained this improbable stance and Brundage played into the charade by choosing to turn a blind eye to this blatant mixture of politics and sport.

Because the communist party sponsored and ran nearly all Soviet sports clubs at all levels, it was impossible to separate politics and sport. While the USOA was an autonomous entity that received very little government funding, particularly during the 1940s, the Soviet Olympic Committee and all other domestic sport organizations were arms of the state. The Kremlin tended to waver on its acknowledgment that its athletes were not exactly playing by the rules, confirming or denying this charge as the situation dictated. This issue had emerged during the Soviet soccer tour to Britain when the local press wondered whether the competition was amateur or professional. The Soviets replied that they were somewhere in the middle.

> They were amateurs in the sense that they each had a trade and that they received no wages under contract for playing. But of course they could neither work nor earn while on tour—or during training for the tour—so the club made up the difference in so-called

traveling expenses. And after the tour they might be rewarded for 'outstanding achievements,' though none of the players could count on that. In other words, the Soviets
claimed, their players were as unpaid as it was possible for them to be.[40]

While American athletes who missed days at work while they competed faced
a proportional loss in wages, their Soviet peers did not face this same conun-
drum.

   This issue only increased in its complexity with time. A 1949 propaganda
brochure not only denied any payment to athletes, but also reminded its audience of the difference between capitalist and communist sport. "In contrast to
capitalist countries, where sport is often either the privilege of the rich, or a
source of profits and livelihood for professional sports promoters and busi-
nessmen, in the Soviet Union millions of working people take part in sport
and no profits are made by it."[41] Ten years later, Moscow-based American television and radio correspondent Irving Levine discussed this inherent contra-
diction between the Soviet and American definitions of amateurism in his book
Main Street, USSR. As he observed, "There is only one status of athletes in the
Soviet Union—amateur by Soviet definition, but with certainly many of the
characteristics of the paid professional."[42]

   Undoubtedly, those outside the Soviet Union reacted with disdain to
these stories and Soviet denials of professionalism charges. The issue of broken
time, how to compensate athletes whose training and competition time cut
into their employment—and therefore their wages—was a lingering issue in
the United States, but the Soviets wasted little time agonizing over it.[43] Despite
IOC rules dictating that athletes not be compensated for their feats or even for
coaching their sport, the Soviets openly admitted that they paid their athletes'
travel expenses and reimbursed their lost wages, even after Moscow agreed to
stop paying its top performers as a condition for membership in the international sporting federations in 1947.[44] Measures like these endlessly frustrated
the USOA and others who either chose to hold themselves to IOC standards
or whom Brundage forced to comply.[45]

   Like the Truman administration, Stalin realized that the world had polar-
ized rapidly after the war and that international athletics was a key means not
only for asserting supremacy but also for keeping his population ready in case
the need to call the Red Army arose. Stalin's distrust of and reluctance to enter
international sporting federations remained, but he also understood the propaganda and physical fitness value of international sport. He sought increasing
competition opportunities, however, the Soviet Union decided against sending
a team to the London Olympics. The reason given for staying home was that
Soviet athletes had not yet risen to the western standard of competition.
Instead, the Soviets sent a number of official observers to the Games to scout

the competition in anticipation of the 1952 Olympics to see what needed to be done in order to field a team that could dominate Helsinki.[46]

Dominance and Manipulation: The Khrushchev and Brezhnev Years

While Stalin's death in 1953 naturally brought changes to the Iron Curtain and the Cold War, his administration had created a solid sporting infrastructure that proved both successful and sustainable. The Soviet Union continued its sporting success throughout the remainder of the 1950s and into the 1960s because of this system. Once this program was in place, there was little need for continued innovation or the same type of heavy Kremlin involvement that had characterized the early years of his reign. This consolidated program carried the Soviet Union through three consecutive Olympiads where they dominated the medal count with few exceptions. Part of this supremacy was due to the Soviet Union's large population from which it could select its Olympic teams. It was an advantage of sheer numbers. Additionally, Stalin had made the decision immediately after World War II to focus national efforts primarily on improvement in Olympic sports.[47] While this included a relatively wide range of athletics, it did allow for some narrowing of focus to concentrate resources and maximize medal chances in a number of prioritized games through this comprehensive and, many would argue, truly professional system.[48]

This focus on the sports most likely to reap international glory reflected the Kremlin's ideology more broadly. While American athletes pursued a wide variety of sports, admittedly with less attention and perhaps fewer resources at their disposal than those competing in the most popular fields, Soviet sportsmen were more limited in their options. The team always came first. Both American and Soviet athletes made sacrifices to pursue their sports at an elite level, but in different forms. While American constraints were largely financial, the limitations that Soviet athletes faced were ideological, as they had to play by the Kremlin's rules in order to represent the Soviet Union. While American audiences tended—then and now—to attach themselves to individual heroes on the field, the Kremlin always dictated a team-first strategy. The national team was always the top priority. Moscow encouraged its constituents to follow team sports like soccer and hockey.[49] Basketball also achieved a substantial increase in spectator interest during the early years of the Cold War, mostly because the United States was the team to beat.[50]

Once the Soviets had successfully competed in their first Olympics, Moscow immediately began looking ahead to the next Games, specifically the ways in which they could win the overall medal count. By this time, the Soviets saw no worth in competing if they could not dominate and win every contest, including the Olympics.[51] One outgrowth of this new focus on the Olympics as a means of displaying communist superiority was the revival of the *Spartakiad* in 1956. These sporting contests were a national version of the Olympics held within the Soviet Union ostensibly as a preparation for the Games themselves.[52] The original *Spartakiad* had begun in Moscow in 1928 during the years of the Sportintern and the Workers Olympics. Their original intent was to provide an alternative to competing in the Olympic Games, an expanded version of the Worker Games. They tied into the contemporary Five-Year Plan in the sense that Soviet athletes were expected to consistently improve their performances in the competition just as Soviet workers were expected to continuously increase their productivity. Twelve countries sent athletes to compete in 1928, which paled in comparison to the forty-six nations represented in the Amsterdam Olympics, but was no small figure when one considered that just fourteen nations had participated in the first Olympics thirty years earlier.[53] Like the newly formed Winter Olympics, the *Spartakiad* also had a cold weather equivalent. It took place later in 1928, though on a much smaller scale than the 1928 events in St. Moritz, Switzerland.[54] Following the Olympic precedent, the next *Spartakiad* transpired in 1932, this time in Leningrad. Like the Sportintern and many other cultural programs, the *Spartakiad* ended in 1937, as Stalin turned increasingly to international politics.

Following a nineteen-year hiatus, the Sports Ministry announced plans to revive the *Spartakiad* in early 1956. The competitions took place in August as a dress rehearsal for the Summer Olympics, scheduled for Melbourne in November. The Sports Ministry instructed all sporting clubs to prepare their athletes for rigorous competition that would not only help select the Soviet teams for Melbourne but which would also demonstrate the superiority of the Soviet sports system to the rest of the world.[55] Although there is no way to calculate an exact number of participants, historians have estimated that perhaps as many as 23 million people competed at the local level for the chance to participate in the national events at Lenin Stadium, with the finals drawing competitors from all fifteen Soviet Socialist Republics. The revamped edition, like the 1920s *Spartakiad* and Workers Olympics, closely resembled the Olympics in terms of ceremony and overt displays of nationalism. Like the Olympics, there was a strong emphasis on and public interest in the track and field events, as they proved extremely popular.[56]

Press coverage of this initial event was intense, with the Soviets encouraging in-depth reporting of both the preparations and the competition itself as a means of building its own prestige and to situate the Soviet Union as medal favorites. New facilities, including a heated pool and a domed stadium incorporating the latest technology, were built around Moscow. This building frenzy led *Sports Illustrated* to speculate that the true intent of this massive construction project was to prepare the city to host the 1964 Summer Games.[57] Pre-*Spartakiad* estimates were that 10,000 competitors would participate with a final count of 9,200 athletes competing from forty countries, making these games even bigger in terms of sheer numbers than the Olympics, though they would not come close to garnering equal world attention or prestige.[58] Nonetheless, the *Spartakiad* served its intended purpose to draw positive press interest to Moscow and to prepare the Soviet team to again impress the world with its athleticism and medal haul in Melbourne.

Following its great success in 1956, the *Spartakiad* became a highly anticipated quadrennial occasion for spectators and athletes alike, as it offered a preview of the Olympics. In a sense, the *Spartakiad* was, as *Sports Illustrated* termed it, "the biggest tryouts ever held by one country." Beginning with the second such event, they moved to the year before the Olympics.[59] This switch was intentional, as it fomented Olympic excitement a year before the Games, and proved to be highly successful. In the words of Soviet gymnast Boris Shakhlin, The *Spartakiad* "are an all-around test of strength and a wonderful way to get into shape for the Olympics.... It gave me confidence, which was very important for me before leaving for the Olympic Games in Rome."[60] This testimonial expressed a common sentiment among Soviet athletes regarding the festival's function and utility.

Even though Stalin had been dead for three years by the time the Sports Ministry revived the *Spartakiad*, his tenet of "every citizen an athlete" continued to dominate Soviet sports ideology. The local levels of the *Spartakiad* were open to anyone and by 1979, an estimated 100 million people trained and tried out for the finals.[61] The Soviets allowed non–Soviet competitors to participate by invitation, though their numbers remained quite small. The focus of these events always remained on the glorification of the Soviet athlete and on building interest in the upcoming Olympic Games.[62] Brundage, on two separate occasions, referenced the *Spartakiad* as a sign of "some hope for the Russians."[63] Throughout their lifetime, which coincided roughly with the height of the Soviet Union, the *Spartakiad* was a quadrennial event that Russians anticipated with great pride. It offered a chance for all to exhibit their athletic prowess in the hopes of advancing to the next round, regardless of whether one was a training school athlete or simply a weekend enthusiast. The sheer number of participants was impressive. Most importantly for Soviet purposes, it was a means of creating a more active population, one which would be ready and able to fight should the Cold War turn hot at any moment. Looking to build off this success, East Germany began hosting its own spartakiads in the 1960s. Like the Soviet events, they were extremely well-planned and attended, held every four years until the 1980s.[64]

As in the United States, the 1950s witnessed a major governmental push toward increased fitness at all levels of society. Just as Eisenhower and later Kennedy increased funding and attention for athletics, the Kremlin devoted more resources to sport as well. According to the British publication *Soviet News Booklet*, the Soviets were spending close to 38 million rubles annually by 1958 to support their school athletics programs, though this paled in comparison to the total expenditure of more than 12 billion rubles between Helsinki and Melbourne to ensure that the Soviet athletes would perform up to the high standards they had set for themselves in 1952.[65] More than 50,000 students graduated from Soviet universities each year with degrees in sports-related fields like physical education and athletic training.[66] This focus on sport as a means of bettering the general population was unabashedly targeted toward Olympic accomplishment, and more blatantly so than contemporary American programs.

Fitness was also a critical component of the Soviet national education system. All elementary school students participated in physical education classes, like those that became mandatory in the United States during the Eisenhower administration. However, there was an added aspect of competition even amongst Soviet students of a young age that was more pronounced than in the United States. Also, by the mid–1950s, the Soviets had begun developing a system of training schools throughout the country to house the most promising young athletes and offer them intense preparation with an eye on their someday representing the hammer and sickle at the Olympic Games. These schools provided the traditional classroom education offered in ordinary schools but coupled it with an increased emphasis on training a particular sport rather than offering the general introduction to all sports found in the schools for the masses. Most of the schools, a total of 1,144 with more than 300,000 attendees throughout the Soviet Union, focused on Olympic sports.[67] As such, there were eventually more than sixty schools scattered across the Soviet Union devoted to soccer alone.[68]

Moscow established national competitions annually in many sports in a system somewhat comparable to the NCAA basketball championships in the United States. They shared similar levels of tension, excitement, and large crowds of spectators; however, Soviet teams tended to be attached to factories, unions, or sporting clubs rather than one's university as under the NCAA system.[69] As in the United States, there were Soviet college sports, but these never received as much attention as the matchups between trade union clubs or on the international level. Instead, the Sports Ministry offered college-age athletes who showed Olympic potential employment that allowed them to maximize their training time while funding their living expenses.[70] In the words of Yuri Brokhin, a former Soviet athlete and defector quite familiar with the system,

> Even if an athlete takes an interest in the treasures of scholarship, he's simply too busy, having to spend six months of the year in training camp and six at tournaments.... An athlete without academic ambitions is set up in a job according to who sponsors his club: electricians, drivers, stonemasons, fishermen, cooks or carpenters. No one ever sees him on the job, even though every month he's handed $160 in a sealed envelope.[71]

Brokhin also noted that money for athletics came from the military budget each year, with the exact amount spent never divulged to the public. As such, it was impossible to know just how much athletes earned or the total spent on trying to ensure Olympic dominance.

The state was at the center of all national sporting organizations. There were no private outlets for sport, as was common in the United States at this time. The Trade Union was the biggest Soviet sports organization and served as an umbrella for many smaller clubs throughout the country. The other sources of competition were Dynamo, run by the Interior Department, and the Army clubs. Taken together, these three units served as the chief overseers for all aspects of sport. Their duties included encouraging mass participation, facilities upkeep, ensuring consistent and positive media coverage, providing experienced coaches and medical staff, and scheduling competitions.[72] The state expected and encouraged Soviet families to pay the minimal membership fees required to belong to any one of these local clubs and to use their facilities on a frequent basis.

The Sports Ministry, like the White House, initiated a number of state-sponsored programs throughout the 1950s and 1960s to improve the physical fitness of the general population for Cold War-related reasons. However, Moscow constantly emphasized sports like cross country, swimming, and triathlons, where there were fewer limits on participation than on sports like hockey or basketball where only a set number of players could take to the ice or court at any one time.[73] Large-scale road races, lake-swimming events, and track meets during which thousands of athletes competed became popular sporting events, though soccer remained the top spectator sport during the early Cold War. The state press covered these events extensively to maximize their propaganda appeal and show the world how fit Soviet citizens were.

While the practice of paying athletes bonuses for sports achievement had been officially discontinued in 1947, the emphasis on athletic achievement continued unabated throughout the Cold War. Just as adult champions reaped material incentives, the Sports Ministry introduced a ranking system to encourage athletic achievement among school children. The primary badge was the GTO, which stood for the Russian-language equivalent of "Ready for Labor and Defense."[74] In order to receive the badge, as 2.5 million students did in 1956, children had to meet a number of fitness standards that corresponded to their age and the sport in which they trained. Once a student received his GTO, he could work his way up a ladder of fitness achievements with criteria tailored to individual sports, culminating in Master of Sports of the USSR, reserved for a select few. According to the Soviet brochure for the 1958 International Exposition, the standards for 1958 were quite rigorous, "It is not easy to achieve it. For example, a Master of Sports in track and field athletics is required to dash 100 meters in 10.4 seconds; a high jumper must clear two meters."[75] These standards became more rigorous as the system evolved in the late 1960s and into the 1970s to provide additional incentive for young Soviet athletes to strive for continuous improvement.

This pressure for constant achievement on both sides led to some fierce yet comical bickering in both the Soviet and American presses. This bashing, like media coverage of Olympic sports more generally, tended to intensify just before and after the Games. Weightlifting became the focal point for this squabbling leading up to Melbourne. The Soviet *Physical Culture and Sports* weekly magazine ran a story in March 1956 in which a Soviet official referred to American weightlifting events as "beauty contests [that] have nothing to do with honest physical culture."[76] The story drew contrasts between Soviet and American athletes, depicting the former as strong and the latter as "sissies who don't practice any sport."[77] This type of criticism flew both ways, as the American press at times mocked the relative unattractiveness of Soviet athletes. The nature of these comments demonstrated the difference in cultural ideals regarding athletes. While the United States championed looks, personality, and athletic prowess in its sporting heroes, contributing to the ideal of the "All-American," the Soviets held a more single-minded focus on results. This reflected the differing needs of the superpowers. While Americans used sports as a measure of pride, the Soviets used sport to gain a sense of legitimacy and acceptance on the world stage.[78]

In addition to officially joining the Olympic Movement and pushing achievement as an important means of demonstrating Russian supremacy, the Soviets visibly increased their efforts to improve their already intense athletic programs throughout the 1950s. Basketball, which had received little national attention until this point, became a major target for improvement. This soon developed into a quadrennial Cold War rivalry, and later a more frequent occasion with the establishment of the annual World Championships. The United States had established strong college and professional programs decades before the Cold War began.[79] The Soviet team traditionally had performed quite well at the European Championships; however, it could not beat the United States. A sound defeat by the Americans in the 1956 Melbourne Olympics motivated an acceleration in this progress toward a more competitive basketball program. *Sports Illustrated* exulted in the American team led by Bill Russell "making monkeys of the Russians in the last gold medal game."[80] The Soviets lost ultimately because none of its players offered even a slight challenge to Russell's pace and athleticism. In response, the Soviets worked over the next four years to remake their national team with bigger, more athletic players specifically to challenge Russell for the Rome Olympics, a highly anticipated rematch in both countries.[81]

While Moscow lost its rematch in Rome, it could take some consolation in having beaten the United States in the 1959 World Championships. Held in Chile in January, the Soviet team—although comprised primarily of newcomers to the elite basketball level—soundly beat the Americans 62–37. This upset gave the Soviets their first ever win over an American squad.[82] While the loss shocked many in the United States, much of the blame was placed on USA Basketball and NCAA officials who would not permit the top stars to travel and "carelessly sent a pick-up team of fifth-rate players to a world championship," in the words of *New York Times* sports columnist Arthur Daley.[83] Instead, a clearly overmatched U.S. Air Force team took the court in Chile, winning a respectable four games before it fell to the Soviets in the semi-finals. The loss was a disappointment at home; however, USA basketball officials acknowledged that this was not a team truly representative America's best. The timing of the world championships, coming in the midst of the NCAA and NBA seasons, prevented the assembly of a team of the caliber of the 1956 gold medal winners.[84] Rather than agonize over these results, USA Basketball set its sights on defending its reputation at the Rome Games.

In addition to developing a basketball team that could compete seriously with the United States, Moscow emphasized the importance of stadium building and facilities improvement throughout the 1950s. The Soviet Union had emerged from World War II facing many of the same struggles as Britain in terms of manpower losses, shortages of food and other necessities, and large numbers of buildings reduced to wreckage. The Kremlin embarked on an all-encompassing national construction project, reinventing the Soviet concepts of housing, commercial buildings, and sporting facilities. However, while housing shortages lingered throughout the 1950s, leaving the Soviets with overcrowding that contributed to one of the highest rates of tuberculosis in the world, Moscow spared no expense when it came to elite sporting venues.[85] The role of sport and the need for impressive venues became priorities following the Dynamo visit to London. One reason was the increased spectator interest resulting from the visit. After seeing their team perform well, many young Soviet athletes began to play or follow soccer, creating the need for more youth leagues and more stadiums for elite teams.[86] As the Soviet Union started to make its debut within various amateur sporting realms, the need for new athletic venues moved to the top of the priority list, similar to what had occurred with the London rebuilding efforts associated with the 1948 Olympics. The Soviet initiatives were highly publicized, both to show sports' importance within the Soviet Union and the superiority of sport under the communist system while preparing to host a future Olympics. The Soviets submitted their first formal bid until 1969 when they tried to bring the 1976 Games to Moscow and later hosted the 1980 summer contests.[87]

Lenin Stadium, a comprehensive and visually imposing structure built ostensibly for the 1956 *Spartakiad*, was a prime example of this rampant construction. It later became a central location for the 1980 Olympics, finally fulfilling the purpose many had speculated a quarter-century earlier.[88] Prior to the Games, Lenin Stadium provided the setting for several important meetings between Soviet and American athletes, including a handful of the famed Soviet-American track meets, which began in 1958. The stadium was innovative in that it was an all-inclusive complex with 500 hotel rooms, restaurants, medical services for athletes, tennis, and basketball courts, all in addition to the main stadium, which could—and on several occasions did—seat an audience of 104,000.[89] Outside the main stadium were an Olympic-sized pool, an ice rink called the Crystal Palace and a Soviet sports museum. To facilitate transportation on a massive scale, the city constructed a metro line to and from the complex. Though this type of comprehensive athletic facility has become relatively common in the United States in the twenty-first century, it was an innovative concept in the 1950s, again underscoring the importance of sport within the Soviet Union and the state's role in supporting sports.[90] Lenin Stadium was certainly the most famous Soviet sports venue, but it was only one of many Cold War construction projects. The residents of Leningrad worked together to build the 96,000-seat Kirov Stadium after their own Lenin Stadium became a World War II casualty.[91]

These centralized building projects were unrealistic at the time in the United States because they would have involved collaborations among the major sporting powers that would have proven unfeasible. It would be implausible to conceive of American organizations like the NCAA, AAU, and USOC all working together to finance, plan, and build a multipurpose stadium that they could share with little squabbling over scheduling or other rights. It was in projects like these where a centralized sporting monopoly was more efficient, as the state handled all of the planning and the funding for such initiatives. At the same time, such a project would likely not have enjoyed the same level of public support and patronage in the United States simply because American ideas of sport were relatively different from the Soviet. While soccer and track were the major attractions behind the Iron Curtain, Americans turned to baseball, basketball, and, increasingly, football, on the college and professional levels for entertainment. These were privately-run leagues. Americans rallied around hometown teams or those of a favorite college, following these more closely than national squads in all but the most highly publicized events like the Olympics.

However, massive construction projects like these, developed more as a spectacle and for their propaganda value than their practicality, came at a cost to the general public who often had to do without simply because there was not enough funding or materials. While it was easy for someone outside the Iron Curtain to conjure up an image of Soviet high schools boasting of Olympic-caliber equipment and pristine fields and pools, these were few and far between. Instead, as many as eighty percent of schools lacked any type of fields, seventy-five percent did not have gyms, and perhaps half lacked enough equipment for the students to participate in regular physical education classes.[92] Instead of sports for all and "every citizen an athlete," the resources were largely devoted to those who had the best chance at bringing home international glory through their achievements. While capitalist societies made it possible for a private entity to finance the necessary facilities with little government funding, the Soviet Union simply did not have the resources to provide for all, which perhaps made its sporting achievements more impressive. The number of athletic opportunities increased for the average American during this era; his Soviet peer could not boast of similar gains.

For those who showed flashes of Olympic-caliber talent, however, the situation was quite different. These gifted few wanted for little, both in terms of training necessities and creature comforts more generally. The Soviet sports bureaucracy was in some senses a self-perpetuating system that capitalized on the inherent love of sport among the Soviet people and also the public realization that athletic achievement could lead to a better life. There was never any shortage of willing applicants to Soviet sport academies because the perks of winning a spot and performing well on the international level were well-known and highly coveted. Simply put, athletes received overall better treatment. Living conditions at the schools exceeded anything the general public could aspire to and offered access to sporting facilities that were scarce elsewhere. While the athletic training was itself was strenuous, it was the primary job for those identified as potential Olympians. Those who had a shot at making the Games often received coveted high commissions in the army or government posts that required little work and essentially paid athletes to improve their fitness.[93] Irving Levine observed, "As soon as a talented high jumper, for example, is discovered in a factory, his life changes. Every encouragement is offered to him— a better apartment, plenty of time away from the assembly line to practice under expert coaches, trips abroad with teams…. He is paid ostensibly for doing a factory job that becomes only secondary to his main job of winning for the club's banner, and, if he's good enough, for the hammer and sickle."[94]

There was a caveat to this special treatment though. The state expected prospective gold medalists to play by the rules and held them to a higher standard of social and political conformity. There was no room for individual superstars as there was in the west. While the rise of the celebrity athlete as had begun in the United States before World War II with baseball player Babe Ruth and boxer Jack Johnson as prime examples, the Soviet government had different ideas about how its sportsmen should behave. The ideal communist athlete was a pillar of his community, a model citizen rather than a dissenter. The Kremlin disliked the term "star" and discouraged its use in conjunction with athletics. Instead, its best athletes were "leaders," who were urged to draw others into their sport.[95] The state punished non-conformers heavily. They were excluded from the rosters for international competitions, like the Olympics, or, in extreme cases, barred from training facilities altogether.[96] These strict policies and the temptation of a better, freer life elsewhere led thousands of athletes to defect, often during or following international travel for events like the Olympics.

This special treatment of athletes for the good of the state stood in sharp contrast to the United States where athletes were often forced to compromise their training in order to make a living, adding to the bitterness that many felt regarding the Soviet domination of the Games. Bob Cleary, star of the 1960 gold medal-winning hockey team recalled, "'I couldn't try out for the Olympic Team at first because I just got married and opened an insurance business…. I couldn't afford to be away for all the time leading up to the Games. When [Coach Jack Riley] asked Bill and I to play later on it was just amazing.'"[97] Having to choose between career and sport was an alien concept to most Soviet athletes simply because they knew that if they showed potential and played by the Kremlin's rules, the system would provide for them.

Just as not all Americans bought into the intense Olympic and Cold War fever that characterized the period at hand, some inside the Iron Curtain lamented this single-minded focus on the Games because it often left non–Olympic competition out in the cold. Additionally, this need to treat all Olympic sports equally rather than focus on a few crowd favorites became a source of frustration by the 1960s. While soccer remained the primary spectator sport at home, Soviet teams could never truly break into the upper echelon and compete seriously either for the World Cup or an Olympic gold medal.[98] Long, harsh winters that cut into outdoor training time remained an insurmountable obstacle. Also, unlike the Olympics, which aside from the Soviet teams, featured mainly competition among true amateurs, the soccer players who competed in the World Cup were mostly professionals who had honed their skills through FIFA play and were simply on a higher level than the Soviets. Although the Soviet Union had joined FIFA in 1946, its international soccer record remained relatively unimpressive. The lack of success became a vicious circle in a sense, as young athletes began to choose other sports over soccer because of its low success rate which limited the pool of naturally skilled players. This kept the national team at a constant disadvantage in terms of talent compared to the rest of Europe and leading to a perpetually disgruntled—though fairly loyal—fan base.[99]

A key component to Soviet sporting success during the 1950s and 1960s was the great enthusiasm shown by faithful spectators. While the Sports Ministry urged everyone to participate to better his own sporting prowess, there was also a great emphasis on patriotism and filling stadiums with boisterous fans as a means of exhibiting national pride. One rationale for the intense focus on sport was its inherent morale building power. Following World War II's destruction and its accompanying staggering loss of life—more than 20 million Soviet people perished—sport provided a means of healing these public wounds and restoring national confidence.[100] As in the United States, society increasingly idolized sports stars and treated them accordingly. Spectator sport in both countries became a huge industry, as the large numbers of seats in the new Lenin and Kirov stadiums demonstrated. The Soviets strove to prevent the lionization of individual athletes over a team approach because this was part of the communist mentality, but success in doing so was limited.

Overall, the spectator experience for Soviet and American fans was fairly comparable during the period at hand. Games sold out, particularly for the most heated rivalries, with heckling and even fighting among opposing fans relatively common. According to *Sovetsky Sport*, "Even the metro has sometimes turned out to be helpful before the unstoppable avalanche of football lovers. Quite often on the days of interesting matches the flow of passengers was so great that it was necessary to close the car doors."[101] During the Cold War, soccer fans became more heterogeneous. Instead of a fan base comprised primarily of lower and working class men, matches began to attract women and members of the upper classes in greater numbers. At times, more than half a million spectators would congregate outside a stadium on game day just to be near the action.[102] This scene would be quite familiar to Americans, if one were to substitute baseball or football in place of soccer. Because soccer was never really a mainstream spectator sport in the United States and several professional soccer leagues failed during the period at hand, the beautiful game never really developed into a Cold War rivalry with the same intensity as either basketball or track.[103]

While *Sovetsky Sport* was already an established and successful publication by the 1960s, there was a perceived need for a second national periodical devoted solely to the athletic conquests of the Soviet Union. This belief led to the creation of *Sport in the USSR* in 1963 to expand coverage of Soviet sport, which tended to be limited outside the country in non–Olympic years. The magazine was published in several languages including Russian, English, and Hungarian. It was a monthly publication that highlighted the sporting exploits of top Soviet athletes, giving special attention to Olympic sports and the *Spartakiad*, both in predicting the outcomes of these contests and in offering detailed post-mortems. At the same time, the magazine pushed increased participation in sport at all levels by the general population, continuing this goal of "every citizen an athlete." And like other Soviet—and American—publications, it was not above blatant political statements and open criticism of rival states, the extent to which will be discussed as it pertained to individual Olympiads. On the whole, however, the magazine was a tribute to athletic accomplishments and a compilation of profiles of the top Soviet stars, often including training regiments meant to inspire Soviet commoners to follow these routines and improve their own athletic prowess. In a sense, *Sport in the USSR* paralleled *Sports Illustrated* because it offered sports coverage on a national level that was deeper in scope than what could be found in local newspapers. However, *Sport in the USSR*, like all Soviet periodicals, was under state control. Therefore, its authors did not have the same freedoms as their American peers, and its bias was quite obvious.

As in the United States, sports were a foreign policy tool and earned additional state attention because they filled this role so well. However, there came a point when Moscow could no longer spend as much time and resources on Olympic glory and sport as Cold War cannon fodder, similar to the situation that Johnson faced after 1964. By the mid–1960s, it was becoming increasingly difficult for Moscow to ignore its burgeoning economic, social, and foreign policy problems, reaching a peak in October 1964 when the Politburo ousted Khrushchev in favor of Brezhnev.[104] Discontent with Khrushchev's leadership had been building for some time even before the Cuban Missile Crisis. It was becoming increasingly difficult for the Soviet Union to deny that it had entered into a period of stagnation. Khrushchev seemed to have no answers to the growing number of pressing issues facing the Kremlin. The Soviet standard of living was falling further behind the west, with the country not even able to provide enough food for its population without buying American grain. The ever-widening Sino-Soviet split garnered a considerable amount of negative press and gave Washington further reason to denounce communism as an untenable form of government. The Soviet public was growing more critical of Khrushchev, even waxing nostalgically for Stalin, particularly in terms of the standard of living.[105] Suddenly in the light of these difficult problems, continuing to strive for Cold War supremacy in cultural matters like the space race or the Olympics were not the top priorities. Spectator sports retained their popularity and interest in the Olympics continued but without the same levels of governmental involvement and pressure to succeed, largely paralleling the situation in the United States during the same period.

Conclusion

Soviet sport underwent a transformation in the 1940s simultaneously as the Cold War replaced World War II. While Stalin had begun to recognize the importance of athletics to foreign politics during the interwar period, the Kremlin maximized its use of sport as a means to achieving set foreign policy objectives during the Cold War. The Olympics became the top priority because they attracted the most global attention and offered the best chance of well-publicized direct competition against the United States. As such, Stalin and his successors strove to ensure that Soviet citizens at all levels understood the importance of athletics and tried to integrate sport into the major aspects of society: work, school, and leisure time. Through this "every citizen an athlete" initiative, sports became ingrained in Soviet society in a comparable fashion to what was occurring in the United States at the same time, though in a more centralized manner. This focus on fitness manifested itself in a national system of training schools for promising athletes, a number of large stadium projects, and an ethically questionable system of financially supporting athletes to allow them to maximize training time.

While the United States also embraced sports as a means of demonstrating national strength during the Cold War, the Soviet emphasis proved a bit more intense because the Kremlin viewed athletics as a means to gaining international recognition and legitimacy. The United States was an established and well-respected global power, especially after World War II, but the Soviet Union was still a relatively new and unknown entity, despite its contribution to the Allied victory. Moscow recognized athletic supremacy was an accepted means of achieving the global legitimacy and acknowledgment that it coveted. As such, Stalin and his successors strove to create and maintain an all-encompassing national sports infrastructure that could compete with and hopefully eclipse the United States to meet two interrelated goals: to gain international acclaim and to win the Cold War on the playing field.

In this sense, sports assumed a critical foreign policy role in the Soviet Union from the late-1920s through the 1960s. The Worker Olympics and early *Spartakiads,* both of which were means of bringing together athletes from a number of communist countries as alternatives to the Olympic Movement, marked the beginning of this phase. Aversion to interaction with the west waned in the early 1930s, leading to some limited involvement with FIFA and other international sporting bodies. Taken together, these efforts show that Stalin recognized the power of athletics to fulfill a highly visible diplomatic purpose nearly two decades before Washington began to ascribe the same importance to American sport. Washington did not follow Moscow's lead in mixing diplomacy and sport until the Cold War began to heat up.

The Soviets intensified their efforts to improve their athletic prowess and tap sport's propaganda potential after the war with the stated intention of becoming the global athletic leader. This renewed focus on sport for political ends was in large part a reaction to Moscow's growing rivalry with the United States. To achieve this end, Stalin was forced to shed some of his reluctance to join western sporting bodies. The Soviet Union joined FIFA and the IOC during the first decade of the Cold War, though not without efforts to manipulate both. This new challenge to its sporting hegemony pushed Washington to use sport for political and propaganda ends in much the same way that their new rivals were.

Their parallel efforts were not identical though. Their often divergent approaches to conquering the sporting world were by and large a direct reflection of their divergent political systems. Because Washington championed freedom and individualism, it was less involved in the quotidian management of American sports, even on the national level. It encouraged a fitter population and used Congressional legislation to support American athletes and later to help bring the 1960 Winter Olympics to Squaw Valley, California, but did not pay athletes or undertake large-scale stadium projects like Moscow. The American press took a strong interest in the Games and in all interactions with the Soviets, proving highly critical of athletes from both countries at certain times.

Behind the Iron Curtain, Moscow kept a close watch on athletics, maintaining a system of national schools to ensure that its top prospects remained competitive on the international level. Those who did not play by the rules of this rigorous program were ostracized. Though Moscow claimed that it had stopped paying its sportsmen for their achievements by 1947, there is little evidence to suggest that this practice ever ended. The press, like its American counterpart, proved fascinated by the Olympics and all interactions with American athletes. Because it was largely an instrument of the state, the Soviet press tended to be highly complimentary of the home team while overly critical of the United States. Moscow encouraged and glorified team sports over individual contests, reflecting the collective approach to society that defined communism. Soccer and hockey became the sports of the masses, though Team Soviet Union had few successes in the former.

The Olympics provided the most visible arena for regular face-offs between these diverging approaches to a shared goal. As Moscow, and soon Washington, perceived Olympic success as the perhaps the most attainable means to Cold War points during its first two decades, both countries organized their national physical fitness campaigns to reflect this. Each ascribed a heightened importance to Olympic achievement through strong rhetoric campaigns. Both superpowers emphasized the need for improvement in all Olympic sports, leading to overall success in the medal counts for both countries and a number of memorable clashes among the superpowers on the field. This shared focus on the Games increased their global visibility and prominence, as the political implication of a major win—or loss—in an Olympic event were more dramatic than they would have been without the strong Cold War undertones that pervaded these competitions.[106]

In studying how Moscow and Washington emphasized athletic diplomacy in similar fashions to promote clashing ideologies, it becomes clear why their shared goal created heated disputes and bitter rivalries on the field. The political intrusions that the Cold War foisted on the IOC and the Olympics themselves demonstrated how seriously both superpowers approached the Games in order to maximize their political and propaganda capacities. The impact of this rivalry on each Olympiad between London in 1948 and Mexico City in 1968 was evident to the athletes, the press, Olympic officials, and the global audience. The extent to which these tensions affected each Olympiad in these years fluctuated based on the contemporary state of relations between the superpowers. The following chapters will demonstrate just how this manifested itself in reference to the individual contests during this intense span.

CHAPTER 3

1948

The Austerity Games

"To resolve differences in a spirit of chivalry is the only way to world-peace. Sporting contests teach this way at a time when the youthful soul is receptive to such teaching."
—IOC president J. Sigfrid Edstrom at the London Olympics
closing ceremonies[1]

The planning for the 1948 Games ushered in a new era for the Olympic Movement, one which brought a unique set of challenges. While the modern Games had found themselves at a crossroads after World War I, circumstances regarding their revival were even less auspicious in 1945 than they had been in 1918. Following the blatant racism and ugly displays of nationalism that marred the Berlin Olympics, many had questioned whether the Games had outlived their purpose even before the war forced a second, longer hiatus. Along with the great athletic feats by American sprinter Jesse Owens and others, the events in 1936 had demonstrated that de Coubertin's objective to use sport as a means of diffusing political tensions was not always effective. While the onset of World War II forced a twelve-year gap between Games, the IOC remained active during this lengthy layoff. Danger and difficulty of travel during the war precluded formal meetings but the committee began preliminary discussions for the 1948 Games via written correspondence more than a year before Germany and Japan surrendered.

The end of World War II and the subsequent Cold War created a new set of political obstacles. The United States and the Soviet Union, former allies, soon found themselves on opposing sides of an entirely novel form of conflict. This uncharted territory spawned much uncertainty on both sides of the Atlantic as the new superpowers learned to coexist through a series of power struggles. With the dividing line between good and evil clearly outlined "from

Stettin in the Baltic to Trieste in the Adriatric," as Churchill famously defined the new Iron Curtain in 1946, it quickly became clear that all collaboration between Washington and Moscow had ended with the war.[2] By the late 1940s, Cold War America readily embraced the portrayal of the Soviet Union as hated rival, both within and away from the political realm. This soon extended to the playing fields.

Despite these growing tensions, the 1948 Games are nostalgically recalled in popular memory for their friendliness and spirit of healing. Planning crises and fears of unfinished venues aside, the London Olympics were lauded almost unanimously for their simplicity and the rampant examples of good sportsmanship throughout the two-week spectacle. In this way, the Games fulfilled de Coubertin's founding mission as a positive outlet for nationalism. The same could not be said of the later Cold War contests, saturated as they were with politics and at times ugly displays of patriotism.

London Sets the Stage

In more ways than one, the 1948 Olympics came at an intersection of prewar tradition and the coming ideological challenge. There was a great deal of uncertainty surrounding the Olympic Movement following the spectacle in Berlin. The twelve-year layoff forced by World War II did little to quell concerns regarding the ongoing feasibility of the Games. The city of London was ill-equipped to host a major athletic event just three years after World War II and to accommodate all of the visitors who would come. While London, and Europe more broadly, had undergone serious physical damage during the war, the postwar political and ideological upheavals were perhaps even more extreme. The London Olympics were the first affected by the Cold War.[3] While the Soviets were not yet IOC members and did not compete in 1948, many of the new political concerns that would dominate the planning and dissemination of the Olympics throughout the next two decades first appeared in 1948. These included the Soviet attempts to control the IOC and the Games, how to treat the two Germanys borne out of the postwar settlement, the issue of the Soviet Socialist Republics clamoring for separate representation, Brundage's struggles with both his own government and the IOC over political matters, and the rampant war of words between the American and Soviet presses. These battles often focused on the Olympics, as they were the most high-profile international sporting event.

In foreshadowing these coming challenges, the London Games, as the first Cold War-era contests, set the overtly political tone for the next five

Olympics. From 1948 through 1968, Cold War politics often took center stage at all levels of the Games: planning, execution, and media coverage. Much to Brundage's chagrin, politics won, as he proved unable to stop current events and ideological concerns from affecting the course of the Games and how the athletes, the press, and the fans perceived them as part of the wider Cold War. At the same time, the additional attention that accompanied this unique political element increased Soviet and American interest in the contests because they became so much more than just a game for all involved. While London became known as the Austerity Games because they were kept intentionally simple and ascribed the purpose of helping the world heal from World War II, there were signs in hindsight that the Olympics had begun to evolve from their prewar counterparts and would continue to do so irreversibly, as the politics became too great a force to ignore.[4]

Even though the Soviet Union did not send a team to London, Moscow managed to stay in the headlines throughout the planning process and the Games themselves. Speculation abounded as to whether or not Stalin would send a team, even after the official entry deadline in June 1948 passed. When a team of Soviet officials arrived during the Games, organizers feared that a delegation of athletes would follow, demanding to compete and touching off a potential diplomatic nightmare.[5] Cold War tensions and the growing western aversion to Stalin played a major role in post–World War II Olympic planning even before Moscow joined the IOC.

Moscow's refusal to play consistently by IOC rules remained a constant throughout the next twenty years. First, the Soviet Union tried to change the IOC in its favor as a condition of its joining in 1951.[6] When this failed, Soviet athletes and officials did the best they could to bend or ignore IOC laws altogether when convenient. In this vein, there was always a question of just how closely—or loosely—the Soviets were following the Olympic requirement that all competitors be amateurs who were not compensated in any for their sporting abilities. The notion of special sports schools and the practice of giving Soviet athletes state jobs that allowed them to train as their main occupation struck many as flaunting the rules, especially in the United States where many athletes were forced to sacrifice training time to work and support their families. Charges of professionalism hurled between the United States and the Soviet Union, particularly in the press, were a constant throughout this period, as both superpowers pursued the podium at all costs.

The issue of German representation, while debated briefly in the planning for London, would became a major source of consternation for Brundage and the IOC in the following decades, particularly once the country's division became seemingly permanent by the early 1950s. While Germany did not receive an invitation to compete in London, there was still some debate over whether there should be a German team in London.[7] A similar conversation had followed World War I in the planning for the Antwerp Olympics with the same end result. However, while the Weimar republic eventually returned to the Games in 1928 with little fanfare, the situation was a bit more complicated following World War II, given both the legacy of the Holocaust and the postwar division of Germany. A revived German NOC comprised entirely of members from the new western section approached the committee before the Helsinki Games asking for reacceptance to the IOC and the right to compete in 1952. This proved problematic because it excluded athletes from the Soviet zone, now the German Democratic Republic. The debate over how to treat the two Germanys spanned the entire twenty years under study here, with Brundage forcing the two countries to compete under one flag until 1964, much to the chagrin of East German and Soviet officials.[8]

The German Democratic Republic was not alone in its struggle to attain separate representation and its own Olympic team. The Ukrainian and Belorussian Soviet Socialist Republics sought to compete independently from the Soviet Union throughout the 1950s, arguing that their separate United Nations membership entitled them to this privilege. Like the ongoing German situation, Brundage refused to acknowledge the political reality, arguing that Ukraine and Belarus would compete as part of the Soviet team or not at all.

Another constant was Brundage as the figure at the center of these and many other political hailstorms. Much maligned in the press for his tenacious refusal to acknowledge the political forces surrounding the Games, Brundage often found himself at odds with both his home government and various IOC members. At times, his attempts to will away diplomatic problems through inaction actually made these political challenges loom even larger. He battled endlessly and ultimately fruitlessly to prevent the Games from modernizing or bowing to the increasingly unavoidable political forces. Despite his status as an American citizen, Brundage strove to remain apolitical, aside from a few select cases, though this approach tended to backfire. Washington and the American sporting establishment found themselves endlessly frustrated with Brundage's unwillingness to serve their best interests or to punish the Soviets for using professional athletes. The lack of consequences for Moscow in the aftermath of its brutal crackdown of the Hungarian Revolution in 1956 rankled many countries while Brundage's unrealistic treatment of the German question caused more than a decade of frustration for the two German delegations fighting to compete on their own terms.[9]

The media on both sides of the Iron Curtain became a major player in Olympic politics throughout the Cold War. The speculation surrounding a potential Soviet presence in London set the stage for the media flurry that would surround future matchups between the United States and the Soviet Union in the Olympics. An ugly battle of the presses accompanied the Cold War on the field, as charges of professionalism, entertaining sportsmanship, and general denouncement of the other ran rampant in the American and Soviet news outlets. Any and all interactions between the two sides were newsworthy, particularly in sports where one of the superpowers traditionally dominated, as did the Americans in track and basketball and the Soviets in hockey. On the American side, columnists Arthur Daley, Shirley Povich, and later Bud Collins of the *Boston Globe*, among others, became the ringleaders for this media circus. These writers proved brutally honest when it came to critiquing not only the Soviets but also the IOC—with Brundage as a favorite target— and the American sports hierarchy. That they were not afraid to offer harsh critiques of American sports stars, and the American sporting establishment more generally, added a level of credibility that was lacking in the state-run Soviet press. While none of these columnists ever had to worry about being called red, their relatively accurate if not always objective analysis of both the national and international sporting scenes provided a means through which the average American fan could follow sports in the days before widespread television coverage. The ability of these writers to link sporting events to the wider Cold War made their frequent columns an invaluable resource in trying to recreate a panorama of the Olympic Games, both from an athletics and a political/cultural standpoint. On the contrary, all news releases from the Iron Curtain had to be treated with a modicum of skepticism, because the Kremlin had final approval over everything printed, making the media a virtual propaganda machine. Nonetheless, Moscow's critiques of the United States often provided an accurate gauge of Cold War hostility.

A New Postwar Order

Despite high-minded sentiments regarding the power of sport to triumph over politics and the IOC's best efforts to achieve this lofty ideal, concerns regarding diplomacy and the Games erupted almost immediately after Japan's surrender. There were few indications in late 1945 that the Cold War would soon dominate international politics for the next forty years, but tensions among the Big Three expanded rapidly. While Stalin, Truman and new British leader Clement Attlee continued to collaborate cordially toward a peace settlement, the absence of a common enemy coupled with mutual skepticism proved too much for an already tenuous alliance to weather. Even before the war ended, Truman had made it clear that he did not trust the Soviet Union and would not be collaborating with or catering to Stalin in the same manner as his predecessor Franklin Roosevelt had. After some deliberation, Truman decided against sharing American knowledge of the atomic bomb, a move that underscored and compounded this sense of mistrust between the former allies. Relations had soured noticeably by early 1946. The Soviet Union did not reciprocate American wartime attempts to portray Stalin as friendly "Uncle Joe." Instead, the Soviet dictator isolated members of Washington's diplomatic corps and forbade his citizens from fraternizing with American liberation forces.[10]

From an objective standpoint, both sides shared the blame for this rapid diplomatic deterioration. Stalin's suspicion of the United States and desire to dominate Eastern Europe did nothing to lessen the growing antagonism between the two biggest powers to emerge from the war. On the American side, Truman chose to follow the advice of what became a very hardline inner circle of advisers in approaching the Soviet Union. These men, including George Kennan, author of "The Long Telegram" in 1947, advocated taking an aggressive stance toward Stalin to showcase American supremacy and discourage any thoughts the Kremlin might have of territorial expansion. These advisers fed into the already prevalent fear of communism that had been sweeping America in intermittent waves since the Russian Revolution thirty years earlier. As such, there was no place for anyone who was "soft" on communism, as tolerance would later be termed, within the White House inner circle.[11]

To this end, the United States introduced what became known as the Truman Doctrine in March 1947 as a deterrent to Soviet meddling in and potential occupation of European states struggling economically as a result of the war. The objective of this financial aid to Greece and Turkey was to sustain states "threatened by the terrorist activities of several thousand armed men, led by Communists, who defy the government's authority at a number of points."[12] Here, Truman conflated terrorists with communism, making obvious his aversion to the latter. In doing so, he created a clear juxtaposition between the United States and the USSR. Rather than working together with the Soviet Union, the only other country in a position to help the crumbling Greek and Turkish economies, the president implied that this was a black and white situation with tremendous stakes. If the United States failed to help, the Soviets were prepared to occupy these countries, as they had already done in Poland, Bulgaria, and most of eastern Europe. His strong rhetoric squelched any notion of compromise and fed into the atmosphere of fear and distrust synonymous with the Cold War. This aversion to communism came to dictate American foreign policy for the next forty years. With Washington denouncing compromise and communism simultaneously, it was all but inevitable that a strong antipathy toward Moscow soon became the new American way. The sentiment "better dead than red" quickly became the modus operandi at the national level.

This flourishing anti–Soviet sentiment soon manifested itself in the major media outlets of the time, perhaps most visibly in the daily newspaper. Writers and columnists across the country made their living analyzing and critiquing the Soviets at all available opportunities. As spectator sports increased in cultural relevance and popularity, they too were drawn into this new and increasingly hostile Cold War. As the Cold War took place during the heyday of the daily newspaper, the papers amplified and provided an outlet for this war of words. Initially through the Associated Press and smaller local papers but later with increasing frequency via radio and television, international sporting events became more accessible and more immediate to spectators than ever before. With sport's growing popularity came a burgeoning market for sports commentary, especially in the United States. Daily and weekly columns analyzing local and international sport competitions were common features in newspapers and magazines across the country. These essays not only spanned the athletic realm but also frequently referenced current affairs, drawing parallels between sport and daily life.[13]

The Olympics, where sports and politics intersected, became a wellspring for this type of writing, bringing international politics to an audience that might otherwise pay only scant attention to global affairs. The need to beat the Russians became all-encompassing, whether in the gym or in the arms race. There was much to critique in the weeks leading up to an Olympics, not to mention during the Games themselves, offering columnists nearly two-months' worth of writing fodder every four years and occasionally during the intervening years as well. By capitalizing on the wealth of information—and speculation—available and on growing public interest, Cold War-era sports columns became another venue for motivational rhetoric encouraging American athletes while simultaneously threatening imminent Soviet domination. In a sense, sports media became a proxy ideological battlefield in its own right, as there were times when this rivalry became even more bitter off the field than on it. The rhetorical battle eclipsed the athletic achievements in terms of garnering attention and inciting anti–Soviet sentiment because it was so biased and downright aggressive in scrutinizing the other. This inflammatory writing soon became emblematic of the Cold War itself, as it fueled an already heated rivalry while encouraging constant comparison and self-examination. Moscow and Washington fed into this sense of antagonism through their perpetual demands for new programs and speeches aimed at motivating their citizens to improve their physical fitness to show supremacy.[14]

Sportswriting assumed a similar role behind the Iron Curtain. Sports journalism, though perhaps equally as important as it was in America, functioned a bit differently in the Soviet Union in the absence of a free press and where television coverage and analysis were a bit more sporadic. For the Soviets and their satellites, sports were never ends in themselves but employed as propaganda tools to promote the spread of communism and demonstrate cultural supremacy. Soviet sports writing reflected and exemplified this objective. The state sponsored all major publications, thereby subjecting them to Kremlin censorship. The anti–American writing that papers like *Sovetsky Sport*, *Izvestia*, and *Pravda* published was always Kremlin-approved and often Kremlin-originated. While this was common knowledge in the United States, American newspapers still reprinted many of these stories, though often with scathing commentary intended to foment and perpetuate further anti–Soviet sentiment.[15]

The examples of this are countless. In the golden age of the daily newspaper and what became a golden age for well-written sports commentary, a few names stand out for their flair for playing to public sentiment on athletic issues that held real world connections. Arthur Daley of the *New York Times* and the *Washington Post's* Shirley Povich are two such writers whose work transcended the sporting realm and demonstrated just how much the Cold War affected athletics. Daley, whose illustrious career as the "Sports of the Times" author spanned the entire period under study here, could in some ways be considered the national sports barometer. Often scathing, but always entertaining and accurate, his columns combined sport and politics in a way that conveyed how hot the Cold War was at any particular moment. One early piece from Daley that stands out for its blatant ridicule on both sides was a column from December 1947 where he mocked a satirical article previously published in *The Daily Worker* that belittled the large funeral thrown for Man O'War, the prizewinning horse. An American diplomat in Bucharest translated and sent this item to Daley, presumably as fodder for such an attack. According to Daley, the paper's scorn for the event showed "why these poor, misguided characters over here behind the Iron Curtain will never understand us, nor be able to compete with us."[16] Daley mocked the Soviets throughout the piece, scoffing that "facts never bothered the Soviets or their satellites…. However, the Red brothers delight in hammering home any wedge which might help to divide the outside world. They've been doing it regularly in affairs of state and yet it still comes as a shock when they take a simple sports item and distort it out of all proportion."[17]

One could make the case that Daley was as guilty of blowing a simple story out of proportion as *The Daily Worker*—or perhaps even more so because his counterattack was so hyperbolic. However, the reality was that this was a fairly accurate reflection of the national mood toward the Iron Curtain. The widening gap between East and West was not merely political; it increasingly permeated all facets of daily life, including sport. Readers probably did not view Daley's column as overblown, though it certainly seems so today. At the same time, it was worth noting that *The Daily Worker* had in some ways played into American hands by publishing such a piece on what was really a fairly minor event in American sports. That it devoted press space to such a story showed that this mockery and increasingly harsh rhetoric was not just an American phenomenon.

Daley's columns were emblematic of how the Cold War affected sports and sportswriting at all levels. He spent more than thirty years, from December 1942 until his death in January 1974, penning columns that encompassed a panorama of sporting events, including the Olympics, that ran five to six days per week in the *Times*. Just the third sportswriter ever to win the Pulitzer Prize, Daley possessed a unique ability to translate Cold War tensions into familiar sporting terms, making the struggle more accessible to the average fan.[18] His work captured the essence of the athletic Cold War, describing both the American and Soviet efforts to win the war on the field without shying away from sharp criticism of both sides. At times acerbic or perhaps overly dramatic but always informative, Daley's columns became an important source for international sporting news and commentary throughout the period under study here. Though he held no special connections to the White House that might have informed his work, Daley's writing gained relevance because it transcended the sporting realm as it drew connections with current affairs that helped to build the image of international sport always being more than just a game throughout the Cold War.

Like the proxy battles that the superpowers would soon wage in the space race and on the playing fields, this consistent anti–Soviet press provided an outlet for deriding Moscow and boosting confidence in American athletics with relatively low stakes. There was virtually no chance that the Soviets would declare war or precipitate a nuclear attack based on what was written in American sports columns. In this sense, the examples offered here and the innumerable others that appeared during the period under study, though blatantly nationalistic, were harmless. One of the benefits of a free press was that it became an instrument for anti-communist sentiment as well as a vehicle for promoting American achievement at the Olympics and in other international sporting competitions, particularly where the Soviets were involved. The Soviet Union also fed into this communist-bashing by publishing many clearly erroneous stories intended to incite anti–American feelings behind the Iron Curtain.

American citizens working as foreign correspondents or in diplomatic posts read these articles and often sent them home, further fueling the already hot anti–Soviet press and perpetuating this ill will on both sides. In this way, a cycle of negative publicity formed that continued even when Cold War tensions were not running as hot.[19]

Brundage and the Soviets were both popular villains for the American sportswriters, though for different reasons. Brundage's unwillingness to use his IOC authority to help the United States coupled with his frequent criticism of American athletes helped build his image as a public adversary. He garnered more than his share of negative publicity for his often unpopular beliefs on how the IOC should act in order to uphold de Coubertin's founding tenets. The *Washington Post's* Shirley Povich was among those who jumped at the chance to criticize Brundage. Povich, like Daley, used his columns to link sports with current events. Povich seized the opportunity to report that Brundage had wanted to invite the Germans to London, remarking, "unfortunately, Brundage has a discus where his heart should be."[20] The inclusion of a snippet like this fed into the growing anti–Brundage sentiment and made the public privy to an item of interest that would not merit its own full-length story. This statement is perhaps the best of the countless examples from the leadup to the 1948 Games of how closely sports and politics were entwined. The sentiment behind these words increased in relevance by 1948, as many American athletes and even IOC members proved reluctant to invite Germany, Japan, or the Soviet Union to the London Games.

Because the press proved to be so receptive to ongoing Soviet critique, even Brundage took to using American newspapers to articulate his stance on various issues. He was particularly vocal regarding his disapproval of the endless political entanglements with the Olympics. By 1946, it was increasingly clear that international sport and global politics were inextricable. The general public had begun to acknowledge that athletes' behavior was considered reflective of their home country, thrusting them into a high-profile role as unofficial diplomats. In this sense, a poor showing on the field was often construed as harmful to the United States' international prestige while poor sportsmanship was costly in diplomatic exchanges with participating nations. Thus, Brundage, still USOA president at the London Games, warned American athletes "not to grouse about little annoyances they may encounter in food-tight England or boast about America's land of plenty."[21]

The 1948 Summer Olympics soon came to be known as the Austerity Games, reflecting the physical condition of the host country following the war.[22] That the United States had emerged from World War II stronger than ever was a point of contention for many Europeans, especially when one remembered that there had been little physical destruction of American soil. While this might seem a bit pedantic, Brundage was well aware that blatant shows of strength or complaints regarding conditions in London might bring adverse diplomatic or public relations consequences and understood that Americans did not want to be cast in a poor light. Brundage's advice served as a stern warning to American athletes competing abroad neither to boast of American surpluses nor to complain about local conditions.[23] As there were a number of ongoing and potentially volatile diplomatic predicaments in 1948, it was commonly understood that American athletes should tread lightly to

In the late 1940s, U.S. aid to western Europe via the Marshall Plan helped revive several national economies while also giving the sense that American dollars were preventing the spread of communism beyond the Iron Curtain (National Archives. Photo No. 286-ME-6[2]).

avoid leaving an adverse impression, including one of being an overfed team in a Games where many of the competitors still suffered from wartime rationing and shortages.[24]

In preparing for the Austerity Games, Washington was very careful to protect its international image while employing the Marshall Plan and overseeing the Berlin Airlift in an effort to prevent the spread of communism. No one wanted to risk provoking yet another international conflict. Journalists and politicians alike recognized this predicament and seized upon sport as an important political means of demonstrating American good will, much to the chagrin of the purists like Brundage, who lamented this entanglement.[25] At this time, Brundage was fulfilling two roles, that of IOC vice president and president of the United States Olympic Association. As such, he often found himself in complex situations. For Brundage, along with mainstream America at this time, there was concern about a Soviet presence in London, but this did not yet overshadow the spectacle on the field. The threat of an Olympics marred by superpower tensions waned once the Soviets decided against sending a team to the Summer Games and allowed the final registration deadline to pass unacknowledged. There was no need for a Cold War mindset when strategizing for the Olympics just yet.[26]

While American athletes heeded orders to be gracious with the threat that failure to adhere might result in their expulsion from the competition keeping them in line, Brundage was unable to exert the same influence over the press. This sporting propaganda war, larger than the Olympic Games, developed simultaneously with the Cold War itself. As relations soured between the Soviet Union and the western world, both the sporting realm and the press began to reflect this growing rift. Non-communist countries expressed their apprehension toward the Soviets by hesitating to schedule matches against Iron Curtain countries. The press increasingly exposed as true what many already believed regarding the professionalism and brutality of Soviet athletes. The role of the press in manufacturing and perpetuating this sense of competition and hostility should not be overlooked when studying Cold War sport and it factors into the narrative presented here.

The beginning of the postwar period saw culture and sports begin to resume their prewar expansion. Both benefitted from the Cold War because they merited more White House attention as this new struggle moved beyond the political realm. While Stalin had begun to recognize the propaganda power of sport before World War II ended essentially all international athletic exchange, Washington proved a bit slower to tap into this potential. However, Truman proved supportive of the American Olympic effort, expressing his encouragement in a 1947 letter to Brundage. "I am particularly pleased that our American boys and girls are to take part in the competitions.... In the spirit of good sportsmanship which I trust our American participants will always maintain, I send best wishes for the success of the Olympic Games next year."[27] The tone of Truman's statement reflected the founding principle of the Olympic Movement, one yet unaffected by Cold War tensions. The political incursions at the Berlin contests had not destroyed the belief that the Games were competitions among individuals and not nations.

Although the media had begun their own tabulation of each country's medal count during the 1920s, the single-minded focus on this total was still another four years away in 1948. Instead, the Olympics were a means of bringing nations together to help move past the war and restore a sense of international goodwill. As Truman paraphrased the USOA charter in his letter to Brundage, the Games were for the youth of all nations "to the end that their health, patriotism, character, and good citizenship may be fully developed."[28] Because the Cold War stakes that debuted with the Soviets in 1952 were not as much a factor in 1948, Truman's statement, like most public figures' remarks pertaining to the Games, highlighted the sportsmanship aspect of the Olympics. There was some suspense over whether Moscow would send a team right up until the registration deadline, but the London Games proved to be the last unaffected by superpower politics until the fall of the Berlin Wall. Truman and others fixated less on the Games as an ideological battleground than as a means of showcasing American athletes and providing an incentive for all-around better fitness among the American public. Truman never threw himself into the burgeoning national fitness movement or the Olympic cause as much as either Dwight Eisenhower or John Kennedy would, but he would acknowledge the heightened stakes in advance of the 1952 Helsinki Games.[29]

Politics Make Their Mark

Despite its oft-stated policy of political indifference, the IOC shared the growing western squeamishness toward the Iron Curtain and it factored into the plans for London. The committee, including President J. Sigfrid Edstrom, seriously debated whether to invite the Soviets to the 1948 Games. On one hand, the Soviet Union had been a critical ally in World War II, helping to defeat Hitler through great sacrifices of men and material. It had aided in the rehabilitation of Eastern Europe, albeit largely through creating communist-friendly governments that were quite unsavory to the west. The Soviet Union was also a charter member of the United Nations. Stalin, while always a looming threat because of his volatility and cruelty even toward his own people, really had not done anything to merit exclusion on political grounds. Realistically speaking, even if his actions had justified sanctioning, it is unlikely that the IOC would have barred him, given the recent example that Berlin provided.[30]

At the same time, the specter of communism was enough to make the IOC very uneasy. Relations between the Soviet Union and the other former Allies had deteriorated quickly after Germany's surrender, perhaps more rapidly than anyone could have anticipated, with the occupation of that country a particular sore spot. The postwar settlement provided for Germany to be split into four zones, each controlled by one of four major Allies—Britain, France, the Soviet Union, and the United States. While the three western powers demonstrated a willingness to work together to the exclusion of Moscow, the status of Berlin, buried deep in the Soviet zone, remained a point of contention between east and west.[31] As Britain, France, and the United States had effectively merged their German zones into one unit by 1948, the Soviets found themselves on the outside looking in. The subsequent western powers' effort at Berlin currency reform—undertaken without Soviet input—further heightened tensions, leading to the Berlin blockade in June 1948.[32] This eleven-month standoff, spanning the London Games, did nothing to dispel the growing hostility or to accelerate the anticipated German reunification process. Instead, relations between east and west crumbled as the sense of mutual suspicion grew between the superpowers.

This affected the Games in that it revived the sentiments that Europe had bigger and more pressing problems than reviving the Olympic Movement. The reports from Berlin were quite dire by 29 June, just five days after the full blockade began. In an appeal to the United Nations, the Berlin City Parliament enumerated the ways in which the former Allies' squabbling over the city had negatively impacted its residents. In addition to the hassles caused by needing different currencies in each zone, citizens—other than those living under Soviet occupation—were beginning to experience shortages in coal, gas, water, and electricity.[33] The parliament feared the blockade would "from about early August onwards, necessarily lead to consequences hardly imaginable at this time in all fields of public, economic, and private life, and in particular in the field of health."[34] The timing of the Olympics, 29 July through 14 August, coincided with this estimate. The start of the Berlin Airlift on 1 July helped to relieve these feared shortages, though the blockade would continue until the following May.[35] British foreign secretary Ernest Bevin addressed the House of Commons as the opening ceremonies were taking place, calling on the Soviets to reopen the routes to Berlin so that negotiations could resume, to no avail.[36] The blockade and associated difficulties between the western powers and Moscow renewed the fear that the Soviets might show up in London unannounced and demand to compete, sparking a new diplomatic wildfire. Luckily for all parties involved, the airlift's lasting effect on the London Games was quite minor, though British and American public sentiment toward Moscow continued to harden.[37]

Though the London Games are now recalled nostalgically as the last Cold War-era Olympiad in which politics did not steal the spotlight, it was during the planning stages for London that the ongoing diplomatic issues that would challenge the IOC endlessly over the next two decades first appeared. As early as 1948, circumstances made it nearly impossible for the committee to maintain its self-imposed directive to avoid politics. With the Soviets as the major obstacle, the organizing committee found itself in a quandary regarding the London invitations. Fortunately for Edstrom, a technicality resolved the issue temporarily. At the time, the Soviet Union did not have a National Olympic Committee (NOC), which is a prerequisite for membership in the IOC and for competing in the Games. Even so, there remained the chance that the Soviets would form an NOC and apply to attend. This possibility grabbed media attention in the United States, since anything involving Moscow had become a matter of curiosity. With the national distaste for communism on the rise, there were many who would have been intrigued by a Soviet presence in London to enhance the sense of competition and offer the world a rare chance to get a glimpse behind the Iron Curtain.[38]

With the rivalry between the superpowers growing on and off the field, the American press kept close watch on this entry deadline. Sportswriters, reflecting the growing antagonism between the superpowers, reported its passing without official Soviet acknowledgment. Associated Press reporter Robert Musel dedicated a column to Moscow's decision to remain on the sidelines, presenting an entirely critical rationale for why the Soviets were not competing. "Soviet Russia, apparently unwilling to suffer a prestige defeat in international competition, allowed its last chance to enter the Olympics pass unnoticed."[39] Here, Musel made clear his belief that the Soviets decided to stay home because they expected to lose, portraying the Soviets as poor sportsmen. In the same piece, however, he foreshadowed imminent Soviet dominance in sport from behind the "athletic curtain," as he termed it. He warned his American audience that the Soviet Union "will keep her stars under wraps for a triumphant entry into the 1952 games when her own satellite nation, Finland, is host."[40] Musel employed a light tone to mock the Soviets for being unwilling to compete when they were not at their best, but the underlying message was clear. The Soviets soon would join the Olympic Movement and were likely to be quite impressive when they deigned to participate in the Games. Despite this warning, Musel's piece also betrayed a sense of disappointment that the United States would have to wait another four years to face its new archrivals.

Although Moscow declined to compete, Stalin was not completely absent from London. There was an awkward moment for all parties when an unannounced committee of Soviet officials arrived in London. Organizers feared that a Soviet team would soon follow and demand to compete, leading to a debate over how to react to a potentially explosive diplomatic situation. Should the Soviets be allowed to compete? Or should the IOC risk an international incident and potential standoff by refusing to admit their athletes because they had failed to play by Olympic rules? The committee was understandably relieved once the representatives announced that they had come alone merely to observe the Games as a means of preparing for future contests.[41] The Soviet observers took copious notes at a variety of events including the track events and basketball games, likely realizing that these were the headline sports as well as the events that offered the best chances for direct competition against the United States.[42]

The Soviet presence was neither the largest nor the most immediate challenge that the London organizers faced. Even before winning the Cold War on all levels became the unofficial American past time, the USOA had tried to replace London as Olympic host in 1948 for more immediate and practical reasons. The 1948 Games were a race against time. Finding a suitable host city for the first Games in more than a decade was the IOC's first priority. Tokyo had planned to host the 1940 Summer Olympics, but Emperor Hirohito withdrew governmental support for the Games even before diplomatic reasons forced the IOC to pick a more neutral site. Helsinki assumed hosting duties; however, Finland was not in a position to consider holding the event after the war. Now there was serious concern over whether the decimated British capital could recover and build the necessary facilities by 1948. Some also feared that the event could turn into a public relations disaster for the British government. Would the British people be angry that the British government devoted so much energy and so many resources to athletics when much of the population was still suffering from wartime shortages? Following the bitterly cold winter of 1947, "food, clothing, and petrol were still rationed, unemployment was high and housing was in very short supply," the combination of which dealt a serious blow to British morale.[43] As such, it was difficult to justify hosting the Games when so many British commoners were doing without basic necessities. There was also serious question as to where the athletes and spectators would stay. The sheer number of obstacles that the wartime destruction posed led many to wonder whether the best course of action might be to pick a less decimated country.

Brundage advised transplanting the Games to Los Angeles, as the city had already hosted in 1932 and therefore had many of the facilities in place.

Additionally, the United States had survived the war relatively unscathed in terms of the physical effects. He wrote in 1944, "London, half destroyed by bombs, will have a lot more important things to do than stage an athletics meeting."[44] However, the British delegation refused to consider a change in venue because the IOC had promised their country a chance to host nearly a decade earlier. More immediate to Britain's circumstances, hosting ensured that the government would turn its attention to improving conditions to meet the 1948 deadline. Organizers argued that keeping the Games in London would promote rebuilding throughout the city and surrounding area that would benefit the British people. The psychological element of the Games was not lost on the organizers either. By 1948, the Olympics were commonly associated with de Coubertin's mission of improving national morale, boosting London's credentials. As *Washington Post* columnist Bob Considine described it, "England, prostrate victor in its worst war, will play host not only because 'It's the sporting thing to do' but because it wishes to give its people a show and with that show a spiritual lift."[45] Bringing athletes from around to world to showcase London was a means of raising British morale in a time when it was quite low.[46]

The Games Begin

Today, the London Olympics are remembered for their simplicity and the spirit of camaraderie fostered among the athletes, especially when compared to the 1936 Berlin contests. The war hiatus and resulting circumstances gave the London organizers a chance to reevaluate its priorities. The goal for London was to lessen the political aspects and grandiose spectacle in favor of a return of the focus to athletic achievement. In retrospect, a city decimated by the war was the perfect venue to remind everyone that the true focus of the Games was on sport, not politics or glamour. As such, the committee's decision to let London host was a wise one. Edstrom and the IOC viewed London's situation as conducive to what the Games were trying to accomplish: restoring the focus on sport and raising Britain's morale.[47] The 1920 Games had set the precedent for using the Olympic Movement as a curative force following the First World War's devastation in Belgium. The accommodations in London were intentionally simple, with many of the events held in venues that predated 1939 and that had survived wartime bombing. This setting lent an atmosphere of austerity that stood in stark contrast to Hitler's Berlin spectacle.[48] It was clear by the closing ceremonies that politics had not won, as some athletes from Czechoslovakia, Hungary, Yugoslavia, and Poland asked for and received permission to become British residents rather than returning home.[49]

In addition to its legacy as a simple and tranquil event, London was the last Olympiad for twenty years during which there was little controversy involving Germany. Because Germany was still divided and under Allied occupation in 1948, few voiced support for a German invitation either to London or to the Winter Games in St. Moritz. Similarly to the Soviet situation, Germany lacked a functioning National Olympic Committee, rendering it ineligible for Olympic competition.[50] There was some controversy though because Edstrom believed that Germany and Japan, also denied an invitation to London, should be allowed to compete and appealed to Lord Burghley, chair of the London Olympic Organizing Committee, on their behalf.[51] In a letter to Burghley, Edstrom chastised the London committee's political mindedness. "I am surprised that you take this attitude three years after the war has ended. We men of sport ought to show the way for the diplomats."[52] This admonishment set the precedent for Brundage's treatment of the German Democratic Republic's future appeals for separate representation at the Games. Brundage's and Edstrom's appeals for German and Japanese invitations for the 1948 Games sparked the ire of many who were not yet ready to forgive the war's instigators but did not convince the IOC to allow them in London.

After a successful Opening Ceremonies, the concerns that had dominated the planning stages largely dissipated. For all of the drama and politics that surrounded their organization, the Games themselves proved largely uneventful in terms of diplomacy. The American team won the total medal count, as had been widely predicted, though it was several European stars from smaller countries who became the iconic figures of the Olympics. Dutch sprinter Fanny Blankers-Koen captured four golds on the track while Czech distance runner Emil Zatopek kicked off a prolific career with a runaway victory in the 10,000 meters.[53] As was tradition, the United States was the team to beat in the sprinting events, with the American men winning the 100-, 200-, and 800-meter golds as well as the 4×100-meter relay.[54] The men's basketball team clinched its second straight gold medal while the Americans made a splash in the pool events also.[55] In all, the Americans left London with thirty-eight gold medals. Sweden finished a distant second the in the final medal count.[56]

While the United States' results were certainly a point of pride, the overall focus was not on the quantifiable but on the immaterial aspects of the Games for the last time during the period under study here—and some might argue for a final time ever. An anonymous *New York Times* editorial revered the Olympics for "creating international amity, they are the supreme test of athletic skill and heart."[57] Friendship and athletic glory shared the stage in London, with politics relegated to the sidelines once the torch was lit over Wembley Stadium. Considine picked up on this theme as well, attributing the Olympic

Movement with building a camaraderie among athletes and nations that trumped the petty diplomatic squabbles that had plagued the organizing committee.[58] For a final time in London, there were few displays of overt nationalism and even fewer gripes about ideologies or cultural differences. Instead, the athletes were the main attraction. Glory and results certainly matter, but as points of individual and national pride instead of ideological victories. The Games achieved their purpose in that they helped revive the city of London and the world after a long and bitter war and because they were able to transcend the growing political friction of their times.

Despite the challenges posed by the Soviet presence, London's physical state, and the dispute over invitations posed, the 1948 Olympics remain as one of the least contentious of the modern era, particularly when compared alongside those of the 1950s and 1960s. Looking closely at London provides the rationale as to why some members of the IOC retained a sense of optimism regarding sport's ability to overcome political obstacles. London demonstrated why the Olympics just might able to resist the taint of national interests. Harping on the theme of diplomacy through sport in a way that would become quite familiar to Olympic fans during Brundage's presidency, Edstrom devoted part of his closing ceremonies speech to the importance using of sport as a teaching tool for diplomacy.

> One does not check nationalism by avoiding comparisons between the peoples, but by learning from one-another to see the good in one's fellow-men, and to accord a just recognition to superiority. A true humanity can be based only upon love of country.... To resolve differences in a spirit of chivalry is the only way to world-peace. Sporting contests teach this way at a time when the youthful soul is receptive to such teaching.[59]

Edstrom ascribed a specific role to nationalism in the tradition that de Coubertin had envisioned when reviving the Games more than fifty years earlier. His conception of the Olympics was a venue where athletes from around the world could come together to compete, learn from each other, and acknowledge greatness. The aim of the Olympics was to provide an idealistic environment of friendly competition where athletes represent their country and to transcend national boundaries. While de Coubertin strove to prevent the outbreak of war by providing an outlet for threatening nationalism, Edstrom saw the London Games as a means by which nations and individuals could recover from "the grey horror of the world-war."[60] Edstrom recognized that nationalism was not a passing phenomenon, but a force that could be channeled into a healthy sense of rivalry to fuel friendly competition when properly contained. While this was perhaps an admirable concept in the abstract, it proved untenable over the long term, particularly once the Soviet Union had joined the Olympic Movement. The same nationalism that Edstrom defended and praised in London would soon become a source of constant frustration for Brundage and the IOC.

The London Olympics were transitional in that they were kept intentionally simple like the pre–World War II contests, excluding Berlin, yet simultaneously, many of the Cold War challenges that would shape the 1950s and 1960s Games surfaced for the first time. They affirmed the founding tenets that de Coubertin had in mind when he looked to use sport as a safe venue for nationalist tensions. The 1948 Games demonstrated that athletics could be a healing force in the aftermath of great tragedy, just as the 1920 contests in Antwerp had shown. London proved that the Olympic Movement could make a successful return after the twelve-year gap after Berlin and grow bigger than ever.

However, the political aspects of the Games now loomed larger as well. Their legacy is decidedly positive, but the off-field issues that would come to define the Brundage era had begun to surface by mid–1948. The Soviets in attendance made clear that they were observing with the intention of dominating in 1952. Although neither Moscow nor the newly divided Germany competed in London, these Games set the stage for much of the political drama that would characterize the Games for the next two decades. The struggle over Berlin, leading to the blockade and subsequent airlift, was only the first of many confrontations between the superpowers over how to share this increasingly divided city. Similar to their battles for Berlin, Moscow and Washington would soon draw the Olympics into their ideological melée. As soon as the Soviet Union announced its intent to compete in 1952, the stakes of the Olympics heightened considerably. During this timeframe, from 1948 through 1968, the United States and the Soviet Union sought to "win" the Games via all possible means, using success on the world's most visible playing field as a Cold War barometer.

Between London and the 1952 Helsinki contests, the Soviets would attain IOC membership, but not before trying—and failing—to reorganize the Committee to better suit their interests. It was also during this span that the question of how to treat the two countries that had resulted from the postwar division of Germany first stymied the IOC. It would not reach final resolution until 1968 when Brundage finally allowed separate representation for the two Germanys. By the mid-1950s, the Ukrainian Soviet Socialist Republic was also clamoring for separate representation from Moscow in the Games, using the country's United Nations membership as validation for this demand. Compounding these issues were the American and Soviet attempts to control the IOC as well as the nearly constant intrusions of superpower politics on the Olympics. Several Cold War standoffs occurred in Olympic years, fueling the already fierce on-field rivalry between the American and Soviet teams and adding to the intrigue of the spectacle. In retrospect, the London Games were the last of their kind because of their relative simplicity and the lack of a politically charged atmosphere. The Helsinki Games, the first in which the Soviets competed—and dominated, would take on an entirely different tone, continuing the transition from athletic competition with discernible political undertones to an overtly political spectacle where the sideline antics at times overshadowed the stars on the field.

CHAPTER 4

1952

The Soviet Debut

"There will be seventy-one nations in the Olympics at Helsinki. The United States would like to beat all of them but the only one that counts is Soviet Russia. The communist propaganda machine must be silenced so that there can't be even one distorted bleat out of it in regard to the Olympics. In sports the Red brothers have reached the put-up-or-shut-up stage. Let's shut them up. Let's support the United States Olympic Team."

—*New York Times* columnist Arthur Daley[1]

While the challenges the IOC faced in planning the London Games had been mostly logistical, those leading up to Helsinki were almost entirely political. The friendly spirit of competition and relative tranquility that IOC president Sigfrid Edstrom had lauded during the London closing ceremonies proved fleeting, both in the sporting world and in international relations more generally. The London Games had represented a triumph for both Great Britain and the IOC, as they demonstrated that sport could overcome monumental obstacles. However, the challenges that the Cold War created proved to be more insuperable, lingering well beyond the 1952 Olympics. In planning for Helsinki, the IOC battled three major issues: Soviet acceptance to the Olympic Movement, representation for the now-partitioned Germany, and fighting the use of the medal count to keep Cold War score. Tangential to this last issue, both the United States and the Soviet Union piloted domestic initiatives intended to boost their medal totals, despite Brundage's insistence that the Games were not political.

Brundage's intent to use sport to transcend politics and accomplish what the diplomats could not confronted its first major challenges between the London and Helsinki Games. The Soviet Union presented a serious quandary to the IOC because many members, including Brundage, were reluctant to bring communists into the Olympic Movement. However, to exclude Moscow based on its government alone would be playing politics. Germany would also prove to be a difficult and lingering test. Though the IOC had not invited the Germans to London, much had changed since 1948. Now there were two German states, each tied to a superpower and clamoring to compete in Helsinki. Politics was a constant factor throughout the planning for the 1952 Games.

The Cold War Heats Up

These new problems reflected the increasingly stormy global climate by the late 1940s and early 1950s. The Cold War tensions that had been building since 1945 reached new heights following the 1948 Berlin blockade and the creation of NATO in 1949. The Kremlin's announcement that Soviet scientists had exploded Moscow's first atomic bomb in 1949 made headlines in the United States and stoked fears that Moscow would not hesitate to use its new weapon.[2] Anxiety regarding the bomb created a sense of impending doom that lingered until the 1980s. New problems arose on the American home front as Washington became mired in a proxy Cold War battle against Chinese and Soviet influence in Korea. What had been intended as a brief intervention soon devolved into an ugly three-year stalemate as Truman's administration tried to showcase American toughness through any means possible. While perhaps comforting to the American public, this strategy came at a high cost. The specter of communism also permeated domestic affairs, as the American people found themselves in the midst of an intense red scare and communist witch hunt. Scrutiny and censorship were the hallmarks of the early 1950s, as Senator Joseph McCarthy led the charge to pick out potential communists from Washington and society at large before they could manage to disturb the established order. The result was a dark period of suspicion and suppression now largely regretted; however, it demonstrated contemporarily just how ubiquitous the threat of communism was.

After observing the 1948 Games, the Soviet Union faced a tough decision. It could either continue to stay aloof from the IOC and lose out on a chance every four years to compete against the best athletes in the world for international glory. Alternatively, Moscow could submit and agree to join the IOC, thereby consenting, at least on paper, to playing by its rules. In the end, Stalin chose the latter, but not without a desperate attempt to tailor the committee to Soviet interests. The first hurdle, though likely a nonissue in Stalin's eyes, was the fact that the Soviet Union did not have a National Olympic Committee as of 1948.[3] This was a requirement for all competing countries. The IOC had used this rule as a means of keeping the vanquished Central Powers out of the 1920 contests and the IOC would invoke this requirement again in the 1950s when the Soviet Union and the leaders of the German Democratic Republic pushed for a separate East German team.

When the Soviets decided to pursue IOC membership in 1950, their representatives brought with them to Lausanne a proposal that the Moscow government be permitted to appoint its delegates to the IOC, that Russian become an official language of the Olympic Movement (joining English and French), and that the Soviet Union be awarded a permanent seat on the Executive Committee. The IOC quickly declined all three of these terms and offered valid reasons as to why they were unacceptable. Regarding representation, the IOC reminded the Soviet Union that de Coubertin had always maintained that IOC members were delegates to their home country on behalf of the Olympic movement and not vice versa. Their primary allegiance was to the IOC and it was a long-established practice that the IOC select a replacement when one of its members from any country either died or resigned. Allowing the Soviets to choose their own delegates would be a clear mixture of politics and sport as Moscow would likely select a member who was more biased toward his home country's interests to the detriment of the Olympic Movement. Regarding language, the IOC argued that there was no need to add a third official language because the current members were all able to speak either English or French, if not both. Adding Russian could set a dangerous precedent, as there would be little to stop other member nations from demanding to use their native language as well. If so, members could become isolated, limiting communication among them if the number of official languages became too numerous and members could not find a common tongue to hold a workable session.[4] This would severely hinder both written correspondence and working sessions

Tangential to these demands, the Soviet Union also asked that Spain's IOC application be refused so long as Franco remained in power, as Stalin loathed fascists. However, the IOC refused this condition as well.[5] Edstrom and Brundage could not concede this demand and deny Spain membership on account of its abhorrent government without acknowledging that politics influenced sport, something which neither was willing to do. The IOC's rejection of these terms forced the Soviet Union to reconsider its application. Was joining the IOC worth making concessions and subjugating its athletes to outside scrutiny? In the end, the Kremlin decided that the foreign policy gains that IOC membership could bring compensated for the compromises that said affiliation required.[6]

Complicating the issue of Soviet membership was the reluctance of several IOC members to admit Moscow to the Olympic Movement. The IOC hesitated when Stalin initially asked for membership. In addition to Moscow's repellent political system, there was serious question over whether Soviet athletes could be considered amateurs. Edstrom asked as much in an open letter to the IOC in October 1950. Tage Ericson, chief of Stockholm Stadium, visited the Soviet Union on behalf of the IOC shortly after Edstrom wrote his letter and reported on the state of sport behind the Iron Curtain. His report confirmed the skepticism surrounding Soviet sportsmen:

> Voluntary athletic movement of the same character as we have in Sweden does not exist. Sport is a tool of the State to bring up physical education for the people, to give the people pastime and to carry on political propaganda. All leaders of sport and all judges and trainers are paid for the work by the State. The active participation in the sport is voluntary. The development of the sport is, however, supported financially by the State through scholarships.[7]

Ericson's visit proved a commonly accepted fact. Soviet athletes were by definition professional and therefore ineligible for Olympic competition, given its strict concept of amateurism. Moscow had admitted to paying Soviet athletes for their achievement as recently as 1947.[8] They assured the IOC that this practice had ended, but Ericson's mention of scholarships contradicted these claims. Later, the Soviets announced unabashedly that their athletes received state subsidies, but the IOC had little recourse. These payments broke IOC rules, which forbade Olympic athletes from even drawing a salary from coaching.

The issue of broken time, when athletes received compensation for time missed at work for training and competing, remained anathema to the IOC throughout Brundage's tenure. Many American athletes worked full time and practiced their sport on evenings and weekends to maintain their Olympic eligibility. While members of the American press and the athletes themselves often protested the unfairness of this issue, Brundage remained adamant that the Games were for amateurs only. The only exceptions were for members of the United States military, who technically trained on paid time.[9] Brundage told the *Washington Post* in December 1951 that college athletic scholarship recipients were eligible, referring to these student athletes as "subsidized."[10] When asked to elaborate, he said, "I mean anyone who is given any scholarship, payments, or anything of value to play football or other sports."[11] His more lenient treatment of Iron Curtain athletes did nothing to lessen the strong anti–Brundage sentiment that had taken hold in the United States by the early 1950s.[12]

Concerns regarding professional athletes continued to follow the Soviet team throughout the early years of the Cold War. In a *New York Times* article analyzing Soviet sport and previewing their Olympic debut in 1952, sportswriter Harry Schwartz bluntly accused the Soviets of not playing by the rules of amateurism.

The Government makes sure that there's plenty of incentive for Soviet athletes to come out on top. The Soviet equivalent of Babe Ruth or Dick Kazmaier in any sport is a pampered darling, rewarded with cash, an automobile, and similar gifts for his prowess. He becomes a member of the Soviet elite.... And in Soviet schools, too, proficiency in studies frequently becomes secondary to an athlete's performance in the field.[13]

Despite the ongoing protests from the United States and other compliant nations, this uneven treatment continued largely unchecked throughout Brundage's tenure. It was not until Lord Killanin, his successor, revised the athletic qualifications that this issue was finally resolved.[14]

Edstrom and Brundage proved willing to accept the Soviets into the Olympic Movement and turn a blind eye to the mix of politics and sport inherent to communist systems. In a letter to Brundage from October 1950, Edstrom wrote, "There is in Russia a central organization of sportsmen and their hope is to take up Olympic matters. I think we can recognize this. Of course everything in Russia is governed by the State and also the sport. What shall we do? Similar organizations exist even now in some countries, e.g. Italy and France, not to speak of Poland, Hungary, Yougoslavia, Tchécoslovaquie etc."[15] Here, Edstrom expressed almost a sense of resignation regarding the intrusion of politics on sport. The Soviets were not the only ones injecting politics into athletics. In his eyes, there was more to gain by accepting the Soviets to the IOC than there was to lose by excluding them indefinitely. There was little chance the Soviets would change their ways, therefore the IOC had to compromise. That the committee did not offer this concession to all members drew ire from the rule-abiders, including the United States. Edstrom realized that several countries were under systems comparable to the Soviet Union where sport and politics mixed and was willing to be flexible regarding their inclusion in the Olympic Movement. Brundage, maintained that this was unacceptable, though he was quietly lenient when he deemed an exception necessary to keep the peace.[16] In exercising this flexibility, Edstrom acknowledged that bringing the Soviets into the Olympic Movement could lead to a new set of problems. He closed out his letter by saying, "I have also been a bit anxious about this Russian competition. It certainly would be much better, if they did not come along."[17]

Over time Edstrom grew more optimistic, agreeing to welcome the Soviets to bridge the political divisions developing via the Cold War. In a letter to IOC chancellor Otto Mayer from April 1951, Edstrom wrote, "I am really glad, if we could have the USSR Olympic Committee recognized, as we otherwise will have the athletic world divided in two big sections—East and West."[18] This letter showed that although Edstrom was as skeptical of communism as many of his peers during the Cold War, he was willing to set aside his personal distaste of Soviet politics to further the international spirit of the Olympic Movement.

He was a stickler for the Olympic rules, but worked to ensure that the IOC did not discriminate politically or racially.[19]

Like Brundage, Edstrom tried to prevent the intersection of politics and sport; however, he was more realistic, as he understood that this was not always possible. He was willing to admit the Soviet NOC to the IOC—only after they met the entrance requirements—and turn a blind eye to the questionable status of their athletes and some of their attempts at tailoring the IOC to the Kremlin's interests. Brundage's adherence to the rules at times drew extra attention to the politics of the Games, detracting from the athletic performances. Brundage bore a heavy burden in mediating the perpetual Soviet and American efforts to use the Olympics as means to their often divergent political ends. The Soviet Union's officially joining the IOC in May 1951 created a new arena for Cold War battles that lasted until the fall of the Berlin Wall in 1989.

Once an official IOC member nation, the Soviet Union benefitted from arranging for Konstantin Andrianov to serve as the IOC's first delegate to the Soviet Union. Andrianov had been president of the Moscow Sports Union until this point and had served as the chief organizer for the new Soviet NOC. As such, his appointment was convenient for all involved because he had experience in sports administration and was quite familiar with his home country's state-run athletics program while also politically well-connected, given his prior employment. Andrianov would go on to a distinguished career within the IOC, serving as vice president under Brundage from 1966 to 1970 and playing an instrumental role on the organizing committee for the 1980 Moscow Games.[20] Despite the political overtones which surrounded the Soviet Union's joining the IOC and Andrianov's subsequent appointment, it became clear in time that this choice was a wise one for all involved.

Moscow wasted little time in using the Games for political ends. While still in the process of obtaining IOC membership, the Kremlin assigned the Sports Ministry to oversee progress toward its new international athletics propaganda goals. It appointed officials to supervise the massive national efforts to meet western athletic standards in time for Helsinki. These high expectations placed a great amount of stress on coaches and trainers to work athletes consistently harder with a singular goal in mind: to demonstrate the glory of the communist way of life over the western capitalists, mainly the United States.[21] Even before the Soviets competed in their first Olympics, the Kremlin strongly emphasized sport as a means of winning Cold War prestige, with the U.S. Government quickly following their lead.[22] By the early 1950s, the White House believed that Soviet ventures abroad were harmful to the United States and its allies, giving the negative propaganda potential. This led to the rapid development of a covert "state-private network" between the government in Washington and American sport governing bodies by the early 1950s, though their efforts always seemed to fall short of Moscow's.[23] In 1950 alone, Moscow spent more than $150 million on cultural exchange projects just in France, more than the United States spent on all of its international culture ventures combined. This disparity led the Truman government to increase their spending to $88 million by 1952, just at the Soviets increased their funding to $1.5 billion.[24] Stalin appealed to all Russians to support the Olympic cause through the "every citizen an athlete" campaign in the months leading up to Helsinki.[25]

The United States countered by stepping up its own efforts to dominate the Games, this time with some help from the White House. Brundage quietly supported these efforts. In a 1951 letter to fellow U.S. Olympic Committee member J. Lyman Bingham, Brundage anticipated the increase in attention and funding that a Soviet entry to the Olympic Movement would spark in the United States, given the growing competition between the superpowers. Brundage predicted that, "The fact that the Russians will send a team should help us considerably in raising money."[26] Brundage followed up this letter with an appeal to American newspaper publishers in advance of the Helsinki Games, the urgent tone of which was unmistakable.

> The year, 1952, is a crucial one for the United States Olympic Team—and the outcome of the competitions at Helsinki will have a definite influence on our nation's political position throughout the world. For the first time, Russia will enter a team of the best athletes she can muster and train. What's more, Stalin will pay all expenses, and issue his usual orders for nothing short of victory. The instructions are to win or else! The reason is obvious. Stalin's big weapon is propaganda—and he hopes—desperately—that the United States team will not be complete—and that he can publicize our weakness in morale as well as in the stamina and ability of the US athletes. We can't let this happen![27]

Brundage's writing here was markedly different in its political charge from his typically neutral stance. This different tone underscored just how important Cold War victories were becoming in all facets of society, as this was a crusade that even Brundage could not help but participate in—albeit behind the scenes.

Truman echoed this concern in a November 1951 letter to Brundage. Referring to athletics as "democracy at work," the president made a clear appeal for a strong performance in Helsinki.[28] Though he did not mention the Soviets by name, the allusion to them was obvious. "Certain countries which have not participated for many years will be represented. Others will take part for the first time."[29] The Soviets' impending debut raised the stakes much higher than they had been in London. While the overarching message in 1948 had been that it would be in poor taste to perform too well and show up the still-recovering European teams, the situation in 1952 was much different. "This competition is not just another event. It requires the finest American athletes we can send, it requires the fullest support Americans can give. The eyes of the world will be upon us."[30] This statement epitomized how perception of the Games changed as soon as the Soviets entered the competition. Now that the Cold War had heated up, the Olympics became another venue open to influence and domination. American athletes arrived in both Oslo and Helsinki with the goal of presenting the United States in the best possible light, as a nation that was both victorious in competition as well as the embodiment of the Olympic spirit.[31] After the Games, several American Olympians went on a U.S. government-funded world tour that focused on the developing world to spread this vision of the United States in the hopes of gaining allies and influence— and thwart Soviet efforts toward the same end.[32]

Despite their shared interest in improving the American team's perform-ance in the Olympics, Brundage's relationship with Washington can be described as contentious at best. Though he was a devoted anti-communist and shared the widespread mentality that keeping Stalin out was in the Olympic Movement's best interest, he believed his primary allegiance was to the IOC and not his country.[33] Brundage tended to vacillate between supporting his home country and trying to uphold the apolitical standards of the Games. His public stance was that he and the Olympic Movement were immune to politics. He perceived himself as the IOC's delegate to the United States with the mis-sion of ensuring that the USOA adhered to Olympic policies. However, there were times when his conservative Republican worldview superseded this posi-tion, leading him to quietly seek more support to help beat the Soviet Union.

Though Brundage prided the USOA in not taking government handouts to fund its athletes, the Olympic fundraising efforts enjoyed great support and endorsement from all levels of society. In addition to stressing the importance of increased physical activity for all Americans to increase their readiness to fight the Cold War, Truman also issued a proclamation in May 1952 declaring an official Olympic week. As such, the president used this occasion as a means of "urging all citizens of our country to contribute as generously as possible to insure that the United States will be fully and adequately represented in the XVth Olympic Games."[34] In the same message, Truman endorsed the USOA's goal of Olympic glory because, "experiences afforded by the Olympic Games make a unique contribution to common understanding and mutual respect among all peoples."[35] This statement highlighted the diplomatic role tacitly ascribed to all American Olympians.

Truman intentionally drew contrasts between the Soviet and American approaches to building fitter constituencies in an address to the U.S. Military Academy in 1952. "The policies of the Soviet Union are exactly the opposite of our own .... The Bolsheviks want physical control of the individual, and they also want to control his thoughts and his soul."[36] The press continued to harp on this point and on the differences between the two societies as the Soviet Union's first Olympic appearance neared. According to the *New York Times* in May 1951, "The Soviet leaders have made no bones about the fact that they want a physically fit population capable of undergoing the extreme rigors of wartime combat as well as hard work in industry and agriculture."[37] The implied contrasts here were quite clear. While the United States encouraged sport for sport's sake and athletic glory, the Soviet Union used athletics to improve production and military preparedness, feeding into the already prevalent popular image of Moscow as building a heartless military-minded society. The implication here was that the Kremlin forced Soviet citizens to take up sports as a means of improving the country's prowess, in contrast to the United States, where both spectatorship and participation in sports were encouraged first and foremost as leisure activities.

As mainstream America began to recognize the Olympics as a means of winning Cold War bragging rights, national celebrities joined the flag-waving bandwagon. Bing Crosby and Bob Hope each took part in the 1952 Olympic Fund Telethon. Crosby routinely declined television appearance requests to the point that the Olympic Telethon marked his small screen debut. He explained his decision to participate: "This is one time I can't refuse. I think every American should get behind our Olympic team and send out athletes across at full strength and in the finest style possible."[38] Hope was equally as enthused about the cause at hand, stating, "I guess old Joe Stalin thinks he is going to show up our soft capitalistic Americans. We've got to cut him down to size. This is the most exciting thing I have ever undertaken, and, brother, Bing and I are going to throw our best punches."[39] The fourteen-hour event in June 1952 featured the two American icons, joined by Dean Martin and Jerry Lewis. It helped to raise more than $1 million in pledges for the Olympic team, despite complaints that Hope and Crosby did little more than read numbers on the air.[40]

Congress jumped into the Olympic fray as well, with legislators realizing the propaganda potential of the Games. Well before the Soviets fielded their first team, Congress approved Public Law 159 in 1947, which created funding for members of the armed forces training for the Olympics through the Office of the Secretary of War. Though this law did not specify a dollar amount, the Secretary of War would now pay "certain expenses incident to training, attendance, and participation of personnel of the Army of the United States and of the naval service, respectively, in the Seventh Winter Sports Olympic Games and the Fourteenth Olympic Games and for future Olympic games."[41] The rationale behind such legislation was that American victories would remind the world that the United States was a cultural as well as a military leader. The stakes became a bit higher once the Soviets officially committed to competing in 1952, leading Congress and Truman to react accordingly. Public Law 344 in 1952 provided support for the Helsinki-bound athletes by declaring a national Olympic week in May to draw public attention to and raise funds for Helsinki-bound athletes. The goal of this legislation was to raise $850,000 "to equip, transport, feed, house, and present in competition over four hundred amateur athletes from all classes of our society and all parts of our country to represent the United States in the 1952 Olympic Games."[42] The city of New York and the Empire State collaborated on a drive to collect $250,000 and to stage a celebratory sendoff for the American team in July "to send a full-strength team" to Helsinki.[43] These types of resolutions and celebrations became customary in Olympic years to raise both money and awareness of the Games' importance to the wider ideological struggle. Though Brundage and many others opposed government subsidies for Olympians, there was a recognized need to offer limited aid to athletes. The word "limited" was key in that this funding usually amounted to only paying for the athletes' housing within the Olympic Village and perhaps covering transportation costs.

While the London Games had received some advance attention mostly from major national publications, their successors benefitted from a dramatic increase in public and media interest. The brunt of this focus centered on the intensifying battle for supremacy between the superpowers. During the 1952 sendoff weekend in New York, the *New York Times* published an editorial encouraging full support for the American Olympic effort, referencing these heightened stakes. "The athletes of all nations this year have equal need of stout hearts, fast finishes and level heads ... [Soviet] victories—and some must be expected, else Moscow wouldn't have sent a team—will be drummed as the triumph of a political system."[44] Political comparisons increasingly appeared in American sportswriting. Journalists routinely adopted a moralistic tone, painting the communists as the rule breakers while reminding readers that their athletes would continue to proudly abide by the amateur code. As columnist Arthur Daley phrased it, "We're not going to abandon our principles of democracy just because the Communists jibe at us and yell louder than we do. Neither should we abandon amateurism just because some athletic crackpots want to change over our brave, new world of tomorrow."[45] The traditionalists argued that the west was the real winner even when the communists were reaping Olympic glory by paying their stars. Soviet assertions that it had ceased payments to athletes for achievements fell on deaf ears outside the Iron Curtain, and perhaps behind it as well. Here, Daley made it clear that he believed the dispute was manifested when "Uncle Joe Stalin's boys began to flex their muscles and cast stray eyes at international competition."[46]

The problem with this American moralism was that it was not completely innocent. In the same piece, Daley called on the United States and Britain to put an end to all such discussions of payments, staking the existence of the Olympics themselves on this proposition as though this were a brand new problem. In actuality, issues regarding true amateurism dated back to the 1912 Olympics in Stockholm where American track star Jim Thorpe was later stripped of his gold medals from the pentathlon and decathlon events because he had played baseball for money before the Games.[47] As the Russian Revolution was still four years away when Thorpe lost the medals in January 1913, Daley's charges that the Soviets were the first to raise the issue of paying athletes for success were false. Moscow acknowledged that it had rewarded athletic accomplishments financially as recently as 1947, but the amateurism debate was much older and already an issue by this point. The Soviets were a convenient scapegoat for a problem nearly as old as the modern Games themselves.

Sports journalism on both sides of the Iron Curtain soon devolved into an ugly war of words, reflecting the growing intensity of the wider Cold War. Denunciations of the Soviet Union in American newspapers were often reported as bad American press behind the Iron Curtain and vice versa. One instance of this was a 1950 *Washington Post* story from a correspondent in Moscow who wrote on Soviet criticisms of the American sporting infrastructure. The original story that ran in *Pravda* in January 1950 argued that until recently only a small number of Americans had the time and means to participate in sport: the wealthy and the professional athletes. This depicted a system comparable to that found in Britain around the turn of the century. While de Coubertin had admired this concept and loosely modeled the Games on the pursuit of sport as leisure, much had since changed. This vision was no longer accurate, especially in the United States. Now *Pravda* charged that Washington was piloting new initiatives to force American youth into sport as a means of preparing them for the military. "To the newly-appeared claimants to world domination, sport is necessary for the preparation of 'good soldiers.' It added that military considerations dictate the kinds of sport played in America, as 'American militarists set their hopes on sport because bourgeois sport kills thought, conscience, humanity.'"[48] Going a step further, the article cited that *Pravda* had alluded to unrest in the United States as the public fought these measures to "militarize sports."[49] The *Post's* clear objective in printing this story was to incite anti–Soviet feeling.

The following day, *Washington Post* columnist Shirley Povich analyzed *Pravda's* report and satirized it in standard Cold War fashion. Povich, like Daley, became synonymous with Cold War-style sarcasm, the voice of concern and hyperbole regarding Soviet domination. "Thus we learn from Moscow that it matters not who won, but how many were killed, unlike in the Soviet which cherishes the lives and welfares of its athletes, except when they sass an official. In America, for that crime, you get put out of the game for unsportsmanlike conduct with your team penalized half the distance of the field. Sass a Soviet official and you get Siberia."[50] Povich's column is a bit exaggerated, but it surely struck a chord with his reading audience, many of whom shared his uneasiness about the Soviet Union.

The press eagerly anticipated the clashes between Brundage and Moscow that were expected to accompany the Soviet debut. The superpowers' conflicting definitions of amateurism and early Soviet attempts to reorganize the IOC to its liking made these heated exchanges inevitable, distracting Brundage from his frequent criticism of the United States. That Moscow agreed to play by the rules—or at least claimed to—merely added to the spectacle, sparking further conjecture regarding Soviet professionalism and imminent domination of the Games. The IOC's ready acceptance of the Soviets, whom few trusted to play by the rules, fed the American media's already strong anti–Brundage stance. By the time he became IOC president, Brundage was a much-maligned figure throughout the world for his staunch adherence to what were viewed as archaic policies regarding Olympic sport. Many were curious as to how this stubbornness would affect Soviet negotiations in joining the IOC. The American press jumped on this possibility eagerly, with Samuel Williamson of the *New York Times* describing Brundage as "irresistible and immovable.... [Soviet Foreign Minister Andrei] Gromyko's insults are cooings of public library pigeons contrasted with what is said about Brundage by hostile sports columnists who are some of the country's most ingenuous wordslingers."[51] The parting shot in this piece was that "in his insistence on amateurism in athletics the man could give Molotov lessons in stubbornness."[52] Even after his death, Brundage remained a favorite target for American sportswriters who disagreed with the IOC's strict amateur policy and outdated insistence on the separation of politics and sport.

Once the Soviets openly acknowledged their intention to dominate Helsinki, it was only natural that the American press soon responded. Soviet news outlets were critical. The already prominent mutual mudslinging increased in pace and hostility as their Olympic debut neared. In January 1952 came false reports from Moscow that the American military establishment had taken control of the USOA in anticipation of the Games. *Sovetsky Sport*, a Moscow-based daily devoted to athletics coverage behind the Iron Curtain, broke the "news" that "the armed forces have converted the formation of the American Olympic team into their monopoly. In this is shown graphically the intensified militarization of the country including American sports which has now reached an unheard-of scope."[53] This article, meant to incite unrest, achieved its intended purpose in both countries. Behind the Iron Curtain, anti–American propaganda couched as news stories spooked Soviet athletes into training harder for the Olympics. On the American side, stories like this demonstrated that the Soviet Union could not be trusted, thereby feeding into the atmosphere of suspicion that helped breed the McCarthyism scare. *Sovetsky Sport* built on this rivalry, predicting a communist victory and boasting of the propaganda fodder that one would provide. "Every record won by our sportsmen, every victory in international contests, graphically demonstrates to the whole world the advantages and strength of the Soviet system."[54]

The *Times* answered via yet another scathing Daley column detailing how misinformed the Soviets were regarding all things American. "The obvious falsehood of the Soviet charge is almost too ridiculous to merit comment…. If the United States whacks the pants off the Russians at the Olympics—as it undoubtedly will—this doesn't even offer an alibi."[55] Even though Daley quickly dismissed the Soviet claims as "almost too ridiculous," he continued with a column-length rant on the subject, all the while expounding upon the Soviet chances of defeat and disappointment in Helsinki. "No one can understand why Russia dared enter the Olympics at so great a risk of having its bubble of invincibility punctured. It's trying to get into the international family of nations at the very top, not even recognizing that it has room for improvement or help."[56] Through his flaming rhetoric, Daley rose to the bait posited by the original *Sovetsky Sport* piece while offering encouragement to aspiring American Olympic hopefuls at a time when many were very curious as to how the Soviets would fare in Helsinki.

The intrigue surrounding the Soviets coupled with the growth of the Games themselves, led to more intense press coverage before Helsinki than any prior Olympiad. Perhaps Daley best captured the American sentiment regarding the Soviet team's presence at the Games when he wrote, "There will be seventy-one nations in the Olympics at Helsinki. The United States would like to beat all of them but the only one that counts is Soviet Russia. The communist propaganda machine must be silenced so that there can't be even one distorted bleat out of it in regard to the Olympics. In sports the Red brothers have reached the put-up-or-shut-up stage. Let's shut them up. Let's support the United States Olympic Team."[57] Daley expressed his rousing support of the American team in the type of blatantly nationalistic rhetoric that made Brundage's blood boil. Nonetheless, it was an accurate gauge of American sentiment in 1952. Though Brundage liked to believe otherwise, the USOA and American audience viewed Moscow as its only real competition. Not only was it the only opponent similar in size and might, but the added intrigue wrought by the clash of ideologies made beating the Soviets even more enticing.

The German Question

   While the Soviets were the main political attraction leading up to Helsinki, Germany provided another Cold War sideshow. The 1952 Olympics were the first in which the status of the two Germanys was open for serious debate. Like the questions surrounding Soviet acceptance to the IOC, the German issue first surfaced between the 1948 and 1952 Olympiads; however, a solution proved a bit more elusive than anyone likely anticipated. Because Germany as constituted before World War II no longer existed, the IOC did not know how to treat the two occupied zones. Britain, France, and the United States merged their occupation zone in May 1949 to create the Federal Republic of Germany. One year later, on 10 May 1950, General Robertson wrote to Lord Burghley, British IOC representative, to ask him to support IOC recognition for the new West Germany. His rationale was the inverse of the reasoning that deterred the IOC from inviting Germany to London. Now an Olympic invite could help move past the memory of the war and to speed the reintegration of Germany into the global community. Robertson argued, "the objective of allied policy towards Germany is that she should become in all senses a member of the community of peace-loving and democratic nations…. After all the terrible things that have happened in Germany during the recent past, it seems clear to me that we must look to the youth of the country to make a new start. They are the leaders of the future."[58] In this view, a West German presence in Helsinki would exemplify Brundage's tenet of using sport as diplomacy. Participating in the Games would offer young Germans a positive example of how to coexist with other nations and would aid in ending the isolation that had characterized the Nazi years. Shortly after Robinson penned his appeal, the IOC offered the Federal Republic of Germany provisional recognition, including the privilege of competing in the 1952 Olympics.

   The Soviet-occupied German zone made its first petition asking for a return to the Games in April 1951. In a letter to IOC chancellor Otto Mayer, the new Comité National Olympique de la République Démocratique Allemande announced its formation and asked the IOC for official recognition.[59] The appeal conveyed the sense that like the partition of Germany itself, the need for separate NOCs and teams was temporary. Hope remained that the two Germanys would reunite, yet plans for reunification soon faded for myriad reasons. At the 1951 IOC session in Vienna, the IOC Executive Committee advised that the Federal Republic of Germany, by then recognized as an autonomous political entity, be allowed admission to the IOC with Karl Ritter von Halt, a prewar German representative, as its representative.[60] Simultaneously, the IOC decided a committee comprised of East and West German sporting officials would meet in May 1951 to discuss the logistics of East German representation. The group held three sessions but failed to reach an agreement before the deadline for the Winter Games in Oslo, leaving eastern athletes on the sidelines.[61]

Edstrom argued that the IOC could not recognize the GDR's committee until other—western—countries recognized the GDR as a separate political entity. The IOC used this same rationale when the Hungarian National Sports Federation appealed to Brundage personally in 1950 asking to compete in Helsinki and later when a Ukrainian Olympic Committee asked for separate representation and the right to compete apart from the Soviets in advance of the 1956 Olympics.[62] Like Brundage and many others, Edstrom was loath to see communism infiltrate the Olympic Movement anymore than was necessary. Fortunately for those who shared this mindset, IOC rules stated that athletes could only compete if they are "certified by a national federation affiliated to an international federation and by a National Olympic Committee both recognized by the IOC."[63] East German athletes did not meet this condition, rendering them ineligible for competition. The IOC appointed Ritter von Halt to lead the commission in deciding a course of action to certify East Germans as members of a unified German team. Despite Ritter von Halt's best efforts, there was not enough time to incorporate a team for Oslo.[64] The IOC decided to reopen the matter at its 1952 Helsinki session should anything change before then.[65]

In February 1952, the East German NOC again appealed directly to Brundage for recognition, arguing that it had reached out to West Germany, only to be ignored. "The NOC of the Federal Republic therefore has no influence on that as it is able to carry through its decisions only on the territory of the Federal Republic (Western Germany). When the affiliation of the West German NOC was decided it happened just without consulting the NOC of the German Democratic Republic."[66] Additionally, the East German NOC argued that it had met all of the requirements necessary for IOC membership. However, Edstrom offered a conflicting report at the Helsinki session, stating that "the O.C. of the East has refused categorically any collaboration with the West."[67]

Alexi Romanov, president of the Soviet NOC, helped to lead the fight for separate East German representation, as the Kremlin hoped to capitalize on the propaganda potential that accompanied Olympic glory. Separate East German representation in Helsinki would have been a great victory for the Soviets because the German Democratic Republic was still technically under Soviet occupation. Therefore, Moscow could boast of even more athletes competing, while increasing its medal chances. Romanov argued that East Germany should be invited since West Germany did not seem to have any objection. He also anticipated a future, united Germany, stating, "this situation cannot last forever and sooner or later Germany will become unified again."[68] Despite this appeal, Edstrom adjourned the matter without a vote, leaving the East without representation in Oslo or Helsinki. The East German distress that this exclusion caused underscored the diplomatic importance of sport. For a marginalized state, Olympic representation signified political legitimacy and an entry into the global community. As such, East Germany reprised its fight to gain IOC admission in time for the 1956 Olympiad shortly after the Helsinki closing ceremonies.[69] Unlike other Soviet satellites, the East Germans would enjoy strong support from Moscow in its quest first for IOC recognition and later in its fight to compete as a separate entity from West Germany.

Helsinki

The Soviet Cold War rhetoric became even more serious in tone as the Helsinki Games opened. According to Soviet newspapers *Pravda* and *Izvestia*, as reported in the *New York Times*, Soviet athletes had a mission to "provide a shining example of the superiority of Soviet culture over that of bourgeois countries."[70] Simultaneously, these papers accused the United States of corrupting the Games by "preparing cannon fodder for a new, aggressive war."[71] This story, appearing in the *Times* two days after the opening ceremonies, demonstrated how quickly the Olympics had become a Cold War proxy battleground. The Soviet press reminded its athletes that they were representatives not just of their country, i.e., unofficial diplomats, but that they should further communist interests by winning their events. Medals were tangible proof of Cold War superiority. At the same time, the Soviet press took the opportunity to denounce the United States for essentially doing the same thing: employing the Games as a means of achieving Cold War glory at a lower opportunity cost than resorting to actual cannon—or atomic—fodder.

There was no doubt that the Soviet debut heightened the level of excitement building up to the Games. Daley summed up the occasion aptly in a column from 16 July 1952, just three days before the opening ceremonies. Drawing comparisons between the overtly political Nazi Games and what was about to transpire in Finland, he wrote that "Soviet Russia has already given everyone the jitters ... [because] the Reds, long a political enigma, have now become a sports one as well."[72] While no one knew quite what to expect from the Soviets, who had long segregated themselves from western competition, the fear was that they would perform quite well. Daley's column, with its obvious anti–Moscow bias, previewed the Soviet team, describing its female athletes as "Amazons" who had barely scraped by with a win at the 1950 track championships.[73] The column went on to discuss other Soviet wins via technicalities, essentially denouncing their chances at sweeping through the Games victoriously. While Daley's column is absurd in its chauvinism, it reflected accurately the aura of curiosity and interest that surrounded the Helsinki Games once the Kremlin decided to send a team.

While in Helsinki, the Soviets were determined to keep their athletes segregated from the other the competitors. The Olympic Organizing Committee inadvertently aided this tactic with their housing arrangements. Only twenty-nine nations had committed to attending the Games when the organizing committee began planning the athletes' village. At this time, it selected the Otaniemi Polytechnic Institute as housing; however, more countries soon decided to compete, increasing the amount of dorm space needed for the athletes, coaches, and officials participating in the Games. The organizing committee planned and built a new village, but the Soviet delegation decided that its athletes and those from the other Iron Curtain countries would remain at Otaniemi apart from everyone else. That they chose to do so despite the cramped conditions there underscored the political aspect of this decision. These dorms "were extremely crowded, with cots having to be put up in halls and lounges. In spite of this, offers by the Finns to supply additional housing elsewhere was refused."[74] The Kremlin was eager to keep its athletes segregated. Isolating communist athletes minimized the possibility of defection and also protected their players from scrutiny from the other competitors, as the Soviets realized that communism was not a popular worldview.[75] In the end, the issue of separate housing proved to be a minor one that did not set any precedent harmful to the Olympic Movement, aside from a few Soviet complaints that the USOA tried to prevent American athletes from interacting with their Iron Curtain peers.[76] These grumbles were puzzling, given the Soviet NOC's insistence on separate accommodations, and went largely unacknowledged. Though the Soviet delegation continued to discourage too much interaction between their athletes and westerners, they would not press for total isolation again until the 1984 Summer Olympics in Los Angeles, an event they eventually decided to boycott.[77]

Turning to the sporting events themselves, many lauded the 1952 Summer Olympics as one of the best of the modern era, due in part to the added intrigue that the Soviet debut rendered. The Games were the largest of any up until that point, with approximately 5,800 athletes representing sixty-nine countries—also a new high.[78] The competition on the field was intense as well, with nineteen world records set in track alone.[79] This contrasted with the Games in

London where morale had been high, but the athletic accomplishments more on par with a world sporting community still recovering from years spent fighting rather than training. The Helsinki Games demonstrated to all just how much progress could be made on the field in four years.

As could be expected, the events that merited the most press coverage, at least from the American media, were the rather frequent superpower matchups. One of the most highly anticipated contests of the two weeks was the basketball gold medal final between the superpowers. In a thrilling contest held the final weekend of the Games, the Americans walked away with a 36–25 victory that was much closer than the final score indicated. Reports of the game described how the Soviets "threw an Iron Curtain around the hole beneath the American basket," keeping the score tight with the Americans ahead 17–15 at halftime.[80] With the win, the United States remained the only country ever to win the Olympic basketball crown.[81]

On the track, the United States ran away with fourteen of a possible twenty-four gold medals.[82] The Soviet harriers, who had expected to make a strong showing, entered every event, running "every name of noted Soviet athletes, which has seeped out of Russia."[83] Czech distance runner Emil Zapotek recorded the communist bloc's strongest showing, as he won both the 5,000 and 10,000 meters before completing the marathon more than six minutes ahead of silver medalist Reinaldo Gorno from Argentina.[84] The United States stole the show on the oval, leading the American press to denounce the Soviet runners as "overrated by non-track journalists as a menace," despite a strong showing by the Soviet women.[85] Moscow captured nearly all of the medals in gymnastics, a sport never embraced within the United States, and held their own in wrestling, weightlifting, and shooting. In all, it was an exciting Games, made more so by the Soviet presence. In reporting on the closing ceremonies, *New York Times* correspondent Allison Danzig reflected,

> There were times before the games got under way when press correspondents wondered whether they were covering a sports event or a political gathering…. But in retrospect these were only minor episodes. They were forgotten once the competition actually got under way and the tremendous crowds thrilled to the unparalleled record breaking performances in track and field and the spectacle of the world's finest athletes contesting for olive wreaths.[86]

While politics were never totally invisible, Danzig's recollections demonstrated the power of sport to transcend seemingly insurmountable boundaries and serve as a unifying force.

The medal count became an object of fascination throughout the two weeks of competition. Tallying medals by nations was nothing new; the media had been doing it since the 1920s. It was the dogged focus on scorekeeping and well-publicized goal of winning this count in Helsinki and all subsequent Olympiads that infuriated the purists, particularly Brundage. In a press conference on the final day of the Games, Brundage warned of the damage such "excess nationalism" could incur on the Games, threatening that, "If this becomes a giant contest between two great nations rich in talents and resources, the spirit of the Olympics will be destroyed."[87] The new IOC president was not alone in his dislike for the official medal table. The major newspapers and television stations covering the Olympics today would almost be remiss without some allusion to this tally, but there was much less focus on the final count and less emphasis on winning before the Soviets began competing.

In addition to fomenting an atmosphere of heated competition, emphasis on the medal count put added pressure on athletes from both sides of the Iron Curtain. In this sense, the 1948 London Games were the last in which American sportsmen and women participated for the sake of sport without larger political implications. In London, the focus for the American team had been on good sportsmanship, an ideal eclipsed by an emphasis on supremacy throughout the next two decades. Though Washington did not begin keeping a close eye on the medal count and urging improvement in nontraditional American sports until 1956 and 1960, the media was vigilant about reporting American successes. While the Soviet Union walked away with the most medals, American newspapers maintained that the United States had "won" the Games because their athletes amassed more points in the system that Associated Press reporter Alan Gould created in 1928. Though this formula predated the Cold War by nearly twenty years, it was not seriously employed until the Soviets' appearance deemed it necessary. Brundage discouraged it openly, to no avail.[88] In this system, a gold medal was worth ten points, a silver medal five, and a bronze four. Fourth, fifth, and six place finishes merited three, two, and one point respectively. Under this system, the United States "won" the Games by accruing more gold medals and more points, finishing with 614, while the Soviets totaled 553.[89] Newspapers across the country printed daily updates on the American and Soviet points totals, noting in particular the results of any direct competition between the superpowers.[90]

Much was made of the inherent contrasts between the American and Soviet athletes as well. The American press lauded the accomplishments of their athletes, praising widely "the greatest comeback in the history of the Olympic games" when the United States pushed past the Soviets in the points total on the final weekend of the spectacle.[91] In the eyes of the press, the American team became "the clearcut winner ... in one of the greatest Olympic games in history."[92] Despite the United States' widely acknowledged sporting prowess before the Games, much of the sports writing during and after the Games depicted the United States' team as David to Moscow's Goliath. These contrasts extended to the physical where "the big-hipped broad-biceped Soviet amazons have demonstrated their superiority to our own svelte lassies" when the Soviet gymnasts outpaced the Americans.[93] The lyrical descriptions of the American victory in the points total stood in clear juxtaposition to discussion of the Soviet team and how conducted itself in Helsinki. While few would dispute the Soviet team's depth and its impressive performance, descriptions of them on and off the field were less than complimentary. *New York Times* correspondent Harrison Salisbury devoted a story on the final day of the Games to how the Soviets had shown poor sportsmanship by dissenting openly with Olympic officials and referees on a number of occasions. "Today's Olympic reports complained against the stalling tactics employed by the American basketball team.... Even sharper criticism was meted out to the boxing judges. The Soviet press was plainly disappointed that their track team, which had been expected by the Russians to win several events, failed to take any championships."[94] While some of the Soviets' gripes may have been valid, the American press was quick to depict them as sore losers, disappointed at their own lack of domination.

There was no question that the Helsinki Games drew added attention and curiosity from the Soviet presence. American athletes admitted that there was a perceived need to perform better for reasons aside from meeting personal goals. According to Bob Mathias, decathlon champion in both London and Helsinki, "There were many more pressures on American athletes because of the Russians than in 1948. They were in a sense the real enemy. You just loved to beat 'em. You just had to beat 'em. It wasn't like beating some friendly country like Australia."[95] This heightened sense of competition lasted through the end of the Cold War, despite Brundage's repeated reminders that the Games were between individuals rather than nations. In his first official speech as IOC president on 14 August 1952, Brundage articulated what would become his doctrine during his twenty-year tenure: The Games "are completely independent and the Olympic Movement owes allegiance to no superior force. It is concerned only with sport and it recognizes no higher power, political or commercial. The Olympic Games must be kept that way, spontaneous and independent. Sport must remain free from dollar signs, and from political intrigue."[96] Brundage's intent, though noble, proved unattainable; there is little question that both politics and financial concerns left indelible marks on the Games under his watch.

The Soviet Union's strong performance at the 1952 Helsinki Olympic Games exacerbated these fears of an imminent communist Cold War victory. Even before the Games, Truman had confided to Brundage that he was concerned about the American team in Helsinki because the Summer Games that year were "especially significant ... certain countries which have not participated for many years will be represented."[97] The Soviets' strong showing on the field and the significance Moscow ascribed to this unofficial measure did nothing to quell these fears going forward. Instead, Truman found himself declaring another National Olympic Week as a means of increasing fundraising efforts for the USOA.[98] These public sector proposals to improve American wellbeing joined the increasing private sector appeals for a more athletic population. One such athletic supporter was Brundage himself. Though he maintained throughout his career that he was the IOC's ambassador to the United States and his allegiance as such was to the IOC over his home country, Brundage expressed concern on several occasions that Americans were falling behind their European—read Soviet—peers. He would continue to voice these anxieties once he became IOC president and Eisenhower moved into the Oval Office.

In all, the Soviet debut at the 1952 Olympics and the associated political drama marked the beginning a new era in terms of the collision of diplomacy and sport. The Olympics became a Cold War pawn even before the Soviets officially joined the IOC because they proved conducive to this purpose. Hitler had set a precedent in using sport for political ends with the Berlin Games, but what happened after 1945 represented a new kind of governmental interference. Though inspired by Hitler at some level—the rationale being that if one man can be allowed to take control of a single Olympiad, a country could do the same across multiple Games—this head-to-head competition between the Americans and the Soviets was novel to the Olympic Movement. Never before 1952 had two countries used the Games as their own venue for direct competition with only one adversary that really mattered in the collective mind. While intense rivalry had been an inherent part of the Olympic Games from their ancient origins, this heated antagonism in all sports with an added political subtext was not found in any of the pre–1949 spectacles. It existed now because the Cold War was a new brand of conflict, one borne out of the post–World War II hostility manufactured on both sides: two exceptionally strong-willed men who eschewed compromise in lieu of nationalism and personal stubbornness. The sense of antagonism prevailed for more than forty years, leaving a legacy of distrust and antagonism between the superpowers for decades to come. The IOC often found itself trapped in the middle of this struggle for supremacy. Throughout the various challenges that these superpower tensions posed, Brundage and the IOC sought to maintain the idea that sportsmen should show the way for the diplomats. This sentiment would soon cause a set of problems all its own in advance of the 1956 Games.

CHAPTER 5

1956

Blood in the Water

"The Olympic Games are contests between individuals and not between nations.... In an imperfect world, if participation in sport is to be stopped every time politicians violate the laws of humanity, there will be few international contests."
—IOC president Avery Brundage, November 1956[1]

Cold War politics were never far from the headlines in the years between the Helsinki and Melbourne Olympiads—and perhaps were never as prominent in the sports pages as during the 1956 Summer Olympics. While there had been some question over how the Soviet Union would behave in 1948 and 1952, these issues paled in comparison to the situation in Melbourne. Timing played a key role in the drama at the Melbourne Games. Because Melbourne is in the southern hemisphere, the Summer Games took place from 22 November through 8 December, rather than during July or August during the northern hemisphere's summer, as was customary. Had the Games transpired during the usual months, much of the drama leading up to these Games might have been avoided because the Hungarian Revolution did not begin until October. Instead the timing of Melbourne led to serious debates over whether the Soviets should be punished for crushing the revolt and boycotts resulting from this uprising, which held obvious Cold War implications.

With the Games occurring less than a month after the Soviet Union sent the Red Army tanks into Budapest, the deadliest event of the Cold War, and days after the first United Nations forces landed at the Suez Canal, in hindsight it is not surprising that the Soviet-Hungarian water polo match devolved into a brawl. Tensions between the two squads were already running high when Soviet player Valentin Prokopov punched Hungarian Ervin Zador in the face during the game's final minutes.[2] Prokopov's attack sparked a riot-like scene in the aquatic center. "Hungarian fans rushed to the parapet that girdled the pool, forcing the referee to intervene and award Hungary a truncated 4–0 victory. The crowd at what came to be called the 'blood in the water' match raised the same cry that had rung through Budapest a few weeks earlier: "*Ruszkik haza!* [Russians go home!]"[3] The Hungarians went on to beat Yugoslavia for the gold medal, though this match was largely deemed anticlimactic. Beating the Soviets represented a clear moral as well as athletic triumph, even overshadowing the gold.

The Soviet presence in Helsinki had been a source of unease for many, including several IOC members, but there had been relatively little hostility exhibited at the Games until Zador's teammates pulled him from the pool, blood streaming down his face, on the penultimate day of competition. However, this one moment came to symbolize the brutality of the Soviet regime and reminded all of the strength with which Moscow had crushed the Hungarians' dreams of a freer society just one month earlier. The animosity between the Moscow government and the rebelling Hungarians had increased the stakes of this semi-final match and the Olympics more generally. The message was clear: politics and sports were inextricable, at least where the superpowers were involved. Never had Cold War tensions been manifested so blatantly in a sports event. After Melbourne, they would not play as critical a role until the United States boycotted the 1980 Moscow Olympics, yet they would remain a tangible part of each Olympics until then, both on field and behind the scenes.

By the mid–1950s, the Cold War had become a fact of daily life. At the same time, the decade-old conflict was so pervasive that there seemed to be few geopolitical issues that were not in some way related to this ongoing struggle. The fear and likelihood of a direct conflict between the super powers lessened without completely dissipating following Stalin's death in 1953. The subsequent change in leadership allowed for a brief loosening of centralized control and limited tolerance of some free thinking behind the Iron Curtain before the Red Army's brutal crushing of the Hungarian Revolution marked the end of all leniency in 1956. Not only were somewhere between 10,000 and 20,000 Hungarians killed, but thousands more were deported or imprisoned in the Soviet Union.[4]

The four years between Helsinki and Melbourme had been quite tumultuous for both superpowers and the IOC even before Suez and the Hungarian Revolution. Washington found itself in the midst of a serious and embarrassing red scare while simultaneously looking to extract itself from an unwinnable and ill-advised war in Korea. Meanwhile, the IOC contended with the ongoing issue of German representation and a new Ukrainian group urging separate Olympic teams for each Soviet republic. When taking all of these pressures into account, it is no wonder that the 1956 Summer Olympics were perhaps the most political between 1948 and 1968.[5] Yet while the politics remained messy behind the scenes, the general benevolence shown in Melbourne and the abilities of the athletes and the press to focus more on the sporting than the diplomatic contests demonstrated to all the unifying power of sport. During these two weeks, on-field antics briefly outshined the sideline bickering. While politics certainly fueled sporting rivalries, diplomatic concerns did not over-shadow them at the Games themselves just yet. Nonetheless, the international climate at the start of the 1956 Melbourne Summer Olympics was one of the most hostile in the modern era.

America Prepares for Melbourne

By November 1956, there was little question that the Soviets' growing athletic prowess had become a real threat to America's athletic hegemony. Rather than continuing to relish their position as the global sporting leader, the United States had to console itself that with the knowledge that its athletes were true amateurs playing by the IOC rules, using this fact to mock the Soviet professionals at all available opportunities. Though their increasingly frequent second-place finishes were a source of lament and created concern that the United States was falling further behind the Soviets (or alternatively, taken as proof that the Soviets were cheating), they served as constant motivation for improvement.

Eisenhower entered office in 1953 with a plan to expand the Cold War outside the diplomatic realm, insinuating along the way that Truman had not gone far enough in the fight at a time when the Soviets were intensifying their propaganda efforts.[6] In an October 1952 campaign speech, he explained what this entailed. "In 'cold war' we do not use an arsenal of arms and armaments. Rather, we use all means short of war to lead men to believe in the values that will preserve peace and freedom. The means we shall employ to spread this truth are often called 'psychological.' ... 'Psychological warfare' is the struggle for the minds and wills of men."[7] It was the Eisenhower administration that really empowered the United States Information Agency to oversee this wider Cold War. The USIA collaborated with the USOA to facilitate the prop-aganda behind the positive image that the United States wished to present to the world, including at the Olympic Games.[8] The Soviets' relatively leniency during the thaw was problematic for the United States because it made Moscow a bit more difficult to vilify. NSC 5501 called for new American cultural infor-mation and exchange programs to better the United States' global image and increase its influence while simultaneously restoring faith at home in the White House.[9]

Oval Office involvement in the Olympic Movement increased steadily between Helsinki and Melbourne, comparable to the Soviet escalation that had followed Stalin's death.[10] After the Soviets' highly successful debut in Helsinki, the United States realized that Iron Curtain athletes were as strong as many had feared. Their near-dominance of the medal tally, official or not, elicited a growing sense in Washington that something had to be done to prevent a similar performance in Melbourne. Additionally, Eisenhower, like Truman before him, did not shy away from openly campaigning for public support for American Olympians. In a letter to USOA president Kenneth Wilson, Eisenhower confirmed that 16 October 1954 would be Olympic Day. He issued a proclamation with language quite similar to Truman's declaration before the Helsinki Games.[11] He wrote, "I urge all citizens in our country to do all in their power to support the XVI Olympic Games, the Winter Games, and the Pan American Games ... [as] these games will afford an opportunity of bringing together young men and women representing more than seventy nations, of many races, creeds, and stations in life and possessing various habits and customs, all bound together by the universal appeal of friendly athletic competition."[12] He also allocated $5 million via the President's Special International Program to ensure than athletes and artists had funding for international tours, building on the exchange programs that had begun at the start of the decade.[13] Taking this a step further, the president wrote to Brundage in June 1955 to inform him that he had signed Senate Joint Resolution 51, to "extend an official invitation to the International Olympic Committee ... to choose an American site" to host an Olympics.[14] This led to the IOC selecting Squaw Valley, California, to host the 1960 Winter Games, giving the United States a chance to draw global interest and visitors from around the world.

Brundage played a key role in raising the Games' profile in his home country. As the new IOC president, Brundage was a fairly public figure, more so than recent president Jacques Rogge or current president Thomas Bach are today. He was a person of considerable influence, both at home and abroad, and his position granted him access to places that might otherwise have been unreachable. One example was the three-week visit to the Soviet Union in 1954 he made on behalf of the IOC.[15] While he had planned a three-day visit to Moscow, Brundage chose to extend his stay and travel throughout the country to take a more comprehensive look at sport under the communist system. He came away with an overwhelmingly favorable impression, though this cast a dark shadow on his perception of the state of American sports. Upon his return, Brundage gave a number of speeches on his trip, using these occasions to warn Americans that they were in grave danger of losing ground to the Soviets.

> No country is stronger than its people, gentlemen, and we had better think a little about our coddled and cushioned youth huddling over television sets.... Things are too soft and too easy. The present generation must ride where we walked when we were boys. They even ride around in carts on the golf course. We amused ourselves, they have to be entertained. In these days of too many automobiles, too many television sets, too many amusements, and in the days to come of push-button existence, we will need the discipline of active sport participation more than ever. Watching someone else play is entertainment, it is not sport.[16]

Brundage's insinuation here that Americans were becoming too soft and physically unfit was a common one during the 1950s, particularly after the Soviet performance in Helsinki.

While most Americans embraced this spirit of competition and saw the push for better Olympic results as healthy, the perceived need to keep pace with the Soviets athletically was not accepted unanimously. There were concerns that such scrutiny of the Games as "cannon fodder for the Cold War" were burying the real meaning of the Olympics and athletics in general.[17] In an article for *Sports Illustrated* from August 1955, Dr. Charles Bucher, a national expert on physical education who penned several works on the subject, tackled the prickly issue of mixing the two. He reasoned that the use of the medal count and associated points system to rank nations—first truly emphasized by the media at the Helsinki Games because of the Soviet presence—put undue pressure on American athletes to perform well, especially the women.[18]

Aside from creating unnecessary stress, Bucher argued that conflating politics and sport would do nothing to improve the global political climate. He claimed, "the games are hampering the achievement of international goodwill. Countries are confusing the winning of sports with national prestige. The honor of the flag is not involved in the winning or losing of a race.... The honor of the flag *is* involved in the success or failure to promote the brotherhood of man and world peace."[19] Bucher argued that wins and losses on the track or the court should not affect national pride or international worth. Instead, the importance of athletics stemmed from the sense of personal accomplishment that individuals should gain merely from participating. Additionally, too much rivalry in sport would hurt the established American amateur athletic infrastructure. If this pressure to win continued unabated, Bucher cautioned that the USOA and Washington could soon turn to a Soviet-style system of state-sponsored athletes. This remark intended to shock an American public quite averse to communism. "Some persons do not seem to understand that our athletes are competing against the boys and girls who are the champions of track and field in Russia—not the leaders in the Kremlin."[20] Here, he warned against transposing Nikita Khrushchev and the Politburo with the young athletes of the Soviet Union, who were mere children and not diplomats, as many assumed athletes to be. Though he made several valid points, Bucher's cautions fell largely on deaf ears, as the American-Soviet rivalry on and off the field persisted through the mid–1960s with growing intensity while Washington pushed through an increasing number of initiatives aimed at improving American fitness and Olympic prowess.

Though seemingly in the minority, several prominent Americans shared this aversion to scrutinizing Olympic results. New York governor Averell Harriman, formerly Roosevelt's ambassador to the Soviet Union, opposed keeping score because it contradicted Olympic ideals. He joined international figures in expressing his thoughts via a *Sports Illustrated* poll just before the opening of the Melbourne Games. "Since most of the competing countries are small and represented by few athletes, the Olympic Committee members should hold true to their ideals and refuse to sanction team scores. It's true that two or three countries dominate the Games, but why give this official recognition?"[21] Harriman, who was more familiar with the Soviet Union than most of his peers given his work there, did not perceive the growing sporting rivalry between the superpowers as something to encourage. L.I. Woolson, Chrysler Motors chief engineer, agreed with Harriman. "In these days, when friendship is so needed between countries, it's probably best to return to the original concept of the Olympics—athlete against athlete—and disregard team scores, which occasionally cause ill feeling. Russia and the U.S. are now bitter Olympic rivals."[22] Even Vice President Richard Nixon was among the ranks of the purists. The "Olympic Games should first promote good will, particularly in these times. The Olympic Committee probably feels that official team scores would make the competitive factor more important than good will. I agree. Anyway, newspapers compile unofficial team scores for those who want them."[23] These responses, among others, showed that not all were as preoccupied with winning the Olympics, so to speak, as was the press.

Despite these high-ranking dissenters, Washington and the American media continued to focus on the differences between the superpowers as a means of proving American superiority throughout the 1950s. There were times when *Sports Illustrated* was the only comparatively objective source on Iron Curtain sports in an otherwise hostile American press. As before the Soviet debut in Helsinki, there were appeals made both in newspapers and in Congress to bar Moscow from the Games, even before the Hungarian Revolution. Republican senator and ardent McCarthy supporter John Marshall Butler charged that the Soviets' obvious non-amateur status should immediately disqualify "Russia and her barbaric goon squads."[24] In an address that likely infuriated Brundage with its overt political tone, Marshall thoroughly excoriated the Soviet Union for its professional athletes and anticipated cheating in Melbourne to increase its medal haul. "The international Communist conspiracy ... has an iron fist ominously pointed at Melbourne, Australia. This athletic gang of cut-throats would do everything and anything, honorable and dishonorable to capture all the honors at that great international amateur athletic event."[25] Butler's harsh rhetoric, considered contemporarily appropriate, gave voice to the prevailing American opinion regarding the Soviets and the lengths to which they would go to win at the Games. The sentiments he expressed captured well the political atmosphere and encapsulated the prevailing western attitude toward Moscow as the Melbourne Games opened.

Germany Renews Its Fight

As in 1952, Germany proved to be a divisive issue leading up to Melbourne, though the circumstances had changed a bit since Helsinki. The Second World War was now further buried in global memory, with time healing some old wounds and erasing resentment toward German athletes. While few would have welcomed a German team in London, many of these harsh feelings faded in the eight years since the Austerity Games. Additionally, much had changed in Germany politically. The postwar occupation had ended; the political division of Germany was complete and an accepted fact. There were two separate countries with functioning governments and membership in rival strategic alliances. Both nations were at least nominally autonomous—though the west more so than the east—which revived the question of Olympic representation for 1956. While only West Germany had competed in Helsinki because the two Germanys could not come to a workable compromise regarding a unified team, East Germany had since created its own NOC and was clamoring for recognition for the Melbourne Games.[26]

Following its exclusion from the 1952 Olympics, the East German NOC worked hard to ensure that its team would be present in Melbourne, even if not on its preferred terms. This fight recommenced almost immediately after Helsinki. In early 1953, the East German NOC protested that its appeal for recognition was not on the agenda for that year's annual IOC meeting in Mexico City. Brundage's response was that East Germany would have to resubmit formal application materials because its leaders had not cooperated during the negotiation sessions with West Germany prior to the 1952 Olympics.[27] The underlying message here was that Brundage still resented that East Germany had refused to play by his rules and collaborate with the west for the sake of sport over politics in 1952. In a letter to Kurt Edel of the East German NOC, Brundage explained his objection as follows: "this lack of courtesy and irresponsibility led some of us to the conclusion that it was a waste of time to deal with them."[28] He ended this letter by advising Edel to apply again in 1954. In response, the East German NOC begged for the resolution of this matter sooner rather than later, appealing to Brundage's lofty idealism regarding the sanctity of the Games. "If the IOC and its President are inspired with the great humane idea of Baron de Coubertin's to grant the youth all over the world the equal right of participation in Olympic life there is no argument to justify a refused discussion and a further delay of our application."[29]

The subject appeared on the agenda for the 1953 Mexico City session. Soviet representative Konstantin Andrianov appealed on behalf of East Germany, arguing that the country had established an NOC to govern sport and ensure that Olympic regulations were followed.[30] However, the failure of the East German NOC to attend a scheduled meeting with members of the IOC executive committee the previous August had hurt its cause. In the committee's view, this spoke to the disorganization of the cause and a lack of seriousness among its members. To make matters worse, the East German NOC had harshly criticized the IOC in the East German press, winning it no favors or sympathy from the wider organization.[31] While East Germany promised to stop the press attacks, the IOC made no formal move toward recognition of its team.

Instead, the committee deferred the matter to the 1954 Athens session, where Brundage reiterated his opposition, offering evidence of noncooperation to justify his disapproval. "In spite of all the goodwill on the part of the IOC no satisfactory understanding has been reached with the Representatives of this part of Germany. On the contrary, the steps we took raised a torrent of abuse from the press of East Germany, this abuse was directed at the IOC and its Representatives."[32] The Soviet delegation countered by strengthening its support for the GDR and confirming that its committee and its sporting federations were in compliance with Olympic regulations. Furthermore, Andrianov expressed regret on Edel's behalf that the chair of East Germany's NOC could not attend the session as he had been unable to secure the proper visa and offered apologies for the ongoing East German press attacks.[33] By this time, most NATO countries had begun to systematically deny entrance visas to East German citizens because NATO did not recognize the GDR diplomatically. These obstacles continued to plague East German athletes and officials through the late 1960s.

In a letter dated 26 May 1954, IOC Chancellor Otto Mayer informed East

Germany's NOC that the committee would address the recognition matter at its next meeting.[34] At this session, Andrianov reported to Brundage and the Committee that the East German NOC "functions perfectly normally and according to the Rules and Regulations of the IOC. The sports are organized in conformity with the traditional precepts of the Olympic spirit."[35] At the same time, Andrianov chastised Brundage and the Executive Board because "we have no right to deprive the youths belonging to that part of the world, from participating in the Olympic Movement, nor can we exclude them from competing in the Olympic Games of 1956."[36] He closed his speech by advising the committee to accept the East German application, playing to the committee's staunch commitment to sport over politics. Karl Ritter von Halt, West Germany's IOC representative, refuted this argument. He appealed to Brundage's apolitical spirit in expressing his wish that there be only one German team representing a unified Germany. Recognition of a separate East German team would render this impossible. Ritter von Halt reminded his peers that "the NOC must be free of all political or religious influence; on the other hand, it must be independent and autonomous.... The NOC of East Germany is a striking example of the opposite."[37] However, Ritter von Halt contradicted himself when he also declared that it would be "impossible" for him to continue talks about bringing the East German NOC into his group because its leaders had continued the negative public relations campaign against him and the IOC that Brundage had denounced the previous year.[38] In doing so, he argued that there should be one German team, comprised solely of West Germans, a solution unacceptable to many. Once again, the IOC adjourned without a vote, leaving East Germany on the sidelines.

The first real sign of progress came in September 1954.[39] On 11 September, Brundage reported that the committee would recognize East Germany provided that it agree to participate in 1956 as part of a unified German delegation. In the letter, he advised that the same representatives who had failed to cooperate with Ritter von Halt and the West German delegation over the course of the previous two years be removed from the NOC so as to avoid further conflict. If the GDR agreed to these terms, Brundage promised to endorse recognition at the 1955 session. While Brundage continued to insist that politics and sport were unrelated, he justified his change of heart in the letter by explaining "since our regulations provide that there shall be only one National Olympic Committee in a country, I do this only to give the youth of the D.D.R., who are not responsible for the political situation, an opportunity to participate in the Olympic Games."[40] Brundage's words were an acknowledgment that politics could not always be ignored.

Following the IOC's promise for provisional recognition, the two Germanys began planning for the 1956 Games. Hans Schobel, new president of the East German NOC, informed the IOC that East Germany would agree to these terms in February 1955. He reported that his committee would grudgingly accept this concession so that its athletes could gain the worldwide exposure and recognition via the Olympics they deserved for their feats.[41] At the IOC's 1955 session, Brundage raised the matter of recognition as promised, though not before first reminding the IOC of the history of noncooperation between the two Germanys.[42] Now he wanted a guarantee that the East German NOC would not rescind its agreement regarding a unified team should it gain acceptance. He made it clear that recognition would be conditional upon collaboration with West Germany. Should this cooperation end, the IOC would rescind its invitation to the 1956 Games.[43] The situation was especially difficult, according to Brundage, because other international sporting bodies had failed to come to a consensus on East German recognition, leaving the IOC without a precedent to follow.

By now, East German recognition had become a race against time with less than a year remaining before the Cortina D'Ampezzo Winter Games' Opening Ceremonies. Brundage presented two options to the committee: it could vote to recognize East Germany immediately based on an understanding that one Olympic committee and team would be formed in collaboration with West Germany or it could wait to accept the GDR until this condition had been met. Waiting would likely prevent East Germany from competing in either of the 1956 Games. A debate ensued during which IOC members voiced their opinions as to how East Germany should be treated. The only member who voiced support for deferring was Ritter von Halt, who again reiterated his unrealistic ideal of a purely West German team. East Germany won provisional recognition by a vote of twenty-seven to seven based on the first option.[44] With this recognition came the privilege of competing in 1956, so long as it cooperated with West Germany.

In an undated letter from early 1956, Ritter von Halt announced that the two Germanys had managed to scrape together a team to represent both countries in at the Winter Games, with fifty-five West German athletes, fifteen from East Germany, and a coaching staff comprised of representatives from both sides.[45] Despite the rapport that Ritter von Halt described, two separate German delegations arrived in Italy ahead of the Games to make arrangements for their respective athletes. Brundage penned a letter to Schobel in March voicing displeasure over this matter and reminding him that only one team and one united delegation would be welcomed in Melbourne. Once again, he argued for the needs of sport over those of politics and urged the two sides to work together. "I am sorry that there are so many technicalities that must be observed, but, as you know, this is a very special situation. I can only repeat what I told both you and Dr. von Halt at Cortina last month. I consider that you have both done a great service to amateur sport and the Olympic Movement and an equally great service to your native land."[46] In response, Schobel made a final fruitless appeal for a separate team in Melbourne before East Germany finally resigned itself to competing as part of a joint team. As outlined at the IOC's 1956 Cortina session, the team competed under one flag while wearing the same uniform. The selection of a hymn in lieu of choosing either country's anthem over the other solved the issue of what anthem to play should a "mixed" team reach the gold medal podium.[47] In the end, the two sides cooperated with few recorded disputes. However, there was little enthusiasm expressed by either German delegation for continuing this joint arrangement at the 1960 Olympics.

The Rise of the Ukrainian Olympic Committee

Hungary was not the only Iron Curtain Country looking to break away from Moscow in 1956. A Ukrainian National Olympic Committee formed between the Helsinki and Melbourne Games and applied for separate Olympic recognition. This Ukrainian Olympic Committee (UOC), which later changed its name to the Ukrainian World Committee for Sport Affairs (UWCSA), established itself in the Washington, D.C., area in the early 1950s. Drawing its members from among the growing ranks of Ukrainian refugees now living in the United States and other western countries, the UOC's main goal was separate Ukrainian representation at the 1956 Olympics and sporting autonomy more generally.[48]

Ukraine had been under Soviet control as one of the Soviet socialist republics (SSRs) since 1922 but had a stronger nationalist contingent than many of the other satellites. Also, it could boast of separate United Nations membership, only one of two SSRs able to claim this privilege. Brundage did not support their efforts for a separate Olympic team. When he learned that the Ukrainian NOC had offices in the United States, Brundage raised the matter in a letter to USOC secretary Asa Bushnell asking him to "undertake a strong action against that so-called OLYMPIC Committee having its seat in Washington."[49] The Ukrainian Olympic Committee wrote to the IOC Executive Board and the Olympic Executive Committee of Australia making a case for why Ukrainian athletes should compete separately from the Soviet team in Melbourne.[50] The UOC listed several reasons as to why the Soviet Union, referring to Russia and its fourteen Soviet Socialist Republics, should not be considered a single nation. The UOC argued that since the Ukraine was an internationally recognized nation given its seat at the United Nations, it deserved separate representation. It claimed that the Soviet Union was an "involuntary" union because "of 15 different Soviet republics, 14 of which have been forced into that union by the Communist Russia."[51] The Soviet Union was comprised of a number of different cultures and ethnicities united only by coercion. As the Hungarian Revolution would soon show, Moscow tended to react harshly when satellites tried to separate themselves.

The UOC's letter appealed not only for separate Ukrainian representation but that "the USSR Olympic team be forbidden to include sportsmen other than those of Russian nationality; and that all its members of non–Russian nationalities compete in the Games as representatives of their respective nations."[52] If this were not possible, the UOC asked the IOC to at least identify Soviet athletes by their individual nationalities rather than referring to them interchangeably as either Russian or Soviet. The group also requested that Ukrainian athletes and those from Belarus—the only other satellite with its own seat at the UN—be allowed free interaction with their western peers, something which the Soviet delegation had sought to prevent in Helsinki.[53] At the end of the letter, the UOC announced that it would soon send a list of Ukrainian athletes who intended to compete under their own flag in Melbourne.

On the surface, some of these requests did not seem that extreme, but IOC precedent made this campaign essentially a lost cause even before the letter was mailed. Taking recent events into account, given that Brundage had been extremely reluctant to allow provisional recognition for the East German team on his terms, there was little hope for his permitting fifteen different nations to replace the Soviet Union. But the UOC's letter and campaign were significant because they exposed signs of unrest behind the Iron Curtain. If the Ukraine were not happy to be competing under the Soviet flag, it was likely that other SSRs were also displeased with the sporting arrangement and the political situation more generally.

Though it was not public knowledge at the time, American spies stationed behind the Iron Curtain sought to capitalize on anti–Moscow sentiment. The forerunners to the Central Intelligence Agency had been building their presence in Ukraine since the end of World War II upon learning of growing unrest and dissatisfaction with Soviet rule.[54] First using solely American spies and later looking to employ local dissenters, American intelligence officials formed several working groups that aimed to exploit this sense of unrest with the hope of fomenting a large-scale resistance movement that could present a serious threat to Moscow.[55] Immediately after the war ended, the Strategic Services

Unit (SSU), a CIA precursor, began collaborating with former Nazi sympa-
thizers in Germany and Ukraine to capitalize on their anti–Stalin sentiment in
a project termed Operation Nightingale. Early failures and a number of agent
defections soured Washington on the utility of the project. The State Department called for a halt to all collaboration with Ukrainians in 1947.[56] The new
CIA, however, decided to recommence building a network of the dissenters in
hope that they would prove useful during a potential war with Moscow. Eventually including some collaboration with British intelligence, the project continued trying to build its presence behind the Iron Curtain into the early 1950s.
While the drawbacks to working with emigres and dissenters were numerous,
the CIA believed that a dubious presence was better than allowing the Soviet
Union to become a complete unknown.[57] The CIA's willingness to associate
with controversial figures underscored how critical winning the Cold War
became.[58]

It is unlikely that Brundage, as a private citizen, would have had any knowledge about the CIA's activities in Ukraine, but the UOC's appeal shed light on
what the IOC had known and chose to ignore: charges that the Soviet Union
was "utilizing this great international event for the purposes of Communist
propaganda and politics, and by controlling its athletes as if they were slaves."[59]
Edstrom had been concerned with the inherent mix of government and sport
when considering the Soviet Union's application for IOC membership in 1951.
At the time, he was content to accept that the Soviets had agreed to stop paying
their athletes for their feats in 1947 and was willing to look the other way in
terms of future infractions so long as they were not too egregious. On the
whole, the IOC proved more willing to bend its rules for the Soviet Union
than for other nations in the name of international harmony and the Olympic
Movement. Once the executive committee had refused the initial terms which
the Soviets tried to impose on their IOC membership, Brundage largely turned
a blind eye toward their mixing politics and sport while remaining overly critical
toward the United States and other western nations for lesser offenses.[60]

After the UOC appealed to several nations for support, the IOC discussed
the Ukrainian request during its 1956 Melbourne session, just one of several
political topics raised there. The members who spoke at the session agreed
that this was a matter of politics rather than sport and as such, the IOC should
not intervene. If Ukraine wished to compete separately from the Soviet Union,
it would first have to become an autonomous country and then apply for membership. Just as the IOC had refused to extend an invitation to Germany in
1948 because it was no longer a recognized country—among other reasons,
it would not admit a Ukrainian team until it was politically separate from
the Soviet Union Since this was impossible to achieve before the start of the

Melbourne Games, the Ukrainians either had to compete as part of the Soviet Union or stay home. Like East Germany, the UOC conceded this fight so that its athletes could take the field in Melbourne, but this attempt for separate representation continued in anticipation of the 1960 Games, much like East Germany's quest.

The Hungarian Revolution

Following Stalin's death, the Soviet Union began a period of transition during which it limited its interference in the affairs of its satellites, granting them a bit more internal control. Under new premier Nikita Khrushchev, the country underwent a period of destalinization, often termed "the thaw." A limited sense of autonomy for the satellites and less social control characterized this brief phase. Khrushchev proved more tolerant toward nationalist sentiments and movements than Stalin had, mostly out of necessity. Stalin's successors simply did not possess the means or the menacing power that the *Vozhd* had to completely squelch these stirrings and maintain an environment of constant fear.[61]

Yet this sense of calm proved fleeting. The harsh Soviet response to the uprisings in Hungary signaled the definitive end of leniency toward nationalistic demonstrations of any kind. Many asked, why should Khrushchev intervene when Hungary, technically not a Soviet satellite, tried to reform? The brutality with which Moscow aborted the Hungarian Revolution proved that the Soviet Union had not changed as much since Stalin's death as many had believed. The crackdown was a forceful reminder to the Unites States—and the rest of the world—that Moscow was quite capable of preserving its dominance, even in the post–Stalin era.[62]

The Hungarian Revolution began with a wave of spontaneous uprisings on 23 October—just one month before the Melbourne opening ceremonies—and continued until the Red Army quelled the last swells of revolt on 10 November. It represented a widespread rejection of Soviet rule and communist oppression centered in Budapest. The revolt immediately grabbed world headlines, particularly in the west, where many were curious as to how the Kremlin would respond to the first real challenge to its authority in the post–Stalin era. Khrushchev reacted quickly and brutally, sending the Red Army to Budapest. Eisenhower issued a statement on 25 October condemning Soviet intervention and frequently repeating the message that "the heart of America goes out to the people of Hungary" throughout the ensuing standoff.[63] The president took advantage of the daily speaking engagements scheduled in conjunction with his reelection campaign to consistently remind the Soviet Union and the world that Washington stood firmly with Hungary and Poland, which was also in the throes of unrest.

With each mention of the turmoil in Hungary, Eisenhower reinforced the inherent contrasts between the American and the Soviet styles of government, portraying the United States as a great liberator of oppressed peoples and drawing on the recent memory of World War II to help create this nostalgic image.

> After World War II, the Soviet Union used military force to impose on the nations of Eastern Europe, governments of Soviet choice—servants of Moscow. It has been consistent United States policy—without regard to political party—to seek to end this situation. We have sought to fulfill the wartime pledge of the United Nations that these countries, overrun by wartime armies, would once again know sovereignty and self-government.[64]

This particular statement, which came during a nationally televised address on 31 October, pressured the Soviet Union to pull its forces out of Hungary while reassuring the Kremlin, at least for publicity's sake, that Washington had no intention of confronting Soviet forces in Budapest or offering more than verbal support to the revolutionaries. Nevertheless, the threat to the Soviets was clear, especially following a subsequent announcement on 8 November that the United States would admit 5,000 Hungarian refugees.[65]

The Hungarian rebellion was an embarrassment to the Kremlin on a number of levels. Though it received less global attention, Poland was also showing signs of dissent concurrently, exposing more cracks in the Soviet system. The free world viewed these uprisings as an indictment of the communist system and proof that it was not a sustainable long-term movement. There had to be some fear in Moscow of a domino effect as well. If Hungary and Poland succeeded in breaking free of the Iron Curtain, what would stop the rest of the satellites from seeking autonomy? Moscow had a tighter hold on the SSRs than it did on the perimeter states, but any nation-wide threat like the Hungarian Revolution had to be taken seriously. Khrushchev reacted quickly by diverting large numbers of military personnel and resources to quell the unrest as efficiently as possible and to minimize the spread of news of the revolt. In a closed-press system like the Soviet Union, any talk of rebellion, even one that appeared to be succeeding even briefly, was a public relations disaster. Hungary's attempt at revolution soon made global headlines and was largely welcomed by the west, as Eisenhower's speeches demonstrated. Countries breaking free from the Iron Curtain represented a clear Cold War victory for Washington.[66]

For the Soviets though, all was not lost. The Red Army managed to crush the rebellion and restore order rather quickly, despite the torrent of bad press that followed. Though it looked every bit the part of harsh dictator in its crushing of the Hungarian Revolution, the outcome for Khrushchev could have been much worse. First, the White House essentially pledged not to intervene unless Hungary was able to rebel successfully on its own and break away from the Iron Curtain. Fortuitously for the Soviets, the revolts failed. Eisenhower felt that he could not provide more than tacit vocal support to the revolutionaries until they had succeeded. In the aftermath of the disaster in Korea, Eisenhower could not risk becoming entangled in what would have been an unpopular and potentially unwinnable war. Broadcasts by Radio Free Europe that seemed to insinuate that American help was on the way sparked some false optimism in Hungary and hurt RFE's reputation.[67] Additionally, it triggered a National Security Council policy revision to prevent future misunderstandings.[68] After 1956, there was no further talk of active liberation of Soviet satellites in the State Department or by Radio Free Europe.[69] The prospect of a standoff over one of the satellites was a risk the United States could not afford. Any clash with the Soviet Union could potentially devolve into nuclear annihilation. These risks forced the United States to merely stand by and watch, offering hopeful sentiments but no material aid without a decisive Hungarian victory, which never came. Eisenhower admitted as much in his 31 October address, where he stated, "we could not, of course, carry out this policy by resort to force. Such force would have been contrary both to the best interests of the Eastern European peoples and to the abiding principles of the United Nations. But we did help to keep alive the hope of these peoples for freedom."[70] In addition to Washington's paralysis on the matter, the Soviets proved able to quash the revolt. Communism survived in Hungary—and the rest of the Iron Curtain—for another thirty years.

The Politics of Melbourne

Politics continued to reign as the opening ceremonies drew near. Like the Hungarian Revolution, timing made the crisis over the Suez Canal a factor in the Melbourne Olympics. Neither Washington nor the British government in London had been pleased to learn in 1955 that Egyptian leader Gamal Abdel Nasser had made an arms-for-cotton deal with Moscow. The United States offered to help fund the Aswam High Dam project in December, but this money was contingent on Egypt making peace with and recognizing Israel. Nasser would not accept these terms and instead chose to nationalize the Suez Canal in July 1956, effectively removing it from British control and using the toll money collected for the Dam.[71] Tensions over the canal ran high through the fall, coming to a head when Britain, France, and Israel staged a joint invasion of the canal zone in late October. Washington refused to help its usual allies, instead remaining on the sidelines so as not to appear imperialist, with Britain and France eventually yielding to United Nations forces in early December.[72] Though both superpowers were involved in the early stages of the Crisis, each had pulled back for different reasons. Moscow became preoccupied with ending the Hungarian Revolution while Washington was wary of being perceived as overly imperialist, like Britain and France. With the height of the crisis occurring as the final preparations were underway for Melbourne, Suez potentially could have impacted the competition. Despite protests from some IOC members at the final meetings before the Games, however, no sanctions resulted and all three aggressor nations were permitted to compete.[73]

Rather than reacting to each situation individually, IOC issued a single statement to express its disapproval of all of the political interferences—the Suez Crisis, the Hungarian revolt, the German and Ukrainian questions—that loomed over Melbourne. "A small number of countries had withdrawn from the Games for reasons other than sport. The International Olympic Committee, an organization concerned solely with sport, expresses its sorrow and regret at these withdrawals, considering that they are not in keeping with the Olympic ideal."[74] This relatively bland statement reminded members that the IOC maintained that politics and sport should not mix without lacking the authority or initiative to enforce this tenet. Its wording was a bit inconsistent with the discussion held during the same session on whether to sanction the Swiss, Spanish, and Dutch Olympic committees for boycotting the Games to protest the IOC not punishing the Soviets for intervening in Hungary, yet this inconsistency followed IOC precedent. The United States only briefly considered a boycott, but quickly decided to compete, not wanting to be seen as supporting Egypt. Also, skipping the Games was all but synonymous with handing Moscow a propaganda victory.[75]

IOC member nations were not immune to bickering amongst themselves, even in the absence of superpower tensions. There was some question in early 1956 as to whether the Soviets would compete in Melbourne because the Australian government had rejected the Soviets' original visa applications. Brundage explained in a March 1956 letter to Andrianov that the Soviets had applied for diplomatic passports, which carry more privileges than regular entry visas.[76] Additionally, Moscow had broken off diplomatic relations with Australia as a result of the 1954 Petrov Affair involving a minor Soviet diplomatic official stationed in Canberra. To the IOC and the Melbourne organizing committee, this breach of protocol was just another Soviet attempt to manipulate the Olympic Movement. Luckily for all parties involved, the matter was cleared up quickly and the Australian government issued general travel visas to the Soviet team in plenty of time for them to travel to Melbourne; however,

Moscow's crackdown in Hungary briefly revived the question of whether the Soviets would be welcomed down under.

Despite protests from several NOCs and outright boycotts from others, Brundage did not punish the Soviets for crushing a revolt in a supposedly autonomous country, demonstrating Soviets' power within the Olympic Movement. The IOC briefly debated whether or not to sanction the Soviets after several countries, including Switzerland and Spain, asked that Moscow be banned from the Melbourne Games in response to the Kremlin's harsh reaction to the events in Hungary. These demands placed the IOC in the difficult position of having to make a last minute decision as to whether the Soviets should be allowed to attend. Brundage held firm to his conviction that "the Games are not concerned with political matters," and ruled that the Soviet team should not be punished for its government's actions, employing the same reasoning that he had embraced during American boycott talks in 1936.[77] Brundage issued a statement to explain the IOC's decision not to sanction the Soviet Union that encapsulated well his sentiments regarding the seemingly endless conflation of politics and sport.

> Every civilized person recoils in horror at the savage slaughter in Hungary, but that is no reason for destroying the nucleus of international co-operation and good will we have in the Olympic Movement. The Olympic Games are contests between individuals and not between nations…. In an imperfect world, if participation in sport is to be stopped every time politicians violate the laws of humanity, there will be few international contests.[78]

This was perhaps the best illustration of his arbitrary nature regarding the intersection of politics and sport. Brundage refused to allow competing in the Games to be a privilege rather than an assumed right for IOC member nations.

Obviously, this was a controversial decision. Many delegations were unhappy with the ruling, but Hungary did not object, possibly because its team was already en route to Melbourme when the IOC announced its decision. The Hungarian delegation chose to compete in Melbourne, but three other nations—Switzerland, Spain, and the Netherlands—stayed home in protest.[79] The Swiss NOC reversed its decision regarding the protest at the last minute but it was too late to arrange transportation for its athletes and officials, forcing them to miss out.[80] Instead of punishing the repressive Soviet Union, Brundage briefly considered sanctioning the Swiss, Spanish, and Dutch NOCs for not conforming with "the spirit of the Olympic Movement."[81] Luckily for all, the Executive Board defeated this proposal. An affirmative vote on the matter would have kept the IOC in international headlines for all the wrong reasons.

The ongoing Hungarian situation remained in the news as the Games opened. *Sports Illustrated* commented: "To say that the Olympics could remain untouched by the world's travail would of course be utter nonsense. One can only wonder what will be in the minds of the Hungarians as they leave Europe."[82] While Moscow's behavior and the subsequent IOC inaction clearly upset the boycotting nations, Hungary did not seem terribly bothered by the lack of Olympic sanctions. Its athletes mostly attended without hesitation and performed quite well in Melbourne. Although there was a brief question of whether the team would be able to travel in late October, this was decided quickly in the affirmative and they set sail for Melbourne with the revolt still underway.[83] Given the turmoil, eleven athletes who had made the team decided to stay home requiring that replacements be found at the last minute.[84] Seventeen athletes sailed to Melbourne with the Soviet team, though they were intentionally kept uninformed regarding the events at home until they arrived in Australia. According to one athlete who spoke to *Sports Illustrated* on the condition of anonymity,

> On the ship there was a chill in the air. One night three of us were talking to a Russian girl. In a few minutes a Russian sailor called out to her sharply. She looked uncomfortable and excused herself suddenly. After that, the Soviet girls stayed away from us. There was no clash between Hungarians and Russians, but this was perhaps due to the fact that at no stage of the voyage were we aware of what really had happened in Hungary. After what I heard on my arrival in Melbourne, I will never mix with those butchers again.[85]

Once the Games began and the Hungarian team learned that the revolution had failed, tensions between the Soviet and the Hungarian delegations rose. Upon realizing that communism was still the modus operandi at home, the Hungarian team showed its displeasure by removing the communist symbol from their flag in the Olympic Village and singing their national anthem loudly.[86] Through all this, the IOC largely ignored the uncomfortable situation.

Despite its lack of support for Hungary and its refusal to sanction Moscow, the IOC took credit for ensuring that Hungarian athletes made it to the Games in its session notes from Melbourne, priding itself on achieving the triumph of sport over politics. "The Chancellor had succeeded in getting the Hungarian team from Budapest to Prague notwithstanding the war in Hungary, the first modern Olympic truce, and subsequently helped it obtain plane accommodations to Melbourne, a great victory for the Olympic Movement."[87] This misplaced adulation only highlighted the IOC's arbitrary approach to the Cold War. The committee was loathe to see politics encroach on the Olympic Movement and yet it consistently congratulated itself on evading the dominant issues rather than taking strong positions when decisive action might have kept these forces in check.

Although Brundage tried his best to ignore the burgeoning force of nationalism, expressions of patriotism, positive and negative, reached new heights in

Melbourne. Hungarian athletes reported a sense of pride in what was happening at home to the extent that it replaced sport as their priority. As one athlete told *Sports Illustrated* during the Games, "We had a duty to come to Melbourne and tell the world about our wonderful revolution. It was that feeling which brought us here. Both in Prague and on the way to Melbourne we could not help but fear that our families might be dead and our homes destroyed."[88] The athletes used this nationalist sentiment to inspire their performance in Melbourne. The Hungarians won fewer medals than they had four years earlier—twenty-six as opposed to forty-two in Helsinki—but won the battle for the world's affection. The Soviets, who again finished atop the medal table, received a considerable amount of bad press during and after the Games, portraying them as Goliath to Hungary's David. As a side note, the Soviets won their lone soccer Olympic gold in 1956 when the Hungarian team, largely considered the favorites, stayed home due to the ongoing political turmoil.[89]

While politics stole the show in months leading up to Melbourne, the feats on the field did not disappoint those hoping for a repeat of Helsinki's thrilling athletic contests. Once again, the Americans all but ran away with the track events, breaking forty-one world records and winning fifteen of twenty-two events on the oval.[90] Bobby Morrow paced the United States with three gold medals in the 100-, 200-, and 400-meter races while the stars and stripes swept the podium in the discus.[91] The Soviet Union again dominated gymnastics and wrestling and took home what remains its only soccer Olympic gold to this day.[92] The basketball gold medal final was a repeat of Helsinki with a comparable outcome. Led by former All-American and future NBA star Bill Russell, the United States routed the Soviets 89–55. After the game, American coach Gerald Turner referred to his team as "the best amateur team—the best ever," a jab that surely did not go unnoticed by Brundage or the Kremlin.[93]

Despite this strong showing on the court and the oval for the Untied States, it was Moscow who "won" both the gold medal count and the unofficial points total.[94] During the Games there was less media fascination than there had been four years prior regarding the ongoing medal race between the superpowers, as Arthur Daley pointed out during the final week of the contests.[95] Daley warned that, unlike in Helsinki, there was little chance for the Americans to come from behind and win the unofficial points total because the Soviets were versatile in so many sports. On the contrary, "the United States once imposing lead has been shrinking steadily and will continue to shrink until it disappears…. If it doesn't happen at Melbourne, it will certainly happen at Rome in 1960."[96] Daley's prediction proved valid in Melbourne, as the Soviets finished more than one hundred points ahead of the United States, 722 to 593.[97]

The United States performed admirably in Melbourne, winning seventy-four total medals, but the fact that the Soviets took home ninety-eight along with the points crown was a cause for concern to many once it became clear that the Soviets had clinched the top spot. A *Washington Post* story from 7 December referred to the American team "as losers for only the second time in a modern Olympiad," lamenting that the United States would finish as runner up for the first time since Berlin.[98] It was clear that the Soviets had "won" because they had diversified the number of sports in which they were medal contenders since Helsinki. There were calls for the USOA to do the same, though these urgings for a more well-rounded performance paled in comparison to those that followed both Helsinki four years earlier and particularly those that would succeed Rome in 1960 when the United States' monopoly over the Olympic basketball title faced its first serious threat.

As the Melbourne Games drew to a close, many Hungarian athletes found themselves facing a difficult decision: whether or not they should return home after the Olympics. The prospect of life in Hungary lost much of its luster with the news that the revolt had failed, leading many to seek asylum in Australia or the United States. However, choosing to relocate came at a high cost: those who left knew they would be leaving their families and lives behind, unlikely to ever be able to return. Despite the high stakes and the punishment they would have faced had they been caught, more than thirty Hungarian Olympians decided to defect. Several of these athletes received American aid and Eisenhower's blessing to resettle in the United States. Though the White House had been unable to offer aid during the actual revolution, it compensated for its relative inaction by welcoming those who wanted a life away from communism after the revolt faltered. Once Moscow had suppressed the uprisings and the stakes were lower, Eisenhower asked the American people to support the American Red Cross, whose efforts to aid refugees included a $5 million fundraising drive aimed at bringing 5,000 Hungarians to the United States.[99] Many of these immigrants spent time at Camp Kilmer in New Jersey, where more than 12,000 political refugees lived for a time in late 1956 and 1957 while they adjusted to life in America and sought more permanent lodgings.[100]

In collaboration with Eisenhower's executive order admitting Hungarian refugees, *Sports Illustrated* agreed to sponsor and aid the defection of Olympic athletes via its powerful publisher and staunch anti-communist Henry R. Luce.[101] Luce was a vocal supporter and personal friend of Eisenhower, whom some have credited with convincing the president to run for office in 1952.[102] Now he used this personal connection to his advantage. With Luce's approval, *SI* staffers covering the Melbourne Games approached Hungarian team members looking to defect and arranged for their transport to America. While there were likely some humanitarian or altruistic sentiments behind this project,

Luce's personal anticommunist crusade and the publicity potential helped drive this mission. In 1956, *Sports Illustrated* was a new publication operating at a deficit. A public relations disaster via the Hungarian efforts might have doomed the magazine or his empire more broadly, but Luce took the risk anyway. The editorial staff at *Sports Illustrated* capitalized on their boss's virulent loathing of all things Soviet aided by the influence of C.D. Jackson, vice president of *Time*, who had worked for the Office of Strategic Services—a forerunner of the CIA—during World War II. For Luce and Jackson, sponsorship of this mission brought great propaganda opportunities.

SI worked out a plan in the intervening week between the end of the Hungarian Revolution and the Melbourne opening ceremonies. Its editors devised a code through which writers stationed in Melbourne could cable the home office detailing how many athletes were planning to defect. The mission proved feasible in part because several of its writers had international experience stemming from World War II missions. In addition to Jackson, Luce had recruited Andre Laguerre, Charles de Gaulle's press officer during the war and now striving to help improve the writing and circulation at the nascent *SI*. Laguerre met with the Hungarian team in Melbourne three times to outline the proposal and make arrangements for those who decided to leave.[103]

Laguerre wrote about his exploits in *Sports Illustrated* once the athletes were safely in the U.S. shortly after the closing ceremonies. The transports had begun even before the Games were over. Hungarian athletes from several sports—including members of the gold medal winning water polo team—seriously considered the matter before fifty-five of them decided to emigrate to the U.S. and elsewhere.[104] This choice was a difficult one to make. Though most team members had not been active revolutionaries, there was a high price for leaving. Those who defected left friends and family behind, along with the fear of government retaliation on their loved ones at home. Also, the prospect of beginning a new life was daunting. There would be a language barrier virtually anywhere they went. Though repressive, the state took good care of its athletes. They had better housing than the average worker and could train without worrying about how to make ends meet, which was not always the case outside the Iron Curtain, as American athletes knew all too well. But seeing and hearing footage of the Soviet reaction to the attempted revolution and knowing that they would not be returning to the free state that seemed likely before they left for Melbourne inspired many to begin new lives elsewhere.

Some, like Hungarian NOC secretary Laszlo Nadori, had been active conspirators in the revolution and therefore felt unsafe returning to Hungary. Laguerre's assurance that *Sports Illustrated* would cover the specific details of their departure proved enticing. He promised that Time, Inc., "would be happy and proud to facilitate their transportation and entry, to sponsor a tour of American cities, and to do all in its power to aid in arranging the permanent settlement of individual athletes…. [I]t seemed our moral responsibility to prevent any decision against going to the U.S. from being taken solely because of some relatively minor material difficulty which we could help overcome."[105] This concept of moral responsibility was one that the United States held dear during the Cold War, as it perceived itself as the global example of freedom and democracy. In the end, thirty-five of the fifty-five members of the Hungarian delegation who defected chose to accept Luce's aid and move to the United States.

While Soviet athletes were often escorted directly from the competition sites to the dock to sail home as a means of preventing defection, Moscow did not extend this type of close surveillance to the Hungarians in Melbourne. The chief of the Hungarian delegation, Gyula Hegyi, knew of the planned defections and did nothing to impede these departures.[106] Four Romanians asked and gained permission to join the list of emigrants, their transport arranged for sheer propaganda purposes. With Eisenhower authorizing the admission of 5,000 Hungarians and Luce sponsoring the Hungarian Athletes' Freedom Tour, as it was termed, the United States reclaimed its reputation as the beacon of freedom for those trapped under repressive governments. The Hungarian situation also gave Washington the opportunity to showcase all that America had to offer on the highly publicized cross-country journey. After landing in San Francisco and visiting New York City, "over 10 weeks the Hungarians met Louis Armstrong backstage in Miami Beach and President Eisenhower in the White House; tried waterskiing in Orlando and inspected an auto plant in Detroit; saw the Hoover Dam, the Grand Canyon and the Las Vegas strip."[107] They met with Vice President Nixon and visited the United Nations.[108] This tour showed them more of the country than most native-born American citizens had personally experienced, all for its propaganda potential.

The tourist experience was a novelty for the defectors. Behind the Iron Curtain, travel was limited even among other communist nations. Athletes who competed internationally did not often have the time or the opportunity for tourism while abroad. Now they realized just how different life was in the United States. For some, the cost of this freedom was too high and they chose to return home once they learned that there would be no retribution for doing so. But twenty of the original thirty-five chose to remain in the United States with another staying until obtaining the promise of a medical pension at home in the late 1990s.[109] This represented a major propaganda coup for both Washington and Time, Inc. The readership of Luce's publications rose, as many began to associate him with the American way and as a champion of freedom.

The United States benefitted simultaneously from a rehabilitated reputation and perhaps stoked the desires of some behind the Iron Curtain to emigrate once they caught of glimpse to the quality of life that could be found outside the Soviet Union. In addition to showcasing the country, the tour raised more than $10,000 for the Red Cross refugee fund to aid other defectors.[110] While there were obstacles along the way, the majority of those who chose to stay thrived in their new lives, some of them later sending for their families to join them. After gaining citizenship, they could to travel back to Hungary with American passports, which represented the best of both worlds for many of them. On the whole, these men and women provided a shining example of hope for those back home looking for a better life, generating a fresh source of American propaganda.

In the end, the political overtones that surrounded the Melbourne Games did not ruin the athletic events but mainly added to the drama and spectacle. While the politics in the weeks leading up to the Games were prevalent, the athletes outshone the diplomats for a brief two-week hiatus while the Olympic torch burned. Even though the Hungarian Revolution was still ongoing when its team arrived in Melbourne, there were few exhibits of animosity between the Hungary and the Soviet delegations. The blood in the water match, though memorable and unsportsmanlike, could have been part of a wider political demonstration. The fact that it remained a relatively isolated incident proved the power of sport to overcome vicious politics. Instead of bitterness, the Hungarian team could instead recall its dramatic victory over the Soviet Union en route to the water polo gold medal.

After Melbourne, politics continued to reign behind the scenes, as the Cold War began to heat up once again. Brundage tried his best to resist these forces from infringing on the Olympic movement to no avail. Rather than placing him "on a cloud above politics," as *Sports Illustrated* described him in 1959, his insistence on retaining the status quo in a rapidly changing global society made him appear outdated and stubborn.[111] Nonetheless, the Games themselves continued to grow in size and global intrigue in the years leading up to the 1960 contests in Squaw Valley, California, and Rome.

CHAPTER 6

1960

The Games in Transition

"Can you imagine the fuss and furor that would result if the United States government sent a group of college science students down to Cape Canaveral to take over the important jobs of beating the Russians in the race for space? This would be sending out a bunch of boys to do a man's mission, but that is what happened in the recent would basketball tournament in Chile in which the United States quintet was soundly trounced by both Russia and Brazil."
—New Hampshire senator Henry Styles Bridges[1]

After the Melbourne Games, ignoring the ongoing political overtones surrounding the Olympics became impossible, especially those pertaining to the Cold War. Nonetheless, the IOC tried to remain above the fray, often a futile pursuit. Many of the same diplomatic quandaries that had plagued the Helsinki and Melbourne Olympiads carried over into the 1960 Squaw Valley and Rome Games. These melded with new problems to create a larger political storm. While there was no single inflammatory incident that defined the 1960 Games like the Soviets' highly anticipated debut in Helsinki or the Soviet-Hungarian water polo match in 1956, political tensions were hard to ignore throughout the Sqauw Valley and Rome contests.

Taken together, the 1960 Games were transitional in the sense that they were the final Olympiads that retained any of the simplicity lauded at the London contests. There was little concern over commercial sponsorship of athletes and no need to cater to network television schedules when planning events. At the same time, the Cold War tensions were obvious, as both superpowers understood that the Games were a critical facet of the flourishing cultural Cold War. Visa problems triggered by the west's refusal to recognize the GDR nearly prevented the East German winter Olympians from competing in Squaw Valley, while the ongoing struggle over Berlin permeated the summer contests.

Throughout the Rome Games, Khrushchev fought to push the western presence out of the city through travel restrictions. There was a sense of general unease present throughout the Rome events that left little doubt of the Cold War's impact on sport. By the closing ceremonies, the USOA had learned that it had a lot of work to do before the 1964 Olympics if it wanted to prevent the Soviets from running away with the medal count—and the Cold War bragging rights—in Tokyo. Meanwhile the American press lamented that the stars and stripes' glory days as global sporting leader seemed to have passed.

The Changing Cold War

As the Cold War evolved, so did the way in which the American government perceived the Olympics. To this end, the Rome Olympics were a turning point because the Games increased their global relevance and saw a correlated rise in Washington's interest in them. As the cultural Cold War heated up, so did the scrutiny of the Games because they were a highly visible means of demonstrating strength. The gradual escalation of tensions in the political realm influenced all direct interactions between the superpowers, including those on the field. The Soviets' strong performance in Melbourne had raised some eyebrows and red flags, as many feared that Moscow was about to unseat the United States as the global sporting leader. An even better showing in Rome—particularly in sports that the United States traditionally dominated—intensified this fear and led to increased calls for American improvement.[2]

The issue of German representation remained problematic. For many, the forced collaboration for a single Olympic team seemed even more contrived by 1960 than it had in 1956, as relations between the two countries had soured noticeably between Melbourne and Rome. The fight over a continued western presence in Berlin doomed any hopes of a lasting peace and reminded both sides that the Cold War was far from over.

While East and West Germany had managed to collaborate fairly successfully for the 1956 Olympics and the hope remained for eventual political reunification, relations between the two sides were fairly stilted in 1960. Bonn was autonomous in its domestic affairs by the late 1950s, but the Soviets consistently interfered in East German governmental matters. The fate of Berlin remained a point of contention between the superpowers. The west had held firmly to West Berlin since the occupation began in 1945, much to Moscow's chagrin. Stalin had tried to force the west out through the 1948 blockade, leading to eleven months of occupation and the Berlin airlift. Now ten years later and tired of the threatening western presence that lured thousands of easterners to defect annually, Khrushchev gave the west a six-month time limit in late 1958 to remove all troops from West Berlin.[3] Naturally, Eisenhower refused, instead assuring the American public that "we stand firm on the rights and the responsibilities that we have undertaken, and that we cannot possibly fail to carry out those responsibilities, because if we did, we would be retreating and abandoning people that have a right to expect the kind of cooperation that we have promised them."[4] This uneasy stalemate lingered, casting a shadow on German Olympic plans and intensifying the Soviet-American rivalry in Rome.

Sandwiched between the Squaw Valley and Rome Games, the U-2 spy incident represented another setback to Soviet-American diplomacy. Relations between Washington and Moscow were already nearing a new low when news broke on 3 May 1960 that the Soviets had shot down CIA pilot Francis Gary Powers and the U-2 plane he had been flying in the Sverdlovsk Oblast region, on the Europe-Asia border two days earlier.[5] A State Department press release issued on 5 May included a disclaimer defending this alleged surveillance activity.

The May 1960 U-2 incident where CIA pilot Gary Powers was shot down while flying over Soviet airspace inflated Cold War tensions just weeks before President Dwight Eisenhower and Soviet premier Nikita Khrushchev were scheduled to meet in France, leading to a moment of lost opportunity (Dwight D. Eisenhower Presidential Library and Museum. Photo No. 75–5–28).

It is certainly no secret that, given the state of the world today, intelligence collection activities are practiced by all countries, and postwar history certainly reveals that the Soviet Union has not been lagging behind in this field. The necessity for such activities as measures for legitimate national defense is enhanced by the excessive secrecy practiced by the Soviet Union in contrast to the free world.[6]

Instead of apologizing for the incident, Washington blamed the Soviet Union's secrecy for its spying, implying that as long as Moscow spied, the United States would too. When Eisenhower met with the press on 11 May, he defended Powers by invoking recent memory. "No one wants another Pearl Harbor. This means that we must have knowledge of military forces and preparations around the world, especially those capable of massive surprise attacks."[7] By associating the Soviet Union with Japan and World War II, Eisenhower cast Moscow as a dangerous aggressor with America as its likely victim. Eisenhower's word choice in this press conference built impressively on the image of Moscow as villain.

Soviet premier Nikita Khrushchev and Vice President Richard Nixon during the infamous kitchen debate at the 1959 American Exhibition in Moscow. Khrushchev's parting words, "We are strong and we can beat you," encapsulate well how each side approached the Cold War (Richard Nixon Library and Birthplace. Photo No. A10–024.43.16.1).

Developments outside the political realm left little hope for ameliorating relations either. Tensions were running high in the cultural Cold War by the end of the 1950s. Each viewed the other as its chief rival in all facets of daily life from the Olympics to the classroom to scientific developments. The space race began in 1957 with the Soviet Union's successful launch of the Sputnik satellite. The United States immediately feared that it was falling behind and looked to compensate via the creation of National Aeronautics and Space Administration (NASA) in 1958. Aside from its critical scientific implications, Sputnik launched a new wide-ranging cultural competition between the super-powers.[8]

There were few direct confrontations between Moscow and Washington during these years aside from conversations over Berlin and U-2, but the Cold War changed fundamentally in the years from Melbourne to Rome. The stand-off continued to expand beyond the political realm. Technology took on an added importance in both societies, as each looked to become the indisputable world leader in all facets of life. The famous 1959 kitchen debate between Khrushchev and Nixon offered a glimpse at how the Cold War had changed since the Truman years. This unplanned and unscripted exchange at the American National Exhibition in Moscow in July turned sharply critical on both sides, with Khrushchev finally taunting Nixon, "We are strong and we can beat you."[9] Though clearly blurted out without premeditation, this comment captured quite well the mindset on both sides of the Iron Curtain. No matter how small the stakes, there now existed a need to always come out on top, if only to convey the message that we can beat you.

The Cultural Cold War

This sense of heightened competition soon manifested itself on the playing field as well. Following strong Soviet performances in 1952 and 1956, the United States government began to realize the propaganda potential of the Olympics, given their growing international visibility and interest. The Eisenhower and Kennedy administrations paid more attention to athletics on both the professional and recreational levels. During Eisenhower's second term, physical education classes became standard curriculum across the country. The President's Challenge became a means of motivating children to meet fitness goals, comparable to the Soviet Masters system, though on a more basic scale. Just as Sputnik had cast doubt on American technological supremacy, the Soviet Union's rising star in international athletics raised the question of whether the United States could remain number one on the playing field.

Consequently, Washington began to offer unsolicited help to the USOA to try to regain this perceived ground loss through added funding and measures to instill the importance of good fitness on all Americans and improve the programs already in place to prepare future Olympians to beat the Soviets.

This fear of Soviet supremacy was one of the few commonalities between liberals and conservatives, as no one wanted to see the United States finish second. The Soviet crackdown in Hungary in 1956 elicited a number of calls for Congressional bills asking the IOC to expel the Soviets, to no avail.[10] When this failed, the legislative branch quickly passed sport and Olympics-related bills and encouraged a level of governmental interference with athletics specific to the Cold War.[11] Congress rushed to allocate funding for Olympic development programs as well as athletic tours to Europe and third-world countries to promote and popularize American sport. However, some feared that this was not going far enough. In a speech to Congress in 1959, New Hampshire senator Henry Styles Bridges, a close associate of Joseph McCarthy, warned that the United States was falling dangerously behind its chief rival, particularly after the recent Sputnik launch.

> The United States is in direct competition with Russia in all aspects and on all fronts. So ... we should not overlook any front on the prestige contest. Can you imagine the fuss and furor that would result if the United States government sent a group of college science students down to Cape Canaveral to take over the important jobs of beating the Russians in the race for space? This would be sending out a bunch of boys to do a man's mission, but that is what happened in the recent would basketball tournament in Chile in which the United States quintet was soundly trounced by both Russia and Brazil. It prompted a Santiago newspaper to comment "When it comes to shooting at the moon or at a basket, the United States can't keep up with the Russians."[12]

Bridges argued that the Olympics were a high stakes Cold War battleground where one defeat could easily trigger a domino effect in the wider war. He made a case for replacing amateur athletes with professionals in international competition to prevent a failure, given the heightened stakes that a second place result brought.

The idea of the cultural Cold War was growing increasingly prominent by the late 1950s. As tensions between Washington and Moscow escalated over Berlin, both sides looked for meaningful ways of competing outside the political realm. Walter McDougall argued in *The Heavens and the Earth* that by the mid–1950s both sides sought to exhibit their strength outside the traditional diplomatic channels in order to replace a daunting confrontation that could potentially annihilate one or both populations. By this time, the Kremlin had achieved most of its original political and diplomatic goals stemming from World War II. While the status of Berlin remained frustrating, the relative stability of its satellites and its nuclear parity with Washington essentially neutralized the threat of a strike. Now the Kremlin could look for other means of demonstrating its all-around superiority. Beating the United States into space was a prime objective because it would make international headlines. Succeeding in the Olympics would render the same level of global visibility that Moscow craved. Conversely, Washington looked for ways of beating the Soviets outside the political realm to atone for its failure in Korea and reverse its perceived loss of athletic dominance. Flaunting the freedom of its citizens and the material advantages that Americans could boast of to their Soviet peers were small victories. Winning at the Olympics was a much higher profile and meaningful way of beating Moscow, so to speak.[13]

In a 1960 news conference on Soviet-American relations, Eisenhower explicitly used the Olympics as an example of the inherent difference between the two countries. While the reporters he addressed here feared that the United States was quickly falling behind the Soviets and was at risk of becoming a second-rate power, the president was quick to defend his country.

> I think here and there you can find that in a country as big as Russia you are going to be certainly second-best; didn't they win the Olympic games last time? ... Now, what we should think about and talk about more in the world are the values which we do treasure. They don't have them. And since we believe that in the long run men do learn to have this same belief about the same values, I believe that there is just as much of the seeds of self-destruction in the Communist system as they claim is in ours—they claim the inherent conflicts within our system are going to destroy it. I think our people ought to have greater faith in their own system.[14]

Eisenhower argued that while the Soviets had won the most medals in 1956, the struggle between capitalism and communism went a bit deeper than simply tallying first-place finishes. This competition would not be won or lost in a single instance, or a single Olympiad, but instead it was a protracted struggle. He pointed out that "there is just as much of the seeds of self-destruction in the Communist system," implying that over time the Soviet Union would collapse while American democracy would continue to thrive. The president preached patience, as "we have a free enterprise; we place above all other values our own individual freedoms and rights; and we believe, moreover, that the operation of such a system in the long run produces more, not only more happiness, more satisfaction, and pride in our people, but also more goods, more wealth."[15] While the United States could not reassert its singular dominance overnight, its methods of training elite athletes would win out in the end because they led to freer individuals who would be less likely to reject the system.

Eisenhower made one final dig at the Soviets, accusing them of not complying with Olympic amateur standards. He reminded the press corps, "Let's remember this: if they find an athlete, they take him, and it's a national responsibility to train him and build him up until he's the best there is in the world, if they can make him such."[16] He exhibited a sense of confidence regarding the future victory of American democracy over Soviet communism that would be realized through faith in the American system and continual improvement at a sustainable pace. He contrasted this method with the Soviets' seemingly untenable push to be the best immediately by embracing all means possible.

While Eisenhower's enthusiasm for Olympic improvement had many supporters, not all embraced the growing politicization of the Games. However, many blamed the Soviets for this development rather than acknowledging America's shared responsibility. Laments of how the Games had changed were a common feature of American sports pages by the late 1950s. In a *New York Times* June 1959 editorial, columnist Arthur Daley discussed how the Olympic Movement, which had survived the Nazi Games relatively unscathed, faced a much tougher challenge in remaining apolitical during the Cold War. "The Red Brothers are tougher than Hitler and more single-minded."[17] This deliberately incendiary comparison betrayed just how negative the American attitude toward Moscow had become. Like the United States, the Soviet Union enjoyed a considerable amount of influence within the IOC, which had heightened the politicization of the Games. Daley lamented, "Ever since the Soviet Union got on the IOC and was able to throw its weight around, things have not been the same."[18] Daley rebuked Moscow for dragging politics in the basketball world championships by refusing to play a team from Nationalist China (Taiwan), but problems with Iron Curtain athletes and delegates in obtaining visas for the Squaw Valley Olympics offered proof that the United States was also guilty of this charge. His complaint that "the Soviet is so entrenched in every sports federation that it will use the IOC as a lever" to grant its political wishes was also true of the United States.[19]

The German Question

Relations between the two Germanys showed few signs of progress during these years, as discussion of reunification all but disappeared. Relations between Khrushchev and the East Berlin government were growing increasingly tense as well. While Andrianov and the Soviet NOC urged cooperation with Brundage's unified German team, the East German NOC began to push harder for separate representation.[20] Meanwhile, there was growing pressure on West German Chancellor Konrad Adenauer to diplomatically recognize the GDR. In 1959, he admitted that he could not continue to postpone this acknowledgment indefinitely without justification.[21] Britain and France were also beginning to waver on the western policy of non-recognition, leaving the United States as its biggest, and at times, only supporter.[22] Concurrently, Khrushchev refused to deal with the Bonn government on an equal basis, turning instead to the western powers, whenever there were matters to discuss. East Germany had expected to be treated as a sovereign nation following the establishment of the Warsaw Pact, but this had yet to occur.[23]

Given the lack of progress in bettering relations between the two sides, it is not surprising that the ongoing tensions between the superpowers affected plans for the 1960 Olympics as much as they had Melbourne. This time, it was the United States playing Cold War politics, which the IOC unintentionally facilitated by selecting Squaw Valley as host city. Just as the Soviet Union had faced visa problems prior to Melbourne, there was question over whether the United States would welcome athletes from Bulgaria and China—two countries with which Washington did not have diplomatic relations. As such, Brundage threatened in 1957 to move the Games to a country that would admit athletes from communist countries.[24] He issued a reminder that both Bulgaria and China were IOC members "in good standing."[25] Secretary of State John Foster Dulles countered by arguing that the United States had the right to deny entry to anyone if they posed a threat to "health and security."[26] However, he also promised to welcome Olympic athletes and not to subject them to routine fingerprinting that was a standard entry procedure in the 1950s.[27] The IOC president had firsthand experience in the strain that this visa situation caused. When Bulgaria hosted the 1957 IOC annual session, Brundage himself had difficulty securing his travel documents as the U.S. State Department did not customarily issue travel visas for American citizens to countries that they did not recognize diplomatically.[28] In the end, Brundage did attend, though he did threaten to retire from the IOC if these travel difficulties continued.

Diplomacy issues frustrated athletes and hindered competition on both sides of the Iron Curtain. In 1957, the United States decided against sending a hockey team to the world amateur championships held in Moscow. This choice created speculation that the State Department had influenced the matter, especially since the team was already in Europe when the decision came.[29] The State Department denied meddling, but noted that players from American-friendly European teams had chosen not to attend the tournament for vague political reasons so that USA Hockey decided that it should follow suit and decline the invitation lest they appear too close to the Soviets. USA Hockey also cited the failed Hungarian Revolution as an excuse for not attending, following a State Department warning that continuing instability could pose a threat to American athletes.[30] The State Department had dissuaded American athletic teams from attending the Moscow World Youth Festival in 1957 because their presence would have been great fodder for the Soviet press. While it did not go as far as refusing to grant passports, Washington strongly discouraged participation because the sporting event was "an instrument of Communist propaganda which serves the purposes of the Soviet Union and its orbit."[31] Now even children were Cold War pawns.

While the State Department allowed some Americans to travel to communist countries for reasons deemed to be of national importance, it remained comparatively more difficult for Iron Curtain athletes to enter the United States. In addition to fingerprinting, visitors had to pass a number of other requirements, including a brief background check and health screening, before entering.[32] These conditions proved trying for athletes long before the Squaw Valley Games. The United States and Soviet Union had scheduled home-and-home track meets in 1957, but the Soviets' refusal to comply with Washington's fingerprinting policy forced their cancellation. The American delegation countered by abandoning its travel plans to Russia.[33]

In light of this, Andrianov wrote to Olympic chancellor Otto Mayer in March 1957, reminding him of the troubles that the Bulgarian delegation faced as it planned for Squaw Valley. He also referenced the plight of the Hungarian figure skating team that the State Department refused to admit for the world championships.[34] He reminded Mayer that "the Olympics belong to the athletes of all countries of the world and if there is a slightest doubt that for reasons having nothing in common with the interests of sport, representatives of any country will not be able to get visas to go to the Olympic Games, the International Olympic Committee is obliged to take the most decisive measures to ensure the conduct of the Games in the spirit of the Olympic rules."[35] Andrianov also asked the IOC to ensure that there would not be any "humiliating procedure in granting visas," referring to the State Department's fingerprinting and background check process.[36] Despite this appeal, visa problems continued for Iron Curtain countries right up through the Squaw Valley Games and surfaced again in advance of the 1968 Winter Games in Grenoble, France.

The few occasions when athletes could pass through the Iron Curtain without political interference allowed fans on both sides to enjoy some rare instances of entertaining head-to-head competition between Olympiads. This reluctance to send American athletes to the Soviet Union did not derail the dual track meet held at Lenin Stadium in Moscow July 26–27, 1958.[37] Competition to make the American squads for this trip was fierce, as many Melbourne Olympians leapt at the chance to see a city that did not often host world events and to compete at a high stakes event in a non–Olympic year. That the Soviet Union was so eager to host such a meet even after plans had fallen apart the previous year showed how much their attitude regarding western interaction and international competition had changed since Helsinki. The American team received a warm reception and both sides deemed the meet such a success that it became a highly anticipated annual event over the next decade. Remarkably, it was unaffected by the several tense standoffs between Moscow and Washington that characterized the late-1950s and the Kennedy years.

In addition to the visa problems, representation issues continued to loom large over the IOC. The Ukrainian Olympic Committee's appeals for its own team in Melbourne lingered into the next Olympiad without moving closer to resolution. The UOC renewed its appeal for recognition in early 1957. Upon learning that this campaign had resumed, Andrianov wrote to Mayer in April 1957 defending the Soviet Union and refuting several of the UOC's incendiary claims. "U.S.S.R. is a voluntary union of 15 Republics which enjoy equal rights.... As for the request, received by you, of which Mr. Brundage also mentioned in Melbourne, it comes from a group of persons who has no right at all to speak in the name of Ukraine and Ukrainian athletes."[38] Andrianov closed out his letter by telling Mayer that the matter was essentially a nonissue since Ukraine already participated in the Olympics as part of the Soviet team, rendering separate representation unnecessary. Andrianov had no cause for concern. Just as Brundage had remained firm that East Germany would compete either as part of a combined German squad—largely under Bonn's control—or not at all, he was not about to permit separate Ukrainian representation. Nonetheless, this campaign was significant in that it demonstrated the ongoing unrest and nationalist stirrings behind the Iron Curtain.

The question of German representation at the Olympics continued without resolution in 1960. Before Melbourne, the IOC had labeled East Germany's presence provisional with the set terms applicable only for 1956. The Olympic flame was likely still smoldering in Melbourne when the East German NOC renewed its fight for separate representation. Relations broke down between the two Germanys in 1957, with the East Germans blaming Bonn for this stalemate.[39] The Soviet NOC did its best to intercede on the part of the East Germans. Andrianov appealed to both Mayer and Brundage in March 1958 recommending that East German Olympic official Hans Schobel be selected as East Germany's first IOC representative because he had done so much to further the Olympic cause there.[40] Schobel had proven himself to be a strong advocate for a separate East German team throughout the previous decade and would continue this mission into the 1960s.

As the fight for two German teams continued, Brundage scolded the East

German NOC for mixing sport with politics. While westerners argued, and validly so, that this was nothing new for an Iron Curtain country, Brundage seemed to take particular exception to East Germany's amateurism violations. In an April 1958 letter to Ritter von Halt and Schobel, Brundage called on both men to stop some "objectionable statements," by which he meant political statements.[41] According to Brundage's letter, the president of the Deutscher Turn and Sport Bund, a group affiliated with but not officially part of the German Olympic movement, had campaigned openly for an atom-free zone in Germany.[42] While a noble sentiment, the IOC president was strongly opposed to any political statement by athletes or officials. Using this issue as a threat, he warned that continued offenses would preempt all discussion of separate German teams. Brundage's intended punishment was more of a burden to the east, as Ritter von Halt had argued vehemently against a separate GDR team in 1956 and endorsed the IOC's implicit message that the west should remain in control.

The squabbling between the two German NOCs only intensified as the Squaw Valley Games drew near. Ritter von Halt wrote to Brundage in June 1959 to complain about the bad press that the German NOC had received recently. He charged that the East Germans had violated Olympic rules as "the leading men are Politicians and have not much knowledge concerning Olympic questions. Furthermore we refuse to have communists correspond for us."[43] Ritter von Halt's politically charged remark showed that Bonn shared this distaste for the united squad. While Brundage had gone out of his way at the Melbourne IOC session to praise the collaboration between the two German NOCs for achieving what the politicians could not, this letter exposed the artificiality of the combined team.

Although recognition of two teams seemed to be a longshot at best, the East German NOC continued to fight for at least the end of its provisional status. The IOC discussed the matter once again without resolution during its 1958 annual session.[44] Ritter von Halt made it clear that he did not support East German recognition. He informed Brundage "the eventual cancellation of the word 'temporary' (provisional) is an enormous danger for the entire German team. Should it be definitely accepted then they demand the drawing-up of an own team and the election of an East-German communist into the IOC. For this we must never give our consent."[45] Without explicitly stating it, Ritter von Halt expressed his belief that East Germany should be excluded from the Olympic Movement altogether. If this was not feasible, then the GDR should at the very least remain under West German control.

His statement questioned the plausibility of this ongoing collaboration between the two sides while also reflecting the widening schism between the two Germanys. The eventual reunification had been all but taken for granted in 1945, yet it had become much less certain by the late 1950s. The economic, political, and cultural divisions between the two countries were growing. As West Germany began to flourish financially and grow into one of Europe's leading industrial powers, the prospect of reuniting with an eastern zone that was almost entirely devoid of industry and under communist control was not an attractive one. The western powers and the Soviet Union lacked a sense of urgency regarding reunification due to the heightening tensions between east and west more generally. Both Germanys were relatively stable in their contemporary states and held the potential of becoming an important ally to its respective superpower. The ongoing bickering over Berlin demonstrated that the two sides were not eager to reunite, as the focus was on division rather than sharing space. Accordingly, it became increasingly evident that this unified Olympic team was much more superficial than Brundage and the IOC realized or were willing to acknowledge.[46]

Nonetheless, Brundage continued to push for collaboration as the 1960 Olympiad drew closer rather than allowing the Games to reflect political realities. In November 1959, the constant battling between the German NOCs focused on the flag to be used during the Games. This time it was the Bonn government overruling its NOC and interfering with Olympic matters. This had had not been a problem for the 1956 Melbourne Games because both countries had retained the flag of the former Germany. Since then, however, East Germany had adopted a new banner, which was the old black, red and gold, with a communist hammer and compass superimposed on the red center band. For the purposes of the unified German team in the 1960 Games, the two sides agreed on a neutral flag. It was red, black, and gold—which were still the colors of both Germanys—with the Olympic rings on the red band in lieu of the communist symbols. The unified team intended to use this banner in both Squaw Valley and Rome until the West German government, under the leadership of Chancellor Konrad Adenauer, decided that not using the West German flag at the Games would be "irreconcilable with national dignity," and therefore could not be allowed.[47] The new East German flag simply underscored the growing disparity between the two countries while West Germany's reaction served as a reminder that "the Bonn government regards itself as the only legal representative of the German people."[48]

When the Bonn government raised this point, West German IOC representative Willi Daume wrote to Brundage explaining the problem and apologizing for his government's inflexibility and meddling.[49] Adenauer, looking to strengthen his country's growing ties to the west, argued that West Germany had already made more than enough compromises to accommodate the East

Germans and that its flag was tied too closely to national pride for it to be sacrificed.[50] East Germany balked and stated that it could not be expected to march under the flag of a different country. As Daume presented Adenauer's argument, "They [the West German government] are of opinion that this would mean a concession from their part only and would rather prefer that the common German team should partake at the Olympic games without any flag at all; in other words there would be no flag in the stadium, no flag when marching in, and no flag when celebrating the winner."[51] The West German contingent agreed with the IOC's ruling that there could be only one German team and understood the reasoning behind the compromise but found itself largely hamstrung by its government.

The resolution of this matter in December saved German participation in Squaw Valley. Both German NOCs voted to accept the previously suggested black, red, and gold flag with the Olympic rings placed on the red band. The Bonn government disliked the solution, but both Olympic committees realized that agreeing was their only option if they wanted to compete. Fortunately, the Bonn government chose to acquiesce rather than trying to block West German participation in the Olympics through a legal injunction or by withholding the funding needed to finance the trips to California and Italy. Conceding was probably the most politically wise option for Adenauer, as the West German athletic federations supported the IOC and Adenauer could have hurt his party's position for the next election had he pursued this fight. There was little chance that Brundage would relent and allow each Germany to bring its own flag or that the East German NOC would agree to march under what was now West Germany's flag.[52]

Despite this reluctant acceptance, the issue of separate flags lingered into the new year. West Germany hosted the ski jumping world championships in January, one month before the opening of the Squaw Valley Games. The West German Ski Association decided that it would not use the flags of any of the competing countries to avoid the obligation of flying the new East German flag. In response, East Germany decided to boycott the event, soon followed by the Soviet Union and Czechoslovakia.[53] Later in January the Soviet and East German flags were stolen at ski events in Austria and Switzerland.[54] Fortunately for all parties involved, bickering over flags did not spoil either the Squaw Valley or Rome Games.

Squaw Valley

Nonetheless, East Germany's troubles with the Squaw Valley Games remained unresolved as late as the opening ceremonies. Members of its delegation reported problems securing American entry visas, despite the State Department's promises to the contrary in 1957. When the unified German team arrived at the Olympic Village in February, there were only forty-five team members present instead of the anticipated fifty-five because the last ten had been unable to obtain the necessary visas.[55] Schobel, now president of the East German NOC, announced that only East German members of the delegation had been barred from traveling. According to Schobel, the American Consulate in West Berlin did not offer any explanation as to why these athletes and officials were not allowed to travel. At the IOC session in San Francisco, the USOA explained that it had provided accommodations and travel visas for eight East German sporting officials before the team announced a plan to bring an extra twenty members. The State Department compromised and provided for an additional four, bringing the East German total up to twelve, equaling the number of West German officials.[56]

The State Department also denied entry to five East German journalists sent to cover the Games. Their situation differed a bit from the team officials' because the IOC did not technically demand that host countries admit all foreign press members who applied for visas, though it was tacitly understood that they would be welcomed. In this case, the State Department tersely explained its decision, "their admission would not be in the interests of the United States."[57] In a follow-up story in the New York Times, the State Department elaborated that it was not unusual to deny communists entry. Also, Washington feared that the East German press would inject an unwanted political element into its sportswriting.[58] This was a highly faulty and hypocritical defense, considering that Cold War politics were the State Department's motivation for excluding the media. Even worse, barring the press and citing politics as the reason only heightened the politicization of the Games and detracted attention from the athletes.

The East German NOC filed a protest against the United States with Brundage. This action was entirely justified, as the United States picked a poor moment to play politics. The IOC supported the protest with Brundage arguing that "all legitimate journalists should be permitted to attend the Games."[59] He told the New York Times that the USOA had assured him that there would not be any such problems involving visas following the issues regarding the Bulgarian team in 1957 and before the committee awarded the Games to Squaw Valley. Following East Germany's complaint, the IOC adopted a resolution stating "its profound belief in the freedom of the press throughout the world in the same way as one of its main Olympic principles is the freedom of the youth of the world to participate in the Olympic Games without any discrimination against any country or any person on grounds of race, religion or politics."[60]

Though relevant, this statement exemplified how the IOC unwittingly facilitated the increasing politicization of sports. The State Department knew that there was little pressure to admit the entire East German delegation because the IOC would not punish the United States for breaking its rules. If Brundage and the IOC wanted to make the Games truly relevant to international relations and to "show the way for the diplomats," as he wrote in 1948, it should have sanctioned the United States for this action.[61] Warning the United States that failure to provide visas would result in the removal of the Games from Squaw Valley in 1957 would have provided justification for such action. However, the IOC feared the implications of angering the United States. It was willing to be political in the sense that it continued to insist on a unified German team and that it refused to accept a separate Ukrainian team, but that resolve was absent here. Its impotence magnified the role of politics at the Games and encouraged all sides to continue to make their own policies rather than to conform to the IOC's arbitrarily enforced tenets. While the committee's statement lamenting the visa issues declared that the Olympic Movement did not discriminate based on politics, it was obvious that the West German NOC—and many others—did.

Sports Illustrated was sharply critical of the State Department and turned its accusation that the East Germans were looking to make the Games political on its head. In the 22 February "Events and Discoveries" piece—a weekly column offering brief commentary on contemporary athletic events with implications beyond the sports world—the publication issued a strong disapproval of the visa denials. "We deplore the presence of that harsh note at Squaw and earnestly hope it will be quickly quenched."[62] While this commentary was in some ways surprising, given Luce's staunch anticommunist stance and his close relationship with the Eisenhower administration, Luce's daily involvement in his publications was on the wane, as was his influence within the White House. This column reflected how important the Olympics were becoming, speaking to the power of sports to transcend politics. "Communist reporters may not be famous for providing completely objective boxscores on democracy's athletes. However, at this point, it scarcely matters. What matters more is that the State Department has already injected a 'harsh, political note' into the friendly competition."[63] While the State Department may have viewed denying visas as a tactical measure intended to show American power, it came across as a poorly judged political move, even within some American circles.

Given the ugly politics surrounding them, it is little wonder that the press watched the Squaw Valley Winter Games closely. These Games proved some of the most acrimonious in terms of this ugly rhetoric. While Secretary of State Christian Herter and his staff were battling the IOC to minimize the

East German presence at the Games, American sportswriters continued to criticize the Soviets' professionalism. Former United States Winter Olympian Irving Jaffee penned a very colorful and chauvinistic Olympic preview for the United Press International wire service which ran in newspapers across the country. In it, he predicted a win for "this army of Commies," because they ignored the IOC's amateur rules.[64] Jaffee painted a clear juxtaposition between the American amateur sportsmen and what he termed as the "massive Russian sports plant."[65] The entire piece drew contradictions between the two systems, accusing the Soviets of taking a militaristic approach to the Games and treating them as a Cold War battlefield. Seemingly lost on Jaffee was the fact that many of his own countrymen, including those at the top in Washington, also regarded the Games as a Cold War proving ground. Both the Eisenhower and Kennedy administrations pushed for better Olympic results and improved all-around physical fitness to stave off the growing communist threat to American sporting dominance.

Luckily for the fans, politics were not the only memorable spectacle in Squaw Valley. As was the case with the superpowers' track meets, a particularly intense atmosphere accompanied Soviet-American hockey games, as players and spectators on both sides were aware of the larger implications of these matchups. The victors celebrated more heartily while the losers faced heavy scrutiny. The 1960 Olympic hockey game was a prime example of these heightened emotions. The United States came away with the 3–2 victory and advanced to beat Czechoslovakia in the gold medal final, its first Olympic hockey championship. The players and coach were all quite exuberant. According to Coach Jack Riley, "It's just been great…. We were so keyed up to beat the Russians."[66] The team felt an added sense of national pride in how they came to the gold. In the words of team member Bob Cleary, "The whole experience was indescribable…. USA won it. It wasn't me, and it wasn't other individuals. It was a team effort for your country."[67] The importance of winning Cold War victory for one's country was one not lost in translation on either side of the Iron Curtain.

The hockey gold medal was just one of many proud moments for the United States. Hosting a Games for the first time since 1932, when both the winter and summer contests took place on American soil, the home team finished third overall behind the Soviet Union and Sweden. Moscow more than doubled Sweden's points total, winning 165.5 to 71.5. The United States was a very close third at 71.[68] American Figure skater Carol Heiss, the silver medalist in Cortina four years earlier, added Olympic gold medalist to her list of achievements. In response, her home city of New York celebrated her homecoming with a parade, with an estimated 250,000 fans attending.[69] While Austria traditionally had dominated the alpine skiing events, the rest of the world seemed to have caught up in the years between Cortina and Squaw Valley. The American team joined Germany, France, and Switzerland as the countries showing the most improvement on the slopes, aided by new metal skis replacing the old wooden models.[70]

With the exception of hockey, a multitude of factors prevented strong Soviet-American rivalries from developing at the Winter Games comparable to the track and basketball standoffs that were so eagerly anticipated during the summer contests. First, the Winter Games never garnered as much fanfare in the United States as did the summer. European athletes with the advantage of proximity to excellent ski mountains and frequent opportunities to practice on these hills tended to dominate the Games. American interest tended to be restricted to hockey and the skating events. The aforementioned Soviet-American hockey rivalry was growing by this time, but it had yet to reach the ferocious heights it would later in the Cold War. Also, the Soviets were still widely considered newcomers to the Winter Games—Squaw Valley was only their second appearance. The American hockey team went out of its way to thank the Soviets for their tips and assistance during the gold medal game against Czechoslovakia, perhaps proving once again that amateur athletes were better diplomats than professional politicians.[71] The *New York Times* said as much in an editorial just after the Games closed. "The Russian athletes are to be congratulated for their fine showing and the Americans spurred on to seek victory in the summer Olympics this year and in subsequent games. How much better it is to strive for athletic perfection than to see who can build the most destructive bomb."[72] Nonetheless, despite the Americans' strong showing, the post–Games analysis rendered the usual calls for improvement and fears that the United States was falling dangerously behind Moscow.[73]

Rome

Much like they had in 1956, heavy political overtones carried over into the Summer Olympics. In the midst of the Games on 30 August, the East German government announced a five-day travel restriction on West Germans forbidding them from entering East Berlin from 31 August until 4 September.[74] This was just the latest in a series of attempts to force the western powers and West Germany out of Berlin. Though the tensions that had built up following Khrushchev's demands for troop removal in 1958 had calmed somewhat, both sides recognized this as only a temporary abatement.

Once again, the State Department refused to panic or to rise to Moscow's bait by countering with its own outrageous demand. In the end, this travel restriction proved ineffective. Rather than hurting West Berlin's relations with Bonn and discouraging the growing number of East Germans defecting via West Berlin, the move instead showcased the ongoing unrest behind the Iron Curtain. The *Washington Post* ran a story in the midst of these restrictions on 3 September reporting that more than 100,000 East Germans had fled the country since 1 January, a dramatic increase over the 61,000 in the period from 1 January to 1 September 1959.[75] East German chancellor Walter Ulbricht made little further attempt at controlling defections until the sudden construction of the Berlin Wall. However, the timing of this battle for Berlin underscored the absurdity of the IOC's insistence on a single German team in Rome.

Superpower tensions remained high throughout the Games. Yet the lack of a defining political incident led many to associate this Olympiad with athletic glory and memorable moments on the field rather than the ongoing political drama off it. From the moment the Games began, the competitive atmosphere between the superpowers was at an unprecedented level, though this antagonism focused on Berlin rather than athletics. While Olympic tradition dictated that nations dip their flags when passing the officials stand during the parade of nations at the Opening Ceremonies, neither superpower complied. American flagbearer Rafer Johnson's statement after the Games that "I didn't dip, but no one told me not to do it," was an obvious political move.[76] The spirit of competition between the superpowers was so high that neither country was willing to show deference to another country or an organization. Each country maintained that it had received more applause and a warmer welcome as it entered Stadio Olimpico, a contest which was nearly impossible to measure objectively, but again highlighted the heated rivalry.

Moscow ratcheted up the political aspect of the Games when it warned its delegation to stay away from their American competition in Rome. The stated rationale behind this counsel was a fear of American spies, particularly following the U-2 incident. In the weeks leading up to the Rome Games, several Soviet newspapers ran stories regarding an influx of American spies, linking them without evidence to Powers.[77] An underlying fear existed that western ideas would infiltrate the Iron Curtain and upset the status quo, triggering a revolt similar to the Hungarian Revolution four years earlier. While the United States worried about finishing second in the medal count and the associated loss of prestige, the Soviets were more insecure politically. There was less criticism of American athletes than there was of the American way of life more generally. While the United States lamented its loss of Olympic domination, it had less to fear in terms of overall stability than the Kremlin did. There were estimates before the Games that somewhere between fifteen and twenty-five

President Dwight Eisenhower and Soviet premier Nikita Khrushchev during Khrushchev's extended visit to the United States in September 1959. Though the two men came to a general sense of agreement on a number of issues during this visit, the U-2 spy incident the following spring and new tensions over Berlin ended this brief thaw in the Cold War (U.S. Navy. Photo No. 67–309–8 U.S. Navy. Dwight D. Eisenhower Presidential Library and Museum).

Hungarian athletes would try to defect via the Rome Games.[78] The CIA employed American track star David Sime to try to convince Soviet long jumper Igor Ter-Ovanesyan to defect, but Ter-Ovanesyan feared that Sime was a double agent and backed out at the last minute.[79]

The United States Information Agency capitalized on this growing Soviet fear and intensified the propaganda war a step further by producing a brochure describing American life for distribution at the Rome Games. Stacks of booklets written in Russian were given to the American delegation to distribute to their Soviet competitors. Though not produced by the USOA, its assistant director, Arthur Lentz, supported the endeavor. "I promised nothing, but brought them along, and I think it's a good idea. So do some of the athletes I talked to," he said in a *Washington Post* story on this initiative.[80] Part of the USIA's new "Books for America" program, which had as its mission to expose oppressed peoples to literary works commonly censored by their home governments, the brochure was intentionally provocative in terms of politics, as it mentioned that members of all parties could stand for election in America.[81] It also referenced the free press and offered a statistic that nearly 900,000 Soviet-born men and women were now living in the United States. The brochure also included a copy of the Declaration of Independence, translated into Russian.[82] While it was customary for athletes to bring souvenirs and patriotic pins from their home countries to trade with their peers, Washington pushed the boundaries by sending pamphlets that were clear examples of democratic propaganda. Iron Curtain athletes arrived in Rome with Soviet sports magazines, a more benign form of nationalist literature, to distribute. There was no press coverage devoted to the Soviets' reaction to the American pamphlets, but perhaps the following quote offered in the *Post* a few days later best summed up the anticipated response. "'We can give 'em to them,' one US official shrugged, 'but whether they'll be allowed to keep them is something else again.'"[83]

Politics continued to haunt the Games. There were reports that Bulgarian wrestler Dmitrio Stoyanov intentionally lost to his Soviet rival Altandil Koridze in the semi-finals of the Greco-Roman wrestling tournament to ensure an Iron Curtain gold medal. While Stoyanov was disqualified, Koridze was permitted to keep his medal following the investigation.[84] This was politically significant because the west often perceived Bulgaria as the most obedient Soviet ally. Cold War sentiments also pervaded the men's basketball tournament, one of the most watched events of the two weeks. With the stands filled to capacity, American athletes from other sports crowded onto the end of the bench to catch the action. While the United States was traditionally the global power on the court, the Soviet Union had begun to catch up in recent years, even beating their biggest rivals in the 1959 World Championships. Their coach, Stepan Spandarian, had predicted a Soviet Olympic victory a few months prior to Rome. On the other bench, American coach Pete Newell ensured that the potential for Cold War bragging rights in this matchup was not lost on his players.[85] The United States walked away with the lopsided 81–57 win and eventually advanced to win the gold medal. While the gold was an accomplishment in itself, it was rather anticlimactic because of the importance and focus that both sides had ascribed to the Soviet game.[86]

The Rome Games marked a critical turning point in attitudes toward the Olympics as well. While many American coaches and sportswriters had zeroed in on the Soviets as their main competition in 1952 and 1956, this sense of a direct rivalry in a global venue like the Olympics became much more pronounced during the Rome Games. This trend continued into the later 1960s contests. The increase in tensions between the superpowers, particularly regarding Berlin and triggered by the U-2 incident, was a main reason for this single-mindedness. Khrushchev only added to these anxieties when he announced during the Games that he would be traveling to New York for the upcoming United Nations session. His intention was to coerce the UN Security Council to oppose the United States on a number of ongoing issues, including the situations in Berlin and Cuba, and to garner support for his idea of a worldwide disarmament conference.[87] The latter reason was widely perceived as purely a propaganda move on Khrushchev's part. The timing of this visit was especially alarming for the United States as it came in the midst of the 1960 presidential campaign season.[88]

The onset of the cultural Cold War was another major factor in this heightened emphasis on Olympic victory. By September 1960, the United States needed a morale boost. The Soviets seemed to be pulling away in the space race. Not only had they scored a major victory with Sputnik, but news broke on 23 August that they had sent a satellite into orbit with two dogs, mice, and rats on board. The vessel had orbited the earth for a day before returning safely to earth.[89] This trial was the precursor to sending a man into space as well as a major source of insecurity for the United States, as the news out of Moscow overshadowed a number of space-related accomplishments that NASA had proudly reported only a week earlier.[90]

Both sides could claim victory in Rome depending on how one studied the results, which meant that there was room for improvement on both sides as well. The Soviets once again claimed the title in the unofficial medal count, just beating the United States 73–71.[91] Not only was this an extremely tight race, but that these medals were concentrated in a number of sports which they had traditionally dominated yet were considered fairly obscure in other countries did little to assuage Soviet concerns.[92] Gymnastics provided the best example. The Soviets had taken nearly all of the medals in the men's and women's competitions since they first entered the Games in 1952 simply because the sport did not attract many athletes in other countries. This maximized the medal potential but also limited Cold War bragging rights. The Soviets were also strong wrestlers and rowers, both considered "minor sports" by *Sports Illustrated*, but

historically had not fared as well in the more popular events like soccer, basketball, and swimming.[93] The Soviets countered this jab with a remark in *Pravda*
from the Olympic coaching staff, "We don't distinguish between important
and non important sports events."[94] Translation: medal quantity mattered, not
the popularity of the individual sport. Moscow intended to win it all. Despite
this relative parity in the final standings, *Pravda* and the other main Soviet
press outlets spun the totals as an outright Iron Curtain victory. A story in
Pravda detailing the Soviet team's return to Moscow boasted of its feats and
definitive position atop the athletic pyramid of nations. "The Soviet athletes
achieved decisive victory in Rome over the team of the leading capitalist country, USA. So now sports fans from all over the world recognize that the Soviet
Union is the first and most powerful country in sports."[95]

Meanwhile, the Americans dominated the swimming competition. While
the Australians were typically the team to beat in the pool, the United States
dominated the water events by winning nine gold medals.[96] Led by teens Dawn
Fraser and Chris von Saltza, a young American squad made great strides from
the two swimming goals it took home from Melbourne. On the track, American
sprinter Wilma Randolph lived up to the pre–Games hype that had surrounded
her, winning both the 100 and 200 meters while helping the gold medal 400-
meter relay team. The American men swept the podium in both hurdles events
and Rafer Johnson won the decathlon event, setting a new world record along
the way.[97] All in all, the United States should have been very proud of its accomplishments. However, the 1960 Olympic results brought more anxiety than
adulation.

In the past, the United States were all but sure gold medalists in a number
of sports, track included. By 1960 though, this tide had begun to turn. The
growing international parity in traditionally American-dominated sports was
a matter of great concern. As Daley wrote in his "Sports of the Times" column
reflecting on the Games, "The disturbing thing about the Russians' success
was the masterful way in which they broadened their base of operations.…
They are spread out in so many directions that they can't help but reap the
richest of harvests. America pays attention to track and to swimming, sneering
at all other sports as 'minor league.' But they are not considered minor league
throughout the world."[98] Daley's was not the only distress signal following
Rome. The United States government began focusing harder than ever on the
Games as a means of showcasing American strength and prowess while reminding the world that the United States was not as soft as some had come to believe.
As the Games grew in size and international exposure, some both within the
U.S. Olympic Movement, like assistant director Lentz, and within the govern-
ment feared that the United States was squandering valuable propaganda

occasions at the Games. Lentz asked that Eisenhower make a public statement about the apolitical nature of the Olympics to counter what many considered blatantly political Soviet propaganda, to no avail.[99] While such a statement might have seemed absurd, it would have been in line with the usual IOC declarations regarding politics, likely assuaging Brundage though earning few accolades from the press.

The growing strength of the combined German team provided added incentive for improvement. While Americans tended to scoff at the professionalism of Iron Curtain athletes, the reality was that Germany was beginning to make its mark on the Games in the same way that the Soviet Union had in 1952. Daley warned that the United States could soon find itself in third place if it did not begin to focus on the "minor league sports," as he termed them. "The Russians are prepared and so is up-and-coming Germany, the most intensely nationalistic nation of any here even though a divided Germany competed under a compromise flag. Worthy of note is the fact that no other group could unite East and West for anything."[100] That sport was the sole unifier in Germany spoke volumes to its propaganda power, something not lost on the Eisenhower administration or the United States more broadly.

As such, the months and years after Rome saw a renewed commitment to the Olympic Movement. Not only did the United States look to shore up its traditional strongholds, but there was a newfound emphasis on improvement in all sports to present a more well-rounded team in 1964. No longer was it acceptable for Washington and the press to use the excuse that its team was all amateurs to comfort themselves for these now customary second-place finishes. Now winning came first, especially in the formerly "minor sports." Incoming president John Kennedy made one of his main goals to improve the fitness of all Americans, in hopes of ending the perceived American decline that many feared. While Vice President Richard Nixon had presided over the first President's Council on Youth Fitness meeting charged with this same goal four years earlier, more than half of American adults failed a basic fitness test in 1960, compared to just ten percent of Europeans.[101]

The events of 1960 showed that politics were more entrenched in the Olympic Movement than ever before. From the ongoing bickering over German representation to the struggles Iron Curtain athletes faced in obtaining visas to the growing emphasis on the superpower rivalry on the podium, issues of diplomacy at times permeated nearly all aspects of the Games, from the planning stages through the closing ceremonies. While Brundage and others lamented this political flood—and rightfully so—at times, it was not an entirely negative force. The strength of the Soviet-American rivalry in hockey and basketball certainly added to the drama and spectator interest in the Games. The added intrigue accompanying the Games' function as a Cold War arena increased the Olympic Movement's international visibility and relevance dramatically. The White House and Congress looked to capitalize on all available opportunities to emphasize the ideals of liberty and democracy, showing Soviet athletes what they were missing behind the Iron Curtain. Succeeding at the Games was a high-profile means of showcasing the best of the west. The Kremlin viewed Olympic victory as vital to demonstrating Soviet strength outside the diplomatic realm, similar to its focus on space exploration. Rome demonstrated that this rivalry was as strong as ever. Though neither could truly be said to be winning the overall Cold War, both sides realized that propaganda potential that accompanied the Games and looked to exploit this resource to its fullest extent. This emphasis on improving Olympic performance would only grow stronger in the years leading up to the 1964 Innsbruck and Tokyo spectacles, as the Cold War pressures threatened to boil over on and off the field.

CHAPTER 7

1964

Politics Take Center Stage

"A national program of physical fitness is as important to our success as a democracy as is a national program for economic growth."
—President John F. Kennedy[1]

By 1964, the Olympics had become virtually unrecognizable to the comparatively simple London contests just sixteen years earlier. Rome had been transitional, but by 1964 there were few signs of the small-scale athletics competition that de Coubertin had envisioned sixty years before. Cold War tensions took center stage, making the Games much more political, but also much more culturally relevant. With the sudden rise of the Berlin Wall and the subsequent western efforts to punish Moscow and East Berlin for this offense, politics were omnipresent before and during the 1964 contests.

There were times when neutral countries like Norway found themselves caught up in the Cold War crossfire and forced to weigh their national interests against those of the international sporting hierarchy. They feared that not appeasing the IOC and other international bodies might ruin their chances to host prestigious sporting events like the Olympics or other world championships.[2] As the Olympic Movement became more open to superpower influence once the IOC tacitly acknowledged the attention that Cold War standoffs brought to the Games, the United States tried—and largely failed—to use the Olympics to demonstrate its cultural supremacy over the Soviet Union. Moscow also pursued this end and placed a strong emphasis on the importance of a strong showing in the 1964 Games to hide some of the glaring problems within Soviet society.[3] Nonetheless, it found itself hindered by growing political concerns in and away from its Olympic committee.

Even aside from Cold War considerations, the Games were bigger than ever by 1964, both in terms of attendance as well as in terms of global interest and relevance. While the early contests had been primarily comprised of European and American athletes, the field of competitors had grown increasingly diverse since London with the Soviet Union, Asian, and African nations increasingly represented. These new teams were also challenging for the medals with greater frequency, threatening the superpowers' shared dominance of the podium.

The IOC's growing list of choices for host cities reflected the increasing globalization of the Games as well. Tokyo became the first Asian setting for an Olympics with the 1964 summer contests. The venue choice was significant in two ways. First, the IOC's decision to hold the Games there symbolized that Japan had successfully reintegrated into the global community less than twenty years after World War II ended. The war itself had begun to recede from public memory by this point. Secondly, this selection demonstrated the changing face of the Games. No longer exclusively Western, the Olympics were attracting more interest and attention around the world. African decolonization was progressing at whirlwind pace, with many new countries applying for IOC membership, increasing the number of participants and spectators at the Games while television further expanded viewership. Now even those who could not be physically present at the Games could follow them closely. Television was a controlling interest for the first time in Tokyo, enabling the events to be viewed worldwide. They increased their audience and the IOC's wealth from selling the broadcast rights, while fueling Brundage's fears that the Olympics were becoming too big.[4]

While satellite television coverage and some of the flags flown during the opening ceremonies were new, politics remained a constant. Neither the Summer Games nor the winter contests in Innsbruck, Austria, took place in a country directly involved in the Cold War, yet there was plenty of diplomatic intrigue during both. By the time the Tokyo Games began in October 1964, the United States had a new leader in Lyndon Johnson and the Soviet Union was on the cusp of the Leonid Brezhnev era. It had been a rocky four years for superpower relations, due to the Bay of Pigs invasion, construction of the Berlin Wall, and the Cuban Missile Crisis, among other minor incidents. Now both nations faced serious challenges, as the Cold War's focus shifted from Europe to the third world. Washington became increasingly bogged down in Vietnam while Moscow confronted a growing schism with China. The Olympics were still important to Cold War prestige, but there were signs of a changing focus in both countries. Simultaneously the superpowers faced both domestic distractions and challenges to their respective hegemonies.

The IOC continued to find itself mired in political issues. The unified German team was an ongoing point of contention, though there were signs that a resolution was near by 1964. East German athletes found themselves facing seemingly endless visa issues when trying to compete in NATO countries, compounding the frustration caused by the IOC's insistence on a single German Olympic team. The interminable sporting war of words between the superpowers remained acerbic, reflecting the Games' high stakes and the growing inextricability of athletics and diplomacy. Despite the intensity of these press battles and the efforts by both superpowers to dominate the Games, both countries found themselves asking what went wrong following relatively disappointing performances. Additionally for Moscow, the increased number of attempted defections by Iron Curtain athletes was a clear sign that though the Soviet sports system produced a lot of Olympic champions, it failed its athletes in other crucial ways.

The Changing Cold War

Both superpowers experienced significant upheaval between the Rome and Tokyo Games. While hopes had been high that Kennedy's election in 1960 would bring a fresh start to Soviet-American relations, these expectations evaporated within three months of his inauguration following the failed Bay of Pigs invasion in Cuba. The eighteen months between the Bay of Pigs disaster and the Cuban Missile Crisis was one of the most volatile periods of the Cold War. Perhaps worse for the anxious publics in both countries, there was no decisive resolution following this nerve-wracking time. Even once tensions lessened following Khrushchev's capitulation in October 1962, it was impossible to state definitively that either side was winning the Cold War.

Despite his public image as the coldest of the Cold Warriors, Kennedy maintained that he was willing to work with the Soviet Union.[5] Yet he was also firm in his resolve that the United States would not be submissive or make unnecessary accommodations to improve relations. In his inaugural address, Kennedy pledged, "We dare not tempt them with weakness. For only when our arms are sufficient beyond doubt can we be certain beyond doubt that they will never be employed…. Let us never negotiate out of fear. But let us never fear to negotiate."[6] While expressing hope for a fresh start with Moscow, Kennedy reassured the American people that Washington would continue to build its strength, calling on the public for support. "Let every nation know, whether it wishes us well or ill, that we shall pay any price, bear any burden, meet any hardship, support any friend, oppose any foe to assure the survival and the success of liberty."[7] Kennedy's inaugural address, still celebrated for its rhetoric more than fifty years later, demonstrated that he was ready to face any

President John F. Kennedy meets with members of the Soviet delegation on October 16, 1962, to discuss the Soviet missiles situated in Cuba. From left to right in foreground are Vladimir S. Semenov, Soviet Deputy Minister of Foreign Affairs, Soviet ambassador to the United States Anatoly Dobrynin, Soviet foreign minister Andrei Gromyko, and Kennedy (Abbie Rowe. White House Photographs. John F. Kennedy Presidential Library and Museum. Boston).

Cold War challenge that might arise. However, as he would soon discover, the best intentions were not enough to win Cold War battles.

Kennedy's brief three-year administration was one of the most tumultuous periods of the "long twilight struggle," as Kennedy poignantly described the Cold War in 1961.[8] Both superpowers struggled to find new means of asserting themselves in what had become an interminable battle of wills. For Kennedy, 1961 was hardly an auspicious first year in office, given the Bay of Pigs disaster in April and the unexpected construction of the Berlin Wall in August. Not only did the Bay of Pigs push Cuban dictator Fidel Castro closer to Moscow, but it led indirectly to the Cuban Missile Crisis eighteen months later, possibly the tensest two weeks of the entire Cold War. In the meantime, the overnight appearance of the Berlin Wall created shock waves on both sides of the Iron Curtain.[9]

The 1962 Cuban Missile Crisis represented a clearer victory for Washington, while simultaneously marking the symbolic beginning of the end for Khrushchev's leadership. On the most basic level, Kennedy won because Khrushchev surrendered first. Negotiating for the removal of the missiles in Cuba without a serious concession in return boosted Kennedy's Cold War record and confidence in dealing with the Soviets. In Moscow, the Politburo began to realize Khrushchev's limitations as a leader. Though he remained in power for another two years, Khrushchev's behavior during the Cuban Missile Crisis and rapid surrender played a large role in the decision to unseat him in October 1964.[10]

The ascendancy of brash Texan Lyndon Johnson to the presidency following Kennedy's death in November 1963 marked a new era in Cold War relations. Johnson inherited a relatively more stable Cold War than Kennedy had. The most recent standoff between the superpowers, the Cuban Missile Crisis, had ended as a decisive American victory. Since that time, the two sides had signed the Nuclear Test Ban Treaty, a truce of sorts. While the Berlin Wall was still standing and West Berliners faced ongoing daily frustration and isolation, the looming fear of confrontation that had characterized late 1950s and early 1960s had dissipated, replaced by a sense of resignation regarding the Cold War and one of permanency regarding the division of Germany that would largely reign until the 1980s. The CIA even ended regulation payments to the Hungarian National Sports Federation in 1962 because they fell victim to all-around funding cuts. Liberating communist nations was not as high on the White House agenda by the Johnson years.[11] While tense confrontations with the Soviet Union had defined Kennedy's tenure, domestic reform and increasingly Vietnam would occupy most of Johnson's attention. Under his watch, the war that he had inherited from Kennedy drained the administration's resources and became a public relations nightmare by 1968.

Domestic concerns preoccupied the Soviets as well. Discontent with Khrushchev's leadership within the Politburo had been building for some time even before the Cuban Missile Crisis underscored his ineptitude. It was becoming increasingly difficult for Moscow to deny that it had entered into a period of stagnation. This unsettling situation became clear at the October 1964 annual communist summit in Moscow where Khrushchev appeared disheartened when questioned on a number of topics, including the space race. He seemed to have no answers to the growing number of pressing issues facing the Kremlin. The Soviet public was increasingly critical of Khrushchev, particularly regarding the standard of living. There was even some misplaced nostalgia for Stalin.[12] This living standard was falling further behind the west, with the country unable to provide enough food for its people without buying

American grain. The widening Sino-Soviet split garnered a considerable amount of negative press and gave Washington further reason to denounce communism. Through all of this, Khrushchev continued to be his cantankerous, stubborn self, constantly trying to increase his own authority within the Kremlin without providing any guidance or ideas on how to reverse these disconcerting trends.[13]

Given these worsening conditions, Khrushchev's fall from power on 14 October 1964—in the midst of the Tokyo Olympics—seemed all but inevitable in retrospect. While the ongoing foreign policy misadventures and economic setbacks were part of the problem, Khrushchev's stubborn adherence to a plan that would have reduced the amount of compulsory education for Soviet children in a time when their students were falling behind their American peers in science and technology was what ultimately doomed him.[14] His administration lacked a clear direction because Khrushchev lacked the vision and leadership skills necessary to pull the Soviet Union out of its slump.[15] News of Khrushchev's removal and the choice of Brezhnev as his successor came as a great surprise in the west.[16] There was understandably a great deal of uncertainty as to how his presence at the top would affect Soviet-American relations, but a more immediate concern behind the Iron Curtain was how Brezhnev would reverse the growing signs of decline.

The Unabated Sporting Cold War

While the end of the Kennedy administration saw some progress in dispelling Cold War tensions, the cultural struggle raged on unabated. This battle for all-around supremacy extended to building a population ready to meet any challenge that might arise, including those on the playing field. As such, improving the fitness of the average American—and especially Olympians—was perhaps more important to Kennedy than to than any other Cold War president. The incoming president penned an article for *Sports Illustrated* in December 1960 to this end, warning of the consequences of a "soft" America. Kennedy argued that a nation's physical health was crucial to its overall strength. "But the harsh fact of the matter is that there is also an increasingly large number of young Americans who are neglecting their bodies—whose physical fitness is not what it should be—who are getting soft. And such softness on the part of individual citizens can help to strip and destroy the vitality of a nation."[17] The president took this point further, drawing comparisons between the Americans and the Soviets, whom he termed a "powerful and implacable adversary."[18]

Kennedy voiced the concerns of many when he targeted the Soviets as the prime competition; those who shared this viewpoint often contrasted the American and Soviet paths to winning. *New York Times* sportswriter Arthur Daley explained the growing Soviet dominance in political terms: "The totalitarian powers have the ability to marshal their youth for what they regard, among other things, as part of the propaganda war. They have said so, bluntly and unashamedly. And the Rome Olympics, on that basis, represented a resounding victory for Soviet Russia."[19] Daley evoked an image of a very militaristic Soviet enemy, reiterating the common critique that Moscow did not play by the rules. Kennedy also drew upon this rather stern portrayal of the Soviets as "determined to show the world that only the Communist system possesses the vigor and determination necessary to satisfy awakening aspirations for progress and the elimination of poverty and want."[20] It would take a grand effort by the United States to keep this pace and reverse the trend toward softness, possible "only if our citizens are physically fit will they be fully capable of such."[21] Daley's and Kennedy's criticisms were intended to inspire Americans to catch up to their European peers to reassert the western way of life as superior. The president penned a second appeal to the American public in *Sports Illustrated* in 1962 with Attorney General Robert Kennedy following suit in 1964. Following the president's death in 1963, the magazine ran a tribute to his athleticism and dedication to improving American fitness as "he showed the Soft American the way of a man with guts."[22]

President Kennedy backed his words with an ambitious legislative agenda intended to encourage better fitness among the general public along with Olympic-caliber athletes. While Eisenhower had put physical fitness on the White House agenda, it was Kennedy who strove to engrain athletic participation into the everyday life of all Americans. He interceded in the long-running feud between the NCAA and the AAU to ensure that American athletes would not miss out on competitive opportunities. He reorganized the President's Council on Fitness to increase its efficacy and encompass all Americans rather than focusing on the young, and was extremely attentive to sporting exploits at all levels, from family football games to recognizing Olympic champions "with an interest that cannot be faked."[23]

Kennedy encouraged the USOC in a letter to its president Kenneth Wilson in 1961. "I urge all Americans to join in this crusade. I ask particularly that our schools and athletic organizations broaden their base of participation to include all those sports in which we must compete in international games. From this greater participation will emerge the caliber of athletes, in all sports, that our position as leader of the Free World demands."[24] Continuing this theme, he referenced the Olympics and expressed concern that the United States was growing complacent at the December 1961 National Football Hall of Fame Banquet. Here, the president again stressed the need for a more athletic nation, specifically to improve Olympic performance.

> Excellence emerges from mass participation. This is shown by the fact that in some areas of our Olympic Games, we have steadily fallen behind those nations who have stressed broad participation in a great variety of sports. I believe that as a nation we should give our full support, for example, to our Olympic development program. We will not subsidize our athletes as some nations do, but we should as a country set a goal, not in the way the Soviet Union or the Chinese do ... generally to produce a standard of excellence for our country which will enable our athletes to win the Olympics-but more importantly than that, which will give us a nation of vigorous men and women.[25]

Kennedy echoed and built upon Eisenhower's concern that the Soviets had outshined the United States in recent Olympics, even in traditionally American-dominated sports. While Eisenhower conceded that a nation or athlete could not be number one all of the time, Kennedy was less willing to compromise. He emphasized that the United States would by no means embrace a state-sponsored athletic system targeted at the elite like Moscow's, but instead the United States would work toward improvement across the population as a means of gaining athletic prowess and Olympic honors in the years ahead.

Kennedy made it a personal goal to reverse America's trend toward spectatorship, again using *Sports Illustrated* as his podium in 1962. He diagnosed the current state of American athletics as "spectating was becoming a national disease."[26] This focus on the entire population differentiated his agenda from the Soviet training program. While the Soviets concentrated their resources on their Olympians and potential world champions to the detriment of the masses, the American government used a more wide-ranging approach to attract young athletes. In the end, both methods proved rather successful as the Soviet Union and the United States finished at or near the top of the medal count for virtually every Cold War-era Olympics. Soviet athletes who showed Olympic potential often reaped monetary benefits and extra training time out of reach of Americans who feared losing their amateur status or who needed to work to support a family.[27] While the Soviets walked away with more Olympic hardware, the average American benefitted more than his Soviet peer did in terms of personal health gains and available resources. Most Soviets attended schools without gyms, but nearly all American children participated in frequent physical education classes. The argument can be made that both systems worked, though there was less skepticism surrounding the Americans' honesty and amateurism while the Soviets reaped more Olympic glory and propaganda fodder.

Mixing politics and sport continued to be a favorite pastime of journalists on both sides of the Iron Curtain. Even as diplomatic tensions began to ebb in

1963 and 1964, the propaganda war in the press remained ugly. Early in 1964, the American press quickly spun the news that the Soviet Union cancelled a planned visit by an NBA all-star team to hide its perceived inferiority.[28] The Kremlin's official reason for rescinding this invitation was to protect its team's amateur status, which was a poor excuse. Moscow feared that its team would lose and did not want to risk embarrassment. American newspapers argued that since the Soviets did not care about true amateurism in the Olympics, why should the concept suddenly become so important in non–Olympic matchups?[29] In the end, the all-star team visited a number of European nations but not the Soviet Union. This compromise limited the tour's spectator appeal but still gave the American team some international exposure.

Sports were not the only facet of the cultural Cold War that received heavy attention and scrutiny from the Kennedy administration. The increased sense of competition extended to the heavens as well. The space race took on an added importance during this period, even appearing in the 1960 Democratic Party Platform as a goal for the new administration.[30] Kennedy made aeronautical achievement one of his first priorities from his campaigning days, using the Sputnik issue to criticize technological stagnation during the Eisenhower years. "They are moving faster than we are," Kennedy said in a Detroit campaign stop in August.[31] "The world's first satellite was called Sputnik, not Vanguard or Explorer. The first vehicle to the moon was named Lunik. The first living creatures to orbit the earth in space and return were named Strelka and Belka, not Rover and Fido. Now let me make it clear that I believe there can only be one defense policy for the United States and that is summed up in the word 'first.'"[32] Kennedy drew parallels between the space race and the missile gap to underscore the importance of rocketry. No one wanted to finish second to the Soviets in technology—or anything else.[33]

Despite this renewed American focus on the skies, the Soviets won the race to send the first human into orbit when Cosmonaut Yugi Gagarin accomplished the feat in April 1961. That an American astronaut, Alan Shepard, echoed Gagarin's feat just weeks later was little comfort, as second place was as good as a loss in terms of Cold War scorekeeping.[34] Fortunately for Washington, NASA began to progress quickly toward achieving Kennedy's goal of putting a man on the moon by end of the decade. When the president addressed Congress on a number of what were pressing needs in his view on 25 May 1961, this ambition made the list. "I believe that this nation should commit itself to achieving the goal, before this decade is out, of landing a man on the moon and returning him safely to the earth. No single space project in this period will be more impressive to mankind, or more important for the long-range exploration of space."[35] Kennedy emphasized that reaching the moon had both scientific and propaganda ends, thereby emphasizing the competitive aspect of walking on the moon.

The United States made up for lost time during the Kennedy years in terms of enthusiasm and government spending on aeronautical research while domestic concerns forced the Soviet Union to scale back. Khrushchev openly announced at the 1963 Politburo annual session that Moscow would not compete with the United States to try to reach the moon.[36] Cracks had begun to appear in the Soviet façade within the past few years, as betrayed by the widening Sino-Soviet split and the end results of the Cuban Missile Crisis. It was obvious that the Soviet Union had other pressing needs.[37] Knowledge of these well-documented issues meant that the news that Yuri Gagarin and a fellow cosmonaut were planning a moonwalk, announced at the six-year anniversary celebration of Sputnik, elicited more skepticism than dread in Washington.[38] The United States had learned by this time to never count out the Soviets, but it was difficult to reconcile this type of expensive project with the country's obvious needs in other areas.

Because Johnson moved into the Oval Office less than a year before the 1964 Olympics, he had little time to make an impact on American athletics before the Innsbruck and Tokyo Games. Johnson did not show the same level of interest or support for the Games or sports more generally as had Eisenhower or especially Kennedy. Even when his advisers reminded him of the propaganda potential that the Olympics brought, especially now that they were televised around the world, he chose not to intervene. It was only when Robert Kennedy raised the subject of the 1964 election and the utility of a strong American performance at the Games to an incumbent candidate that the president demonstrated any inclination to offer more than limited verbal support to American Olympians.[39] Even then, Johnson's involvement with the Olympic Movement before the 1964 Games was quite limited. His influence on the Games, while still less than Kennedy's, occurred before Mexico City rather than Tokyo.

Johnson did issue the now standard Oval Office congratulatory statement recognizing the Olympic team for their performance in the Tokyo Games. In it, he emphasized the role that American athletes had played as diplomats, expressing appreciation for what had been accomplished both on and off the field. "We are all proud of the record that you have made and the way in which you have served as ambassadors of good will for our country. You have made clear the vigor and the fair play that best represent our own national character.... Healthy competition can be a spur to bring out the best in all of us, and international understanding that leads to peace is possible even in the presently troubled world."[40] Like Eisenhower and Kennedy before him, Johnson clearly underscored the differences between the American and Soviet approaches, as he referenced "the vigor and clear play that best represent our own national character." He also expressed hope that the Games might be used as a starting point for improved international relations at a time when several issues that threatened to upset the delicate Cold War balance. These included Khrushchev's ouster and related Soviet unrest, the impending American presidential elections and growing domestic reaction to the civil rights movement and Vietnam. While the Games gave the United States a chance to demonstrate their prowess and athleticism, they were also an opportunity to spread the seeds of good will in an effort to calm rising global tensions.

Politics Reign at the IOC

Though superpower tensions had begun to abate slightly by the end of Kennedy's term, the IOC continued to face a number of Cold War political quandaries. The volatile issue remained the ongoing German saga. The artificiality of the united team was clearer than ever, given the open hostility that East Germany faced from the west. Could Brundage continue to insist on a unified German team even after the Berlin Wall made the division of the two Germanys seem more permanent than ever? Even the IOC could not ignore the worsening tensions between east and west by the early 1960s. Though the two countries had competed together as required in 1960, the East German squad had been at a clear disadvantage in Squaw Valley because several members of its delegation were refused American entry visas. Between 1960 and 1964, visa problems arose whenever East Germans tried to compete in NATO countries, with the IOC seemingly powerless or totally ambivalent toward this problem.

The IOC announced in 1961 that a unified German team would once again compete in Innsbruck and Tokyo; however, the ongoing political antagonism between the two countries made this unrealistic even before the wall went up. East German leader Walter Ulbricht even went as far as to mention Bonn's stranglehold over the combined team in a long list of grievances sent to Khrushchev in June 1961. Ulbricht wrote that Bonn "even tried to prevent the participation of the German Gymnastics and Sports Club in the Olympic games. [West German chancellor Konrad] Adenauer categorically stated that the Federal Republic is the German state and on this basis no sports competition of GDR teams can occur in which the national flag or coat of arms of the GDR is displayed."[41]

There were reports in mid–August following construction of the Berlin Wall that the west would refuse to continue this collaboration and would

West Berlin residents protest the closing of the border with East Berlin on August 13, 1961. The Wall remained the most prominent physical symbol of the Cold War and made the unified German team appear increasingly farcical by the early 1960s. (National Archives. Photo No. 306-PS-D-61–11295).

boycott all events held in East Germany.[42] Part of the problem, according to Daume, was that the government was only allowing a very small number of East German athletes to leave the country, "only the really certain communists," as he termed them in a November 1961 letter, due to the high defection rate.[43] Because of this and the offense to which West Germany had taken to the Wall, continuing business as usual with East German sporting federations was all but impossible. Nonetheless, Daume remained hopeful that the matter would be resolved. He termed the temporary break in relations "a transitory measure," with the expectation that the athletes would again show the politicians how to play nicely.[44] As such, there was no immediate need to discuss disbanding the unified team.

In the same letter, the West German NOC renewed its charges that the east was using sport for political propaganda purposes. Daume argued that this meant East Germany should retain only provisional recognition. "The recent resolutions and measures of the East-German sports management, which adhere naturally to the tended political situation, offend absolutely against the statutes of the International Olympic Committee, so that already by this reason a definite recognition could not be justified. Such a step would cause for us a very difficult situation, and we then could not any longer plead for the united German team."[45] Daume also reminded Brundage that mixing sport and politics was inevitable in a communist state and as such, East Germany did not merit recognition. This defense failed when one recalled that the IOC had conceded this point when it admitted the Soviets in 1951. But Daume played his hand well in that he threatened to abandon the unified team, something of which Brundage was quite proud and unwilling to concede.[46] This pressured Brundage to maintain East Germany's provisional status or risk losing his most important allies on his pet project.

Writing before the IOC's 1962 session in Moscow, Daume reminded Brundage that West German support for a unified team hinged on conditional status for the east. Continuing the unified team was growing increasingly unpopular at home, Daume warned Brundage, so the IOC had better tread carefully in its decision-making. "The public opinion in Germany and in the main ports of Europe is, that the united German Olympic team seems not to be possible any longer. Equally there are many voices to pronounce, that under these circumstances we, the free part of Germany, should not participate at all in Innsbruck and Tokyo. We both remain true to your conviction and to this of the IOC. But we are forced to proceed with caution."[47] In addition to providing a gauge of West German public sentiment, the warning was a thinly veiled threat against upsetting the status quo. Daume also advised that Brundage leave any discussion of East Germany off the 1962 meeting agenda. While the IOC did address the matter in Moscow, it earned only a brief mention in the official session minutes, confirming that East Germany's provisional status would continue.[48] Both Brundage and West German representative Karl Ritter von Halt then voiced support for the continuation of the unified team in 1964. The IOC settled the matter with virtually no input from East Germany.[49]

The issue of German representation at the Games continued to make the headlines. News broke in December 1962 that while the two Germanys would march under the same flag in 1964, this would be the extent of their unity. The teams would compete separately while wearing the same uniform, reflecting the continuing animosity between the two countries.[50] Rather than forming a combined entry for team sports as they had in the 1956 and 1960 Games, east and west teams would square off before the Games to earn the right to represent Germany in 1964. For example, the East German field hockey team won a best-of-three playoff with West Germany and therefore went to Tokyo while the West German squad stayed home.[51] The IOC's tolerance of a limited amount of separation was a tacit acknowledgment that the division of Germany was increasingly permanent. Even the West German NOC was beginning to reject the unified team arrangement because it was unworkable. Even so, Brundage clung to this settlement, regardless of the political reality. At the 1963 IOC session, he once again waxed poetically on the German question. "The spectacle of East and West German athletes in the same uniform marching behind the same leaders and the same flag is an inspiration under the present political conditions and a great service to all the German people who wish for a united country…. We must convince the cynical politicians that sport, like the fine arts, transcends politics. It can be done—in fact, it has been done."[52] Read today, this speech is striking for its idealism and its prescience, as Germany is again one country. However, it seemed unrealistic in its time, reminding both sides just how far removed Brundage and the IOC were at times from the political reality.

The two Germanys continued to squabble throughout 1963, bickering over tryout sites for the 1964 Games as well as the proceedings for team selection. Brundage himself moderated a meeting between the two NOCs in August 1963 and witnessed firsthand how tenuous their relationship had become, yet he continued to force cooperation.[53] While North Korea, another communist state that NATO refused to recognize, gained permanent recognition at the 1963 session, the IOC rejected Andrianov's proposal that the same right be extended to East Germany and so the charade of a unified team continued.[54] Relations between the two sides had grown so hostile by mid–1964 that East Germany again petitioned the IOC for separate representation in Tokyo, violating its 1961 agreement to compete on a unified team. The East German NOC had complained about ice skating trials being hosted in West Berlin in 1963 because it feared for its athletes' safety.[55]

IOC Chancellor Otto Mayer replied to the East German NOC's appeal in July 1964 but deferred the matter until after the Games. "In view of the interest of the Olympic spirit and so as not to mar the positive achievement of the

United German team in the Tokyo Games, it was hoped that your National Olympic Committee would agree to postpone its request until the session following the Games, that is to say in 1965."[56] This meant that German athletes could either play by the rules or stay home. The East German team finally won a concession from Brundage when he declared at the 1964 Tokyo session that the IOC would address the matter of separate and permanent representation in 1965.[57] Brundage reasoned that as the IOC had demanded that NATO countries stop barring East German athletes, it would be consistent and treat East Germany as a separate and recognized entity, but only after the Tokyo Games.[58]

Tangential to the ongoing German problem, the issue of visas for Iron Curtain athletes continued without resolution. Once again, it was East Germany left out, as Britain, France, and the United States all denied its athletes entry in 1962. In January, the Soviet Union filed a complaint with the World Hockey Federation because the State Department had refused visas for the East German team to attend the March world championships in Colorado. According to the State Department, East Germany needed to file applications with the American consulate in West Berlin to secure entry, because it claimed "that had been normal procedure for years."[59] While the World Hockey Federation could have elected to move the championships to a neutral country in response, the event remained on American soil, tacitly endorsing this petty diplomacy.[60] The East German ski team faced similar obstacles in February with the world championships in Chamonix, France. When the French government refused to reverse its decision, the federation decided to hold the meet anyway but announced that it could not be termed a true world championship. Instead, the event became the world games with the assurance given by one official that "Just the label will be changed. It will still be the unofficial world championship."[61] The rest of the Iron Curtain countries responded by boycotting the event, leaving the United States to dominate in their absence.[62] Britain hosted the 1961–1962 European Cup in soccer but refused entry to the East German squad. Its matches, important because they served as World Cup qualifiers, were moved to Malmo, Sweden, inconveniencing both the East Germans and their opponents.[63]

The political overtones were obvious. It was no coincidence that the three most powerful nations who barred East German athletes were the leaders of NATO who opposed the communist de facto takeover of Berlin and the wall.[64] Tensions escalated between east and west as these instances became more frequent. The East German government continued to limit West Berlin travel rights, making it increasingly difficult to pass through the city. The IOC refused to punish any of the NATO countries. Brundage issued only a limited statement similar to the release following the East German difficulties at the Squaw Valley

Olympics that "occurrences of this kind are most regrettable and may have more and more violent repercussions that will threaten the very existence of organized amateur sport and the Olympic Games."[65]

Simultaneously, the IOC warned that any country that refused entry to athletes for political reasons would not host the Games. However, the committee then awarded the 1968 Winter Games to France, the same country that had barred the East Germans in February. As Cold War tensions became too pervasive to ignore, the IOC's stance regarding political affairs was increasingly untenable. The press picked up on how easy it would be to evade the promise to extend visas for all athletes that Brundage forced all cities vying for the Games to sign. As Daley put it, "Once the Games have been organized and the money has been paid out and most teams and tourists are on the scene, agreements can be repudiated with impunity."[66] It was tacitly understood that the IOC had to tread carefully around the United States and other major IOC players because these countries held more influence within the Olympic Movement. An Olympic Games without the Americans or the Soviets would not garner nearly as much interest.[67]

A "Failure" at Innsbruck

Despite President Kennedy's efforts to the contrary, the United States' performance in the 1964 Winter Games was disappointing. The Soviets again topped the medal count, while the United States finished a lackluster eighth. Moscow amassed a total of twenty-five medals to the Americans' paltry six. While considered a major defeat, *Boston Globe* sportswriter Red Smith cautioned his readers against panic, reminding them that American skiers and skaters had only taken home ten medals from Squaw Valley.[68] However, one of these ten was the hockey gold medal, arguably worth more than a single tally in Cold War box score. The Soviets beat Canada for the gold in 1964 with the United States compiling a dismal 2–5 record in Olympic play.[69] This one big loss overshadowed any modest gains that the Americans made in other sports.

Meanwhile, Moscow had little time to bask in its hockey gold or any of its other twenty-four medals, as this success was tempered by the growing problem of its athletes seeking greener pastures. In an indictment of the harshness of the communist system, the 1964 Games boasted of a spike in the number of attempted defections during both the Innsbruck and Tokyo events. The two nations with the most publicized cases were the two satellites that perhaps had experienced the most political upheaval since 1945: East Germany and Hungary. The unrest that the Berlin Wall intended to quell actually spurred a spike in East German defections during the 1964 Olympics. Following the September 1960 travel restrictions, East German residents, particularly East Berliners, had begun to consider the partition of Germany as permanent. With the increasing strictness of the rules and the relatively fewer opportunities open to them, particularly in comparison to their western peers, the impetus to defect was greater than it had been a decade earlier when the reunification of Germany appeared more likely. Though athletes received better treatment than the average East German worker, some still chose to leave each year, often escaping while traveling for international competition.

The Kremlin knew that sending athletes to any competition outside the Iron Curtain brought risk of defection. This had motivated Moscow's insistence on near isolation for all Iron Curtain athletes in Helsinki and explained why the medal winners in Melbourne were escorted directly from the medal podiums to the ships or planes waiting to take them home. But even these drastic measures failed to prevent defections. Just as a small number of East Germans risked their lives each year trying to flee communism through the Berlin Wall, there would always be a small number of athletes willing to sacrifice seeing their family again or competing at the Games in return for a better life away from communism.[70] Several such cases made headlines following the 1964 Games. In Innsbruck, it was women's tobogganer Ute Gaehler who reportedly reached West Germany safely. She had made the unified German team as an alternate but was not needed to race, so her leaving did not necessarily hurt the team.[71] When queried on the matter, the East German delegation said that it had prohibited its athletes from contacting the defector or speaking to her should she reach out to them, reminding the world of the isolation that those who left faced. At the same time, thirteen other Iron Curtain residents, who were not Olympic athletes, asked the Innsbruck police department for political asylum while in Austria for the Games.[72]

Between Innsbruck and Tokyo

The Americans' relative disappointment in Innsbruck rendered more than the typical number of post–Winter Games appeals for improvement. Washington led the campaign for a stronger American team. Senate Majority Leader Hubert Humphrey asked Johnson to advocate for a White House commission on sport. In Humphrey's words, the United States "should never again ... run a mere eighth as we, unfortunately, did in Innsbruck."[73] USOC assistant executive director Lentz echoed this sentiment when he asked Washington to help fund better training facilities. Lentz argued that while the Americans would never have the same advantages in the Winter Games as the Scandinavian countries who benefitted from more snow and longer training seasons, there was much that could be done to help American skaters and hockey players.[74] Even President Johnson, who did not promote national athletics as much as either Eisenhower or Kennedy, understood the need for overall improvement.

Nicholas Rodis, State Department special assistant for athletics and a former baseball and football player at Harvard University, agreed with Humphrey and Lentz. He told the *Boston Globe*, "No sport which involves international competition is a minor sport. We've got to do something to stimulate gymnastics and water polo and cycling, for example, as well as the others. That means interesting athletes in them and providing the facilities for them."[75] Rodis appealed to corporate America to help provide funding and suggested creating an American Olympics, which the Soviet *Spartakiad* might have inspired, to prepare its athletes for tough competition abroad.[76] These possibilities were part of a wider plan that also included reconsidering the infrastructure of the amateur athletics program more broadly. Though quite ambitious, his ideas reflected the level of concern that the Innsbruck results had raised nationwide.

In July 1964, Attorney General Robert Kennedy embraced this cause, penning an article for *Sports Illustrated* that evoked his brother's words from two years earlier. Now Kennedy reminded the American public of the Olympics' political importance. From his blunt opening line, "part of a nation's prestige in the cold war is won in the Olympic Games," he made the obvious connection between politics and sport.[77] Kennedy articulated his belief that the United States was falling behind the Soviets and warned of serious repercussions should this continue. He, like Brundage and others, feared that Americans were growing complacent and could lose their status as world leader—at least in perception if not reality—should their Olympic performance not improve. "In this day of international stalemates nations use the scoreboard of sports as a visible measuring stick to prove their superiority over the 'soft and decadent' democratic way of life. It is thus in our national interest that we regain our Olympic superiority—that we once again give the world visible proof of our inner strength and vitality."[78]

Kennedy reiterated the importance of the Olympic Games as a proxy Cold War battleground less than three months before the opening of the Tokyo Games, employing some of the Soviets' own anti–American rhetoric to serve his point. One of the Kremlin's favorite arguments was that the United States was soft and complacent. Their decadence would lead to Soviet triumph in the Cold War. Kennedy reviewed the composite American performance in the Games since World War II, to show that the United States trailed the Soviets in the medal count and arguing that this relative backslide could be interpreted to mean that the Soviets were winning the overall Cold War. Writing in the context of the Bay of Pigs disaster and the Cuban Missile Crisis, he argued that sports were more critical than ever to diplomacy. "During a military or nuclear stalemate such as the world is now experiencing, athletics can become an increasingly important factor in international relations."[79] While neither the United States nor the Soviet Union could conceivably claim total Cold War victory in 1964, he argued that a better showing at the Olympics would keep Washington in the race, at least temporarily.

Kennedy outlined an action plan for improved physical fitness among all Americans. Admittedly, several of his suggestions such as the formation of "a comprehensive, nationwide program to recruit and train athletic talent," were Olympic-driven, yet he also called for a wide-ranging program to increase fitness among American children.[80] Kennedy did not neglect the Olympics as an end in themselves and expounded on the need to improve American performance in all sports at the Games. He echoed Rodis' appeal for improvement across the board. "Hopefully, interest in athletics in this country can be broadened to include some of the so-called nonindigenous sports. Cycling, canoeing, judo, soccer, luge, Nordic skiing, and gymnastics are just a few examples.... Other countries have taken up sports identified with us—baseball, basketball, and volleyball, for instance—with success. We need to interest young people in unfamiliar sports or concede further slippage in international competitions."[81] Without explicitly mentioning the Soviet Union, Kennedy clearly tied Olympic achievement to Cold War victory.

Kennedy, whose influence within the Johnson administration was waning, pushed for more governmental involvement in sport, in a sense negating the ongoing American critique of the Soviets tainting their athletes with politics. "A sympathetic government at all levels would help to encourage overall effort. While participation in amateur athletics is up to individuals and private groups, cooperative governments can ease the way."[82] Again summoning Rodis, he proposed what he termed "a kind of national Olympics," which one could easily compare to the Soviet *Spartakiad*, their quadrennial athletic competitions which served as training events for Olympic hopefuls. American derisions of state-sponsored Soviet athletes to the contrary, Kennedy spoke for many when he articulated the need for a system that resembled Moscow's. He suggested that perhaps this was the best chance of reclaiming traditional American dominance at the games. In other words, if you can't beat them, join them. While it may seem strange today for the attorney general to write in a sports magazine that more Olympic medals in judo or luge are critical to American diplomatic success, Kennedy's piece was a reflection of his times and an indicator of the Cold War's reach.

Many shared Kennedy's opinion that not only should the United States embrace the same tactics as the Soviets, but that they would have to if they wanted the chance of ever beating them. Humphrey had remarked in 1963, "If the Battle of Waterloo was won on the playing fields of Eton, the Cold War can be won in the schools, gymnasia, and playgrounds of this nation."[83] These words epitomized just how important the Olympics became during the Cold War. However, committees formed with the objective of Olympic fundraising, such as the one chaired by former U.S. Army Officer and future USOC president Franklin Orth, were denounced as frivolous because "it is difficult to believe that democracy can be saved only by speed of foot."[84] Another later abandoned suggestion was a campaign intended to pressure the IOC to end its ban on professional athletes. This in turn would allow the USOC to recruit professional hockey and basketball players and would level the playing field with the Soviet Union. It would save Washington from spending millions of dollars developing amateur sports on the same level of the pros with only the earning prospects separating the two.[85] Despite a plethora of suggestions and appeals, there were few changes made to America's sporting infrastructure before Tokyo. Johnson proved less interested in promoting White House involvement in athletics or increasing American medal chances in Tokyo, as he needed to focus more on the impending 1964 election.

Tokyo

As usual, the sporting propaganda war heated up in the weeks before the Tokyo Games. Articles ran in newspapers across America criticizing Moscow's focus on Olympic glory, including the following from the *New York Times* in early October. "The USSR exhorts its athletes ideologically. *Soviet Sport* criticizes any lack of an 'aggressive, militant character.' ... There are no amateurs in organized Communist athletics."[86] The charges against Soviet professionalism here were nothing new; by this point, it was commonly accepted that Brundage was willing to accept professionals from the Soviets only while holding the Americans to a higher standard. This unequal treatment infuriated American sportswriters and fueled other complaints regarding politics and the Games, eliciting a shared sense of frustration that there was little recourse. In expounding the inherent differences between the two societies and griping about how the Soviets were cheating and tainting the Olympic spirit through their tactics, the press used politics to excuse what were becoming consistent American second-place finishes in the Olympic medal count.

Meanwhile, behind the Iron Curtain, the Soviets extolled their relative improvement in basketball. In the Tokyo Olympic preview, the Soviet Olympic committee reminded its chief competition, "It is not so long ago that Soviet basketballers were inferior to the sportsmen of the USA, the original home of basketball. But, today, Soviet teams—not only the selected team of the country, but also those of Soviet republics—frequently beat their American rivals."[87] Arthur Daley warned in March 1964 that though the American men's basketball team had yet to play a truly close game in Olympic competition, the rest of the world was catching up. "The gap has narrowed tremendously. The Americans can no longer laugh their way to victory. They have to work for it."[88] Olympic team coach Hank Iba echoed these concerns and warned against overconfidence going into the tournament. "I'm afraid that the American people think this will be easy…. It won't be. International basketball is improving at such a phenomenal rate that other countries are either catching up with us or—this scares me—have already caught up."[89] Nonetheless, the American team had the last laugh and won bragging rights for the next four years when it defeated the Soviets in the gold medal game. The Americans started sluggishly in the finals, betraying a sense of nervous energy that had been largely absent in prior gold medal contests. With the United States never having never lost a game in Olympic play, it was the Soviets who played like they had nothing to lose in the opening minutes.[90] By halftime though the stars and stripes were up 39–31. They never looked back after that, running away with a 73–59 win, its forty-seventh straight Olympic victory.[91] Despite the double-digit triumph, concern abounded that the United States was witnessing the end of its monopoly on the Olympic basketball gold medal.

When looking past the seemingly relentless political struggles that had prefaced the 1964 Olympiads, the Games themselves were notable in that the actual athletic events were less tainted by nationalism than either the 1956 or 1960 contests had been. As could be expected, the United States and the Soviet Union perceived each other as its main competition in Tokyo. In its preview of the Games, the *New York Times* highlighted a number of anticipated Soviet-American matchups to watch for and warned the American public that its most hated rival could take home as many as fifty gold medals. Moscow anticipated podium finishes even in sports where they did not traditionally factor into the medal count, because its team planned to compete in every event except field hockey and soccer.[92] Again, the emphasis was on medal quantity, not necessarily on the sports that drew the biggest audiences.

The USOC also tried to widen the range of sports in which it hoped to medal. The White House had taken to heart pledges made after Rome to increase medal chances in non-indigenous sports. The superpowers continued to fight for all-around Olympic dominance and to fixate on the medal count, yet there were fewer instances of direct competition between the superpowers on the playing fields than in past Games, with one exception being the American-Soviet men's basketball game. The Americans finished only six medals behind the Soviets in the final medal tally—but again, many feared that the Soviets matched America's sporting prowess and would soon eclipse the United States altogether, if they had not already. Perhaps Iba said it best when he told Arthur Daley, "the day of the soft touch in Olympic competition is over.... We, as a nation, can no longer take for granted the fact that all we need to do to win is enter a team. The rest of the world is catching up with us fast, and they'll overhaul us if we don't watch out."[93]

While Iba feared that the rest of the world would soon eclipse the United States on the court, the Soviets were looking over their shoulders at a much improved American squad from the one they had beaten soundly in Innsbruck. The Soviet Union amassed an impressive ninety-six medals in Tokyo with the United States finishing with ninety. Not lost on Shirley Povich and his American sportswriting peers was that the Americans had accumulated more gold medals than Moscow. Povich argued the Soviets technically won the medal count but they "needed a slew of silver and bronzes to firm up this claim.... It serves the Russians well to use their ruble count to show they won the Olympics. But actually there is no unanimity in Moscow that they did."[94] But even Moscow was less than enthused with the final tally. *Pravda* declared their ninety-six medals, down slightly from the 109 they had amassed in Rome, "disappointing."[95]

In addition to its sixth straight basketball gold medal, the stars and stripes dominated a relatively small number of sports, despite the Kennedys' appeals for diversification. All thirty-six of its golds came in only six sports: basketball, track, boxing, rowing, shooting, and swimming.[96] While Moscow was a bit more even in its medal distribution, the Soviets collected nearly twenty percent of its medals—nineteen—in gymnastics. However, the Japanese team was beginning to cut into Moscow's monopoly on this sport.[97] As usual, the Americans were the ones to beat on the track. Their twenty-four medals—including fourteen gold—represented a slight decline from Rome, but one that merited little press scrutiny.[98] Al Oerter won the discus gold medal for the third straight Games while Wyomia Tyus took home the women's 100-meter gold, earning her the title fastest woman alive.[99] The Americans' performance in the pool inspired Povich to fawn over "the greatest track and swimming teams that America ever sent to any Olympics."[100] The men's team won nine of a possible twelve gold medals while the women collected seven of their own.[101] This commanding performance went a long way in dulling the sense of failure that many felt following the Innsbruck Games and in restoring faith in the American athletic establishment. While there was always room for improvement—and beating the Soviets outright remained the main goal—there was less anxiety and fewer demands for improvement following Tokyo than there had been the previous winter.

While the American team left Tokyo in much better spirits than it had Innsbruck—or any Games since the Soviets began competing, the Soviets went home wondering where they had gone wrong. They found themselves in a position comparable to the Americans after Rome—deliberating how to fix their Olympic team and meet the high expectations they had set for themselves before the Games, a situation not lost on American sportswriters. The Soviets had won the overall medal count once again, yet they did not perform nearly as well as most had anticipated. Arthur Daley phrased this letdown bluntly. "Humiliating is the only word that fits the Soviet debacle. The Russians won only two men's events. The United States won 12, which is as many as the rest of the world combined…. It had to be close to disaster for the Red brothers. They have slipped back, and it has to be mortifying for them to realize that the American way is the better way."[102]

The demanding Soviet government had not only predicted but had come to expect excellence in all sports. That the Americans had taken home the gold in both top visibility sports—track and basketball—made this sense of failure even more bitter. To make matters worse, the Soviets could not help but glance over their shoulder to see their satellites catching up to them in athletic prowess and medal haul. Unlike in Rome, Bulgarian wrestlers were no longer throwing matches to ensure a Soviet gold medal. Instead, these smaller countries helped the United States to chip away at the Soviets' stranglehold on the medal count.[103]

Compounding its disappointments in the field and on the court, Moscow still had to grapple with the growing defection problem in Tokyo. The west reaped coveted propaganda fodder, spinning these cases as indicators of ongoing discontent behind the Iron Curtain. The *Washington Post* ran a story in advance of the Tokyo Games depicting escape attempts as part of life for athletes in communist countries. East Germany had become a real problem for the Kremlin because its forced alliance with the West German delegation eased defection, forcing team officials to emulate the Soviets' isolation in Helsinki.[104] With the number of defections increasing, team officials made a concerted effort to prevent athletes from socializing, traveling, or even dining with western peers so that arrangements could not be made for desertion. East German authorities accused West Germany of trying to steal its athletes by tempting them into defecting, but the IOC deigned not to react.[105]

While the Kremlin identified East Germans as most likely to defect, they were not the only ones. News of Khrushchev's fall from the Soviet premiership reached Tokyo during the Games, inspiring those who feared a crackdown under a new leader to seek asylum in Japan or elsewhere rather than returning home.[106] A Hungarian athlete and two tourists also took advantage of Tokyo's relative proximity to Alaska and sought political asylum in Anchorage during the Summer Games.[107] A security cordon met the trio to shield them from any possible Soviet efforts to recapture them, though Moscow chose not to pursue them. Those who came to the United States often benefitted from this type of protection intended to deter any possible action by their home governments to force their return home. These defectors, and another separate group, all confirmed that they had family or other connections already in America. The west continued to publicize these stories as anti-communist propaganda, yet there was less fanfare surrounding these emigrations than there had been in 1956, a reflection of how the Cold War had changed since Melbourne.

In the end, the 1964 Games contained their share of Cold War intrusions, though perhaps these tensions were not as ubiquitous as they had been in either Melbourne or Rome. The German question remained largely unsettled, though the animosity between east and west hinted at a coming showdown. Once again, neither superpower could truly claim victory, though there was somewhat of a shift in the summer contests, as the United States inched closer to Moscow in terms of the total medal count. In some ways, the Soviets' relative decline in the production of dominant athletes and commanding performances at the Olympics was both a symptom of the increasingly turbulent political situation in Moscow and a sign of even greater turmoil to come in the years between Tokyo and Mexico City. At the same time, the United States could take heart in its continued strength in basketball and swimming. These gains paralleled how the Kennedy administration had renewed its confidence in dealing with the Kremlin following its successes with the Cuban Missile Crisis and the signing of a nuclear test ban treaty. However, this sense of resurgence proved fleeting, as the next four years would prove as tumultuous in Washington as they would be behind the Iron Curtain.

CHAPTER 8

1968

Politics as Main Event

"Olympic officials tell you that they will allow no politics in their playpen, yet instead their very format encourages tasteless nationalism and stifling of individualism. Maybe it runs fairly smoothly, but it's not what the Olympics was meant to be, and not what it should be."
— *Boston Globe* sportswriter Bud Collins[1]

The United States won the overall medal count at the 1968 Summer Olympics in Mexico City for the first time since 1952. While this should have brought great pride, the accomplishment was largely forgotten in the aftermath of the Black Power demonstration, which distracted the American press and infuriated the IOC. Even today, the most lasting image of the Games is the clenched fist salute exhibited by two American track stars, Tommie Smith and John Carlos, on the podium when receiving their medals for their respective first and third place finishes in the 200-meter final.[2] This brief yet unmistakable gesture was a clear reminder of the growing politicization of the Games and the domestic unrest in the United States. Rather than the demonstrations of patriotism that were quite common during Olympic medal ceremonies, Smith and Carlos used a very visible global stage, made even more so by television, to show that all was not well either at the Games or at home. Suddenly, their protest quickly overshadowed their feats on the track and the Americans' performance in Mexico City more broadly, stirring up a political and media storm that today is still synonymous with the 1968 Games.

In many ways, 1968 marked a turning point for the Olympic Movement and for the Cold War more generally. By this time, politics had become impossible for the IOC to ignore. While high-intensity confrontations like the Bay of Pigs invasion and the Cuban Missile Crisis were the hallmark of the four years between the Rome and Tokyo Games, transition characterized the period

During the 1968 medal ceremony for the men's 200-meter race, Australian runner Peter Norman faces forward as American track stars Tommie Smith and John Carlos give the Black Power salute to draw attention to the ongoing civil rights crisis. Civil rights was just one problem President Johnson faced in the waning days of his administration (© 2016 / Comité International Olympique (CIO) / United Archives).

from Tokyo to Mexico City. Both superpowers experienced a number of significant domestic changes that in turn affected the course of the Cold War so that by the fall of 1968, the conflict had evolved greatly to something nearly unrecognizable to the Kennedy-Khrushchev years. Yet, the intense competition between American and Soviet athletes remained palpable at the Mexico City Games. The strength of this rivalry reminded all that both sides still perceived the Olympics as a Cold War battleground. Meanwhile, politics continued to haunt the IOC. In addition to the dramatic Black Power display in Mexico City, politics reigned behind the scenes. While the question of German representation was finally resolved, the IOC now grappled race issues and the seemingly endless East German visa issues.

Wars at Home

Increasing domestic upheaval and Vietnam War drama made United States a volatile place by the latter half of the Johnson administration. The Democrats seemingly could do nothing right, with Johnson pulling out of the presidential race early and leading presidential candidate Robert Kennedy's untimely death leading to the default selection of Vice President Hubert Humphrey to run against Nixon in 1968. The outcome was the first Republican presidential victory in twelve years, ostensibly a condemnation of Johnson's mismanagement in Vietnam and a call for a change in Washington. Nixon's ascent to the presidency marked another turning point in the Cold War, as his presidency ushered in the brief era of détente. Together Soviet general secretary Leonid Brezhnev and Nixon proved more devoted to lessening the Cold War strain through a relaxing of tensions than to renewing the rivalry.

Also distracting attention from the Cold War was the ongoing American civil rights struggle. African American activists were growing increasingly militant, hoping to speed the road to racial equality. This intensification of efforts soon spread to the Olympic Movement, as several prominent black athletes threatened to boycott the Mexico City Games to protest the lack of progress. Opinions about the efficacy of a boycott were mixed though, among both black and white athletes and officials. Many of these men and women had spent their whole lives training for the chance to compete at the Games. They did not want to miss this once in a lifetime opportunity. For others, beating the Soviets was more important than the limited gains they anticipated from a protest.[3] By 1968, the Johnson administration was so mired in Vietnam that there was much less focus on civil rights than there had been at the beginning of his tenure.[4]

Like the United States, the Soviet Union was mired in a number of ongoing challenges, as political unrest shook Eastern Europe. Similarly to the Hungarian Revolution twelve years earlier, the Prague Spring exposed serious cracks in the Iron Curtain. Americans reacted with horror to Brezhnev's dispatch of the Red Army to Prague in August, but Washington was in no position to intervene. The Kremlin later explained its response with what became known as the Brezhnev Doctrine, arguing that a threat to socialism in one country was a threat to socialism in all countries and must be treated as such. Therefore, Moscow needed to take decisive action to prevent a domino effect. While Washington worried that the Soviets might use this policy to create new satellites, the White House's growing list of concerns limited the American response. Having decided not to run for reelection, Johnson was a lame duck with limited recourse. The White House had few options in part because of its timing but also because no one wanted another confrontation with Moscow. The United Nations denounced Moscow's brutality, but took no action. As the Brezhnev Doctrine effectively deterred dissent until Poland began to push for reform in 1980, there proved to be little need for enforcement throughout the 1970s.[5] After 1968, the instances of active protest behind the Iron Curtain waned for more than a decade, as the Moscow government passed a series of measures intending to quell the unrest. These included stricter passport control and harsher punishment of those accused of hooliganism, but at the same time, they passed wage increases that the country could not afford, turned a blind eye toward the flourishing black market, and even used bribery to retain a sense of order.[6]

Washington's inaction marked a definitive change of course from the early years of the Cold War and it demonstrated how the priorities in Washington had changed since the Truman years. The White House had its hands full already with the losing battle in Vietnam and an American public that was unlikely to tolerate another foreign war, especially one with the Soviet Union that could potentially involve nuclear weapons. Instead, the Soviets felt comfortable and justified in interceding in Prague; however, Brezhnev's attention was also divided among a multitude of other problems. He was personally reluctant to send tanks into Prague, and delayed assertive action because he feared a UN or American counterstrike. Nonetheless, the Politburo decided that the military was necessary when negotiations with the Czechs failed.[7]

Together the Prague Spring, the United States' ongoing Vietnam nightmare, American racial unrest, and Nixon's subsequent victory explained why the Cold War was not the same all-consuming conflict by 1968 that it had been just five years earlier. Johnson never approached the Cold War with the same gusto and fiery rhetoric as his predecessor in part because of Vietnam, but also because he was more interested in domestic policy issues like civil rights and

This photograph from the October 1967 March for Peace in front of the Pentagon shows just how unpopular the Vietnam War had become by the latter half of Lyndon B. Johnson's administration. Fallout from Vietnam and other domestic struggles distracted Johnson from the same type of commitment to the Cold War and the Olympic Movement that Kennedy had shown (LBJ Library Photo by Frank Wolfe).

the war on poverty. While the Soviet response to the uprisings in Prague horrified Washington and the American public, there was much less external criticism than there had been in 1956. It was clear by 1968 that both superpowers were facing the most serious challenges to their respective hegemonies since 1945. Another factor was the worldwide unrest now commonly associated with that year. A confluence of forces that largely originated during the first half of the decade caused so much upheaval that the superpowers largely found themselves at a loss as to where to reassert control. Each had more than enough to concern them at home without renewing hostilities.[8]

The theory behind détente stemmed from the Cuban Missile Crisis. Following this tense altercation, both sides realized how close they had come to using nuclear weapons and how much they wished to avoid another similar situation. The 1963 Nuclear Test Ban Treaty was a first step in this direction. The subsequent changes in leadership on both sides also helped to calm Cold War tensions for the remainder of the decade. Brezhnev proved to be a less volatile leader than Khrushchev, while Johnson was more interested in his domestic agenda and became mired in Vietnam. By August 1968 when the

Warsaw Pact countries invaded Czechoslovakia to quell the Prague Spring demonstrations, the Cuban Missile Crisis was a distant memory as both countries increasingly dealt with challenges to their domestic authority.

Détente was an outgrowth of this focus on the mass uprisings at home. It was a tacit agreement between Moscow and Washington to work together to present a united front against the popular upheaval that each faced. It emphasized stability and continuity in lieu of reform or change as a means of preventing further disturbances.[9] This policy, which Nixon and Brezhnev employed through the early 1970s, definitively altered the tone of the Cold War. There was less competition for science and military breakthroughs than during the Eisenhower administration and little of the warlike rhetoric of the Kennedy years. There was no mention of reviving the Truman Doctrine to help save the Czechs from communist oppression. Instead, Radio Free Europe received specific instructions that "no direct appeal be made to the Russian troops and that no change in the program be made which would differentiate it from the broadcasts that regularly go to the Soviet Union. He asked that we be particularly careful to comply with this policy requirement."[10] The rationale for this caution was the evolving Cold War, coupled with the changes at home. Simply put, the Johnson administration could not afford to become entangled in Soviet affairs.

While Moscow's and Washington's implicit agreement to leave each other alone led to an extended period of calm, détente simultaneously stifled any potential progress toward improving relations or in evolving communism to better fit the needs of its constituents. Rather than taking diplomatic risks, both sides became more invested in preserving the status quo to prevent relations from deteriorating further or breaking down altogether.[11] As a result, Moscow largely ignored or quickly suppressed the satellites' appeals for more freedoms without fear of American recourse. The White House largely overlooked Soviet human rights violations to avoid disturbing this new calm. Moscow and Washington toned down their rhetoric, using offers of peace to calm domestic tensions and diverting attention from the widespread unrest that has come to characterize 1968.[12] There was much less emphasis on competition between the superpowers, including the Olympics, for roughly ten years following the 1968 Games. Nonetheless, politics and the Olympic Movement would remain entwined throughout the 1970s and the superpowers' struggles to control the Games would reappear in advance of the 1980 contests.

The Mexican government was also dealing with widespread upheaval throughout the summer of 1968. A vibrant student movement eventually numbering 200,000 rocked the country in advance of the Games.[13] One reason for this burgeoning unrest was the great amounts of money and resources that the Mexican government devoted to hosting the Olympics at a time when the country had so many other pressing needs. Nonetheless, leaders declared that the Games would go on. Students promised not to interfere with the Games themselves, yet labor unions strikes were hindering final preparations, something to which the national government did not take kindly.[14] Events turned tragic on 2 October when police officers began firing into a crowd of student protesters in Tlatelolco Plaza, Mexico City, killing and injuring hundreds of people, the exact numbers of which remain unknown.[15] Now declassified United States National Security Administration documents later showed that the Mexican government was concerned that the student and labor upheaval would disturb the Games in April and asked the Pentagon to supply materials to help quell the protests, should they turn violent.[16] Washington complied, as it associated the demonstrations with a nascent communist movement in Mexico rather than rejection of the Olympics. According to U.S. Embassy documents from July 1968, the Mexican government was blaming "indications of Soviet Embassy complicity" for the growing violence and disruption, an easily accepted claim in Cold War-era Washington.[17]

Media reports throughout the summer linked discontent with the Games to the protests, building speculation that the Olympics might not occur as planned.[18] The upheaval and the harsh reaction by law enforcement on 2 October sanctioned by the Mexican government prompted further uncertainty as to whether the Games would still begin as scheduled ten days later. They did, but the deadly protests cast a long shadow over the events and prompted Washington to increase its security presence at the Games. Fortunately for all, there were no further demonstrations during the Olympics themselves or after the fact.[19] Following the declassification of NSA material in the 1990s, it became public knowledge that Mexico's growing financial concerns had been a contributing factor to these demonstrations.[20] This was another indicator of both how big the Games had become and how entwined they were with politics, even those not directly tied to the Cold War.

The Olympics on the American Homefront

Personality and the changing landscape of the Cold War shaped the White House's relationship with the national sporting establishment during the Johnson years. While Eisenhower and Kennedy had both been enthusiastic participants in and supporters of American sports, Johnson did not share this affinity. As such, he never ascribed the same importance to sports, either recreationally or on the elite/professional level, as his predecessors had. Consequently, he made little impact on the Olympic Movement during his first year in office, which spanned the Innsbruck and Tokyo Games, beyond issuing the standard adulatory message following the Games. With the Tokyo Games transpiring during the 1964 campaign season, it is understandable that Johnson had more pressing concerns than urging Olympic improvement. The president proved fairly apathetic toward American sports even after he was reelected.[21] The American press picked up on this, with *Washington Post* columnist Bob Addie commenting that sports were "an acquired taste" for the commander in chief.[22] Robert Lipsyte of the *New York Times* devoted an entire column to "the present Administration's poor record in sports."[23]

The Johnson years did witness limited attempts to keep the United States competitive in the Olympics before other concerns overshadowed these efforts. Encouraged by a 1965 report demonstrating that American youth had made considerable progress in fitness since the late 1950s, the President's Council on Fitness began to offer annual awards to students ages ten to seventeen who achieved certain levels of physical acuity. Johnson remarked, "It is essential that our young people develop their physical capabilities as well as their mental skills. Sports and other forms of active play promote good health and help provide our country with sturdy young citizens equal to the challenges of the future."[24] The allusion to future challenges lent a Cold War tone to his address. A 1966 U.S. Olympic Development Committee report advised that American athletes needed to diversify their medal prospects or risk losing their status as an athletics superpower. While the United States dominated a few major sports, "the rest of the world was rapidly improving in these sports while becoming dominant in others. Aside from improving performances in its strong sports, the report declared that the American athletes 'must give greater attention to the so-called minor sports, improving our performance in these events in an effort to make up the inevitable losses in sports where we have excelled in the past."[25] The committee specifically asked for improvement in individual sports with multiple medal opportunities, like swimming, gymnastics, and track, over team sports like soccer and basketball with fewer medals there for the taking. The message was that quantity, not quality, mattered in the Cold War medal count, ultimately advising the same strategy that the Soviets had employed for more than a decade—and for which they had earned harsh criticism from the American press. Despite these recommendations, the Johnson White House took few steps to implement any form of widespread campaign.[26]

In light of the president's relative disengagement with the American sporting establishment, it was Vice President Humphrey who assumed Eisenhower's and Kennedy's advocacy mantle. He urged the American public to "buckle down to the task of giving our young people a chance to compete," in an NBC sports special in 1966.[27] He appealed for leniency for full-time workers training for the Games, resurrected the notion of a biannual American sports festival and for the construction of more facilities open to the public, particularly those that would encourage female athletes.[28] That these measures also sounded vaguely like the Soviet program was no coincidence. Catching Moscow was clearly in Humphrey's sights. He reminded the American public after the Tokyo Games that the Soviets "are hardly satisfied that their overall medal total— gold, silver and bronze—surpassed ours 96 to 90…. In the future, we Americans should not be satisfied with anything less than the best possible opportunities for participation by amateur athletes."[29] Humphrey openly campaigned for more Olympic funding as well, following the examples set by Truman, Eisenhower, and Kennedy.[30]

Nonetheless, the Johnson administration made little lasting impact on the sporting Cold War, especially once the growing debacle in Vietnam and rising domestic unrest reached fever pitch. By 1968, Humphrey's enthusiasm had cooled slightly as well. There was little use denying that the country had much bigger problems than improving its medal haul at the Olympics. The State Department sponsored fewer athletes' tours than it had during the 1950s or the first half of the 1960s, both out of a need to tend to more pressing concerns as well as the programs increasingly falling victim to funding cuts.[31] One casualty of the changing Cold War during the Johnson years was the annual Soviet-American track meet. Moscow stirred up fresh controversy in July 1966 when it backed out of the event scheduled in Los Angeles to protest ongoing American involvement in Vietnam.[32] The western media speculated that the issue was a bit different than presented because Soviet track was going through a transition following its relative letdown in Tokyo. The press assumed that Moscow was afraid of losing to the United States yet again, which would translate as an American propaganda victory.[33] These meets had survived the era of the U-2 spying incident, the Berlin crisis, and the Cuban Missile Crisis yet could not weather a conflict in which Moscow had no direct stakes. This meant the next major matchup between the superpowers would wait until the Olympics. Ironically, despite this decline in White House involvement, the Americans performed even better in Mexico City than they had in Tokyo. Their accomplishments attracted little fanfare as politics stole the show, overshadowing this achievement and reminding all that Washington faced as much upheaval as its biggest rival.

Two Germanys, More Politics

Turning to IOC politics, the committee grappled with the German question for a final time in the years between Tokyo and Mexico City, though now the focus turned to exacting the separation of the two teams. While Brundage had acknowledged the need for two German teams in Tokyo, he tried once more to urge a joint team for the 1968 contests. Calling it "in the best interests of the German people," he continued to believe at the end of the 1964 Summer Games that the unified team was the IOC's crowning achievement.[34] However, now even West Germany was unwilling to continue the charade of a joint entry to the Games because the negotiations between the two sides were so hostile and time-consuming. There was little sporting consensus and a slim chance for political reunification, making this combined team an antiquated and idealistic concept. The onset of détente would eventually help in calming tensions between the two Germanys, but at the same time, their division had slowly attained a new sense of permanence over the past few years. Beginning in April 1968, the East German government enacted a new list of travel restrictions aimed at punishing the Federal Republic and forcing the recognition issue. These included barring West German cabinet members from traveling through GDR territory, demanding passports or visas for all western citizens traveling to West Berlin.[35] Détente cooled political fires but also lessened the chances for progress toward better working relationships between east and west.[36]

The new division of German athletes was one side effect of the political changes. A new Soviet sport periodical entitled *Sport in the USSR*, first published in 1963, and notorious for its political-mindedness, soon jumped on the issue. In addition to its reporting on domestic sporting feats, Olympic performances, and Spartakiads, the monthly magazine voiced the official Soviet opinion on the ongoing German question. In a 1965 appeal for separate representation, Soviet NOC member Roman Kiselyov took to its pages in much the same manner that the Kennedys used *Sports Illustrated* to voice their concerns regarding American fitness.

> Unfair though the IOC decision was, the sports organizations of the German Democratic Republic carried it out to the letter.... Athletes of the German Democratic Republic compete as independent teams in all European and world championships, but not in the Olympics. Furthermore, to win an Olympic berth they have to go through a series of strenuous qualifying meets with the athletes of another country, the situation is clearly abnormal.[37]

Finally the IOC began to accept the political reality, with this admission helping East Germany to earn the right to its own team for the 1968 Games.

Schobel wrote to Brundage before the 1965 IOC session to remind him that he had affirmed the need for two teams in Tokyo. He emphasized that even Daume, who until very recently had championed the unified team as a means of keeping the East German NOC under his control, now favored separate representation. Schobel argued that East Germany met all of the IOC's membership requirements because it had a stable government and because IOC recognition "does not imply political recognition, as this is outside the competence of the International Olympic Committee."[38] He reasoned that the IOC should not withhold recognition simply because Bonn and the NATO countries refused to establish diplomatic ties. Schobel recalled the problems that joint representation had posed in 1964, from bickering over Olympic trial venues to a long disagreement over the selection of a flag for the joint team. He closed his letter by turning Brundage's token statement of the unified team showing up the diplomats on its head. "Contrary to your view that the combined German Olympic team is a victory of sport over politics, our NOC, on the basis of its experiences made in recent years, arrived at the conclusion that under the present political conditions in Germany, it would be a victory of sport over politics, if independent teams would compete in the Olympic Games."[39] Continuing the unified team had become an exercise in futility while allowing two teams would let sport take center stage without as many political distractions.

When the IOC convened in Madrid in October 1965, East Germany applied a final time for official and separate recognition. Brundage feared the implications of granting this before the Grenoble Games because France remained unwilling to admit an East German delegation.[40] He threatened again to move the Olympics if the Paris government would not change its position, leading a member of the French delegation to assure that there would not be a problem. A desire to bring the 1972 Summer Olympics to Paris was the likely rationale for this sudden change of heart, as the IOC would surely reject this bid should the French government bar East Germany from Grenoble.[41] The status of divided Berlin was another tangential concern to the wider German problem. If each Germany achieved separated recognition, would West Berlin push for its own team because it was isolated from the rest of the country?[42] The larger question quickly eclipsed this matter, but it was a logical outgrowth of the German situation, given the incessant bickering over rights to the city throughout the past two decades.

A long debate on the first day of the annual session failed to resolve the issue, as the board was divided rather evenly. While West Germany had pushed for the continuity of the current arrangement as recently as 1964, it had grown tired of the constant bickering with the east and the organization quandaries surrounding the unified team. The IOC discussed the possibility of a compromise where a unified team would compete in Grenoble to evade the visa issue with full East German recognition promised for the Mexico City Games.[43] However, Schobel firmly opposed this scenario, telling the committee, "There has been no talk of a compromise as far as we know. We want an East German team in both Mexico City and Grenoble."[44] The IOC decided the following day that "there will be separate teams however they will march under the same banner, use the same hymn and the same emblems."[45] In this settlement, the committee designated West Berlin part of West Germany and East Germany as inclusive of East Berlin.

The East German NOC scored another victory in 1967 when IOC secretary general J.W. Westerhoff announced that beginning with the 1972 Games, the German teams would be completely separate. As such, each team would use its own flag and play its own anthem at the medal ceremony whenever one of its athletes won gold.[46] The IOC voted on this policy and made it official at its Mexico City session in 1968.[47] Brundage acknowledged this change in a letter to Schobel where he announced that beginning 1 November 1968, the East German NOC would be referred to formally as Germany DR going forward."[48]

The politicization of sport continued relentlessly even once the German matter reached conclusion. While the West German NOC had supported separate German teams, its sporting federations balked when it came to executing this new policy. In this regard, 1966 proved to be a particularly trying year. The Bonn government filed a protest in March when the European Track and Field Commission announced its decision to provide for two German teams competing under separate flags at the European championships.[49] The Commission overruled these objections and allowed both German teams to compete. East Germany walked away with seventeen medals to lead all nations. In October, the Bonn government discussed an official policy regarding sporting events where two German teams were invited to compete. Under consideration was whether to boycott these occasions, though this could prove problematic because it could isolate West German athletes from the world stage. Even though West Germany and NATO refused to establish diplomatic ties with the GDR, most international federations and the IOC had begun to recognize East Germany, limiting the efficacy of this stubborn resistance. Additionally, there were few who wished to risk West Germany either boycotting or facing an IOC ban in either the 1968 or the 1972 Games.[50]

Sport in the USSR's critiques of IOC politics continued even once the committee decided to allow two German teams in 1968. Next, the Soviets took issue with the IOC using the name "East Germany" in lieu of its preferred "German Democratic Republic," blaming Brundage's western bias for this infraction. "On orders from their political bosses the supporters of the cold war in sport zealously continue to discriminate against the sports organizations of the German Democratic Republic.... This is overt political interference in the internal affairs of sovereign countries. This situation clearly hinders the development of international sport and lowers the significance and level of major competitions."[51] Here, the Soviets took a cue from Brundage in portraying themselves as above politics, painting a divide between those who were fighting for East German sovereignty, and those who were not, the alleged "supporters of the Cold War."[52]

East Germany's seemingly endless visa problems resurfaced in 1965. France announced that it would not issue visas for a separate East German team for the 1968 Winter Games because it did not recognize East Germany diplomatically. While IOC regulations required the host country for the Games to welcome all delegations, Germany had been still competing as a single entity when the IOC selected Grenoble as host. At the time, French Prime Minister Georges Pompidou had guaranteed that there would not be any issues. Now that there were two Germanys, the French were unwilling to uphold this vow.[53] Instead, France informed the Bonn government that it would not accept East German athletes.

The IOC had begun deliberating potential host cities for the 1972 Summer Olympics concurrently with the issue of German representation. Munich had submitted a bid and many considered it a frontrunner, but there was understandable concern surrounding the prudence of its selection.[54] With so much controversy already surrounding Germany, was it smart to bring the Games to West Germany? Would the Munich organizers or the Bonn government subject East German athletes to the same troubles that had thwarted their attempts to compete in other NATO countries? Also, would East Germany take offense to this selection or refuse to send athletes out of a fear that they would try to defect? With the continued bickering over two teams, there was little chance that the two sides would cooperate enough to present a joint German bid to host. Both East Germany and the Soviet Union opposed Munich for obvious political reasons. The IOC raised its own questions even after Brundage addressed some of these concerns in a letter to Daume in May 1966. At this time, he informed the West German NOC that "Munich would have to receive all National Olympic Committees recognized by the IOC, and that since East Germany is now independently recognized it would be entitled to have its own flag and hymn…. If there is any doubt on this we should know about it now, since we awarded the Games with the understanding that all NOCs would be welcomed with their own flags and hymns."[55]

Brundage asked Britain in 1966 to lift its ban on East German sportswriters in advance of the FIFA World Cup. He also reminded the NATO countries of the impending 1972 host selection. He warned, "they will not be given to any city unless the Government agrees to permit the entry of all countries recognized by the IOC."[56] This threat lost its potency, however, when Brundage and the IOC awarded Munich the Summer Games without first resolving East Germany's ongoing visa problems. Many speculated that this decision would backfire and prove detrimental to the Olympic Movement because an East German travel ban would likely trigger an Iron Curtain boycott. The heightened sense of competition between east and west was one of the most anticipated features of the Games and removing this aspect would kill much of their appeal.[57] As it turned out, the 1972 Games would become memorable for their political overtones, but for more tragic reasons than those that had plagued other Cold War-era contests.

After remaining a background matter for a number of years, the South African apartheid quandary began to wreak havoc on the Olympic Movement during the planning for Mexico City. Though neither the United States nor the Soviet Union was directly involved, apartheid, like many contemporary international politics issues, had tangential Cold War connections. The South African NOC's refusal to allow black athletes to compete had surfaced originally at the 1959 Munich Session when the Soviet NOC complained about discriminatory practices of its team. South African representative Reginald Honey explained the dearth of black athletes on his country's team: "There are 10 and ½ million colored men in this country. These have started to show an interest in Olympism for the last 2 or 3 years only."[58] While the IOC accepted this reasoning, many read Honey's statement as implying that the number of black athletes on the South African team would increase over the next couple of Olympiads. When this failed to occur, the issue arose again in the sessions leading up to the 1968 Games. The IOC had not allowed South Africa to compete in Tokyo but did not suspend its IOC membership either.[59] By 1968, the outcry against South Africa had grown into a global movement, largely because many associated apartheid with colonialism. When the IOC took up the issue, the Soviet Union was firmly in support of dismissing the South Africa delegation from the Olympic Movement while the American delegation opposed this action.

The Soviet Union found itself at the center of this issue, as it correlated South African apartheid with the American involvement in Vietnam and colonialism, disapproving of both strongly. The Soviets called a press conference the day before the Grenoble opening ceremonies to protest the American presence in Vietnam, stating, "The Soviet sportsmen are profoundly disgusted by the American aggression in Vietnam. It is inhuman that the world's youth should die on battlefields instead of competing pacifically in sporting events."[60] The editorial staff at *Sport in the USSR* tackled the issue as well:

> One of the main Olympic aims is the building of a better and more tranquil world. However, some IOC leaders, contending that 'sport and politics do not mix,' have evaded a principled stand on the most important issue of our time, the preservation and consolidation of peace, without which neither sport in general nor the Olympic Games in particular

would be possible.... Soviet sportsmen condemn the US aggression in Vietnam, aggression which every honest minded person in the world regards it as his duty to oppose.[61]

What made this statement particularly inconsistent was its allusion to a principled stand regarding aggression, as the Soviets had a history of brutality toward any attempt at liberalization behind the Iron Curtain. Moscow had used extreme force against its own ally in Hungary in 1956 and would do so again before Mexico City when it crushed the Prague Spring demonstrations.

The Soviet NOC also indicated in Grenoble that it would boycott the Summer Games if South Africa were allowed to compete.[62] When the IOC voted to reinstate South Africa for Mexico City provided it bring an integrated team, a number of nations, mostly African, immediately announced plans to boycott.

The Soviet Union found itself on the fence regarding this issue because the Kremlin was loath to forgo Olympic propaganda opportunities. As columnist Arthur Daley phrased it, "the Soviet Union and other Iron Curtain countries have assiduously been wooing the African countries for years and they could join such a boycott because they are pragmatists and always have used sport for political purposes."[63] While a boycott would likely gain the Soviets some African allies, the cost of staying home was steep. There was a lot of international prestige at stake in the Olympics, particularly when Moscow defeated the United States. Any Iron Curtain medal was a victory for the communist movement as a whole. Additionally, the Soviet NOC did not want to jeopardize its relatively privileged standing within the IOC by upsetting Brundage. By 1968, everyone knew that the Soviet Union was mixing politics and sport, but the IOC largely turned a blind eye to this offense.

The South African dilemma left the Soviet Union in a difficult position in the months between Grenoble and Mexico City. It did not want to commit to a boycott too early, thereby angering Brundage and drawing IOC scrutiny, yet neither it could not wait until the last minute when it was too late for compromise, as doing so would likely sideline its athletes while the South Africans competed.[64] The Soviet vacillation led Brundage to reconsider the IOC's decision to let South Africa compete. Moscow formally asked the committee to ban South Africa in March, offering a veiled threat to boycott and perhaps keep the rest of the Iron Curtain countries home too.[65] A boycott could prove detrimental to the Olympic Movement not only because of the layer of intrigue that U.S.–USSR competitions brought but also because it would have encompassed enough athletes to shrink the Games to a fraction of their normal size. The IOC avoided this potential letdown by voting in a special session to disallow South African participation by a wide margin.[66]

While this ban ended the Soviet boycott threat, political intrusions continued to plague Mexico City. The Soviet-led invasion of Czechoslovakia in August triggered cries that the Soviets should be banned from the Games. These calls were similar to the protests that had followed the Soviet putdown of the Hungarian Revolution, drawing uneasy parallels between the two situations.[67] Once again, Brundage proclaimed that "the Games cannot be used as a political tool."[68] Those who opposed Soviet participation argued that if the IOC banned South Africa for political offenses, the Soviet Union deserved punishment, to no avail. A number of European nations, including Norway and several Iron Curtain countries, threatened to skip the Games if the IOC did not intervene even though the committee had proven extremely reluctant to do so in the past. Since the IOC had refused to act in Berlin in 1936 and in Melbourne in 1956, there was no reason to expect anything different in 1968.[69] In the end, the Soviets competed with little ostensible protest from other countries, apart from the Czech athletes' refusal to sit with the Russians in the dining hall.[70] This was a non-event in comparison to the bloody water polo match that had followed the Hungarian Revolution twelve years earlier, much to the IOC's relief. The lack of repercussions spelled victory for the Soviet Union in that it reinforced Moscow's clout within the IOC and behind the Iron Curtain.

Grenoble

Like Tokyo four years earlier, the Grenoble Games were a relative Soviet disappointment. Though its hockey team won gold again while the American skaters performed poorly, Moscow failed to win the medal count. America newspapers jumped on this, though few noted just how close the final totals were. Norway just edged out the Soviets fourteen medals to thirteen. According to the *Washington Post*, "The rest of the world is just catching up, says Igor Kazanski, vice president of the Soviet National Olympic Committee, borrowing an excuse from bourgeois America."[71] This relative disappointment compounded Soviet fears that they were losing ground in the wider Cold War. This decline was not lost on the American press, as the *Post* referred to it as one of the "features" of the Grenoble Games and in their analysis of the final day of competition, referred to Team Soviet Union as "the fading Russians."[72]

French skier Jean-Claude Killy largely stole the show in Grenoble, winning three gold medals in the downhill, giant slalom, and special slalom events.[73] On the ice, figure skater Peggy Fleming won the first American gold in Grenoble, while three American speed skaters—Dianne Holum, Mary Meyers, and Jennifer Fish—all tied for the silver medal in the 500-meter event.[74] These successes helped to erase some of the disgrace of having eight out of fourteen American skiers fall and injure themselves either in practice runs or during the competition.[75] In all, the United States did not fare much better than it had four years earlier in Innsbruck, yet the fact that the Soviets left without fulfilling lofty expectations tempered this disappointment.

Politics and Protest in Mexico

By 1968, the landscape of global sports had changed dramatically from that surrounding the 1948 Austerity Games just twenty years earlier. While London had been noteworthy for its simplicity and its role in helping the world heal from the horrors of the war, the Mexico City Olympics were distinguished by their size and the elements of pessimism that characterize them even today. Part of this evolution was due to the growth of the world sporting community as more countries became competitive on an international level. More than 7,000 athletes competed from over one hundred countries on six continents.[76] Not only were there more nations—including those behind the Iron Curtain— represented at events like the Olympics and the World Cup, but these nations were increasingly challenging for titles. As *Sports Illustrated* reported in its Mexico City preview, "More and more, the so-called lesser countries are moving into the Olympic spotlight, and others are making an impact in events that historically have not been their province."[77] While it was still Moscow and Washington leading the race for the overall medal count, other countries increasingly forced them to share the spotlight, particularly the East German squad. In short, the Olympics were truly becoming a global competition. This widening of the Games' scope attracted new audiences around the world while also paving the way for the growing commercialization that made the Olympics the lucrative entity they are today. At the same time, the growing global parity in sport lessened the instances of direct one-on-one competition between the superpowers just as détente was taking hold.

While the increasing diversity of the competition had a definitive impact on the Games, television and commercialization wrought even more dramatic effects. The Mexico City contests were the first seen globally on live television.[78] The advent of satellites able to show live pictures around the world helped to multiply the number of spectators for these events, drawing greater interest even from those unable to physically attend the events. Television networks began to compete heavily and to pay large sums of money to the IOC and other sporting administrations for the rights to broadcast sports, farming these costs out to advertisers who proved ready and willing to use this new avenue of promotion.

ABC invested $2 million to show the Grenoble Games, anticipating that advertising revenue would exceed this then-daunting figure and turn it into a worthwhile risk.[79] Understandably, these networks wanted to maximize their viewership to make these considerable expenses pay off and to lure advertisers. The growing television revenue stream meant that the networks began to exercise greater control over major sporting events. Within the span of a decade, "the geography, the economics, the schedules, the esthetics, the very ethos of sport has come to depend upon television's cameras and advertising's monies," as *Sports Illustrated* phrased it in 1969.[80]

Because of the money that television brought, suddenly it was the deciding factor in nearly all aspects of planning major events. Money had become crucial to the Games by this time, with an estimated one billion viewers in North America, Europe and Asia watching some portion of the Mexico City events.[81] The onslaught of television coverage meant that Brundage lost some of his control over the Games, with the tradeoff that television greatly increased spectatorship. Athletic industries were not alone in looking to gain a piece of the pie. Nixon became the first politician to pay for television ads during a sporting event, effectively making his campaign a sponsor of the Games and further complicating the relationship of politics and sport.[82]

With television beginning to make its imprint on the Olympic Movement, rumors that certain marquee countries might not compete in the Games elicited waves of panic among sponsors and advertisers. Growing fears that the IOC might ban the Soviets from Mexico City largely hinged on anticipation of the attention and revenue that these U.S.–USSR matchups attracted, especially now that they were so much more accessible to the general public. Reading the recap in the newspapers was interesting, yet it could not beat actually watching the Games in real time or on tape delay. Simply put, a match between Bulgaria and Norway would never draw half the interest or viewership that a clash of the superpowers would. In this way, television added another layer of drama to the ongoing Cold War on-field feud. As *Washington Post* writer Shirley Povich phrased it, "There are 18 other sports on the Olympic program, but it is the track and field events, pitting Russia vs. the US, that sells out the big stadium for the most revenue. So much of the rest of the Olympic program is carried on the back of track and field, swimming, and boxing."[83] These were the events in which the Soviets and Americans won almost all the golds; the public's familiarity with and the quantity of individual events within these sports made them particularly entertaining for spectators, as there was more pride at stake.

In drawing the most viewership, these major sports also received the most scrutiny on both sides. Soviet and American sportswriters alike continued to critique their rival's way of life as a means of belittling their athletic achievements.

Boxing was a prime example of this in the weeks leading up to Mexico City. A piece appeared in the *New York Times* during the opening days of the Games attributing Soviet weight lifter Leonid Zhabtinsky's anticipated Olympic gold to the advantages reaped by athletes training under the socialist system. "We must realize that his feat cannot exist without space and time, and it was the product of a particular society within a particular culture. There must be some interrelation between Zhabotinsky's feat and the advantages of a socialist system that gives possibilities to workers, students and peasants to practice sport and go to the Olympic Games."[84] His expected victory was a direct result of the system from which he benefitted and not attributable to his own skill and hours of practice. This implied a contrast with the United States where American athletes had to work for a living and train in their limited free time. Soviet athletes had fewer such worries and more practice time.

The quadrennial appeals for changes to the Games to make them fairer to true amateurs and more relevant internationally surfaced in the *Times* as well. "It seems pretty for fencers or weight lifters, say, to represent America while they have been scrounging for four years to get in shape and to get trained in a country unaware of their existence until they are beaten by Eastern Europeans who have done nothing but work out since the last Olympics."[85] In other words, it was futile for Americans to compete and expect to fare well in non-traditional sports against socialist athletes simply because the playing field was so uneven. The American excuses seemed petty, coming as they were from a country where athletes were still so much better off financially and had many other advantages over the majority of their communist and non–Iron Curtain competitors alike, yet many bought into this rhetoric without a second thought.

Press critique was rampant as the Games approached, though perhaps a bit less so than during past Olympiads. One notable American barb came from an Art Buchwald column in September 1968 where he criticized the sloppiness with which the Soviets had invaded Prague, linking this to the Games. "Boganski suggests we announce that the reason the Soviets invaded Czechoslovakia was to scout the Czech Olympic team…. We should say the Soviet soldiers manning the tanks are really Soviet track men in disguise, who did not want to call attention to the real purpose of their visit."[86] While the dialogue here from Buchwald's editorial was clearly farcical, it reflected the changing tone in relations between the superpowers. The piece demonstrated that politics and sport were more entwined than ever before, but also that this rivalry was evolving. Buchwald's was not an obvious criticism of Soviet athletes or their training system. It mocked the Czech invasion more than it did Soviet sport, but also drew attention to the growing anxiety within the Soviet Union regarding its Olympic team, which was not predicted to fare as well as it had in years past.

While Moscow received its share of criticism and bad press during the Prague Spring, the United States was simultaneously grappling with its own problems at home, primarily involving race. Black American athletes had debated boycotting the Games throughout the summer in protest of the lack of sanctions against South Africa and the USOC's position against expelling the South African NOC from the Olympic Movement. Even after the IOC formally banned South Africa from Mexico City, African American athletes continued to mull the possibility of skipping the Games because they opposed the IOC's indifference toward racism, the ongoing American involvement in Vietnam, and American civil rights violations.[87]

In the end, this contingent of black athletes decided to compete, though sprinter John Carlos warned of possible demonstrations which "won't be anything serious but will be dramatic and they will go on throughout the Games."[88] The most brazen display came during the medal ceremony for the 200-meter dash on 16 October where Tommie Smith, the gold medalist, and Carlos, who finished third, each wore a single black glove and raised his fist in a Black Power salute while "The Star-Spangled Banner" played.[89] Brundage, historically insensitive to racial issues, wasted no time in demanding Smith's and Carlos's removal from the Olympic Village and even threatened more serious action against the USOC if the pair did not obey his orders.[90] The USOC complied because it feared that all of its athletes would be expelled from the Games, but made clear that its disappointment pertained to the timing of Smith's and Carlos's statement and not the action itself.[91] The USOC reluctantly apologized for the incident and promised that there would not be any further protests under pressure from Brundage, but would have preferred to pretend that nothing had happened.

The demonstration put the White House in a tough position. On the surface, it was negative publicity at a time when the Johnson administration was already drowning in a sea of bad press. Many within his inner circle had been reluctant to address the obvious race issues before the Games, now this hesitation backfired. The administration went to great lengths to publicize Johnson's meeting with gold medalist George Foreman after the Games, but released no official statement regarding the Black Power salute.[92] Fear of both foreign and domestic repercussions led the White House to ignore the incident, echoing the USOC's stance. Johnson, a lame duck president with much bigger concerns distracting him, had few options. Instead of promoting the outstanding black athletes to refute the Kremlin's frequent charges that the United States was a nation of racial inequality, Johnson had stood by idly as tensions between black American athletes and the IOC had grown throughout 1968. Now, his administration found itself facing the consequences of this inaction.

The Soviets tried to spin on the Black Power demonstration to their advantage. As track coach Gabriel Korobkov put it, "It's too bad.... They are supposed to [be] free people. It wouldn't happen to us. We don't mix sport and politics."[93] *Sport in the USSR* did not let this golden opportunity to critique American politics pass unnoticed. Writer Boris Bazunov exalted in the incident, as it disproved the idea of a unified, harmonious United States. "What courage it must have taken to deliver such an open challenge to the American establishment and hated racism.... All this—the clenched fists, the black berets and gloves—is a silent cry of pain and protest by talented athletes at the moment of their highest sporting achievement."[94] This reaction was just one of many in support of Carlos and Smith, though one of the few exclusively critical of the United States. Other negative reactions were more focused on the choice of venue or the meaning of the gesture rather than on ongoing American racial tensions. For the Soviets, this was a chance to atone for their loss in the medal count. Even though the Americans made more appearances on the podium, Moscow could take comfort in the fact that all was not well on the American home front. Just as the Kremlin faced opposition in Prague, the White House was drowning in its own struggles both in Vietnam and among its own people.

Just as Americans had reveled in the chinks in the Soviet armor as revealed by the Hungarian and Czech uprisings, Moscow now had its chance to exploit signs of unrest among Washington's constituency. On the whole, world reaction to the demonstration was mixed, as many perceived it as a just political statement in a poorly selected venue. In the emergency meeting that Brundage called to discuss the protest, one of the Soviet representatives actually went as far as to state, "The Soviet Union has never used the Olympic Games for political propaganda."[95] The whole experience only served to remind the IOC of just how political the Mexico City Games were from start to finish, with the Black Power salute providing one more distraction along the way.

Brundage's overreaction and demands that the offending pair be expelled from the Games took what was a minor incident in the Black Power salute and blew it out of proportion. While the IOC consistently described itself as apolitical, its actions in 1968 refute this claim. Bud Collins described this discrepancy quite aptly when he wrote, "Olympic officials tell you that they will allow no politics in their playpen, yet instead their very format encourages tasteless nationalism and stifling of individualism. Maybe it runs fairly smoothly, but it's not what the Olympics was meant to be, and not what it should be."[96] Brundage took issue with these athletes drawing attention to themselves for something other than their feats on the field. While the United States finally managed to eclipse the Soviet Union's medal total, the protest diverted global attention from this accomplishment. Perhaps the Associated Press best captured the essence of these Games when it termed them "an event born in chaos and nurtured in bitterness."[97] More than forty years later, these Games are not remembered for the athletic feats but for their politics.

While denouncing the so-called Soviet professionals, the American press steered clear of the ongoing race wars in stories reflecting American triumphs at the Games, as well as the fallout from the Black Power salute on the medal stand. Instead, newspapers focused on the fact that the Soviet women failed to win any track gold medals while "even the Kenyans, with their miniscule squad, outscored the Russian men."[98] When the United States won the medal count for the first time since the Soviets' debut in 1952, it voiced its glee with a series of self-congratulatory remarks that must have rankled Brundage. Some of these smug outpourings turned downright chauvinistic. "Observers noted that the Soviet women were not of the masculine, thick-shouldered type that marked previous Games but were trim and pretty with natural feminine weaknesses for lipstick, rouge and nice coiffeurs. They couldn't throw as far but they turned more eyes."[99] This demeaning remark was just one example of how the superpowers tended to stereotype and degrade the other, even as the Olympic Games were changing and their shared monopoly on the medal stand was disintegrating.

Given the growing trouble at home, the United States could have used a strong and uncontroversial performance in Mexico City to boost its morale. However, events at the Summer Games only added to this sense of chaos. The demonstration on the medal stand showcased to all, including the Soviets, the growing discontent and unrest within the United States.[100] The Mexico City Games marked a point of transition for the U.S. Olympic Movement, as overriding domestic and Vietnam concerns really detracted from the amount of time and resources that the White House could devote to winning the Games. Coming changes in Washington and shifts in the Cold War would radically alter how both superpowers would treat sport, and especially the Olympics after 1968.

Following the Games, the Kremlin called for a reorganization of the Soviet Olympic program under a new leader as a means of preparing better for 1972.[101] Even the moment from which it could have gained the most propaganda fodder, the controversy surrounding the Black Power salute, was not as fruitful as it might have originally seemed because only the IOC—and particularly Brundage—was truly appalled by the demonstration. Other NOCs, including the United States, had a more temperate reaction, feeling that while the timing was wrong, the sentiments expressed were not out of place. The one taunt the

Soviets did slide into post–Olympic reflections was to exalt in the accomplishment of separate East German and North Korean teams with permanent representation on the IOC.

> After a long and persistent battle by progressive elements, the rights of athletes from the German Democratic Republic and the Korean People's Democratic Republic were acknowledged. Proponents of the Cold War tried at length to depreciate these two sovereign nations. They gave the GDR and the KPDR teams artificial designations and demanded that their national anthems should not be played, nor their national flags raised at official contests. But justice triumphed![102]

The unnamed author's inflammatory rhetoric ostensibly linked the IOC with western control and the Cold War. However, the decision to finally grant East Germany permanent recognition was the proper one, as it was increasingly evident that German reunification was far from imminent. All sides finally acknowledged that the cooperation that Brundage had lauded countless times since the mid–1950s had become totally artificial. Still, the Soviet Union took credit for two communist nations achieving IOC membership and reveled in the opportunity to expand Iron Curtain influence within the Olympic Movement.

The events in 1968 proved that the political aspects of the Games were beyond IOC control. While Brundage and the committee strove to extinguish political fires before they could detract attention from events on the field, this proved an impossible task. Finally permitting two German teams and excluding South Africa from Mexico City helped to quell some of these issues, but there was simply no way to eradicate them completely. While there were many who did not want the politics eliminated because they added intrigue to the events, particularly when the superpowers were involved, it was obvious that politics stole the show in 1968. The feats on the field were impressive, particularly for the American team, but it is the Black Power demonstration that has become synonymous with Mexico City. Politics would be front and center once again in Munich, but unrelated to the Cold War and in a much more tragic sense.

Just as the Cold War rivalry itself changed noticeably after 1968, politically-charged sportswriting gradually diminished as well. While American columnists continued to insult and stereotype Soviet athletes and the Soviet press advocated for the superiority of the communist training system, these exchanges abated for roughly a decade as the super powers grappled with more pressing concerns. Sporting news in the United States became a bit more absorbed in American professional sports than the international scene. At the same time, the deaths of eleven Israeli athletes in Munich rightfully eclipsed the superpowers' Olympic rivalry at the 1972 Games. Brundage's decision to step down as IOC president effective after the Munich Games was another important factor in this transition period, as his successor, Lord Killanin, proved much more willing to oversee widespread change to the Olympic Movement. Famed *New York Times* columnist Arthur Daley, who possessed a unique ability to combine sport and current events consistently and thoughtfully, passed away in 1974.[103] It was not until the Games came to Moscow in 1980 and President Jimmy Carter chose to boycott in protest of the Soviet presence in Afghanistan that Cold War politics returned to the fore on the Olympic political scene with the same intensity as during the period discussed here. The events in Munich showed that politics were always part of the Games, even when the superpowers were not on the frontlines, but after Mexico City, Moscow and Washington remained relatively quiet within the Olympic Movement until the late 1970s.

CHAPTER 9

Post–1968 Experience and Conclusion

"I am sure that the public will agree that we cannot allow a handful of terrorists to destroy this nucleus of international cooperation and goodwill we have in the Olympic movement. The Games must go on and we must continue our efforts to keep them clean, pure, and honest, and to try to extend the sportsmanship of the athletic field into other areas."
—IOC president Avery Brundage, Munich Games 1972[1]

As the previous chapters have shown, the Olympic Movement experienced unprecedented growth in the twenty-year span from 1948 to 1968. During these years, the Soviet Union made its Olympic debut and several former colonies in Africa and Asia began fielding teams regularly. The Games themselves, once largely a European phenomenon, expanded to include Australia and Asia as host sites. The growth of politically-charged sports commentary followed by widespread television coverage dramatically increased spectator and media interest in the events on and off the field. National governments, particularly those in Moscow and Washington, began to devote more attention and resources to Olympic glory, as they tied athletic achievement to Cold War dominance. Taken together, these factors created by 1968 a global athletics spectacular with thousands of competitors televised to an international audience estimated at one billion—a far cry from the Austerity Games just two decades earlier.

Yet, there are many ways in which 1968 represented the end of an era for the Olympics. First, Avery Brundage announced his retirement in 1968 and the IOC selected Lord Killanin as his successor, effective after the Munich Summer Games. Because Brundage had ruled for so long and was such a strong personality, the Olympic Movement was bound to change once he was no longer at its helm. He had managed, albeit briefly, to force the superpowers to adhere to his will in a unique manner that other international bodies simply could not replicate. Although the results were not always as expected nor were they easily accepted, he possessed a singular ability to dominate the IOC. Change was inevitable following his retirement. Lord Killanin proved more receptive to calls to modernize the Games and to working within the political reality.

The discernable shift in global politics caused by the onset of détente also makes 1968 a natural end point for this project. Détente was a conscious choice to reduce tensions between the superpowers in all areas. Therefore, there was less emphasis on beating the other and fewer allusions to the Games being a clash of ideologies during the 1970s than during the previous two decades. The superpowers did not approach the 1970s-era Olympiads with the same enthusiasm or competitive spirit as had become customary. There were simply too many other problems that preoccupied the governments in Washington and Moscow, preventing them from expending high levels of energy and resources on their Olympic teams. This harsh rhetoric would return by 1980, but in the meantime, the political incursions of the 1970s assumed a different tone.

Finally, the Games themselves had changed. They had grown to encompass more than a hundred nations on six continents by 1968 and were seen on television by an estimated audience of one billion people worldwide. This was a far cry from the fourteen nations that had participated in 1896 and even the fifty-nine represented in 1948. With so many athletes and a global audience, there were more storylines to follow and a wider range of competition—both on the playing fields and in terms of media attention. As such, there was bound to be less focus on the east-west battle for supremacy that had characterized the early Cold War Olympiads. Therefore, while superpower tensions were not absent from the post–1968 Games, they were not as pervasive.

After Mexico City

The Olympic Games continued to evolve after 1968 to become today's quadrennial spectacle. Without the same Cold War stakes, the Olympics grew and made headlines in different ways, with new questions replacing the German issue. With the signing of the Basic Treaty between the two Germanys in 1972, the NATO countries finally recognized the government in East Berlin, calming tensions and ending the obstacles that had kept East German athletes on the sidelines far too often. The awarding of the 1972 Summer Games to Munich demonstrated the political legitimacy of the GFR. Though there were concerns about whether the East German team would be welcomed in Munich, there were very few issues. The problems that did arise in Munich were quickly over-shadowed by the Black September attacks.[2] Despite this progress, issues with organizing the Games remained a constant.[3] Now the IOC grappled increas-ingly with financial concerns, those pertaining to allegations of steroid use, and the visibility of corporate sponsorships. While détente slowed the outright Cold War politicization of the Olympics for a time, the Games of the 1970s proved controversial in different ways. The boycotts in 1980 and 1984 were obvious reminders that politics were an inherent aspect of the Games; however, the superpowers' decisions to stay home made a different statement. Rather than using the Olympics to demonstrate Cold War prowess, Moscow and Wash-ington chose to use the Games to take an overtly political stance, proving that the politics off the field could still eclipse the athletic feats on it.

The unprecedented growth and change that Brundage lamented through-out the 1960s has continued since with few signs of abatement. Not only were there more countries than ever entering the Games and winning medals, but the number of people present at each event, including the coaches, officials, spectators, and members of the press corps, multiplied. The advent of live tel-evision coverage brought with it new prospects for advertisers and sponsor-ships, which in turn led to increasing opportunities for commercialization and corruption. The £1500 that the BBC had paid to the IOC in 1948 for moving image rights at the London Games was pocket change compared to the figures thrown out by American networks vying for broadcast rights in the 1970s and 1980s.[4]

Another major change to the Olympics after Mexico City was Brundage's decision to step down as IOC president. After twenty years, Brundage, who was eighty-four years old by the time he relinquished his post, chose retirement at a time when his popularity had bottomed out. His refusal to accept change within the Olympic Movement led many, especially members of the press, to revile him. In a *Sports Illustrated* story divulging Brundage's extramarital affairs published after his death, William Oscar Johnson excoriated his subject: "until he retired from the presidency in 1972, he strode the earth as if he were a crowned monarch, and he ruled the Olympic movement as if it were his fief-dom, dictating policy and passing judgment with an arrogance, a stubbornness and an outspokenness that earned him the soubriquet Old Discus Heart."[5] When he retired, Brundage went on the record warning the world that the Games had become so big that political and commercial interests had buried their ideals. He recommended the elimination of basketball and soccer from the Summer Olympics and the end of the Winter Games altogether, brazen remarks that were unlikely to win him many fans, particularly as the Soviet-American basketball games remained among the most highly anticipated and most watched events of the Games.[6] Lord Killanin, viewed widely as the Olympics' savior as well as the anti–Brundage, came to be revered for the changes he brought to what many feared was a dying movement. Nonetheless, it cannot be disputed that Brundage certainly left his mark on the Games.

However he is perceived, Brundage was an influential figure within the Olympic Movement for more than three decades, dating back to his days as USOA president during the Great Depression. His departure created a turning point in Olympic leadership. There were some who questioned openly whether the Olympics had run their course by this time. Was the looming amateur problem too difficult to solve? Had the Games simply become so big as to make them nearly impossible for all but a handful of the world's major cities to accommodate? Throughout the 1960s, host cities had built increasingly extravagant venues, setting an expensive precedent that put the Games out of reach for many smaller metropolises and leaving behind stadiums with little ongoing utility to fall into disrepair. There were also concerns as to whether politics had become too much of an impediment.[7]

Lord Killanin's willingness to modernize the Games stifled talk of their possible extinction. He acknowledged that change was inevitable. There was no plausible means of keeping television out of the Games after 1964 and few desired this, as it offered good exposure for the athletes and brought in millions of dollars through broadcasting rights. While there were valid concerns that too much money could lead to corruption and wreck the Games, discontinuing television was impractical and unwise. There were fears that spectator interest in the Olympics was waning by the early 1970s. Taking the Games off television would only have hastened their decline. Instead of presiding over their undoing, Lord Killanin—and his successor Juan Antonio Samaranch—helped to revive the Games by embracing initiatives that Brundage would not have considered.

While many of the old problems that had plagued the IOC during the 1950s and 1960s had finally abated, the rest of the Cold War-era Games were far from drama-free. There will never be a perfectly executed or seamless Olympic Games even now that the Cold War is over, simply because the Games are not an isolated event. They draw their relevance and some of their intrigue from external political dynamics. Though the athletic feats are the main attraction, the international competition component is part of their entertainment value. It would be impossible to extricate nationalism from the Olympic Movement, nor are there many who wish to do so. While some Olympiads are more tranquil than others, there are too many outside factors at play and too many political aspects for there to be a completely flawless event from the initial planning stages through the closing ceremonies. Politics and the Olympics, whether superpower-related or not, are forever intertwined.

Following the drama that plagued the 1968 Olympiad, there was hope that the 1972 Games in Sapporo, Japan, and Munich would prove quieter and less politically charged. While Sapporo proved relatively tranquil, Munich took a tragic turn with the Black September attack. While the major political event was not Cold War-related, just the choice of Munich as an Olympic host was political in itself, given the trouble that many East German athletes had faced for more than a decade in trying to enter NATO countries for international sporting events.[8] Fortunately, East Germany faced no such obstacles in Munich.[9] Given the American success in Mexico City and the temporary abatement in Cold War tensions, there were fewer appeals for improvement and less athletic propaganda.[10]

The IOC faced a much sadder problem, however, when the Black September group, an arm of the PLO, took hostage and later killed eleven Israelis at the Games on 5 September.[11] This type of violence was unprecedented at an Olympics, leading many to call for the cancellation of the remaining events. The IOC responded by suspending that day's contests to allow time to mourn and to give its Executive Committee a chance to decide how to proceed. After the one-day hiatus and a memorial service for the fallen athletes, the Olympics resumed, over the protests of those who perceived this decision as disrespectful to the victims as well as to the Egyptian and Syrian delegations, who feared retaliation would soon follow.[12] In response to the question of why the IOC decided against cancelling, Brundage made his now famous statement. "I am sure that the public will agree that we cannot allow a handful of terrorists to destroy this nucleus of international cooperation and goodwill we have in the Olympic movement. The Games must go on and we must continue our efforts to keep them clean, pure, and honest, and to try to extend the sportsmanship of the athletic field into other areas."[13]

For some, this statement was a final reminder that the retiring Brundage was both insensitive and unwilling to compromise. It was an indication that the IOC president did not understand the contemporary political reality. However, there were many who defended the decision to continue. These supporters included the surviving members of the Israeli team, who argued that cancelling the Games would be a victory for the PLO. Instead, they believed that resuming the Olympics following the mourning period would show the importance and strength of the Games.[14] Given this tragedy and the ensuing controversy, there was serious question by the closing ceremonies if Munich should be the final Olympics.

This moment perhaps more than any other in Olympic history served as a powerful reminder that sport and politics were inseparable. Had the time come when political costs outweighed the gains and the glory achievable through the Games? It seemed so, given that the $700 million and the six years that the Munich organizing committee had invested in preparing for the Olympics quickly became irrelevant after such tragedy, in addition to the seemingly heartless way in which Brundage and the IOC reacted. If the Games were to continue, they needed major changes. As *New York Times* sportswriter Red Smith phrased it, "the Olympics may or may not have outgrown their sweatpants, but the International Olympic Committee as now constituted has truly outlived its time…. The Olympics have been described, not always without reason, as an orgy of nationalism that exacerbates international relations."[15] Taking into account the rapidly inflating costs of hosting the Games, the unflagging commercialism that surrounded the spectacle, and the endless political turmoil, it was understandable why many wondered whether the Olympic Movement had become unsustainable.

Brundage yielded to Lord Killanin following the Munich Games, giving some hope that the IOC would modernize and perhaps recapture its viability, yet the problems continued. Unfortunately for Killanin and the IOC, the 1976 Innsbruck Winter Games also proved problematic. In January, one month before the Winter Olympics were to open, there were concerns that a snow shortage would interfere with the skiing events, forcing organizers to import snow to the mountains to prevent this disruption.[16] Another dilemma arose regarding television rights for the Games, which for a time made it likely that much of the European audience would not be able to watch the events.[17] While this was eventually settled, the IOC's decision not to allow American-based Radio Free Europe to broadcast the Winter Games led to a charge by the U.S. State Department that the Kremlin was to blame, briefly resurrecting Cold War tensions. Lord Killanin informed the United States that the move was made to prevent the Games from being used as political propaganda. This explanation largely fell on deaf ears in Washington, particularly since everyone knew Moscow and East Berlin constantly used the Games for political ends. Nonetheless, the IOC refused to intervene, leaving RFE out of the Games.[18]

The 1976 Games in Montreal proved problematic from the start of the planning process, but in a financial rather than a political sense.[19] The Summer Olympics were a public relations disaster to the extent that the IOC considered moving them as late as 1975. An extended ironworker strike in January 1975—just eighteen months before the opening ceremonies—delayed work on the main stadium long enough that there were legitimate fears that the city would not be prepared for the 17 July 1976 starting date.[20] Compounding anxiety over the labor stoppage were the skyrocketing costs of the associated building projects. While Montreal had budgeted roughly $350 million for construction, that price tag had reached $653 million by January 1975 with a new final estimate of $1 billion. This news was not welcome in Canada, where many had opposed the selection of Montreal as host from the start.

As the IOC grappled with last-minute issues in Innsbruck, it also learned that the Montreal price tag had climbed to $1.2 billion, most of which would be passed on to Quebec residents, with still no guarantee that the facilities would be ready in time. Rather than postpone, Lord Killanin said that the Summer Olympics would simply be canceled for that year, offering Montreal an ultimatum, "either have them on time, or don't have them at all."[21] At a time when the IOC had pushed for a scaling back of the Olympic villages and facilities so as not to leave host cities with "white elephant" stadiums, as Lord Killanin termed them in 1973, Montreal clearly failed.[22] However, the IOC chose to carry on despite these obstacles, a decision that perhaps might have been different had its leaders known what was ahead in the 1980s.

The 1980 Summer Olympics were the only Games held in the Soviet Union. Moscow fought hard to host for many of the same reasons as Munich: to prove that the Soviet Union was a respected member of the IOC as well as "a member in good standing of the world of nations."[23] Despite these lofty aims, the 1980 Games were overtly political from the start. The Soviet Union announced in 1977 that teams from South Africa and Rhodesia would not be welcome because of their unsavory racial policies. This contradicted the Soviets' earlier assurance that all IOC member nations would be permitted to compete.[24] Already by 1978, there were widespread concerns that the Soviets would try to completely monopolize coverage of the Games and prevent American media outlets from broadcasting, evoking memories of Radio Free Europe's problems in Innsbruck.[25] The Kremlin had a history of arbitrarily evicting American and western writers who were critical of socialism, substantiating these fears. Soviet anti–Semitism and its strong anti–Israel stance were troubling. There were valid concerns that the Kremlin would find a reason to exclude Israel from competing at the last minute. Simultaneously, the debate over a potential American boycott first surfaced in July 1978, more than a year before the Soviets invaded Afghanistan. The idea gained widespread press support, but there was little belief that the Jimmy Carter administration or the USOC would follow through.[26]

After nearly a decade of calm between the superpowers, tensions escalated in the late 1970s. Carter had made human rights an important piece of his platform and a priority for his administration. The Soviet Union was infamous for its violations and Carter's scrutiny did not go unnoticed. At the same time, Moscow began building its armaments supply, much to Washington's chagrin.

Washington perceived Moscow's invasion of Afghanistan on Christmas Eve 1979 as open aggression in a place where the Soviets had no business interfering, disputing Moscow's claim that it was boosting an ally needing outside aid.[27] The Carter administration immediately denounced this assault and urged the Soviets to withdraw, to no avail. The president's first public threat of a boycott came in an address to the American people on 4 January 1980.[28] For the United States, it was a low-risk means of encouraging the Soviets to leave Afghanistan. By mid–January, national opinion polls showed that more than half of the American public was in favor of an Olympic boycott.[29]

Carter announced in early February that the United States would not compete in Moscow. This decision proved quite unpopular with the athletes who had devoted so many years training for the opportunity to compete on their sport's biggest stage. American public support quickly dissipated following the unexpected men's hockey gold medal in the "Miracle on Ice." The surprising victory reinvigorated interest in the Olympic Games as a national morale booster at a critical juncture.[30] Now many in the press and among the American public doubted whether a boycott was the best means of protesting the Soviets' interference in Afghanistan. But American efforts to meet with Killanin and the IOC to force the Soviets' hand failed, leaving Washington in a tough position. It could either withdraw its threat, therefore risking embarrassment by appearing submissive to the Soviets, or it could stand firm and risk public outcry and the wrath of summer athletes around the country. The Carter administration chose the latter course in what Washington Post writer Ken Denlinger termed "a dramatic miscalculation of American passion for Olympic sport."[31]

The Games went on. Carter failed in his efforts to force Moscow's hand and hundreds of American athletes missed their chance to compete on their sport's biggest stage. Only West Germany and Japan joined the boycott, giving Moscow the Cold War victory.[32] In the end, the American athletes and audience were the real losers, as Moscow still had its moment in the spotlight and the IOC picked Moscow over Washington in this contest of wills, though the U.S. did not face any IOC sanctions for their boycott.

With Los Angeles selected to host the 1984 Summer Olympics before the Carter administration first considered boycotting Moscow, speculation about a Soviet reprisal began immediately after the 1980 Games. Incoming IOC president Juan Antonio Samaranch, a veteran member of Spain's National Olympic Committee who chaired the IOC until 2001, urged Moscow to compete. Samaranch was more aware and accepting of the relationship between politics and sport than either Brundage or Lord Killanin. As he said in 1980, "We are aware of the need to try and separate politics and sport. But we are also realists. We are fully aware that in this world, and in a world without conflict, the Olympic movement certainly will not suffer as it did at this time."[33] The message here was clear: politics and sport remained entwined, but the IOC would do all it could to prevent another high-profile boycott for the next Olympics.

While the United States saw its influence in the Olympic Movement wane as a result of the Moscow protest, Samaranch pledged to move past the boycott and make the 1984 Games the most successful yet.[34] At the same time, the Soviet Union exerted its newfound influence to push for more favorable conditions for its team, including private lodging for its athletes.[35] Rather than immediately announcing a counter boycott, the Soviets vowed to outnumber the American delegation in Los Angeles.[36] However, Moscow began to hedge on its commitment to attend in July 1983, one year before the opening ceremonies.[37] Speculation continued throughout the fall and winter over a potential Soviet boycott, though the majority believed Moscow would attend. Soviet complaints about the organization of the Games began to escalate in early 1984, obscuring Moscow's intentions.[38]

The Soviets waited until the last minute by announcing their decision to skip the Summer Games on 9 May. Part of their change in policy was due to the change in leadership at the top. Konstantin Chernenko, who became General Secretary in February, advocated a hard line approach toward Washington. The Kremlin took offense when the State Department refused to grant a visa for a Soviet Olympic official in March for reasons pertaining to "international security."[39] The Soviets continued to disparage the city of Los Angeles for its history of crime and gang activity and charged that the work of the organizing committee was "motived solely by profit."[40] They followed these charges with demands for an emergency IOC session in April to discuss the Games' apparent anti–Soviet bias.[41] From this point, speculation grew that the Soviets were preparing to boycott. The text of this statement, published in the *New York Times*, cited "the cavalier attitude of the US authorities to the Olympic charter, the gross flouting of the ideals and traditions of the Olympic Movement," as the main reasons why the Soviet NOC felt it had no choice but to protest.[42] Two days later, East Germany followed the Soviet lead and pulled out of the Games, followed piecemeal by the other satellites throughout May.[43] American attempts to lure the Soviets back failed.

In the absence of its chief rival, the Games were essentially an American party, as it amassed 174 medals, yet there was a nagging sense that something was missing. As many had feared before the boycott was official, the quality of the competition was weaker than most other Olympics, robbing the Games of some of their glory. Even some American athletes felt that their victories were a bit watered down without the Soviets. This realization tempered their excitement at participating in their first Summer Games since Montreal. Yet at the same time, many athletes savored their chance to compete more than they otherwise would have because of their lost opportunity in Moscow. For some, LA was their last shot at Olympic glory. In this sense, the home team did not disappoint, walking away with a record number of medals.[44]

The Soviet boycott resurrected the quadrennial discussion over whether the Olympics had run their course. The Olympics, more than ever, appeared to have reached a crossroads. Now that both superpowers had used the Games as political protest, was there any future to a movement that strove to remain apolitical? There were concerns over the 1988 host, Seoul, South Korea, and whether the Soviets would attend, given South Korea's ties to the west.[45]

Between 1984 and 1988, the Olympic Movement changed considerably, transforming the Games into the spectacle they are today. The IOC openly acknowledged its commercial interests and the role of television in staging the Games for the first time. Ironically, television and commercialization, once vilified by Brundage and other purists, became the saving graces for the Games because they widened their international appeal and made them more available around the world. One of the IOC's biggest changes was shifting the Winter Games to the intervening even year between Summer Olympiads beginning in 1994 to make them more marketable to television networks and increase sponsorship opportunities, which in turn increased advertising profits.[46] A number of sports openly welcomed professional athletes beginning in 1992. These updates, contrary to Brundage's vision for the Games, came with Samaranch's blessing. He seemed to realize more than any of his predecessors that the Olympics could not survive as a stagnant entity. They had to change with the times to continue to be viable, even when some of these changes seemed to contradict the original tenets of the Olympic Movement.

Both superpowers played nice in the years leading up to Seoul, reflecting the thaw between Ronald Reagan's and Mikhail Gorbachev's governments. An unprecedented 160 nations took part in the 1988 Games, and though no one knew it at the time, they were the last to feature teams from East Germany and the Soviet Union. The last Cold War Olympics are remembered for their relative harmony, at least in comparison to the two previous Summer Games. While North Korea and some of its key allies chose to boycott, politics remained firmly on the sidelines for the first time since the early days of the Cold War. The IOC sessions leading up to Seoul lacked the drama that had largely characterized these annual meetings for more nearly four decades. As usual, there were some black marks on the Games—the first major steroid busts and the now-customary ugly displays of chauvinism—but on the whole, the Seoul Games were notable for their lack of Cold War clashes. Again, this became clear only with hindsight and after the Soviet Union dissolved, but the

1988 events were later identifiable as a transition to the post–Cold War Games, remarkable for their relative tranquility. The Soviet Union and East Germany, the only two countries to break the hundred-medal plateau, finished in first and second place in the overall medal count with the United States a close third. The 1992 Games would be the true transition, with the former Soviet republics combining one more time as the Unified team in Barcelona for the Summer Olympics and Albertville, France, for the Winter contests.

In this way, the Cold War-era Olympics came to an end with much less fanfare than they had begun four decades earlier. Though the always intriguing Soviet-American rivalry ended with the Cold War, the Games continued to evolve throughout the 1990s and into the new millennium. More and more nations joined the IOC with the medals spread across an ever-growing number of countries, adding to the global appeal of the Games. In this sense, the Olympics did not die out as many had feared following the tumult of the 1970s and 1980s, but changed fundamentally and for the benefit of the worldwide audience as the Games neared their centennial anniversary in Atlanta. While politics continued to define the post–1968 Cold War games, they did so in a different sense than from 1948 to 1968. The earlier period had been marked by intense on and off the field competitiveness between the superpowers, leading to riveting matches that drew global interest. By the 1970s, new questions created doubts about the Games' viability. Although there were moments when it appeared the Olympic heyday had passed, the movement's ability to modernize and adapt to global change under Samaranch's direction ensured their survival and flourishing so that any suggestion today that the Olympics are on the verge of collapse is met with skepticism.

Conclusions

The period between 1948 and 1968 offers a unique window during which the Cold War and the Olympics converged in such a way that was beneficial for both the superpowers and the IOC. By the late 1940s, all interactions between Moscow and Washington had become headline news. Struggling over global influence, competing ideologies, and the administration of occupied Germany, the United States and the Soviet Union quickly proved that their wartime collaboration was a thing of the past. This growing rivalry soon encompassed cultural, academic, technological, and sporting grounds, creating a scenario where Moscow and Washington competed to dominate all facets of daily life. The Olympic Movement was drawn into the Cold War when the Soviets joined the IOC in 1951 and announced their intent to compete in Helsinki.

Washington's response was to beef up American efforts to make a strong impression at the Games. When Moscow lived up to USOA official Richard Ritter's billing as "the potent dark horse" of Helsinki, Washington, the American press, and even Brundage countered with stronger urgings to beat the Soviets.[47] Despite their contrasting approaches to sport, the United States and the Soviet Union shared a belief that the Olympics could play a critical role in the Cold War. While the Soviet Union employed a centralized approach, the United States remained largely privatized. Moscow looked to win in all sports, while the United States largely focused its efforts on traditional strongholds and fan favorites like track, swimming, and basketball.

Some Americans, most notably Brundage, lamented the influence of geopolitics on the Olympics, but the reality was that this element increased the Games' relevance. Washington's and Moscow's shared focus on the Games hastened their politicization but also heightened spectator interest. Media outlets on both sides of the Iron Curtain offered more coverage before, during, and after the events, than prior to the Soviet debut. The public followed the Games more closely because they were perhaps the most accessible element of the flourishing cultural Cold War. Moscow and Washington both embraced the Olympics as crucial ideological proving grounds. And at times when superpower diplomacy was at a standstill, the Olympics were a means of proving a nation's strength without risking serious consequences. As Robert Kennedy wrote in 1964, "During a military or nuclear stalemate such as the world is now experiencing athletics can become an increasingly important factor in international relations."[48] A strong American performance would remind the world of its strength on and off the field. The superpowers profited from having a low-stakes venue for their Cold War battles while the Olympic Movement reaped the benefits of a larger audience and greater attention.

This period also demonstrated the curative power of sport. London was the most obvious example, but the 1956 Olympics offered a sense of redemption to the Hungarians after they arrived in Melbourne only to find out that their revolution had failed. Their water polo team beating the Soviet Union en route to winning the gold medal gave them a victory over Moscow in a different sense. After the Games, more than thirty Hungarian athletes benefitted from the chance to move to the United States and escape communism. The Olympics also demonstrated that sports could be a healthy outlet for nationalism. The Soviet-American basketball game in the 1960 Olympics is proof of this. Coaches of both teams invoked politics and ideology as motivating forces and the game itself was one of the most watched contests of the two weeks, because of the heightened stakes. In these cases, and many others, the political sideshows at the Olympics added to their drama and appeal.

Granted, the politics behind the scenes at times made it easy to lose sight of the Olympics' true purpose. Brundage proved just as vulnerable to political forces as the countries he worked so hard to keep under his control. One of the key factors in the over-politicization of IOC events was his inconsistency and refusal to operate the Games within the political reality. He strove to stage an apolitical Olympics every four years; however, in doing so, he disregarded one of de Coubertin's motivations in reviving them: to give countries, particularly the great powers, a venue in which they could express their nationalism to avoid war. De Coubertin failed in his mission to prevent war among the great powers; yet, even he was conscious of the growing ties between national pride and sport.

Brundage's conception of de Coubertin's vision of the Games was an admirable one, however, it was not entirely accurate. Politics had always been part of the Olympic Movement, though perhaps not at the level that they were present during the Cold War. There were times when Brundage would acknowledge and even play to the political reality. One example was his advocacy for better fitness and a stronger American team after he spent three weeks observing Soviet sport. Try as he might, he could not completely shed his conservative American outlook. At other times, he proved insensitive to the plight of groups like the Ukrainians or the East Germans, whose unfortunate political circumstances often left them on the sidelines. Rather than minimizing these challenges by facing them "to show the way for the diplomats," Brundage chose to disregard the political reality.[49] In doing so, he unwittingly allowed these encroachments to overshadow the events on the field at certain junctures.

This disconnect between Brundage's vision and the frustration experienced by many IOC member nations belied a deeper difference in approach to the Olympic Movement. For Brundage and the IOC, the Games were ends in themselves. Their purpose was to provide a quadrennial sporting festival with the field comprised of the best amateur athletes in the world. Even though each competitor was required to represent his home country, there was a bit of an incongruity in that Brundage and others touted the Games as a contest of individuals, not nations. On the contrary, the superpowers treated the Olympics as means to an end: to demonstrate political strength. For the Iron Curtain countries, most notably the Soviet Union and East Germany, the Games were a means of gaining legitimacy and international respectability following World War II. For the United States, the Games were a stage for showing that they were still the world's leading power, on and off the playing field. The superpowers together pulled the Olympics into the Cold War, by using the contests as low-stakes battlefields and by taking the overall medal count quite seriously. The athletes, fans, and media in both countries embraced this fight

on the playing fields, increasing its legitimacy. Because athletics were so acces-
sible to the general public and already a source of interest on both sides of the
Iron Curtain, the Olympics proved quite conducive to inclusion in the wider
Cold War.

In the end, Brundage lost the battle of wills to keep politics out of the
Olympics. The Black Power demonstration in 1968 was perhaps the clearest
example of this. Despite strong efforts keep the Games apolitical, the onset of
television and the IOC's refusal to take decisive action toward ending racism
at the Games created the perfect storm for the raised fists seen around the
world. Part of the rationale for the Black September group using the Munich
Games as the stage for their massacre of Israeli athletes was the global visibility
of the Olympic Movement. As the Games grew, they naturally grew out of
Brundage's control. There were simply too many factors and too many diverse
interests at stake. The IOC often found itself in a very difficult position, trying
to balance the interests of its member nations with those of the Olympic Movement. The Committee's treatment of the lingering German question was proof
of this. The IOC was willing to admit the Soviet Union in 1951, despite its fla-
grant disregard for amateurism, and to turn a blind eye to its inhumane reaction
to the Hungarian Revolution. However, it would not tolerate a separate East
German team until 1968 when it was more than a decade overdue and its previous refusals had already caused seemingly endless and unnecessary hardship
to East German athletes and officials. Brundage attempted to enforce his own
ideals on the Olympic Movement, to show that sport could achieve what the
politicians could not. He failed because the divide between the two Germanys
was deeper than he realized. The presence of two German delegations at the
Grenoble Games signified that political concerns outweighed athletic idealism
at times.

By 1968, it was clear that politics had won. The need for German teams
was just one indication that much had changed with the Olympic Movement.
Even the IOC could no longer ignore the fact that there were two entirely separate German states. The Olympics themselves had changed too. Now the
countries challenging for medals were increasingly diverse and the Committee
found itself grappling with new problems. Commercialism, increased professionalism, and the new avenues opened by television were all forces that would
outlive Brundage. He stepped down, but politics continued to influence the
Games. Even with superpower tensions on hiatus throughout the 1970s, the
IOC grappled with Israeli-Palestinian drama and continued racial unrest,
among other issues. What Brundage never realized was that the Olympics draw
some of their appeal from the external forces at play, something that continues
today.

Simply put, the Cold War was, in the final balance, a positive force on the Olympic Movement because superpower drama heightened the Games' international importance and their relevance to the average spectator. Without these tensions, the events on the field would not have garnered as much governmental attention or large-scale press interest. The genuine sports fans and a curious public would still watch, but there would not have been the same diplomatic stakes tied to these contests. The Cold War raised the bar for politics at the Games and at times overshadowed the athletes themselves, particularly by 1968. And while the athletes should always be the main spectacle at the Olympics, these external politics helped to draw added attention to the sports stars and to boost the Games' appeal.

More than twenty years after the official end of the Cold War, politics and nationalism continue to play critical roles in the Olympic Movement, just as they did before and during the Cold War. The politicization of the Games predated the Iron Curtain and has outlived it as well. The former Soviet republics combined one final time to compete on a unified team in 1992 while the 1996 Atlanta Games survived a bombing incident. The 2006 Winter Games in Torino, Italy, were plagued by a figure skating judging scandal that resurrected east-west tensions reminiscent of the 1960s. In the months before the 2014 Winter Olympics in Sochi, Russia, Prime Minister Vladimir Putin's strong anti-gay legislation raised the question of whether Russia should be allowed to host. Fortunately, there were few reported incidents of homophobia or anti-gay bias during the Games. Had there been, the results would have been a public relations nightmare for a nation already quite unpopular on the world stage. The Olympics remain a critical means by which countries can demonstrate their international worth and legitimacy. Brazil, in hosting the 2016 summer contests in Rio de Janeiro, became the first South American nation to host and hopes to capitalize the accompanying publicity and tourism opportunities, but it faced several of the same organizational quandaries that plagued Montreal.[50] Nonetheless, athletes around the world—and particularly throughout South America—remain eager to represent their country and compete for their chance at Olympic glory. While the exact circumstances change, international relations and politics remain a constant factor in planning for the Games. External factors like nationalism and diplomacy continue to add to the global appeal of the Games, as hosting the contests remains a point of national pride while Olympic medals often are accompanied by outpourings of patriotic sentiment. The perpetuation of these themes demonstrates that political considerations did not begin or end with the Cold War or with Brundage's tenure as IOC president.

The Games continue to go on with few signs of flagging interest, more than a century after de Coubertin's first efforts to revive them. Though it is lamentable when the antics on the sidelines overshadow the feats on the field, politics remain an integral facet of the Olympic Movement. It took the world wars to force the cancellation of the Games and in seventy years since the Allied victory in 1945, nothing has stopped them. The Olympics have demonstrated a great sense of resiliency, recovering from seemingly endless challenges and surviving exponential growth that has made them the lucrative and popular entity they are today. Part of their continued viability and interest comes from the Olympic Movement's ability to weather political storms even when it cannot completely eliminate them. In response to the Soviet invasion of Czechoslovakia in 1968, Brundage pronounced, "The world, alas, is full of injustice, aggression, violence and warfare, against which all civilized persons rebel, but this is no reason to destroy the nucleus of international cooperation and good will we have in the Olympic Movement."[51] This is true, but in the end perhaps these outside forces only increase the Games' appeal as well as the stakes of the events on the field.

Chapter Notes

Introduction

1. Baron Pierre de Coubertin, "Why I Revived the Olympic Games," 1908, in *Olympism, Selected Writings* (Lausanne: International Olympic Committee, 2000), 545.

2. David Maraniss, *Rome 1960: The Olympics That Changed the World* (New York: Simon & Schuster, 2008), 235–236.

3. *Ibid.*, 234.

4. *Ibid.*, 235–238.

5. Barbara Keys, *Globalizing Sport: National Rivalry and International Community in the 1930s* (Cambridge: Harvard University Press, 2006), 134–136.

6. *Ibid.*, 4.

7. *Ibid.*

8. Maraniss, *Rome 1960*.

9. Alfred E. Senn, *Power, Politics and the Olympic Games: A History of the Power Brokers, Events and Controversies That Shaped the Games* (Champaign, IL: Human Kinetics, 1999), x.

10. *Ibid.*

11. Richard Espy, *The Politics of the Olympic Games* (Berkeley: University of California Press, 1979), 4.

12. Nicholas Evan Sarantakes, *Dropping the Torch: Jimmy Carter, the Olympic Boycott, and the Cold War* (New York: Cambridge University Press, 2011).

13. Walter McDougall, *The Heavens and the Earth: A Political History of the Space Race* (Baltimore: Johns Hopkins University Press, 1987).

14. Roy Clumpner, "Federal Involvement in Sport to Promote American Interest or Foreign Policy Objectives, 1950–1973," *Sport and International Relations* 1, no. 1 (March 1983).

15. Sam Lebovic, "From War Junk to Educational Exchange: The World War II Origins of the Fulbright Program and the Foundations of American Cultural Globalism, 1945–1950," *Diplomatic History* 3, no. 2 (April 2013), 280–312; See also Sam Lebovic, "The Fulbright: History's Greatest War Surplus Program," *Boston Globe*, 11 August 2013.

16. Jeremi Suri, *Power and Protest: Global Revolution and the Rise of Détente* (Cambridge: Harvard University Press, 2003).

17. Clive Gammon, "Lord of the Games," *Sports Illustrated*, 9 February 1976.

18. David Clay Large, *Nazi Games: The Olympics of 1936* (New York: W.W. Norton, 2007), 7.

19. Keys, *Globalizing Sport*, 30.

20. John J. MacAloon, *This Great Symbol: Pierre De Coubertin and the Origins of the Modern Olympic Games* (Chicago: University of Chicago Press, 1981), 5–7.

21. To read de Coubertin's writings on the Games and the utility of physical fitness more broadly, see *Olympism, Selected Writings*.

22. MacAloon, *This Great Symbol*, 4–5.

23. *Ibid.*, 39–41.

24. Louis Menand, "The Critics at Large: Glory Days," *The New Yorker*, 71.

25. Pierre de Coubertin, "English Education," in *Olympism: Selected Writings* (Lausanne: International Olympic Committee, 2000), 114.

26. Jim Reisler, *Igniting the Flame: America's First Olympic Team* (Guilford, CT: Lyons Press, 2012).

27. Keys, *Globalizing Sport*, 4.

28. Jacques Rogge, "The Legacy of the Modern Olympic Games' Founder Lives On," *Sports Illustrated*, 1 January 2013.

29. *Ibid.*

30. Guy Walters, *Berlin Games: How the Nazis*

Stole the Olympic Dream (New York: William Morrow, 2006), 4.

31. Robert Lipsyte, "Olympics: Evidence Ties Olympic Taint to 1936 Games," *New York Times,* 21 February 1999.

32. *Ibid.,* 5–6.

33. Allen Guttmann, *The Olympics: A History of the Modern Games* (Urbana: University of Illinois Press, 1992), 86.

34. Walters, *Berlin Games.*

35. Robert Lipsyte, "Olympics: Evidence Ties Olympic Taint to 1936 Games."

36. "Olympic Team Sure, Brundage Asserts," *New York Times,* 25 October 1935, page 1.

37. For more on Brundage's anti-Semitic stance during discussions regarding a Berlin boycott, see the letters in Box 153, Avery Brundage Collection, LA84, and Allen Guttmann, *The Games Must Go On: Avery Brundage and the Olympic Movement* (New York: Columbia University Press, 1984), 63–78.

38. Keys, *Globalizing Sport,* 37–38.

39. *Ibid.,* 4.

40. Robert Creamer, "Of Greeks—And Russians," *Sports Illustrated,* 6 February 1956.

41. Jeremiah Tax, "An In-Depth Look at Both the Seemly and Seamy Sides of Avery Brundage," *Sports Illustrated,* 16 January 1984.

42. John Lardner, "Letter from the Olympics," *The New Yorker,* 8 December 1956, 157. In response to Moscow's brutal crushing of the Hungarian Revolution, Brundage released the following statement, almost universally reviled for its insensitivity: "Every civilized person recoils in horror at the savage slaughter in Hungary, but that is no reason for destroying the nucleus of international cooperation and good will we have in the Olympic Movement. The Olympic Games are contests between individuals and not between nations. We hope that those who have withdrawn from the Melbourne Games will reconsider. In an imperfect world, if participation in sport is to be stopped every time politicians violate the laws of humanity, there will be few international contests. Is it not better to try to expand the sportsmanship of the athletic field into other areas?" Melbourne Session Notes, 19 November–4 December 1956, Avery Brundage Collection, Box 78, LA84 Foundation, Los Angeles, hereafter LA84.

43. "Portrait: Amateurs," *The New Yorker,* 23 July 1960, 30.

44. International Olympic Committee, "The Olympic Movement," 2007. Available 17 November 2012. http://www.olympic.org/Documents/Reports/EN/en_report_670.pdf.

45. *Ibid.*

46. Brundage to IOC in Wolf Lyberg, *The Meetings Between the IOC Executive Board and the National Olympic Committees 1952–1994: Study Made for the IOC* (Lausanne: International Olympic Committee, 1994), 18.

47. International Olympic Committee, "Revenue Sources and Distribution," olympic.org, 2007. Available 17 November 2012. http://www.olympic.org/ioc-financing-revenue-sources-distribution?tab=sources.

48. Reisler, *Igniting the Flame,* 184.

49. *Ibid.*

50. Large, *Nazi Games,* 28–29.

51. Allen Guttmann, *The Games Must Go On: Avery Brundage and the Olympic Movement* (New York: Columbia University Press, 1984).

52. Large, *Nazi Games,* 41.

53. Keys, *Globalizing Sport,* 188–189.

54. *Ibid.,* 92, 96.

55. *Ibid.,* 92.

56. *Ibid.,* 105–106.

57. Walters, *Berlin Games: How the Nazis Stole the Olympic Dream,* 122.

58. *Ibid.,* 117.

59. Martin Kane, "The White Sepulcher," *Sports Illustrated,* 4 September 1972.

60. Kevin B. Witherspoon, *Before the Eyes of the World: Mexico and the 1968 Olympic Games* (DeKalb: Northern Illinois University Press, 2008), 30.

61. Guttmann, *The Olympics: A History of the Modern Games,* 129.

62. David B. Kanin, *A Political History of the Olympic Games* (Boulder, CO: Westview Press, 1981), 64.

63. Bo Schoenfeld, "Olympics Seen as Prestige War," *Oakland Tribune,* 19 November 1961, 1.

64. Melbourne Session Notes.

65. Janie Hampton, *The Austerity Olympics: When the Games Came to London in 1948* (London: Aurum Press, 2008), 40.

Chapter 1

1. John F. Kennedy, "Remarks to the Delegates to the Youth Fitness Conference," 21 February 1961, *American Presidency Project.* Available 7 April 2013. http://www.presidency.ucsb.edu/ws/index.php?pid=8455&st=physical&st1=.

2. Robert F. Kennedy, "A Bold Proposal for American Sport," *Sports Illustrated,* 27 July 1964.

3. David Mandell, *Sport: A Cultural History* (New York: Columbia University Press, 1984), 187–191.

4. Keys, *Globalizing Sport,* 4; Warren I. Susman, *Culture as History: The Transformation of American Society in the Twentieth Century* (New York: Pantheon Books, 1984), 172–180.

5. Susman, *Culture as History,* 141–42.

6. James Riordan, *Soviet Sport: Background to the Olympics* (Oxford: Basil Blackwell, 1980), 17.

7. Thomas M. Domer, *Sport in Cold War America: The Diplomatic and Political Use of Sport in the Eisenhower and Kennedy Administrations* (Dissertation, University of Wisconsin-Milwaukee, 1976), 3.

8. *Ibid.,* 25.

9. Walter A. McDougall, *The Heavens and the Earth: A Political History of the Space Age* (Baltimore: Johns Hopkins University Press, 1987), 139.

10. Kathryn Jay, *More Than Just a Game: Sports in American Life Since 1945* (New York: Columbia University Press, 2004), 50.

11. Ibid.

12. Mike Rywkin, *Soviet Society Today* (Armonk, NY: Me Sharp, 1989), 166.

13. Bill Henry and Patricia Henry Yeomans. *An Approved History of the Olympic Games* (Los Angeles: The Southern California Committee for the Olympic Games, 1984), 225.

14. Jim Reisler, *Igniting the Flame: America's First Olympic Team* (Guilford, CT: Lyons Press, 2012), 61–62.

15. United States Olympic Committee, *Olympic Dreams: 100 Years of Excellence* (New York: Universe Publishing, 1996), 43.

16. Reisler, *Igniting the Flame,* 90.

17. "Athletes Well Pleased: Americans Enthusiastic Over Their Reception," *The Boston Daily Globe,* 12 April 1896, Page 1.

18. "Athens 1896 Medal Table," International Olympic Committee, Archived, Accessed 21 February 2013. http://www.olympic.org/athens-1896-summer-olympics.

19. Reisler, *Igniting the Flame,* 90.

20. *Ibid.,* 195–197.

21. Mandell, *Sport: A Cultural History,* 191; Jay, *More than Just a Game,* 24.

22. David E. Kyvig, *Daily Life in the United States, 1920–1940* (Chicago: Ivan R. Dee, 2004), 158.

23. *Ibid.,* 160–161.

24. *Ibid.*

25. *Ibid.,*87.

26. Kathryn Jay, *More than Just a Game: Sports in American Life Since 1945* (New York: Columbia University Press, 2004), 50.

27. David B. Kanin, *A Political History of the Olympic Games* (Boulder, CO: Westview Press, 1981), 64–66.

28. Jay, *More than Just a Game,* 12, 50.

29. Ying Wushanley, *Playing Nicely and Losing: The Struggle for Control of Women's Intercollegiate Athletics, 1960–2000* (Syracuse: Syracuse University Press, 2004), 23.

30. Harry S. Truman, "Remarks to the President's Advisory Commission on Universal Training," December 20, 1946. Online by Gerhard Peters and John T. Woolley, *The American Presidency Project.* http://www.presidency.ucsb.edu/ws/?pid=

31. Ernest Lindley, "Truman's Message: Universal Military Training," *Washington Post,* 24 October 1945, Page 5.

32. Harry S. Truman, "Special Message to the Congress Recommending a Comprehensive Health Program," 19 November 1945. Available 7 April 2013. http://www.presidency.ucsb.edu/ws/index.php?pid=12288&st=physical&st1=.

33. Harry S. Truman, "Remarks to the President's Advisory Council on Universal Training," 20 December 1946. *American Presidency Project.* Available 7 April 2013. http://www.presidency.ucsb.edu/ws/index.php?pid=12565&st=physical&st1=

34. Lucy Freeman, "Truman Board Hit on Athletics Lack," *New York Times,* 9 April 1948, 28.

35. Shirley Povich, "This Morning with Shirley Povich," *Washington Post,* 9 December 1949, B4.

36. *Ibid.*

37. Domer, *Sport in Cold War America,* 3, 25.

38. Amy Bass, *Not the Triumph but the Struggle: The 1968 Olympics and the Making of the Black Athlete* (Minneapolis: University of Minnesota Press, 2002), 8.

39. *Ibid.,* 162.

40. Dwight D. Eisenhower, "Message to the President' S Conference on the Fitness of American Youth," 19 June 1956, *American Presidency Project.* Available 7 April 2013. http://www.presidency.ucsb.edu/ws/index.php?pid=10514&st=physical&st1=.

41. *Ibid.*

42. Henry R. Luce, "The American Century," *Life*, 17 February 1941.

43. *Ibid.*

44. Alan Brinkley, *The Publisher: Henry Luce and His American Century* (New York: Alfred A. Knopf, 2010), 401.

45. *Ibid.*, 361–362.

46. Toby C. Rider, *The Olympic Games and the Secret Cold War: The U.S. Government and the Propaganda Campaign Against Communist Sport, 1950–1960*. Thesis / Dissertation ETD, n.d.<http://doc.rero.ch/record/29394/files/Thesis_Toby_Rider.pdf>.

47. *Ibid.*, 147.

48. *Ibid.*, 220–22.

49. *Ibid.*, 255–67.

50. Alexander Wolff, "Revolution Games," *Sports Illustrated*, 18 June 2012.

51. Dorothy Stull, "The Point of Fitness," *Sports Illustrated*, 9 September 1957.

52. *Ibid.*

53. *Ibid.*

54. Kanin, *A Political History of the Olympic Games*, 64.

55. "Distaff Diplomats on the Mark," *Sports Illustrated*, 7 April 1958.

56. "Dulles Calls Soviet Price for Conference Too High," *Toronto Blade*, 25 March 1958, Page 1.

57. Dirk Bank, "A Slight Blow for Extremism in Sport's Cold War," *Sports Illustrated*, 27 July 1964.

58. "Soviets Risk Olympic Ban," *Boston Globe*, 12 July 1966, 21, Kanin, *A Political History of the Olympic Games*, 66.

59. Roy Terrell, "The High Meet the Mighty," *Sports Illustrated*, 24 July 1961.

60. "Why Can't We Beat This Girl?" *Sports Illustrated*, 30 September 1963.

61. Al Monaco, "A History of Volleyball Relations Between the Russian and American People," (*USA Volleyball*: 2009), 1–2.

62. Frederick Kempe, *Berlin 1961: Kennedy, Khrushchev, and the Most Dangerous Place on Earth* (New York: G.P. Putnam and Sons, 2011).

63. John Soares, "Cold War, Hot Ice: International Ice Hockey, 1947–1980," *Journal of Sport History* 24, no. 2 (Summer 2007), 211–212.

64. John F. Kennedy, "Remarks to the Delegates to the Youth Fitness Conference," 21 February 1961, *American Presidency Project*. Available 7 April 2013. http://www.presidency.ucsb.edu/ws/index.php?pid=8455&st=physical&st1=.

65. John F. Kennedy, "Remarks on the Youth Fitness Program," 19 July 1961, *American Presidency Project*. Available 8 April 2013. http://www.presidency.ucsb.edu/ws/index.php?pid=8248&st=physical&st1=.

66. *Ibid.*

67. Domer, 256–257.

68. John F. Kennedy: "Executive Order 11117—Establishing an Interagency Committee on International Athletics," August 13, 1963. Online by Gerhard Peters and John T. Woolley, *The American Presidency Project*. http://www.presidency.ucsb.edu/ws/?pid=59056.

69. John F. Kennedy, "Progress Report by the President on Physical Fitness," 13 August 1961, *American Presidency Project*. Available 8 April 2013. http://www.presidency.ucsb.edu/ws/index.php?pid=9371&st=physical&st1=.

70. McDougall, *The Heavens and the Earth*, 8.

71. President's Council on Youth, Fitness, and Nutrition, "Our History," *United States Government*. Available 9 April 2013. http://www.fitness.gov/about-pcfsn/our-history/.

72. John F. Kennedy: "Article by the President: The Vigor We Need," July 16, 1962. Online by Gerhard Peters and John T. Woolley, *The American Presidency Project*. http://www.presidency.ucsb.edu/ws/?pid=8771.

73. *Ibid.*

74. *Ibid.*

75. *Ibid.*

76. John F. Kennedy, "The President's News Conference," 12 December 1962, *American Presidency Project*. Available 9 April 2013. http://www.presidency.ucsb.edu/ws/index.php?pid=9054.

77. Lyndon B. Johnson, "Statement by the President on Receiving a Progress Report of the Council on Physical Fitness," 30 July 1964, *American Presidency Project*. Available 9 April 2013. http://www.presidency.ucsb.edu/ws/index.php?pid=26410&st=physical&st1=.

78. *Ibid.*

79. Lyndon B. Johnson," "Remarks at a Ceremony Honoring Physical Fitness Winners," 3 May 1965, *American Presidency Project*. Available 10 April 2013. http://www.presidency.ucsb.edu/ws/index.php?pid=26933&st=physical&st1=.

80. *Ibid.*

81. Robert Dallek, *Flawed Giant: Lyndon Johnson and His Times, 1961–1973* (New York: Oxford University Press, 1998), 519.

82. John F. Kennedy: "Inaugural Address," January 20, 1961. Online by Gerhard Peters and John T. Woolley, *The American Presidency*

Project. http://www.presidency.ucsb.edu/Ws/?
Pid=8032.

Chapter 2

1. "Russia Plans Other Visits," *New York Times,* 21 November 1945.
2. Andre Gounot, "Between Revolutionary Demands and Diplomatic Necessity: The Uneasy Relationship Between Soviet Sport and Worker and Bourgeois Sport in Europe from 1920 to 1937," in Pierre Arnaud and James Riordan, ed., *Sport and International Politics* (New York: E and FN Spon, 1998), 190.
3. William Taubman, *Khrushchev: The Man and His Era* (New York: W.W. Norton, 2004).
4. "Paris 1900," *International Olympic Committee,* 2012. Available 22 April 2013. http://www.olympic.org/paris-1900-summer-olympics.
5. "London, 1908," *International Olympic Committee,* 2012. Available 22 April 2013. http://www.olympic.org/london-1908-summer-olympics.
6. "Stockholm 1912," *International Olympic Committee,* 2012. Available 22 April 2013. http://www.olympic.org/stockholm-1912-summer-olympics.
7. *Ibid.*
8. Keys, *Globalizing Sport,* 19.
9. James Riordan, "The Sports Policy of the Soviet Union, 1917–1941," in Pierre Arnaud and James Riordan, ed., *Sport and International Politics* (New York: E and FN Spon, 1998), 68.
10. *Ibid.*
11. William D. Frank, *Everyone to Skis! Skiing in Russia and the Rise of Soviet Biathlon* (DeKalb: Northern Illinois University Press, 2013), 62.
12. E.H. Carr, *A History of Soviet Russia: Socialism in One Country, 1924–1926: Volume 3, Part 2* (London: Macmillan, 1964), 957.
13. James Riordan and Arnd Krüger, *The International Politics of Sport in the Twentieth Century* (London: Routledge, 1999), 107.
14. Riordan, "The Sports Policy of the Soviet Union," 69.
15. *Ibid.,* 109.
16. Gounot, 201.
17. Barbara Keys, "Soviet Sport and Transnational Mass Culture in the 1930s," *Journal of Contemporary History* 38, no. 3 (July 2003), 423.
18. Susan Grant, *Physical Culture and Sport*

in Soviet Society: Propaganda, Acculturation, and Transformation in the 1920s and 1930s (New York: Routledge, 2013), 35–37.
19. Robert Service, *A History of Twentieth-Century Russia* (Cambridge: Harvard University Press, 1998), 140.
20. *Ibid.,* 191.
21. Barbara Keys, *Globalizing Sport: National Rivalry and International Community in the 1930s* (Cambridge: Harvard University Press, 2006), 164.
22. *Ibid.,* 165.
23. *Ibid.,* 170.
24. *Ibid.,* 170–171.
25. "About Sovetsky Sport," *Sovetsky Sport,* 2013. Available 25 April 2013. http://www.sovsport.ru/about/.
26. James Riordan "The Role of Sport in Soviet Foreign Policy," *International Journal* 43, no. 4, Sport in World Politics (Autumn 1988), 570–571.
27. Keys, *Globalizing Sport,* 165.
28. *Ibid.,* 164–167.
29. Riordan and Kruger, *The International Politics of Sport in the Twentieth* Century, 76–77.
30. James Riordan, "The Worker Sports Movement," in *the International Politics of Sport in the Twentieth Century* (London: F&N Spon, 1999), 114.
31. Victor Peppard and James Riordan, *Playing Politics: Soviet Sport Diplomacy to 1992* (Greenwich, Conn.: JAI Press, Inc., 1993), 62.
32. David Downing, *Passovotchka: Moscow Dynamo in Britain* (London: Bloomsbury, 1999), 51–52.
33. Robert Edelman, *Serious Fun: A History of Spectator Sports in the USSR* (New York: Oxford University Press, 1993), 87.
34. Downing, *Passovotchka,* 188.
35. "Russia Plans Other Visits," *New York Times,* 21 November 1945.
36. Edelman, *Serious Fun,* 94–95.
37. Downing, *Passovotchka,* 253–254.
38. Riordan, *Sport in Soviet Society,* 168.
39. *The Soviet Olympic Team, 1964* (Moscow: Novosti Press Agency Publishing House, 1964), 3.
40. Downing, 105–106.
41. *Sport in the USSR* (Moscow: Soviet News Publication, 1949), 5.
42. Irving R. Levine, *Main Street, USSR* (Garden City, NY: Doubleday and Company, 1959), 375.
43. Espy, *The Politics of the Olympic Games,* 71.

44. Allen Guttmann, *The Olympics: A History of the Modern Games* (Urbana: University of Illinois Press, 1992).

45. Irving Jaffee, "Why America Can't Win the 1960 Olympics," *Washington Post*, 17 January 1960, AW4; Randy Roberts and James Olson, *Winning Is the Only Thing: Sports in America Since 1945* (Baltimore: Johns Hopkins University Press, 1989), 11–13.

46. Peppard and Riordan, *Playing Politics*, 67–68.

47. Alfred E. Senn, *Power, Politics and the Olympic Games: A History of the Power Brokers, Events, and Controversies That Shaped the Games* (Champagne, Il.: Human Kinetics, 1999) 90.

48. Edelman, *Serious Fun*, 126.

49. *Ibid.*, 201.

50. Carson Cunningham, *American Hoops: U.S. Men's Olympic Basketball from Berlin to Beijing* (Lincoln: University of Nebraska Press, 2009), 110.

51. Frank, *Everyone to Skis!*, 58.

52. Riordan, *Sport in Soviet Society*, 173–174.

53. Mike O'Mahony, *Sport in the USSR: Physical Culture-Visual Culture* (London: Reaktion Books, 2006), 30–31.

54. James Riordan, *Sport in Soviet Society* (Cambridge: Cambridge University Press, 1977), 110–111.

55. *Ibid.*, 173–174.

56. Edelman, *Serious Fun*, 150.

57. Horace Sutton, "The Olympian Fields of Moscow," *Sports Illustrated*, 15 April 1956.

58. *Ibid.*

59. "Current Week and What's Ahead," *Sports Illustrated*, 30 January 1956.

60. *Highlights of Soviet Sport*, 25.

61. Anatoli Kolassov, "From the Spartakiad to the Olympiad," *Olympic Review* 143, (September 1979), 502.

62. *Ibid.* 502–503.

63. Avery Brundage, Speech given 29 September 1967, *Olympic Review*, November 2 (1967), 7.

64. Mike Dennis and Jonathan Griz, *Sport Under Communism: Behind the East German 'Miracle'* (Basingstoke: Palgrave Macmillan, 2012), 72–74.

65. Alan R. Platt, *The Olympic Games and Their Political Aspects: 1952–1972* (Dissertation, Kent State, 1976), 17.

66. *Soviet Sports Handbook, 1958*, London: "Soviet News" booklet no. 28, *Soviet News Booklet* 28 (1957), 5.

67. *Ibid.*, 5.

68. Richard Stites, *Russian Popular Culture: Entertainment and Society Since 1900* (Cambridge: Cambridge University Press, 1992), 175.

69. Harry Schwartz, "Stalin Trains His Olympic Teams," *New York Times*, 20 April 1952.

70. Riordan, *Sport in Soviet Society*, 345–346.

71. Yuri Brokhin, *The Big Red Machine: The Rise and Fall of Soviet Olympic Champions* (New York: Random House, 1977), 106.

72. Frank, *Everyone to Skis!*, 58.

73. Schwartz, "Stalin Trains His Olympic Teams."

74. *Physical Culture and Sport in the USSR* (Brussels: Brussels Universal and International Exposition USSR Section, 1958), 9.

75. *Ibid.*, 55.

76. "U.S. Weightlifters Called Sissies by Reds," *Washington Post*, 26 March 1956, 12.

77. *Ibid.*

78. Edelman, *Serious Fun*, 151.

79. Cunningham, *American Hoops*, 33–34.

80. "Golden Melbourne," *Sports Illustrated*, 10 December 1956.

81. Carson Cunningham, "The Russell Model: Melbourne 1956 and Bill Russell's New Basketball Standard," *Olympika: The International Journal of Sports Studies* Volume XV (2006), 81.

82. "U.S. Routed by Russians," *Washington Post and Times Herald*, 29 January 1959, D1.

83. Arthur Daley, "Sports of the Times: Seeing Red," *New York Times*, 3 February 1959, 39.

84. Juan de Onis, "Loss to Russia Costs U.S. Basketball Prestige," *New York Times*, 30 January 1959, 23.

85. Levine, *Main Street, USSR*, 144.

86. Wright Miller, *Russians as People* (New York: EP Dutton and Co., 1961), 148–49.

87. Edelman, *Serious Fun*, 152.

88. *Physical Culture and Sport in the USSR*, 23.

89. Speak and Ambler, *Physical Education, Recreation and Sport in the USSR*, 73.

90. *Ibid.*, 73–74.

91. *Ibid.*, 78–79.

92. James Riordan, *Soviet Sport: Background to the Olympics* (London: Washington Mews Books, 1980), 16.

93. William J. Baker, *Sport in the Western World* (Urbana: University of Illinois Press, 1988) 267.

94. Levine, *Main Street, USSR*, 375.

95. Riordan, *Soviet Sport: Background to the Olympics*, 17.

96. *Ibid.*

97. Caracappa, "The Original Golden Boys."

98. Edelman, *Serious Fun*, 130.

99. *Ibid.*, 129–134.

100. Riordan, *Sport, Politics and Communism*, 127–138; JT Dykman, "The Soviet Experience in World War II," *The Eisenhower Institute*. Available 1 November 2014. http://www.eisenhowerinstitute.org/about/living_history/wwii_soviet_experience.dot.

101. Edelman, *Serious Fun*, 100.

102. Robert Edelman, *Spartak Moscow: A History of the People's Team in the Workers' State* (Ithaca: Cornell University Press, 2009), 138–142.

103. *Ibid.*, 197.

104. Aleksandr Fursenko and Timothy Naftali, *Khrushchev's Cold War: The Inside Story of an American Adversary* (New York: W.W. Norton, 2006), 535–537.

105. Harry Schwartz, "Khrushchev Under Fire: New Leaders' Charges May Portend Campaign Similar to De-Stalinization," *New York Times*, 18 October 1964, 32.

106. Roberts and Olson, *Winning Is the Only Thing*, 19.

Chapter 3

1. Sigfrid Edstrom, Speech, 14 August 1948, Speeches of Sigfrid Edstrom 1936.01.01–1953.12.31, Olympic Studies Centre, Lausanne, Switzerland, hereafter OSC.

2. Winston Churchill, "Iron Curtain Speech," 5 March 1946, *Modern History Sourcebook*. Available 20 November 2013. http://www.fordham.edu/halsall/mod/churchill-iron.asp.

3. Matt Rogan and Martin Rogan, *Britain and the Olympic Games: Past, Present, Legacy* (Leicester, UK: Matador, 2011), 42.

4. Hampton, *The Austerity Olympics*.

5. Richard Espy, *The Politics of the Olympic Games* (Berkeley: University of California Press, 1979), 26–29.

6. Nicholas Evan Sarantakes, *Dropping the Torch: Jimmy Carter, the Olympic Boycott, and the Cold War* (New York: Cambridge University Press, 2011), 22.

7. Espy, 28.

8. *Ibid.*, 32–36.

9. Carson Cunningham, *American Hoops: U.S. Men's Olympic Basketball from Berlin to Beijing* (Lincoln: University of Nebraska Press, 2009), 147–148.

10. Frank Costigliola, *Roosevelt's Lost Alliances: How Personal Politics Helped Start the Cold War* (Princeton: Princeton University Press, 2012).

11. *Ibid.*

12. Harry S. Truman: "Special Message to the Congress on Greece and Turkey: The Truman Doctrine," March 12, 1947. Online by Gerhard Peters and John T. Woolley, *The American Presidency Project*. http://www.presidency.ucsb.edu/ws/?pid=12846.

13. For examples of this type of writing, see the *New York Times* and *Washington Post* sports pages throughout the period at hand, 1948–1968.

14. Walter Hixson, *Parting the Curtain: Propaganda, Culture, and the Cold War, 1945–1961* (New York: St. Martin's, 1997); Stephen Wagg and David L. Andrews, eds., *East Plays West: Sport and the Cold War* (London: Routledge, 2007).

15. *New York Times* was the newspaper that most frequently republished Soviet news paired with its own commentary, though by no means was it the only press outlet to do so. Even before the Soviets joined the Olympic Movement, anti-Moscow sentiment had begun to run rampant as part of the developing superpower rivalry. For one example, see Ferdinand Kuhn, Jr., "Red Newspapers Build Up Foreign Conspiracy Theme," *Washington Post*, 18 May 1947, M10.

16. Arthur Daley, "Sports of the Times: From Behind the Iron Curtain," *New York Times*, 23 December 1947, 34.

17. *Ibid.*

18. Red Smith, "Arthur Daley, Sports Columnist, Dies," *New York Times*, 4 January 1974, 32.

19. Examples of this are numerous and can be found in a multitude of American publications throughout the Cold War. One such example is Daley's Man O'War piece from 1947. Daley, "Sports of the Times: From Behind the Iron Curtain."

20. Shirley Povich, "This Morning with Shirley Povich," *Washington Post*, 26 August 1945, M6.

21. Shirley Povich, "This Morning with Shirley Povich," *Washington Post*, 18 July 1948, C1.

22. Hampton, *The Austerity Olmypics*, 8.

23. Povich, "This Morning with Shirley Povich," 18 July 1948.

24. Shirley Povich, "This Morning with Shirley Povich," *Washington Post*, 21 January 1948, 19.

25. Hampton, *The Austerity Olympics*, 38, 75–76.

26. Robert Musel, "Russians Ignore Olympic Deadline, Stick to Bragging from Behind 'Iron Curtain,'" *Washington Post*, 17 June 1948, 21.

27. Harry S. Truman to Avery Brundage, 7 November 1947, Brundage Papers, Box 332 Important Letters To and from Heads of State, USA, LA84 Foundation Library, Los Angeles, hereafter LA84.

28. *Ibid.*

29. Harry S. Truman to Avery Brundage, 10 November 1951, Box 332, Important Letters to and from Avery Brundage, Brundage Papers, LA84.

30. Hampton, *The Austerity Olympics*, 38–40.

31. "Russians Start Berlin Rail Lines but Restrict Food," *The Daily Boston Globe*, 1 July 1949, 13.

32. Espy, *The Politics of the Olympic Games*, 24.

33. "Appeal by the City Parliament to the United Nations," 29 June 1948, in Wolfgang Heidelmeyer and Guenter Hindrichs, eds., *Documents on Berlin, 1943–1963* (Munich: R. Oldenbourg Verlag, 1963), 80–83.

34. *Ibid.*, 82.

35. "More Food Being Flown into Berlin than Needed," *Washington Post*, 3 July 1948, 1.

36. "Bevin Says Crisis May Cause Britain to Peg Army," *Washington Post*, 30 July 1948, 1.

37. Rogan and Rogan, *Britain and the Olympic Games*, 42; Hampton 39.

38. Espy, *The Politics of the Olympic Games*, 26.

39. Robert Musel, "Russians Ignore Olympic Deadline, Stick to Bragging Rights from Behind 'Iron Curtain,'" *Washington Post*, 17 June 1948, 21.

40. *Ibid.*

41. Hampton, 39; "Brundage Sees Soviets, Germans, Japs in Olympics," *The Daily Boston Globe*, 16 August 1948, 8.

42. "Big Athletics Program," *New York Times*, 16 August 1948, 15.

43. Hampton, *The Austerity Olympics*, 2.

44. *Ibid.*, 22.

45. Bob Considine, "Olympic Games, with or Without Their Squabbles, Inspire Millions," *Washington Post*, 19 July 1948, 11.

46. Richard Espy, *The Politics of the Olympic Games*, 24.

47. Hampton, *The Austerity Olympics*, 22.

48. Hampton, *The Austerity Olympics*, 29–

30; Robin Tait, *The Politicization of the Modern Olympic Games* (Ann Arbor, MI: UMI, 1984), 80.

49. Tait, *The Politicization of the Modern Olympic Games*, 80.

50. Hampton, *The Austerity Olympics*, 317.

51. *Ibid.*, 39–40.

52. *Ibid.*, 40.

53. *Ibid.*, 6.

54. Bill Haley, *An Approved History of the Olympic Games* (New York: G.P. Putnam and Sons, 1976), 211.

55. *Ibid.*, 211–214.

56. Gayle Talbot, "Pageantry Marks End of Olympics," *Washington Post*, 15 August 1948, C1.

57. "Olympic Laurels," *New York Times*, 5 August 1948, 20.

58. Considine, "Olympic Games, with or Without Their Squabbles, Inspire Millions."

59. Sigfrid Edstrom, Speech, 14 August 1948, Speeches of Sigfrid Edstrom 1936.01.01–1953.12.31, OSC.

60. *Ibid.*

Chapter 4

1. Arthur Daley, "Sports of the Times," *New York Times*, 10 June 1952, 32.

2. Espy, *The Politics of the Olympic Games*, 31.

3. Hampton, *The Austerity Olympics*, 39.

4. Wagg and Andrews, *East Plays West*, 35.

5. "Brundage Says U.S. Olympic Team Will Fly All or Part of the Way to Helsinki Games," *New York Times*, 13 June 1951, 51.

6. Victor Peppard and James Riordan, *Playing Politics: Soviet Diplomacy to 1992* (Greenwich, Conn.: JAI Press, Inc., 1993), 67–68.

7. Tage Ericson, "Some Impressions from Sporting Life in Sovjet Russia," October 1950, Recognition request of the NOC of USSR: correspondence and recognition 1935.01.01–1951.12.31, OSC.

8. Wagg and Andrews, *East Plays West*, 30.

9. "Brundage Says Russians Promise to Heed Rules, Use No Pro Athletes," *Boston Globe*, 6 February 1952, 10.

10. "Ban on 'Subsidized' Athletes May Ruin U.S. in Olympics," *Washington Post*, 2 December 1951, C5;

11. *Ibid.*

12. Robert Creamer, "The Embattled World of Avery Brundage," *Sports Illustrated*, 30 Janu-

ary 1956; Harold Kaese, "Brundage Should Scan AAU Court, Track Ranks, If He Must Bar Someone," *Boston Globe,* 4 January 1952, 18.

13. Harry Schwartz, "Stalin Trains His Olympic Teams," *New York Times,* 20 April 1952, SM19.

14. Allen Guttmann, *The Olympics: A History of the Modern Games* (Urbana: University of Illinois Press, 1992), 142.

15. Letter from Edstrom to Brundage, 25 October 1950, Recognition request of the NOC of USSR: correspondence and recognition 1935.01.01–1951.12.31, OSC.

16. This remained a sticking point for many within the American sporting establishment and the press, who bemoaned the ongoing uneven treatment. Sources on this are numerous. See David Maraniss, *Rome 1960: The Olympics That Changed the World* (New York: Simon & Schuster, 2008), 330–331; "Brundage Says Russians Promise to Heed Rules, Use No Pro Athletes," *Boston Globe,* 6 February 1952, 10.

17. *Ibid.*

18. Letter from Edstrom to Mayer, 24 April 1951, Recognition request of the NOC of USSR: correspondence and recognition 1935.01.01–1951.12.31, OSC.

19. Tait, *The Politicization of the Modern Olympic Games,* 82.

20. "Constantin Andrianov Obituary," *Olympic Review* 245 (March 1988), 135.

21. Carson Cunningham, *American Hoops,* 63.

22. Damion L. Thomas, *Globetrotting: African American Athletes and Cold War Politics* (Urbana: University of Illinois Press, 2012), 78–82.

23. Toby C. Rider, "Political Warfare in Helsinki: American Covert Strategy and the Union of Free Eastern European Sportsmen," *The International Journal of the History Of Sport* 30, no. 13 (2013), 3–5.

24. Thomas, *Globetrotting: African American Athletes and Cold War Politics,* 78–82.

25. Harry Schwartz, "Stalin Trains His Olympic Teams," *New York Times,* 20 April 1952.

26. Brundage to J. Lyman Bingham, 18 June 1951, Box 20, Lyman Bingham Individual File, Brundage Papers, LA84.

27. Brundage to publishers, undated, Olympic Funds, 1952, Box 140, 1952 Olympic Games, Brundage papers, LA84.

28. Harry S. Truman to Avery Brundage, 10 November 1951, Box 332, Important Letters to and from Avery Brundage, Brundage Papers, LA84.

29. *Ibid.*

30. *Ibid.*

31. Rider, "Political Warfare in Helsinki," 147.

32. *Ibid.*

33. Toby Rider, "'It Is Not a Simple Matter to Keep Aloof': Avery Brundage and the U.S. Government in the Early Cold War Years," in Janice Forsyth and Michael K. Heine, *Problems, Possibilities, Promising Practices: Critical Dialogues on the Olympic and Paralympic Games* (Los Angeles: LA84 Foundation, 2012), 13–14.

34. Harry S. Truman, "Proclamation 2976—Olympic Week," 16 May 1952, *American Presidency Project.* Available 10 April 2013. http://www.presidency.ucsb.edu/ws/index.php?pid=87330&st=olympic&st1=

35. *Ibid.*

36. Harry S. Truman: "Address at the Sesquicentennial Convocation of the United States Military Academy," May 20, 1952. Online by Gerhard Peters and John T. Woolley, *The American Presidency Project.* http://www.presidency.ucsb.edu/ws/?pid=14119.

37. Harry Schwartz, "Moscow's Olympians: Soviet Competitors in the 1952 Olympics Are Likely to Be Tough and Competent," *New York Times,* 6 May 1951, SM30.

38. Bing Crosby in William O. Johnson, *All That Glitters Is Not Gold: The Olympic Game* (New York: G.P. Putnam and Sons, 1972), 223.

39. *Ibid.*

40. Jack Gould, "Radio and Television: Hope and Crosby, Latter in His TV Debut, Receive $1,000,020 in Pledges on 'Telethon' for Olympics, the *New York Times,* 23 June 1952, 27.

41. House Resolution 2276, Public Law 159, 80th Congress, First Session (1 July 1947), *Calendars of the United States House of Representatives and History of Legislation,* 62.

42. Harry S. Truman: "Proclamation 2976—Olympic Week, 1952," May 16, 1952. Online by Gerhard Peters and John T. Woolley, *The American Presidency Project.* http://www.presidency.ucsb.edu/ws/?pid=87330.

43. "City Charts Plans for Olympic Fund," *New York Times,* 1 April 1952, 39.

44. "Olympic Weekend," *New York Times,* 5 July 1952, 14.

45. Arthur Daley, "Sports of the Times: In Pursuit of an Ideal," *New York Times,* 12 August 1946, 26.

46. *Ibid.*

47. "'Jim' Thorpe Professional, Pleads Guilty to Charge," *Washington Post,* 28 January 1913, 8.

48. Tom Whitney, "Only Rich Students, Few Pros Can Afford to Engage in U.S. Sports, Says Soviet Paper," *Washington Post,* 17 January 1950, 11.

49. *Ibid.*

50. Shirley Povich, "This Morning with Shirley Povich," *Washington Post,* 18 January 1951, 17.

51. Samuel T. Williamson, "Headliners," *New York Times,* 20 May 1951, SM10.

52. *Ibid.*

53. "Military Heads Control Olympians from U.S., Soviet Paper Charges," *New York Times,* 27 January 1952, S1.

54. *Sovetsky Sport,* 8 March 1952.

55. Arthur Daley, "Sports of the Times: How Stupid Can They Get?" *New York Times,* 30 January 1952, 29.

56. *Ibid.*

57. Daley, "Sports of the Times," 10 June 1952.

58. Letter from Robertson to Lord Burghley, 10 May 1950, Recognition Request of the NOC of the German Democratic Republic: Correspondence and Statutes: 1951.01.01–1962.12.31, OSC.

59. Letter to Otto Mayer from le Comité National Olympique de la République Démocratique Allemande, 22 April 1951, Recognition Request of the NOC of the German Democratic Republic: Correspondence and Statutes: 1951.01.01–1962.12.31, OSC.

60. IOC Session Minutes, Vienna, 7–10 May 1951, Avery Brundage Collection, Box 76, LA84.

61. "Decision of the Executive Committee of the International Olympic Committee Regarding the German Situation," 11 February 1952, Recognition Request of the NOC of the German Democratic Republic: Correspondence and Statutes: 1951.01.01–1962.12.31, OSC.

62. Rider, "Political Warfare in Helsinki," 171, 208.

63. "Decision of the Executive Committee of the International Olympic Committee Regarding the German Situation."

64. *Ibid.*

65. Vienna Session Minutes.

66. Letter to Avery Brundage from Comité National Olympique de la République Démocratique Allemande, 12 February 1952, Recognition Request of the NOC of the German Democratic Republic: Correspondence and Statutes: 1951.01.01–1962.12.31, OSC.

67. IOC Session Minutes, Helsinki, 16–18 July 1952, Avery Brundage Collection, LA84.

68. *Ibid.*

69. Martin Barry Vinokur, *More than a Game: Sport and Politics* (New York: Greenwood Press, 1988), 61–62.

70. Harrison E. Salisbury, "Pep Talks by Soviet Press Urge Red Athletes to Annex Crowns," *New York Times,* 21 July 1952.

71. *Ibid.*

72. Arthur Daley, "Sports of the Times: The Olympic Enigma," 16 July 1952, 29.

73. *Ibid.*

74. Tait, *The Politicization of the Modern Olympic Games,* 180–181.

75. *Ibid.,*

76. Platt, *The Olympic Games and Their Political Aspects,* 149.

77. Sarantakes, *Dropping the Torch,* 248.

78. Bill Henry, *An Approved History of the Olympic Games* (New York: G.P. Putnam and Sons, 1976), 224.

79. *Ibid.,* 228.

80. "Soviet Uses Stall, Holds Score Down," *Washington Post,* 3 August 1952, C4.

81. *Ibid.*

82. "Olympics End; U.S. Scores 4 More Points," *Washington Post,* 4 August 1952, 38.

83. "Soviet Has Full Entry in Track," *Washington Post,* 11 July 1952, 17.

84. Henry, *An Approved History of the Olympic Games,* 229.

85. Jesse Abramson, "Olympics End; U.S. Scores 4 More Points," *Boston Globe,* 28 July 1952, 1.

86. Allison Danzig, "70,000 See Colorful Closing of Helsinki Olympic Games," *New York Times,* 4 August 1952, 1.

87. Abramson, "Olympics End; U.S. Scores 4 More Points."

88. Bill Henry, *An Approved History of the Olympic Games,* 226.

89. Abramson, "Olympics End; U.S. Scores 4 More Points."

90. Robert Musel, "U.S. Comeback Beats Russia in Olympics," *Washington Post,* 3 August 1952, M1.

91. *Ibid.*

92. Abramson, "Olympics End; U.S. Scores 4 More Points."

93. "Olympics and Politics," *Washington Post,* 29 July 1952, 10.

94. Harrison E. Salisbury, "Russians' Note of Joy at Showing Soured by Complaint on Officials," *New York Times,* 3 August 1952, 19.

95. Espy, *The Politics of the Olympic Games,* 38.

96. Avery Brundage, *The Speeches of Presi-*

dent *Avery Brundage, 1952–1968* (Lausanne: Comité Olympique Internationale: 1968), 6.

97. Thomas M. Domer, *Sport in Cold War America: The Diplomatic and Political Use of Sport in the Eisenhower and Kennedy Administrations* (Dissertation, University of Wisconsin-Milwaukee, 1976), 37.

98. *Ibid.,* 37.

Chapter 5

1. Melbourne Session Notes, 19 November-4 December 1956, Avery Brundage Collection, Box 78, LA84.

2. Simon Burnton, "Fifty Stunning Olympic Moments N07: Hungary V Soviet Union: Blood in the Water," *The Guardian,* 28 December 2011. Available 1 October 2014. http://www.theguardian.com/sport/blog/2011/dec/28/olympic-hungary-soviet-union-blood-water.

3. Alexander Wolff, "Revolution Games," *Sports Illustrated,* 18 June 2012.

4. Arch Puddington, *Broadcasting Freedom: The Cold War Triumph of Radio Free Europe and Radio Liberty* (Lexington: University Press of Kentucky, 2000), 89.

5. *Ibid.,* 42–43.

6. Kenneth Osgood, *Total Cold War: Eisenhower's Secret Propaganda Battle at Home and Abroad* (Manhattan: University Press of Kansas, 2006), 46.

7. Damion L. Thomas, *Globetrotting: African American Athletes and Cold War Politics* (Urbana: University of Illinois Press, 2012), 63.

8. *Ibid.,* 125.

9. Osgood, *Total Cold War,* 74.

10. Thomas, *Globetrotting,* 85.

11. Dwight D. Eisenhower: "Proclamation 3069—National Olympic Day, 1954," October 2, 1954. Online by Gerhard Peters and John T. Woolley, *The American Presidency Project.* http://www.presidency.ucsb.edu/ws/?pid=107217.

12. Dwight D. Eisenhower, "Remarks to Members of the Olympic Committee, Denver, Colorado," 12 October 1954. *The American Presidency Project.* Available 10 April 2013. http://www.presidency.ucsb.edu/ws/index.php?pid=10082&st=olympic&st1=

13. Thomas, *Globetrotting,* 90.

14. Dwight D. Eisenhower to Avery Brundage, 17 June 1955, Box 332, Important letters to and from Avery Brundage, Volume 1, Avery Brundage Collection, LA84.

15. Jenifer Parks, "Verbal Gymnastics: Sports, Bureaucracy, and the Soviet Union's Entrance into the Olympic Games, 1946–1952," in Wagg and Andrews, *East Plays West,* 27.

16. Avery Brundage, "Three Weeks Behind the Iron Curtain and What I Saw There," Speech given to the Detroit Economic Club, 15 October 1954, Box 245, Avery Brundage Collection, LA84.

17. Charles A. Bucher, "Are We Losing the Olympic Ideal?" *Sports Illustrated,* 8 August 1955.

18. *Ibid.*

19. *Ibid.*

20. *Ibid.*

21. Jimmy Jemail, "The Question: Should Team Scores Be Kept in the Olympics? (Asked of Big Shots)," *Sports Illustrated,* 19 November 1956.

22. *Ibid.*

23. *Ibid.*

24. Shirley Povich, "This Morning with Shirley Povich," *Washington Post,* 5 April 1956, 53.

25. *Ibid.*

26. Espy, *The Politics of the Olympic Games,* 52–53.

27. Brundage to Professor Jerzy Loth, 28 March 1953, Recognition Request of the NOC of the German Democratic Republic: Correspondence and Statutes: 1951.01.01–1962.12.31, OSC.

28. Brundage to Kurt Edel, 30 March 1953, Recognition Request of the NOC of the German Democratic Republic: Correspondence and Statutes: 1951.01.01–1962.12.31, OSC.

29. National Olympic Committee of the German Democratic Republic to the International Olympic Committee, 31 March 1953, Recognition Request of the NOC of the German Democratic Republic: Correspondence and Statutes: 1951.01.01–1962.12.31, OSC.

30. IOC Session Minutes, Mexico City, 17–20 April 1953, Box 79, Avery Brundage Collection, LA84.

31. *Ibid.*

32. IOC Session Minutes, Athens, 12–15 May 1954, Box 79, Avery Brundage Collection, LA84.

33. *Ibid.*

34. Letter from Mayer to the National Olympic Committee of the German Democratic Republic, 26 May 1954, Recognition Request of the NOC of the German Democratic Republic: Correspondence and Statutes: 1951.01.01–1962.12.31, OSC.

35. IOC Session Notes, Athens, 12–15 May 1954, Box 79, Avery Brundage Collection, LA84.

36. *Ibid.*

37. *Ibid.*

38. *Ibid.*

39. Letter from Brundage to the Nationales Olympisches Komites, 11 September 1954, Recognition Request of the NOC of the German Democratic Republic: Correspondence and Statutes: 1951.01.01–1962.12.31, OSC.

40. *Ibid.*

41. Letter from the Nationales Olympisches Komitee to the International Olympic Committee,28 February 1955, Recognition Request of the NOC of the German Democratic Republic: Correspondence and Statutes: 1951.01.01–1962.12.31, OSC.

42. IOC Session Minutes, Paris, 13–18 June 1955, Box 80, Avery Brundage Collection, LA84.

43. *Ibid.*

44. *Ibid.*

45. Karl Ritter von Halt, "Our Decision of Paris Was the Following," 1956, Recognition Request of the NOC of the German Democratic Republic: Correspondence and Statutes: 1951.01.01–1962.12.31, OSC.

46. Letter from Brundage to Schobel, 21 March 1956, Recognition Request of the NOC of the German Democratic Republic: Correspondence and Statutes: 1951.01.01–1962.12.31, OSC.

47. IOC Session Minutes, Cortina d'Ampezzo, 24–25 January 1956, Box 80, Avery Brundage Collection, LA84.

48. Toby C. Rider, "The Distant Fight Against Communist Sport: Refugee Sports Organizations in America and the International Olympic Committee," in Robert Knight Barney, Janice Forsyth, et al, *Rethinking Matters Olympic: Investigations into the Socio-Cultural Study of the Modern Olympic Movement* (London, Ontario: International Centre for Olympic Research, 2010), 118.

49. Mayer to Asa Bushnell, 16 October 1956, Correspondence of the NOC of the United States of America: 1955.01.01–1966.12.31, OSC.

50. Ukrainian Olympic Committee to the IOC Executive Board, 1956, Correspondence of the NOC of the United States of America: 1955.01.01–1966.12.31, page 2, OSC.

51. *Ibid.,*1.

52. *Ibid.,*2.

53. *Ibid.*

54. Kevin C. Ruffner, "Cold War Allies: The Origins of CIA's Relationship with Ukrainian Nationalists," Central Intelligence Agency. Available 23 June 2014. http://www.foia.

cia.gov/sites/default/files/document_conversions/1705143/STUDIES%20IN%20 INTELLIGENCE%20NAZI%20%20REL-ATED%20ARTICLES_0015.pdf, 19.

55. *Ibid.,* 29.

56. *Ibid.,* 30–32.

57. *Ibid.,* 35–43.

58. Tim Weiner, *Legacy of Ashes: The History of the CIA* (New York: Doubleday, 2007), 41.

59. Ukrainian Olympic Committee to the IOC Executive Board, 1956, 1.

60. Robert Creamer, "The Embattled World of Avery Brundage," *Sports Illustrated*, 30 January 1956; Jeremiah Tax, "An In-Depth Look at Both the Seemly and Seamy Sides of Avery Brundage," *Sports Illustrated*, 16 January 1984.

61. Jorg K.Hoensch, *A History of Modern Hungary: 1867–1986* (London: Longman, 1988), 208.

62. William Taubman, *Khrushchev: The Man and His Era* (New York: W.W. Norton, 2004), 300–301.

63. Dwight D. Eisenhower: "Statement by the President on the Developments in Hungary," October 25, 1956. Online by Gerhard Peters and John T. Woolley, *The American Presidency Project*. http://www.presidency.ucsb.edu/ws/?pid=10672.

64. Dwight D. Eisenhower: "Radio and Television Report to the American People on the Developments in Eastern Europe and the Middle East," October 31, 1956. Online by Gerhard Peters and John T. Woolley, *The American Presidency Project*. http://www.presidency.ucsb.edu/ws/?pid=10685.

65. Dwight D. Eisenhower: "Statement by the President Concerning the Admission of Refugees From Hungary," November 8, 1956. Online by Gerhard Peters and John T. Woolley, *The American Presidency Project*. http://www.presidency.ucsb.edu/ws/?pid=10700.

66. Taubman, *Khrushchev*, 300–301.

67. Puddington, *Broadcasting Freedom*, 90.

68. Thomas, *Globetrotting*, 272.

69. Kenneth Osgood, "Hearts and Minds: The Unconventional Cold War," *Journal of Cold War Studies* 4, no. 2 (Spring 2002), 85–107, 98.

70. Eisenhower, "Radio and Television Report to the American People on the Developments in Eastern Europe and the Middle East."

71. Douglas Little, *American Orientalism: The United States and the Middle East Since 1945* (Chapel Hill: University of North Carolina Press, 2008), 168–172.

72. *Ibid.,* 176–181.

73. IOC Session Notes, Melbourne, 19–21 November, 4 December 1956, Box 80, Avery Brundage Collection, LA84.

74. Melbourne Session Notes.

75. Thomas, *Globetrotting*, 275.

76. Brundage to Konstantin Andrianov and Vladimir Stoytcheff, 29 March 1956, Correspondence of the NOC of the USSR: 1951.01.01–1969.01.01, OSC.

77. "Events and Discoveries," *Sports Illustrated*, 12 November 1956.

78. Melbourne Session Notes.

79. *Ibid.*

80. Platt, *The Olympic Games and Their Political Aspects*, 194.

81. Melbourne Session Notes.

82. "Events and Discoveries."

83. *Ibid.*

84. Wolff, "Revolution Games."

85. "Hungary's Heroes in Their Hour of Staggering Strain," *Sports Illustrated*, 3 December 1956.

86. Platt, *The Olympic Games and Their Political Aspects*, 194.

87. Melbourne Session Notes.

88. "Hungary's Heroes in Their Hour of Staggering Strain."

89. Robert Edelman, *Spartak Moscow: A History of the People's Team in the Workers' State* (Ithaca: Cornell University Press, 2009), 228–229.

90. Bob Holbrook, "Jenkins, Connolly, Tenley Winners: U.S. Lost Olympics, but Broke or Tied World Marks 41 Times," *Boston Globe*, 30 December 1956, B19.

91. Ted Smits, "Morrow, U.S., Complete Olympic Track Rout," *Washington Postand Times Herald*, 2 December 1956, C1; Ted Smits, "Morrow Wins Two Gold Medals in Olympics," *Washington Postand Times Herald*, 28 November 1956, D1.

92. "Russia Captures Soccer Final, 1–0," *New York Times*, 8 December 1956, 23.

93. "U.S. Quintet Routs Russia in Melbourne Final, 89–55," *New York Times*, 2 December 1958, 81.

94. "Wait 'Til 1960," *New York Times*, 9 December 1956, 226.

95. Arthur Daley, "Sports of the Times: Long Range Look," *New York Times*, 5 December 1956, 53.

96. *Ibid.*

97. Alison Danzig, "Brundage Praises Games' Host City as Olympics End," *New York Times*, 9 December 1956, 235.

98. "Reds Win 12 Wrestling, Gymnastics Gold Medals," *Washington Post*, 7 December 1956, D1.

99. Dwight D. Eisenhower: "Statement by the President in Support of Red Cross Disaster Appeal for Relief in Hungary and to Hungarian Refugees in Austria," November 29, 1956. Online by Gerhard Peters and John T. Woolley, *The American Presidency Project*. http://www.presidency.ucsb.edu/ws/?pid=10710.

100. Philip Benjamin, "Hungarians Tour Jersey Factory," *New York Times*, 27 December 1956, 4.

101. Wolff, "Revolution Games."

102. Brinkley, *The Publisher*, 374.

103. Wolff, "Revolution Games."

104. Andre Laguerre, "Down a Road Called Liberty," *Sports Illustrated*, 17 December 1956.

105. *Ibid.*

106. Wolff, "Revolution Games."

107. *Ibid.*

108. Benjamin, "Hungarians Tour Jersey Factory."

109. Alexander Wolff, "What Became of 1956 Hungarian Olympians?" *Sports Illustrated*, 13 June 2012.

110. Wolff, "Revolution Games."

111. "Brundage on a Cloud Above Politics," *Sports Illustrated*, 15 June 1959.

Chapter 6

1. Henry Styles Bridges, U.S. Congress, Senate, 86th Congress, 1st session 24 April 1959, Cong. Record 105; A919.

2. David Maraniss, *Rome 1960: The Olympics That Changed the World* (New York: Simon & Schuster, 2008).

3. Taubman, *Khrushchev*, 396–397.

4. Dwight D. Eisenhower: "The President's News Conference," December 10, 1958. Online by Gerhard Peters and John T. Woolley, *The American Presidency Project*. http://www.presidency.ucsb.edu/ws/?pid=11294.

5. State Department Press Release #249 Concerning U-2 Incident, May 6, 1960, [Christian Herter Papers, Box 20, U-2 (1)]

6. State Department Statement 7 May 1960, Department of State Bulletin, May 23, 1960, p. 818–819.

7. Dwight D. Eisenhower: "The President's News Conference," May 11, 1960. Online by Gerhard Peters and John T. Woolley, *The American Presidency Project*. http://www.presidency.ucsb.edu/ws/?pid=11778.

8. Walter A. McDougall, *The Heavens and*

the Earth: A Political History of the Space Age (New York: Basic Books, Inc., 1985), 8.

9. William Safire, "The Cold War's Hot Kitchen," *New York Times*, 23 July 2009.

10. Thomas M. Domer, *Sport in Cold War America: The Diplomatic and Political Use of Sport in the Eisenhower and Kennedy Administrations* (Dissertation, University of Wisconsin-Milwaukee, 1976), 157.

11. John Soares, "Cold War, Hot Ice: International Ice Hockey, 1947–1980," *Journal of Sport History* 24, no. 2 (Summer 2007), 139.

12. Henry Styles Bridges, U.S. Congress, Senate, 86th Congress, 1st session 24 April 1959, Cong. Record 105; A919.

13. McDougall, *The Heavens and the Earth*, 57.

14. Dwight D. Eisenhower, "The President's News Conference," 3 February 1960, *American Presidency Project*. Available 11 April 2013. http://www.presidency.ucsb.edu/ws/index.php?pid=11884&st=olympic&st1=.

15. *Ibid.*

16. *Ibid.*

17. Arthur Daley, "Sports of the Times: The Inscrutable Orient," *New York Times*, 1 June 1959, 32.

18. *Ibid.*

19. *Ibid.*

20. Jenifer Parks, *Red Sport, Red Tape: The Olympic Games, the Soviet Sports Bureaucracy, and the Cold War, 1952–1980* (Dissertation, University of North Carolina), 210.

21. William Glenn Gray, *Germany's Cold War: The Global Campaign to Isolate East Germany, 1949–1969* (Chapel Hill: University of North Carolina Press, 2003), 97.

22. *Ibid.,* 42.

23. *Ibid.,* 30–31.

24. "Red Issue May Bar '60 Olympics in U.S.," *The New York Times*, 2 July 1957.

25. "Brundage Tells U.S. Its Stand on Visas Can Imperil Olympics," *New York Times*, 13 July 1957.

26. Donald J. Gonzales, "U.S. to Admit Reds for Winter Olympics," *Washington Post*, 18 September 1957, A3.

27. *Ibid.*

28. "Brundage Tells U.S. Its Stand on Visas Can Imperil Olympics."

29. Russians Voice Surprise at Decision of U.S. Hockey Team to Cancel Visit, *New York Times*, 17 February 1957.

30. *Ibid.*

31. John M. Hoberman, *The Olympic Crisis: Sport, Politics, and the Moral Order* (New

Rochelle, NY: Aristide D. Caratzas, 1986), 78.

32. Espy, *The Politics of the Olympic Games*, 62.

33. Gordon S. White, "Track Meets Between United States and Russia Canceled," *New York Times*, 19 June 1957, 45.

34. Andrianov to Mayer, 28 March 1957, Correspondence of the NOC of the USSR: 01.01.1951–12.31.1969, OSC.

35. *Ibid.*

36. *Ibid.*

37. Arthur Daley, "Sports of the Times: En Route to Moscow," *New York Times*, 19 June 1958, 42.

38. Andrianov to Mayer, 9 April 1957, Correspondence of the NOC of USSR: 1951.01.01–1969.12.31, OSC.

39. Platt, *The Olympic Games and Their Political Aspects*, 222.

40. Andrianov to Mayer, 22 March 1958, Recognition Request of the NOC of the German Democratic Republic: Correspondence and Statutes: 1951.01.01–1962.12.31, OSC.

41. Brundage to Ritter von Halt and Schobel, 15 April 1958, Recognition Request of the NOC of the German Democratic Republic: Correspondence and Statutes: 1951.01.01–1962.12.31, OSC.

42. *Ibid.*

43. Ritter von Halt to Brundage, 18 June 1959, Recognition Request of the NOC of the German Democratic Republic: Correspondence and Statutes: 1951.01.01–1962.12.31, OSC.

44. IOC Session Minutes, Munich, 25–28 May 1959, Box 81, Avery Brundage Collection, LA84.

45. *Ibid.*

46. Espy, *The Politics of the Olympic Games*, 67.

47. Sydney Gruson, "Reds' Flag Snags Bonn Olympics Bid," *New York Times*, 23 November 1959, 7.

48. Sydney Gruson, "German Flag Set for Olympics," *New York Times*, 7 December 1959, 3.

49. Willi Daume to Brundage, 27 November 1959, Recognition Request of the NOC of the German Democratic Republic: Correspondence and Statutes: 1951.01.01–1962.12.31, OSC.

50. Gruson, Reds' Flag Snags Bonn Olympics Bid."

51. Daume to Brundage, 27 November 1959.

52. Gruson, "German Flag Set for Olympics."

53. "Skiing to Be Boycotted," *New York Times,* 28 December 1959, 28.

54. "Soviet Flag Is Stolen at Austrian Ski Meet," *New York Times,* 15 January 1960, 20.

55. "15 East Germans Denied U.S. Visas," *New York Times,* 6 February 1960.

56. IOC Session Minutes, San Francisco, 15–16 February 1960, Box 81, Avery Brundage Collection, LA84.

57. "U.S. Refuses Visas," *New York Times,* 11 February 1960, 47.

58. "German Reds Assail U.S. Olympic Curb," *New York Times,* 12 February 1960, 3.

59. San Francisco Session Minutes.

60. "Free Press Gets Olympic Support," *New York Times,* 16 February 1960, 2.

61. Hampton, *The Austerity Olympics,* 40.

62. "Events and Discoveries," *Sports Illustrated,* 22 February 1960.

63. *Ibid.*

64. Irving Jaffee, "Why America Can't Win the 1960 Olympics," *Washington Post,* 17 January 1960, AW4.

65. *Ibid.*

66. "We Did It Is Cry of U.S. Jubilation," *New York Times,* 28 February 1960.

67. Matt Caracappa, "The Original Golden Boys," *USA Hockey Magazine,* February 2010. Available 3 May 2013. http://www.usahockey magazine.com/article/2010-02/original-golden-boys.

68. "U.S. Teams Finish 3d in Olympics," *Boston Globe,* 29 February 1960, 1.

69. "250,000 Welcome Carol Heiss Home," *New York Times,* 10 March 1960, 15.

70. Roy Terrell, "The Heroes of Squaw Valley," *Sports Illustrated,* 29 February 1960.

71. "The Spirit of the Game," *Boston Globe,* 29 February 1960, 6.

72. "The Winter Games," *New York Times,* 29 February 1960, 26.

73. Michael Strauss, "U.S. Performance Teaches a Lesson," *New York Times,* 1 March 1960, 38.

74. Maraniss, *Rome 1960,* 155.

75. "100,025 Go West," *Washington Post,* 4 September 1960, B3.

76. Maraniss, *Rome 1960,* 106.

77. Harry Schwartz, "Propaganda Drive: Moscow Tells Its People to Be Wary of Contact with Americans," *New York Times,* 21 August 1960, E3.

78. Rider, *The Olympic Games and the Secret Cold War,* 355–357.

79. *Ibid.,* 372.

80. Eddy Gilmore, "A Struggle for Men's Minds in Olympics," *Washington Post,* 20 August 1960, A13.

81. Nicholas J. Cull, *The Cold War and the United States Information Agency: American Propaganda and Public Diplomacy, 1945–1989* (Cambridge: Cambridge University Press, 2008), 174–175.

82. *Ibid.*

83. Oscar Fraley, "Uncle Sam Sends 305 into Games," *Washington Post,* 25 August 1960, D1.

84. "Bulgar Accused of Wrestling Fix," *New York Times,* 3 September 1960, 10.

85. Maraniss, *Rome 1960,* 234–236.

86. *Ibid.,* 238–239.

87. "Why Khrushchev Is Coming to UN," *Washington Post,* 4 September 1960, E4.

88. Maraniss, *Rome 1960,* 194.

89. "2 Satellite Dogs Shown in Moscow," *New York Times,* 23 August 1960, 3.

90. Dwight D. Eisenhower: "Statement by the President on U.S. Achievements in Space," August 17, 1960. Online by Gerhard Peters and John T. Woolley, *The American Presidency Project.* http://www.presidency.ucsb.edu/ws/?pid=11911.

91. Maraniss, *Rome 1960,* 426.

92. *Ibid.,* 387.

93. Martin Kane, "Splendor and Spleen," *Sports Illustrated,* 5 September 1960.

94. Maraniss, *Rome 1960,* 385.

95. *Ibid.,* 394.

96. Kenneth Rudeen, "Dangerous When Wet," *Sports Illustrated,* 12 September 1960.

97. Maraniss, *Rome 1960,* 416, 427–430.

98. Arthur Daley, "Sports of the Times: Somber Second Thoughts," *New York Times,* 13 September 1960, 42.

99. Maraniss, *Rome 1960,* 308–309.

100. Arthur Daley, "Sports of the Times: Somber Second Thoughts."

101. John Sayle Watterson, *The Games Presidents Play: Sports and the Presidency* (Baltimore: John Hopkins University Press, 2006), 210.

Chapter 7

1. John F. Kennedy: "Statement by Senator John F. Kennedy on National Sportsmen for Kennedy Committee," October 21, 1960. Online by Gerhard Peters and John T. Woolley, *The American Presidency Project.* http://www.presidency.ucsb.edu/ws/?pid=74147.

2. Heather L. Dichter, "A Game of Polit-

ical Ice Hockey," in Heather L. Dichter and Andrew Johns, eds., *Diplomatic Games: Sport, Statecraft, and International Relations Since 1945* (Lexington: University Press of Kentucky, 2014), 38–41.

3. William D. Frank, *Everyone to Skis! Skiing in Russia and the Rise of Soviet Biathlon* (DeKalb: Northern Illinois University Press, 2013), 193.

4. Guttmann, *The Olympics*, 110.

5. Andreas Wenger, *Living with Peril: Eisenhower, Kennedy, and Nuclear Weapons* (New York: Rowman and Littlefield, 1997), 238.

6. John F. Kennedy: "Inaugural Address," January 20, 1961. Online by Gerhard Peters and John T. Woolley, *The American Presidency Project*. http://www.presidency.ucsb.edu/ws/?pid=8032.

7. *Ibid.*

8. *Ibid.*

9. Aleksandr Fursenko and Timothy Naftali, *Khrushchev's Cold War: The Inside Story of an American Adversary* (New York: W.W. Norton, 2006), 379–83.

10. Taubman, *Khrushchev*, 536–537.

11. Rider, *The Olympic Games and the Secret Cold War*, 378.

12. Harry Schwartz, "Khrushchev Under Fire: New Leaders' Charges May Portend Campaign Similar to De-Stalinization," *New York Times*, 18 October 1964, 32.

13. *Ibid.*

14. Fursenko and Naftali, *Khrushchev's Cold War*, 531–32.

15. Vladislav M. Zubok, *A Failed Empire: The Soviet Union in the Cold War from Stalin to Gorbachev* (Chapel Hill: University of North Carolina Press, 2007), 193–94.

16. Lyndon B. Johnson: "Radio and Television Report to the American People on Recent Events in Russia, China, and Great Britain," October 18, 1964. Online by Gerhard Peters and John T. Woolley, *The American Presidency Project*. http://www.presidency.ucsb.edu/ws/?pid=26627.

17. John F. Kennedy, "The Soft American," *Sports Illustrated*, 26 December 1960.

18. *Ibid.*

19. Arthur Daley, "Sports of the Times: Somber Second Thoughts," *New York Times*, 13 September 1960, 42.

20. Kennedy, "The Soft American."

21. *Ibid.*

22. "The President Who Loved Sport," *Sports Illustrated*, 3 December 1963.

23. *Ibid.*

24. Domer, *Sport in Cold War America*, 228.

25. John F. Kennedy, "Address in New York City at the National Football Foundation and Hall of Fame Banquet," 5 December 1961, *American Presidency Project*. Available 11 April 2013. http://www.presidency.ucsb.edu/ws/index.php?pid=8473&st=olympic&st1=.

26. John F. Kennedy, "The Vigor We Need," *Sports Illustrated* 16 July 1962.

27. Robert Edelman, *Serious Fun: A History of Spectator Sport in the USSR* (New York: Oxford University Press, 1993), 125–126, 151.

28. Harold Kaese, "Russia Afraid of U.S. Aces?" *Boston Globe*, 10 April 1964, 23.

29. "Russians Turn Down NBA Tour," *Washington Post*, 10 April 1964, D6.

30. Democratic Party Platforms: "Democratic Party Platform of 1960," July 11, 1960. Online by Gerhard Peters and John T. Woolley, *The American Presidency Project*. http://www.presidency.ucsb.edu/ws/?pid=29602.

31. John F. Kennedy: "Speech of Senator John F. Kennedy, VFW Convention, Detroit, MI—(verbatim Text)," August 26, 1960. Online by Gerhard Peters and John T. Woolley, *The American Presidency Project*. http://presidency.ucsb.edu/ws/?pid=74216.

32. *Ibid.*

33. McDougall, *The Heavens and the Earth*, 218–219.

34. "Cheering Sailors Greet Astronaut," *New York Times*, 6 May 1961, 8.

35. John F. Kennedy: "Special Message to the Congress on Urgent National Needs," May 25, 1961. Online by Gerhard Peters and John T. Woolley, *The American Presidency Project*. http://www.presidency.ucsb.edu/ws/?pid=8151.

36. Schwartz.

37. John F. Kennedy: "The President's News Conference," October 9, 1963. Online by Gerhard Peters and John T. Woolley, *The American Presidency Project*. http://www.presidency.ucsb.edu/ws/?pid=9460.

38. Chalmers M. Roberts, "What Are the Russians Up To?" *Boston Globe*, 5 October 1963, 5.

39. Thomas M. Hunt, "American Sport Policy and the Cultural Cold War: The Lyndon B. Johnson Presidential Years," *Journal of Sport History* 33, no. 3 (2006), 275.

40. Lyndon B. Johnson: "Recorded Remarks Congratulating the U.S. Olympic Team and the Members of the U.S. Olympic Committee," October 23, 1964. Online by Gerhard Peters and John T. Woolley, *The American Pres-*

idency Project. http://www.presidency.ucsb. edu/ws/?pid=26641.

41. "Letter from Ulbricht to Khrushchev," June 1961, History and Public Policy Program Digital Archive, SED Archives, IfGA, ZPA, J IV 2/202/129. CWIHP Working Paper No. 5, "Ulbricht and the Concrete 'Rose.'" Translated for CWIHP by Hope Harrison. http://digital archive.wilsoncenter.org/document/117149

42. "Sports Ties Ended," *New York Times,* 17 August 1961, 10.

43. Daume to Brundage, 10 November 1961, 6.

44. *Ibid.,* 7.

45. *Ibid.*

46. *Ibid.*

47. Daume to Brundage, 15 February 1962, Recognition Request of the NOC of the German Democratic Republic: Correspondence and Statutes: 1951.01.01–1962.12.31, page 1, OSC.

48. IOC Session Minutes, Moscow, 5–8 June 1962, Box 82, Avery Brundage Collection, LA84, 6.

49. "Unified German Team Competes in Olympics," *Washington Post,* 6 June 1962, D4.

50. "One Germany for Olympics, Partly Anyway," *Boston Globe,* 9 December 1962, 62.

51. "East Germans in Olympic Berth," *New York Times,* 6 July 1964, 24.

52. Brundage, *The Speeches of President Avery Brundage,* 67–68.

53. "Meeting of the Two German Olympic Committees Presided Over by Mr. Avery Brundage, President of the International Olympic Committee," 20 August 1963, Box 129, Avery Brundage Collection, LA84.

54. IOC Session Minutes, Baden Baden, 16–20 October 1963, Box 82, Avery Brundage Collection, LA84, 10.

55. "East-West Rift Threatens Winter Team," *New York Times,* 29 July 1963, 25.

56. Mayer to NOK, 8 July 1964, Recognition Request of the NOC of the German Democratic Republic: Correspondence and Statutes: 1963.01.01–1968.12.31, OSC.

57. IOC Session Minutes, Tokyo, 4–5 October 1964, Box 83, Avery Brundage Collection, LA84, 13.

58. *Ibid.,* 25.

59. "Soviet Charges U.S. Bars German Team," *New York Times,* 7 January 1962, 14.

60. "U.S. Is Assured Visa Trouble Will Not Shift World Hockey," *New York Times,* 27 January 1962, 25.

61. "World Ski Event Still on but Name Is Changed," *Washington Post,* 6 February 1962, A16.

62. "Communists Withdraw from Ski Championship," *Washington Post,* 7 February 1962, C3.

63. Ed West, *Don't Mention the World Cup: A History of England-Germany Rivalry from the War to the World Cup* (Chichester, UK: Summersdale, 2006).

64. Max Frankel, "West Bars East Germans in Retaliation for the Wall," *New York Times,* 27 January 1962, 1.

65. "Cold War Called Olympic Threat," *New York Times,* 29 March 1962, 36.

66. Robert Daley, "Olympics Insist on 1968 Bias Ban," *New York Times,* 16 March 1963, 8.

67. Espy, *The Politics of the Olympic Games,* Mr80–82.

68. Red Smith, "U.S. Skiers Draw Praise for 'Major Breakthrough,'" *Boston Globe,* 10 February 1964, 21.

69. "Russia Tips Canada, Wins Hockey Crown," *Boston Globe,* 9 February 1964, 73.

70. "Defections at Innsbruck," *New York Times,* 10 February 1964, 4; "East German Athletes Practice Disappearing Act for Olympics," *Washington Post, Times Herald,* 20 September 1964, C6.

71. "E. German Girl Defects from Olympic Team," *Washington Post,* 10 February 1964, A8.

72. *Ibid.*

73. "LBJ Backs Drive to Improve Olympic Prestige," *Boston Globe,* 15 March 1964, 79.

74. Dave Brady, "Lentz Asks Federal Help for Olympics," *Washington Post, Times Herald,* 8 March 1964, C5.

75. "U.S. Vows to Refurbish Olympic Image," *Boston Globe,* 11 February 1964, 31.

76. *Ibid.*

77. Robert F. Kennedy, "A Bold Proposal for American Sport," *Sports Illustrated,* 27 July 1964.

78. *Ibid.*

79. *Ibid.*

80. *Ibid.*

81. *Ibid.*

82. Robert F. Kennedy, "A Bold Proposal for American Sport."

83. Domer, *Sport in Cold War America,* 208.

84. Red Smith, "U.S. Olympic Win Not Worth Billions," *Boston Globe,* 6 May 1964, 39.

85. C.L. Sulzberger, "Foreign Affairs: 'Open' Olympics—And Grimmer Games," *New York Times,* 10 October 1964, 8.

86. C.L. Sulzberger, "Foreign Affairs: 'Open' Olympics—And Grimmer Games."

87. *The Soviet Olympic Team, 1964* (Moscow: Novosti Press Agency Publishing House, 1964), 23.

88. Arthur Daley, "Sports of the Times: En Route to Tokyo," *New York Times*, 31 March 1964, 45.

89. Arthur Daley, "Sports of the Times: The Cautious Approach," *New York Times*, 5 April 1964, S2.

90. Will Grimsley, "U.S. Basketball Team Overcomes Early Jitters, Swamps Russians," *Washington Post, Times Herald*, 24 October 1964, B4.

91. Emerson Chapin, "Americans Keep Title by Downing Soviet Quintet, 73 59," *New York Times*, 24 October 1964, 21.

92. Theodore Shabad, "Soviet Union," *New York Times*, 27 September 1964, S6.

93. Arthur Daley, "Aloha Instead of Sayonara," *New York Times*, 27 October 1964, 50.

94. Shirley Povich, "This Morning with Shirley Povich," *Washington Post, Times Herald*, 26 October 1964, B1.

95. *Ibid.*

96. Bill Henry, *An Approved History of the Olympic Games* (New York: G.P. Putnam and Sons, 1976), 312–323.

97. Jesse Abramson, "U.S. Tops USSR by Six Gold Medals," *Boston Globe*, 24 October 1964, 73.

98. "U.S. Dominates Track—24 Medals," *Boston Globe*, 22 October 1964, 45.

99. "U.S. Rakes in More Olympic Medals," *Boston Globe*, 16 October 1964, 19.

100. Shirley Povich, "This Morning with Shirley Povich," *Washington Post, Times Herald*, 26 October 1964, B1.

101. Henry, *An Approved History of the Olympic Games*, 315–317.

102. Arthur Daley, "Sports of the Times: The Red-Faced Reds," *New York Times*, 23 October 1964, 47.

103. Arthur Daley, "Sports of the Times: Sayonara Means Farewell," *New York Times*, 25 October 1964, S2.

104. "East German Athletes Practice Disappearing Act for Olympics," *Washington Post*, 20 September 1964, C4.

105. *Ibid.*

106. "Hungarian Defector Fears New Red Acts," *Washington Post*, 25 October 1964, A22.

107. "Three Hungarians Flee to U.S. from Tokyo," *Boston Globe*, 24 October 1964, 3.

Chapter 8

1. Bud Collins, "The Olympic Protesters Have Been Too Few," *Boston Globe*, 23 October 1968, 27.

2. Richard Hoffer, *Something in the Air: American Passion and Defiance in the 1968 Mexico City Olympics* (New York: Free Press, 2009), 159–161.

3. Thomas, *Globetrotting*, 140.

4. *Ibid.*, 162.

5. Zubok, *A Failed Empire*, 207–209.

6. Vladimir A. Kozlov, *Mass Uprisings in the USSR: Protest and Rebellion in the Post-Stalin Years* (Armonk, NY: M.E. Sharpe, 2002), 308–309.

7. Zubok, *A Failed Empire*, 207–209.

8. Jeremi Suri, *Power and Protest: Global Revolution and the Rise of Détente* (Cambridge: Harvard University Press, 2003).

9. *Ibid.*, 5.

10. "CIA-State Consultations on Czechoslovak Crisis" August 22, 1968, History and Public Policy Program Digital Archive, Obtained and contributed to CWIHP by A. Ross Johnson. Cited Ch5 n14 in his book Radio Free Europe and Radio Liberty, CIA mandatory declassification review document number C01441043. http://digitalarchive.wilsoncenter.org/document/115111

11. Suri, *Power and Protest*, 5.

12. *Ibid.*, 213.

13. Kevin Witherspoon, *Before the Eyes of the World: Mexico and the 1968 Olympic Games* (DeKalb: Northern Illinois University Press, 2008), 112–115.

14. Lauren Harper, "The Declassified Record on the Tlatelolco Massacre That Preceded the '68 Olympic Games," *The National Security Archive*, 28 January 2014. Available 26 October 2014, https://nsarchive.wordpress.com/2014/01/28/the-declassified-record-on-the-tlatelolco-massacre-that-preceded-the-68-olympic-games/.

15. Kate Doyle, "The Tlatelolco Massacre: U.S. Documents on Mexico and the Events of 1968," *The National Security Archive*. Available 26 October 2014, http://www2.gwu.edu/~nsarchiv/NSAEBB/NSAEBB99/

16. *Ibid.*

17. Department of State Telegram, 30 July 1968, Lyndon B. Johnson Library, National Security Files CO-Mexico, Vol. IV, Box 60, "Mexico, memos & misc., 1/68–10/68," page 1.

18. Witherspoon, *Before the Eyes of the World*, 121.

19. *Ibid.,* 122.

20. *Ibid.,* 120.

21. Bob Addie, "An Acquired Taste..." *Washington Post, Times Herald,* 20 January 1965, F3.

22. *Ibid.*

23. Robert Lipsyte, "Sports of the Times," *New York Times,* 10 October 1968, 65.

24. Lyndon B. Johnson: "Statement by the President Upon Announcing the Creation of the Physical Fitness Awards Program," December 11, 1965. Online by Gerhard Peters and John T. Woolley, *The American Presidency Project.* http://www.presidency.ucsb.edu/ws/?pid= 27402.

25. Platt, *The Olympic Games and Their Political Aspects,* 291–292.

26. Thomas M. Hunt, "American Sport Policy and the Cultural Cold War: The Lyndon Johnson Presidential Years," *Journal of Sport History* 33, no. 3 (Fall 2006), 283.

27. "Match USSR in Sports, Humphrey Urges U.S.," *Washington Post, Times Herald,* 24 May 1966, D5.

28. *Ibid.;* "U.S. Amateur Festival Proposed by Humphrey," *New York Times,* 10 May 1966, 35.

29. "Humphrey Urges Drive for Olympics," *Washington Post, Times Herald,* 26 October 1964, B4.

30. "Match USSR in Sports, Humphrey Urges U.S."

31. Hunt, "American Sport Policy and the Cultural Cold War: The Lyndon Johnson Presidential Years," 283.

32. "Soviets Risk Olympic Ban," *Boston Globe,* 12 July 1966, 21.

33. Jerry Nason, "Russians Pull Track Booboo," *Boston Globe,* 25 June 1967, 45.

34. "One German Team Urged," *New York Times,* 25 October 1964, 52.

35. William Glenn Gray, *Germany's Cold War: The Global Campaign to Isolate East Germany, 1949–1969* (Chapel Hill: University of North Carolina Press, 2003), 206.

36. *Ibid.,* 147.

37. Roman Kiselyov, "Now It's Up to the IOC," *Sport in the USSR,* 1965 6 (28), 3.

38. Schobel to Brundage, 23 June 1965, Recognition Request of the NOC of the German Democratic Republic: Correspondence and Statutes: 1963.01.01–1968.12.31, OSC.

39. *Ibid.*

40. IOC Session Minutes, Madrid, 6–8 October 1965, Box 83, Avery Brundage Collection, LA84, 11.

41. "France Is Said to Assure IOC She Will Admit East Germans in '68," *New York Times,* 7 October 1965, 13.

42. Madrid Session Minutes, 12.

43. *Ibid.*

44. "Olympic Unit's 'Heated Discussion' Fails to Decide German Problem," *New York Times,* 8 October 1965, 10.

45. Madrid Session Minutes, 24.

46. "2 Germanys May Compete in Olympics After '68 Games," *New York Times,* 30 April 1967, 206.

47. IOC Session Notes, Mexico City, 7–11 October 1968, Box 89, Avery Brundage Collection, LA84, 22.

48. Brundage to NOC, 24 October 1968, Recognition Request of the NOC of the German Democratic Republic: Correspondence and Statutes: 1963.01.01–1968.12.31, OSC.

49. "Protest by West Germany," *New York Times,* 1 September 1966, 60.

50. Philip Shabecoff, "Erhard Weighs Demand to Alter Policy on East German Athletes," *New York Times,* 9 October 1966, 29.

51. "Legitimate Demands," *Sport in the USSR,* 1968 8 (66), 6–7.

52. *Ibid.*

53. "Utah Renews Bid for Winter Olympics in '68," *Washington Post,* 18 April 1965, C3.

54. "Detroit Bid Boosted for Olympics," *Washington Post,* 21 April 1966, C4.

55. Avery Brundage to Daume, 13 May 1966, Correspondence of the NOC of the Federal Republic of Germany: 1961.01.01– 1967.12.31, OSC.

56. "World Olympic Body Fights British Ban on East Germans," *New York Times,* 29 March 1966, 52.

57. Otto Zausmer, "Beyond the Wall, What Future?" *Boston Globe,* 26 January 1967, 17.

58. IOC Session Minutes, Munich, 25 May 1959, Box 81, Avery Brundage Collection, LA84, 16.

59. Espy, *The Politics of the Olympic Games,* 84.

60. "Soviet Injects Politics into Olympics," *New York Times,* 6 February 1968, 50.

61. "International and Olympic Problems," *Sport in the USSR,* 1967 6 (52), 19.

62. "South Africa Ok'd for Olympics," *Boston Globe,* 16 February 1968, 17.

63. Arthur Daley, "Sports of the Times: Dark Shadows," *New York Times,* 18 February 1968, 173.

64. "Soviet Stand Undecided," *New York Times,* 27 February 1968, 48.

65. "Soviets Ask Olympic Ban on S. Africa," *Washington Post*, 6 March 1968, E1.

66. IOC Executive Board Session Minutes, Lausanne, 20–21 April 1968, Box 87, Avery Brundage Collection, LA84.

67. Arthur Daley, "Sports of the Times: Jostling the Applecart," *New York Times*, 23 August 1968, 48.

68. Robert Lipsyte, "Sports of the Times: Doomed to Survive," *New York Times*, 24 August 1968, 37.

69. Shirley Povich, "This Morning with Shirley Povich," *Washington Post*, 29 August 1968, G1.

70. John Underwood, "The Long Long Jump," *Sports Illustrated*, 28 October 1968.

71. "Russians Not Faring Well at Grenoble," *Washington Post*, 16 February 1968, D3.

72. *Ibid.*, "Russia Wins Ski Jump Finale." *Washington Post*, 19 February 1968, D1.

73. Fred Tupper, "Beloussov Wins 90-Meter Ski Jump as 10th Winter Olympics End at Grenoble," *New York Times*, 19 February 1968, 53.

74. Bob Ottum, "The Perils of Peggy and a Great Silver Raid," *Sports Illustrated*, 19 February 1968.

75. Dan Jenkins, "Over the Scattered Bones Came Jean-Claude," *Sports Illsutrated*, 26 February 1968.

76. "'Go-Go' Olympics Termed 'Best Ever' by Old-Timers," *Washington Post*, 27 October 1968, C2.

77. "The Third Force," *Sports Illustrated*, 30 September 1968.

78. Jesse Abramson, "Olympus Was Never So Good."

79. William Johnson, "TV Made It All a New Games," *Sports Illustrated*, 22 December 1969.

80. *Ibid.*

81. Jesse Abramson, "Olympus Was Never So Good," *Washington Post*, 1 October 1968, D3.

82. "Scorecard," *Sports Illustrated*, 23 September 1968.

83. Povich, "This Morning with Shirley Povich," 29 August 1968.

84. Robert Lipsyte, "Sports of the Times: Here We Go Again," *New York Times*, 12 October 1968, 45.

85. *Ibid.*

86. Art Buchwald, "Soviets Cover Story for Czech Invasion," *Boston Globe*, 10 September 1968, 13.

87. Espy, *The Politics of the Olympic Games*, 102–106.

88. "Olympic Demonstrations Possible, Says Carlos," *Boston Globe*, 7 October 1968, 31.

89. "2 Accept Medals Wearing Black Gloves," *New York Times*, 17 October 1968, 59.

90. Espy, *The Politics of the Olympic Games*, 120.

91. Shirley Povich, "This Morning with Shirley Povich," *Washington Post*, 19 October 1968, C1.

92. Thomas M. Hunt, "American Sport Policy and the Cultural Cold War: The Lyndon Johnson Presidential Years," 287–288.

93. Bass, *Not the Triumph but the Struggle*, 268.

94. Boris Bazunov, "Olympic Echo," *Sport in the USSR*, 1968 12 (70), 11.

95. Arthur Daley, "Sports of the Times: The Incident," *New York Times*, 20 October 1968, S2.

96. Bud Collins, "The Olympic Protesters Have Been Too Few," *Boston Globe*, 23 October 1968, 27.

97. "'Go-Go' Olympics Termed 'Best Ever' by Old-Timers."

98. *Ibid.*

99. *Ibid.*

100. Witherspoon, *Before the Eyes of the World*, 88.

101. "Soviet Council Names a Minister of Sports," *New York Times*, 10 November 1968, S15.

102. "What They Discussed in Mexico," *Sport in the USSR*, 1968 No. 12 (70), 3.

103. Red Smith, "Arthur Daley, Sports Columnist, Dies," *New York Times*, 4 January 1974, 32.

Chapter 9

1. Red Smith, "Again the Sandbox," *New York Times*, 8 September 1972, 21.

2. Kay Schiller, and Christopher Young, *The 1972 Munich Olympics and the Making of Modern Germany* (Berkeley: University of California Press, 2010), 2.

3. Gray, *Germany's Cold War*, 218.

4. Bass, *Not the Triumph but the Struggle*, 100.

5. William Oscar Johnson, "Avery Brundage: The Man Behind the Mask," *Sports Illustrated*, 4 August 1980.

6. "Brundage: Games Getting Too Big for Ideals," *New York Times*, 23 July 1972, S6.

7. Clive Gammon, "Lord of the Games," *Sports Illsutrated*, 9 February 1976.

8. IOC Session Minutes, Tehran, 2–8 May 1967, Box 86, Avery Brundage Collection, LA84, 6.

9. David Clay Large, *Munich 1972: Tragedy, Terror and Triumph at the Olympic Games* (Lanham, MD: Rowman and Littlefield, 2013), 6.

10. Platt, *The Olympic Games and Their Political Aspects*, 317.

11. Simon Reeve, "Olympics Massacre: Munich—The Real Story," *The Independent*, 22 January 2006.

12. Alvin Shuster, "'Despicable Act' Decried at Arena Rites," *New York Times*, 7 September 1972, 1.

13. Red Smith, "Again the Sandbox," *New York Times*, 8 September 1972, 21.

14. Bernard Kirsch, "At Memorial Service, Plea That Games Continue," *Washington Post*, 7 September 1972, A16.

15. Red Smith, "Six Days Late, the Gas Man Cometh," *New York Times*, 11 September 1972, 49.

16. "Odds '50–50' on Opening of Olympics," *New York Times*, 7 January 1976, 59.

17. "Europeans Face TV Blackout for Olympics," *Boston Globe*, 25 May 1975, 69.

18. Richard M. Weintraub, "Olympics Reject U.S. RFE," *Washington Post*, 12 February 1976, A19.

19. Espy, 143.

20. "Olympics Concern Montreal," *New York Times*, 11 January 1975, L25.

21. Peter Ward, "Montreal May Be Forced to Cancel Olympics," *Boston Globe*, 10 January 1976, 2.

22. William Guildea, "In Quest of a Human-Sized Olympiad," *Washington Post*, 1 April 1973, A1.

23. Murray Seeger, "Russians Try Harder for 1980 Games," *Washington Post*, 5 September 1972, D6.

24. Byron Rosen, "Moscow Games Go Political; Wings Pick Up Czech," *Washington Post*, 16 November 1977, D7.

25. Dave Kindred, "Moscow Politics Seem Inevitable," *Washington Post*, 8 April 1978, D1.

26. George F. Will, "Playing Games with the Games," *Boston Globe*, 20 July 1978, 19.

27. Sarantakes, *Dropping the Torch* 60.

28. *Ibid.*, 81–82.

29. *Ibid.*, 86–87.

30. Sarantakes, *Dropping the Torch*, 11.

31. Ken Denlinger, "White House Words Have Slushy Feel," *Washington Post*, 14 February 1980, F1.

32. Sarantakes, *Dropping the Torch*, 226–227.

33. *Ibid.*

34. Bart Barnes, "Ioc Leader: '80 Boycott Won't Affect Olympics," *Washington Post*, 29 January 1982, C6.

35. Sarantakes, *Dropping the Torch*, 247.

36. Byron Rosen, "Soviets LA-Bound in '84,"*Washington Post*, 20 May 1982, D5.

37. "USSR to Decide in May About Olympics," *Washington Post*, 23 July 1983, D2.

38. "Soviet Officials Issue Objections," *New York Times*, 20 January 1984, A19.

39. "U.S. Tells Why It Barred Soviet Olympic Official," *New York Times*, 3 March 1984, 4.

40. Serge Schmemann, "No Nice Words in Moscow," *New York Times*, 3 April 1984, D9.

41. Serge Schmemann, "Moscow Charges Anti-Soviet Bias," *New York Times*, 10 April 1984, D1.

42. "Text of Soviet Statement on Olympic Games," *New York Times*, 9 May 1984, A16.

43. "East Germany Joins Soviet in Boycotting Games," *New York Times*, 11 May 1984, A12.

44. Sarantakes, *Dropping the Torch*, 255–257.

45. William Oscar Johnson, "Is There Life After Los Angeles?" *Sports Illustrated*, 21 May 1984.

46. William Oscar Johnson, "Goodbye Olive Wreaths; Hello, Riches and Reality," *Sports Illustrated*, 9 February 1987.

47. "Russia Is Building Secretly for Olympics, Official Says," *Washington Post*, 22 May 1952, 21.

48. Robert F. Kennedy, "A Bold Proposal for American Sport," *Sports Illustrated*, 27 July 1964.

49. Hampton, *The Austerity Olympics*, 40.

50. Juliet Macur, "Rio Wins 2016 Olympics in a First for South America," *New York Times*, 2 October 2009.

51. Avery Brundage, Untitled Speech, Box 176, 23 August 1968, Avery Brundage Colllection, LA84.

Bibliography

Primary Sources

The American Presidency Project.

Avery Brundage Collection.

The Boston Globe.

Brundage, Avery. *The Speeches of President Avery Brundage, 1952–1968.* Lausanne: Comité Olympique Internationale, 1968.

Bushnell, Asa S., and Arthur G. Lentz, eds. *United States 1956 Olympic Book: Quadrennial Report of the United States Olympic Committee.* New York: United States Olympic Association, Inc., 1957.

_____. *United States 1960 Olympic Book: Quadrennial Report of the United States Olympic Committee.* New York: United States Olympic Association, Inc., 1961.

Churchill, Winston. "Iron Curtain Speech." 5 March 1946. *Modern History Sourcebook.* Available 20 November 2013. http://www.fordham.edu/halsall/mod/churchill-iron.asp.

de Coubertin, Pierre. *Olympic Memoirs.* Lausanne: Comité International Olympique, 1931.

_____. *Olympische Erinnerungen.* Frankfurt, 1959.

_____. *Olympism: Selected Writings.* Lusanne: International Olympic Committee, 2000.

The Guardian.

Heidelmeyer, Wolfgang, and Hindrichs Guenter, eds. *Documents on Berlin, 1943–1963.* Munich: R. Oldenbourg Verlag, 1963.

Highlights of Soviet Sport. Moscow: Novosti Press Agency Publishing House, 1972.

Levine, Irving R. *Main Street, USSR.* Garden City, NY: Doubleday, 1959.

The 1980 Summer Olympic Games: Hearings and Markup Before the Committee on Foreign Affairs, January 23 and February 4, 1980, 96th Congress, Second Session. Washington, D.C.: Government Printing Office, 1980.

Olympic Games London 1948 Official Souvenir. London: Futura Publications, 1948.

Olympic Review.

Physical Culture and Sport in the USSR. Brussels: Brussels Universal and International Exposition USSR Section, 1958.

Rubien, Frederick William, United States Olympic Committee. *Report of the American Olympic Committee: Games of the XIth Olympiad.* New York: American Olympic Committee, 1936.

Shteinbakh, Valeri. *The Soviet Contribution to the Olympics.* Moscow: Novosti Press Agency Publishing House, 1980.

The Soviet Olympic Team, 1964. Moscow: Novosti Press Agency Publishing House, 1964.

Soviet Sports Handbook, 1958. London: "Soviet news" booklet no. 28, *Soviet News Booklet* (1957) no. 28.

La Spartakiade, 1955. Prague: Le Comité d'État pour la Culture physique et les Sports, 1955.
Sport: The Soviet Union Today and Tomorrow. Moscow: Novosti Press Agency Publishing House, 1980.
Sport in the USSR. Moscow: Soviet News Publication, 1949.
Sports Illustrated.
Time.
United States. Congress. House of Representatives. Committee on Energy and Commerce. *1984 Summer Olympics: Hearing Before the Subcommittee on Commerce, Transportation, and Tourism of the Committee on Energy and Commerce,* House of Representatives, 98th Congress, 1st Session, September 27, 1983. Washington, D.C.: Government Printing Office, 1983.
_____._____. _____. Committee on the Judiciary, Subcommittee on Administrative Law and Government Relations. *Amateur Sports Act of 1978: Hearings Before the Subcommittee on Administrative Law and Governmental Relations of the Committee on the Judiciary,* House of Representatives, 95th Congress, 2nd Session, on H.R. 12626 and H.R. 12920 ... June 21 and 22, 1978. Washington, D.C.: Government Printing Office, 1978.
_____._____. Senate. 86th Congress, 1st session 24 April 1959. Congressional Record (1945–1970).
_____. Department of State. Telegram, 30 July 1968, Lyndon B. Johnson Library, National Security Files CO-Mexico, Vol. IV, Box 60, "Mexico, memos & misc., 1/68–10/68."
US News and World Report.
USA Volleyball.
The Washington Post.

Secondary Sources

Allison, Lincoln, ed. *The Politics of Sport.* Manchester: Manchester University Press, 1986.
Anderson, Sheldon. *The Politics and Culture of Modern Sport.* Lanham, MD: Lexington Books, 2015.
Arnaud, Pierre, and James Riordan. *Sport and International Politics.* New York: E and FN Spon, 1998.
Baker, William J. *Sport in the Western World.* Urbana: University of Illinois Press, 1988.
Bass, Amy. *Not the Triumph but the Struggle: The 1968 Olympics and the Making of the Black Athlete.* Minneapolis: University of Minnesota Press, 2002.
Berlioux, Monique. "The Quiet Irishman—A Final Portrait of Lord Killanin." *Journal of Olympic History* 12 (2015), 7–13.
Bernhard, Nancy E. *U.S. Television News and Cold War Propaganda, 1947–1960.* Cambridge: Cambridge University Press, 1999.
Booker, Christopher. *The Games War: A Moscow Journal.* London: Faber and Faber, 1981.
Bowers, Matthew T., and Thomas M. Hunt. "The President's Council on Physical Fitness and the Systemisation of Children's Play in America." *The International Journal of the History of Sport* 28, No. 11 (August 2011), 1496–1511.
Brasher, Christopher. *Tokyo 1964:A Diary of the XVIIIth Olympiad.* London: Stanley Paul, 1964.
Brinkley, Alan. *The Publisher: Henry Luce and His American Century.* New York: A. A. Knopf, 2010.
Brokhin, Yuri. *The Big Red Machine: The Rise and Fall of Soviet Olympic Champions.* New York: Random House, 1977.
Caracappa, Matt. "The Original Golden Boys." *USA Hockey Magazine,* February 2010. Available 3 May 2013. http://www.usahockeymagazine.com/article/2010–02/original-golden-boys.

Carr, E. H. *A History of Soviet Russia: Socialism in One Country, 1924–1926s.* London: Macmillan, 1964.

Cary, Noel D. "Olympics in Divided Berlin? Popular Culture and Political Imagination at the Cold War Frontier." *Cold War History* 11, no. 3 (August 2011), 291–316.

Clumpner, Roy. "Federal Involvement in Sport to Promote American Interest or Foreign Policy Objectives, 1950–1973." *Sport and International Relations* 1, no. 1 (March 1983).

Collins, Douglas. *Olympic Dreams: 100 Years of Excellence.* New York: Universe Publishing, 1996.

Costigliola, Frank. *France and the United States: The Cold Alliance Since World War II.* New York: Twayne, 1992.

_____. *Roosevelt's Lost Alliances: How Personal Politics Helped Start the Cold War.* Princeton: Princeton University Press, 2012.

Cull, Nicholas J. *The Cold War and the United States Information Agency: American Propaganda and Public Diplomacy, 1945–1989.* Cambridge: Cambridge University Press, 2008.

Cunningham, Carson. *American Hoops: US Men's Olympic Basketball from Berlin to Beijing.* Lincoln: University of Nebraska Press, 2009.

_____. "The Russell Model: Melbourne 1956 and Bill Russell's New Basketball Standard," *Olympika: The International Journal of Sports Studies,* Volume XV (2006), pp. 59–85.

D'Agati, Philip. *The Cold War and the 1984 Olympic Games: A Soviet-American Surrogate War.* New York: Palgrave Macmillan, 2013.

Dallek, Robert. *Flawed Giant: Lyndon Johnson and His Times, 1961–1973.* New York: Oxford University Press, 1998.

Dichter, Heather L., and Andrew L. Johns. *Diplomatic Games: Sport, Statecraft, and International Relations Since 1945.* Lexington: University Press of Kentucky, 2014.

Domer, Thomas M. *Sport in Cold War America: The Diplomatic and Political Use of Sport in the Eisenhower and Kennedy Administrations.* Dissertation, University of Wisconsin-Milwaukee, 1976.

Downing, David. *Passovotchka: Moscow Dynamo in Britain.* London: Bloomsbury, 1999.

Doyle, Kate. "The Tlatelolco Massacre: U.S. Documents on Mexico and the Events of 1968." *The National Security Archive.* Available 26 October 2014. http://www2.gwu.edu/~nsarchiv/NSAEBB/NSAEBB99/.

Drevon, André. *Les Jeux olympiques oubliés: Paris 1900.* Paris: CNRS Éditions, 2000.

Dykman, J.T. "The Soviet Experience in World War II." *The Eisenhower Institute.* Available 1 November 2014. http://www.eisenhowerinstitute.org/about/living_history/wwii_soviet_experience.dot.

Edelman, Robert. *Serious Fun: A History of Spectator Sport in the USSR.* New York: Oxford University Press, 1993.

_____. *Spartak Moscow: A History of the People's Team in the Workers' State.* Ithaca: Cornell University Press, 2009.

Espy, Richard. *The Politics of the Olympic Games.* Berkeley: University of California Press, 1979.

Findling, John E., and Kimberly D. Pelle, eds. *Encyclopedia of the Modern Olympic Movement.* Westport, CT: Greenwood Press, 2004.

Fink, Carole, et al., eds. *1956: European and Global Perspectives.* Leipzig: Leipzig University, 2006.

Frank, William D. *Everyone to Skis! Skiing in Russia and the Rise of Soviet Biathlon.* DeKalb: Northern Illinois Press, 2013.

Fursenko, Aleksandr, and Timothy Naftali. *Khrushchev's Cold War: The Inside Story of an American Adversary.* New York: W.W. Norton, 2006.

Garrett, Kenneth. *The International Olympic Committee and the German Question: A Case Study of the Role of Transnational Organizations in the International System.* Palo Alto: StaNford University, 2002.

Gorman, Robert F. *Great Debates at the United Nations: An Encyclopedia of Fifty Key Issues, 1945–2000.* Westport, CT: Greenwood Press, 2001.

Grant, Susan. *Physical Culture and Sport in Soviet Society: Propaganda, Acculturation, and Transformation in the 1920s and 1930s.* New York: Routledge, 2013.

Granville, Joanna. *The First Domino: International Decision Making During the Hungarian Crisis of 1956.* College Station: Texas A&M University Press, 2004.

Grose, Peter. *Operation Rollback: America's Secret War Behind the Iron Curtain.* Boston: Houghton Mifflin, 2000.

Guttmann, Allen. *The Games Must Go On: Avery Brundage and the Olympic Movement.* New York: Columbia University Press, 1984.

_____. *The Olympics: A History of the Modern Games.* Urbana: University of Illinois Press, 1992.

Gygax, Jérôme. *Olympisme et Guerre Froide Culturelle: Le prix de la victoire américaine.* Paris: Harmattan, 2012.

Hampton, Janie. *The Austerity Olympics: When the Games came to London in 1948.* London: Aurum Press, 2008.

Harper, Lauren. "The Declassified Record on the Tlatelolco Massacre that Preceded the '68 Olympic Games." *The National Security Archive.* 28 January 2014. Available 26 October 2014. https://nsarchive.wordpress.com/2014/01/28/the-declassified-record-on-the-tlatelolco-massacre-that-preceded-the-68-olympic-games/.

Harrison, Hope M. *Driving the Soviets Up the Wall: Soviet-East German Relations, 1953–1961.* Princeton: Princeton University Press, 2003.

Henry, Bill. *An Approved History of the Olympic Games.* New York: G.P. Putnam and Sons, 1976.

Henry, Bill, and Patricia Henry Yeomans. *An Approved History of the Olympic Games.* Los Angeles: The Southern California Committee for the Olympic Games, 1984.

Hill, Christopher R. *Olympic Politics.* New York: Manchester University Press, 1996.

Hixson, Walter. *Parting the Curtain: Propaganda, Culture, and the Cold War, 1945- 1961.* New York: St. Martin's Press, 1997.

Hoberman, John M. *The Olympic Crisis: Sport, Politics, and the Moral Order.* New Rochelle, NY: Aristide D. Caratzas, 1986.

Hoffer, Richard. *Something in the Air: American Passion and Defiance in the 1968 Mexico City Olympics.* New York: Free Press, 2009.

Hunt, Thomas M. "American Sport Policy and the Cultural Cold War: The Lyndon B. Johnson Presidential Years." *Journal of Sport History* 33, no. 3 (2006).

Jay, Kathryn. *More Than Just a Game: Sports in American Life Since 1945.* New York: Columbia University Press, 2004.

Johnson, William Oscar. *All That Glitters Is Not Gold: The Olympic Game.* New York: G.P. Putnam and Sons, 1972.

_____. *The Olympics: A History of the Games.* Birmingham, AL: Oxmoor House, 1992.

Kanin, David B. *A Political History of the Olympic Games.* Boulder, CO: Westview Press, 1981.

Kempe, Frederick. *Berlin 1961: Kennedy, Khrushchev, and the Most Dangerous Place on Earth.* New York: G.P. Putnam and Sons, 2011.

Keys, Barbara J. *Globalizing Sport: National Rivalry and International Community in the 1930s.* Cambridge: Harvard University Press, 2006.

Kieran, John, and Arthur Daley. *The Story of the Olympic Games: 776 B.C. to 1968.* Philadelphia: J.B. Lippincott, 1969.

Killanin, Lord. *My Olympic Years.* New York: William Morrow, 1983.

Kolassov, Anatoly. "From the Spartakiad to the Olympiad." *Olympic Review* 143 (September 1979), pp. 502–503.

Kozlov, Vladimir A. *Mass Uprisings in the USSR: Protest and Rebellion in the Post- Stalin Years.* Armonk, NY: M.E. Sharpe, 2002.

Kyvig, David E. *Daily Life in the United States, 1920–1940*. Chicago: Ivan R. Dee, 2004.

Large, David Clay. *Munich 1972: Tragedy, Terror and Triumph at the Olympic Games*. Lanham, MD: Rowman and Littlefield, 2013.

_____. *Nazi Games: The Olympics of 1936*. New York: W.W. Norton, 2007.

Lennartz, Karl. "The Exclusion of the Central Empires from the Olympic Games in 1920." *Global and Cultural Critique: Problematizing the Olympic Games*. London: Fourth International Symposium for Olympic Research, 1998.

Levermore, Roger, and Adrian Budd, eds. *Sport and International Relations: An Emerging Relationship*. London: Routledge, 2004.

Levine, Irving R. *Main Street, USSR*. Garden City, NY: Doubleday and Company, 1959.

Little, Douglas. *American Orientalism: The United States and the Middle East since 1945*. Chapel Hill: University of North Carolina Press, 2008.

Lowe, Benjamin, David B. Kanin, et al. *Sport and International Relations*. Champaign, IL: Stipes Publishing Co., 1978.

Lucas, Scott. *Freedom's War: The American Crusade Against the Soviet Union*. New York: New York University Press, 1999.

MacAloon, John J. *The Great Symbol: Pierre de Coubertin and the Origins of the Modern Olympic Games*. Chicago: University of Chicago Press, 1981.

Mandell, David. *Sport: A Cultural History*. New York: Columbia University Press, 1984.

Maraniss, David. *Rome 1960: The Olympics That Changed the World*. New York: Simon & Schuster, 2008.

Marvin, Carolyn. "Avery Brundage and American Participation in the 1936 Olympic Games." (Annenberg School for Communication Departmental Papers, 1982), 81–106.

McDougall, Walter A. *The Heavens and the Earth: A Political History of the Space Age*. Baltimore: Johns Hopkins University Press, 1987.

Mechikoff, Robert A., and Paula R. Lupcho. "The Emergence of the Cold War Olympics: 1948 London Games." Fourth Canadian Symposium on the History of Sport and Physical Education. Proceedings. Vancouver, June 24–26, 1979.

Miller, David. *The Official History of the Olympic Games and the IOC: 1894–2008*. Edinburgh: Mainstream Publishing, 2008.

Miller, Geoffrey. *Behind the Olympic Rings*. Lynn, MA: H.O. Zimman, Inc., 1979.

Miller, Wright. *Russians as People*. New York: E.P. Dutton, 1961.

Mitrovich, Gregory. *Undermining the Kremlin: America's Strategy to Subvert the Soviet Bloc, 1947–1956*. Ithaca: Cornell University Press, 2000.

Morton, Henry W. *Soviet Sport: Mirror of Soviet Society*. New York: Collier Books, 1963.

O'Mahony, Mike. *Sport in the USSR: Physical Culture-Visual culture*. London: Reaktion Books, 2006.

Osgood, Kenneth. "Hearts and Minds: The Unconventional Cold War." *Journal of Cold War Studies* 4, no. 2 (Spring 2002), 85–107 (Review).

_____. *Total Cold War: Eisenhower's Secret Propaganda Battle at Home and Abroad*. Manhattan: University Press of Kansas, 2006.

Parks, Jenifer. "'Nothing but Trouble': The Soviet Union's Push to 'Democratise' International Sports During the Cold War, 1959–1962." *The International Journal of the History of Sport* 30, no. 13 (2013), 1554–1567.

_____. *Red Sport, Red Tape: The Olympic Games, the Soviet Sports Bureaucracy, and the Cold War, 1952–1980*. Dissertation, University of North Carolina.

Payne, Michael. *Olympic Turnaround: How the Olympic Games Stepped Back from the Brink of Extinction to Become the World's Best Known Brand*. Westport, CT: Praeger, 2006.

Peppard, Victor, and James Riordan. *Playing Politics: Soviet Sport Diplomacy to 1992*. Greenwich, CT: JAI Press, Inc., 1993.

Phillips, Bob. *The 1948 Olympics: How London Rescued the Games*. Cheltenham, England: Sports Books Limited, 2007.

Pigman, Geoffrey Allen. "International Sport and Diplomacy's Public Dimension: Governments, Sporting Federations and the Global Audience." *Diplomacy & Statecraft* 25 (2014), 94–114.

Platt, Alan R. *The Olympic Games and their Political Aspects: 1952–1972.* Dissertation, Kent State, 1976.

Pound, Richard W. *Inside the Olympics.* Etobicoke, Ontario: John Wiley and Sons Canada, 2004.

Puddington, Arch. *Broadcasting Freedom: The Cold War Triumph of Radio Free Europe and Radio Liberty.* Lexington: University Press of Kentucky, 2000.

Reeve, Simon. *One Day in September: The full story of the 1972 Munich Olympics Massacre.* New York: Arcade Publishing, 2003.

Reich, Kenneth. *Making It Happen: Peter Ueberroth and the 1984 Olympics.* Santa Barbara, CA: Capra Press, 1986.

Reisler, Jim. *Igniting the Flame: America's First Olympic Team.* Guilford, CT: Lyons Press, 2012.

Renson, Roland. *The Games Reborn: the VIIth Olympiad, Antwerp 1920.* Antwerp: Pandora, 1996.

Richmond, Yale. *Cultural Exchange and the Cold War: Raising the Iron Curtain.* University Park: Pennsylvania State University Press, 2003.

Rider, Toby C. "The Distant Fight Against Communist Sport: Refugee Sports Organizations in America and the International Olympic Committee," in Robert Knight Barney, Janice Forsyth, et al., *Rethinking Matters Olympic: Investigations into the Socio-Cultural Study of the Modern Olympic Movement.* London: International Centre for Olympic Research, 2010, 116–126.

_____. "'It Is Not a Simple Matter to Keep Aloof': Avery Brundage and the US Government in the Early Cold War years," in Janice Forsyth and Michael K. Heine, *Problems, Possibilities, Promising Practices: Critical Dialogues on the Olympic and Paralympic Games.* Los Angeles: LA84 Foundation, 2012, 12–18.

_____. "Political Warfare in Helsinki: American Covert Strategy and the Union of Free Eastern European Sportsmen." *The International Journal of the History of Sport* 30, no. 13 (2013), 1493–1507.

Riordan, James. "The Role of Sport in Soviet Foreign Policy." *International Journal* 43, no. 4, Sport in World Politics (Autumn 1988), 569–595.

_____. *Soviet Sport: Background to the Olympics.* Oxford: Basil Blackwell, 1980.

_____. *Sport in Soviet Society.* Cambridge: Cambridge University Press, 1977.

_____. *Sport, Politics, and Communism.* New York: St. Martin's Press, 1991.

Riordan, James, and Arnd Krüger. *The International Politics of Sport in the Twentieth Century.* London: F&N Spon, 1999.

Roberts, Randy, and James Olson. *Winning Is the Only Thing: Sports in America since 1945.* Baltimore: Johns Hopkins University Press, 1989.

Rogan, Matt, and Martin Rogan. *Britain and the Olympic Games: Past, Present, Legacy.* Leicester, UK: Matador, 2011.

Ruffner, Kevin C. "Cold War Allies: The Origins of CIA's Relationship with Ukrainian Nationalists." Central Intelligence Agency. Available 23 June 2014. http://www.foia.cia.gov/sites/default/files/document_conversions/1705143/STUDIES%20IN%20INTELLIGENCE%20NAZI%20-%20RELATED%20ARTICLES_0015.pdf.

Sarantakes, Nicholas Evan. *Dropping the Torch: Jimmy Carter, the Olympic Boycott, and the Cold War.* New York: Cambridge University Press, 2011.

Schaffer, Kay, and Sidonie Smith, eds. *The Olympics at the Millennium: Power, Politics, and the Games.* New Brunswick: Rutgers University Press, 2000.

Schiller, Kay, and Christopher Young. *The 1972 Munich Olympics and the Making of Modern Germany.* Berkeley: University of California Press, 2010.

Segrave, Jeffrey, and Donald Chu, eds. *The Olympic Games in Transition.* Champagne, IL: Human Kinetics Books, 1988.

Senn, Alfred E. *Power, Politics and the Olympic Games: A History of the Power Brokers, Events, and Controversies That Dhaped the Games.* Champagne, IL: Human Kinetics, 1999.

Service, Robert. *A History of Twentieth-Century Russia.* Cambridge: Harvard University Press, 1998.

Sheffer, Edith. *Burned Bridge: How East and West Germans made the Iron Curtain.* New York: Oxford University Press, 2011.

Shteinbakh, V., ed. *Soviet Sport: The Success Story.* Moscow: Raduga Publications, 1987.

Simpson, Christopher. *Blowback: The First Full Account of America's Recruitment of Nazis, and Its Disastrous Effect on Our Domestic and Foreign Policy.* New York: Collier Books, 1988.

Smyser, W.R. *Kennedy and the Berlin Wall.* New York: Rowman & Littlefield, 2009.

Soares, John. "Cold War, Hot Ice: International Ice Hockey, 1947–1980." *Journal of Sport History* 24, no. 2 (Summer 2007), 207–230.

Stevenson, Matthew, and Michael Martin, eds. *Rules of the Game: The Best Sports Writing from Harper's Magazine.* New York: Franklin Square Press, 2010.

Stites, Richard. *Russian Popular Culture: Entertainment and Society Since 1900.* Cambridge: Cambridge University Press, 1992.

Strenk, Andrew. "Diplomats in Track Suits: Linkages Between Sports and Foreign Policy in the German Democratic Republic." In *Sport and International Relations.* Champaign, IL: Stipes Publishing Company, 1978.

Suri, Jeremi. *Power and Protest: Global Revolution and the Rise of Détente.* Cambridge: Harvard University Press, 2003.

Susman, Warren I. *Culture as History: The Transformation of American Society in the Twentieth Century.* New York: Pantheon Books, 1984.

Tait, Robin. *The Politicization of the Modern Olympic Games.* Ann Arbor: UMI, 1984.

Taubman, William. *Khrushchev: The Man and His Era.* New York: W.W. Norton, 2004.

Thomas, Damion L. *Globetrotting: African American Athletes and Cold War Politics.* Urbana: University of Illinois Press, 2012.

Tomlinson, Alan, and Christopher Young, eds. *National Identity and Global Sports Events: Culture, Politics, and Spectacle in the Olympics and the Football World Cup.* Albany: State University of New York Press, 2006.

Trory, Ernie. *Munich, Montreal and Moscow: A Political Tale of Three Olympic Cities.* Hove Sussex: Crabtree Press, 1980.

United States Olympic Committee. *Olympic Dreams: 100 Years of Excellence.* New York: Universe Publishing, 1996.

USSR–USA Sports Encounters. Moscow: Progress Publishers, 1977.

Vinokur, Martin Barry. *More Than a Game: Sports and Politics.* New York: Greenwood Press, 1988.

Wagg, Stephen, and David Andrews. *East Plays West: Sport and the Cold War.* New York: Taylor and Francis, 2006.

Walker, James Russell. *The Politics of Performance: Soviet Participation in the Olympic Games,1952–1984.*Ann Arbor: UMI, 1988.

Walters, Guy. *Berlin Games: How the Nazis Stole the Olympic Dream.* New York: William Morrow, 2006.

Watterson, John Sayle. *The Games Presidents Play: Sports and the Presidency.* Baltimore: John Hopkins University Press, 2006.

Weiner, Tim. *Legacy of Ashes: The History of the CIA.* New York: Doubleday, 2007.

Wenger, Andreas. *Living with Peril: Eisenhower, Kennedy, and Nuclear Weapons.* New York: Rowman & Littlefield, 2007.

West, Ed. *Don't Mention the World Cup: A History of England-Germany Rivalry from the War to the World Cup.* Chichester, UK: Summersdale, 2006.

White, Mark J. *Missiles in Cuba: Kennedy, Khrushchev, Castro and the 1962 Crisis.* Chicago: Ivan R. Dee, 1997.

Witherspoon, Kevin B. *Before the Eyes of the World: Mexico and the 1968 Olympic Games.* DeKalb: Northern Illinois University Press, 2008.

Wushanley, Ying. *Playing Nicely and Losing: the Struggle for Control of Women's Intercollegiate Athletics, 1960–2000.* Syracuse: Syracuse University Press, 2004.

Young, Candy Cartwright. *United States Olympic Politics: A public Policy Case Study.* Ann Arbor: UMI, 1982.

Zubkova, Elena. *Russia After the War: Hopes, Illusions, and Disappointments, 1945–1957.* Armonk, NY: M.E. Sharpe, 1998.

Zubok, Vladislav M. *Failed Empire: The Soviet Union in the Cold War from Stalin to Gorbachev.* Chapel Hill: University of North Carolina Press, 2007.

Index

Page numbers in **_bold italics_** indicate pages with illustrations.

Adenauer, Konrad 148, 152–153, 175
Addie, Bob 195
Afghanistan 8, 32, 212, 219–220
All-Union Committee for Physical Culture and Sports Activities (Sports Ministry) 27, 57, 60, 61, 63, 69, 100
Amateur Athletic Union (AAU) 14, 27, 29, 33, 38, 41, 44–45, 46, 66, 171
American Broadcasting Company (ABC) 206
"The American Century" 37
American National Exhibition 144
American Olympic Association 14, 33
American Red Cross 136, 139
Andrianov, Konstantin 100, 123–124, 132, 147, 149, 150, 178
Associated Press (AP) 80, 88, 113, 210
Athens 11–12, 16, 18, 29–30, 50, 123
Attlee, Clement 78
The Austerity Olympics 7
Australia 16, 114, 122, 132, 134, 136, 162, 213
Austria 153, 156, 166, 181

Bach, Thomas 21, 119
Basic Treaty 10, 214
basketball 1, 31, 40, 59, 62, 63, 64–65, 67, 70, 78, 89, 91, 112, 114, 135–136, 140, 145, 147, 157, 160, 162, 163, 183, 184, 185, 186, 187, 188, 196, 215–216, 224
Bay of Pigs invasion 50, 166, 167, 168, 183, 189
Belgium 19, 90
Belorussian Soviet Socialist Republic 77
Berlin 7, 10, 13, 19, 87, 90, 93, 96, 140, 141–142, 144, 145, 147, 152, 154, 157–158, 159,
161, 165, 176, 178, 181, 197, 198, 199–200, 204, 214
Berlin Airlift 7, 85, 87, 93, 96, 141
Berlin Wall 20, 86, 100, 158, 165, 166, 168, 169, 175–176, **_176_**, 179, 180–181
Bevin, Ernest 87
Bingham, J. Lyman 101
Black Power movement 23, 189–191, 208–211, 226
Black September 217, 226
Bonn 10, 141, 148, 150, 152–153, 158, 175, 199–201
Boston Globe 30, 78, 180, 182, 189
boycott 6, 14, 20, 21, 32, 40, 111, 117, 132–134, 153, 176, 177, 191, 200, 202–203, 208, 212, 215, 219–222
Brezhnev, Leonid 10, 47, 50, 59, 70, 166, 170, 191, 192, 193–194
Brezhnev Doctrine 192
Bridges, Henry Styles 140, 145
Brokhin, Yuri 63
Brundage, Avery 3–4, 6, 8, 10, 11, 12, 13–18, 20–22, 23–24, 36, 57, 58, 61, 75–78, 83–86, 89–90, 92–93, 95–96, 97–100, 101–102, 104, 106, 108–09, 113, 114–115, 116, 119–120, 122–126, 128, 132–134, 135, 139, 147–148, 150–153, 154–155, 163, 166, 175, 177–180, 182, 184, 198–201, 203–204, 206, 208–210, 211, 213, 215–218, 220, 222, 224, 225, 226, 227, 228
Bucher, Charles 120–121
Buchwald, Art 207
Bulgaria 79, 148, 149, 154, 160, 187, 206
Burghley, Lord 91, 108
Bushnell, Ava 126
Butler, John Marshall 121–122

Carlos, John   24, 189, *190*, 208, 209
Carter, Jimmy   8, 32, 212, 219–220
Castro, Fidel   168
Central Committee of the Communist Party   57
Central Intelligence Agency (CIA)   37, 38, 127–128, 142, 159, 169
Chernenko, Konstantin   221
China   8, 40, 71, 148, 166, 172
Churchill, Winston   55, 75
civil rights   7, 46, 175, 190, 191, 192, 208–209
Cleary, Bob   68, 156
Collins, Bud   78, 189
Communist Youth International (Comintern)   52
Conference on the Fitness of American Youth   36, 41
Connolly, James   30
Considine, Bob   90, 91
Crosby, Bing   103
Cuba   161, 169
Cuban Missile Crisis   48, 50, 70, 166, 167, 168–169, 174, 183, 188, 189, 193, 194, 197
Czechoslovakia   21, 24, 54–55, 90, 99, 153, 156, 157, 192, 194, 204, 207, 209, 228

Daily Worker   81–82
Daley, Arthur   38, 65, 78, 80, 81–83, 95, 104–105, 107, 110–111, 135, 147, 162–163, 171, 180, 185, 186, 187, 203, 212
Danzig, Allison   112
Daume, Willi   152–153, 176–177, 198–199, 201
de Balliet-Latour, Henri   13
de Coubertin, Baron Pierre   1, 4, 6, 10–13, 14, 16–19, 23, 29, 30, 52, 74, 75, 83, 90, 92, 93, 97, 105, 123, 165, 225, 228
Denlinger, Ken   220
détente   9–10, 191, 193–194, 198, 205, 214, 215
Deutscher Turn and Sport Bund   151
Dobrynin, Anatoly   *168*
Dropping the Torch   8
Dulles, Allen   37
Dulles, John Foster   37, 39, 148

East German National Olympic Committee (NOC)   109, 122–125, 147, 150–154, 178, 198–200
Edel, Kurt   123
Edstrom, J. Sigfrid   13–14, 74, 86–87, 88, 90, 91–93, 95, 97–100, 109–110, 128
Eisenhower, Dwight   8, 9, 35–38, 41, 43–44, 47, 62, 86, 115, 118–119, 129–131, 136, 138, 142–143, 144, 146–147, 155, 156, *159*, 163, 171, 172, 173, 174, 182, 194, 195, 196–197

Emergency Fund for International Affairs   35
Ericson, Tage   98
Espy, Richard   8
Executive Order 11117   42

FIFA   5, 51, 53–54, 55–56, 69, 201
Five-Year Plan   60
Ford, Gerald   10
Foreman, George   208
France   11–12, 50, 55, 87, 99, 101, 108, 131–132, 142, 148, 157, 179, 180, 201
Fulbright program   9, 25

German Democratic Republic (GDR)   10, 41, 50, 62, 77, 91, 97, 109–110, 122–126, 127, 129, 140–142, 148, 151–156, 157–158, 175–177, 178, 179–181, 187, 191, 198, 199–201, 205, 211, 214–215, 217, 221, 222, 223, 225, 226; East German National Olympic Committee (NOC)   109, 122–125, 147, 150–154, 178, 198–200
German Federal Republic (GFR)   108, 109–110, 122–126, 141, 148, 157, 175–177, 181, 187, 198, 199–200, 201, 214, 220; West German National Olympic Committee (NOC)   77, 109, 151–153, 155, 177–178, 200, 201
German representation   8, 20, 24, 41, 75, 76–77, 90–91, 93, 96–97, 108–110, 117, 122–126, 127, 128–129, 132, 140, 141, 142, 147–148, 150–155, 158, 163, 166–167, 175–180, 188, 191, 197–202, 205, 211, 214–215, 217, 226
Germany   3, 7, 8, 10, 13, 20, 32, 50, 52, 55, 74–75, 83, 87, 91, 93, 96, 108, 122, 128, 152, 157, 163, 169, 178, 214
Globalizing Sport: National Rivalry and International Community in the 1930s   5–6
Gorbachev, Mikhail   222
Great Britain   2, 12, 14, 20, 26, 55–56, 57, 65, 87, 89–90, 95, 105, 108, 131–132, 148, 179, 201
Great Depression   19–20, 32
Greece   18, 29, 30, 79
Griffiths, Martha W.   *43*
Gromyko, Andrei   106, *168*
GTO badge   64
gymnastics   55, 112, 135, 161, 183, 186, 196

Hampton, Janie   7
Harriman, Averell   121
Hart, Philip A.   *43*
Harvard University   18, 30, 182
The Heavens and the Earth   8, 145
Hegyi, Gyula   138
Heiss, Carol   156

Herter, Christian 155–156
Hitler, Adolf 6, 13, 14, 20, 86, 90, 93, 115, 147
hockey 2, 29, 40–41, 53, 59, 63, 68, 73, 78, 148, 156, 157, 163, 179, 180, 182, 184, 204, 220
Honey, Reginald 202
Hoover, Herbert 20, 32
Hope, Bob 103
House of Commons 87
Humphrey, Hubert 181–182, 184, 191, 196–197
Hungarian Athletes' Freedom Tour 138
Hungarian National Sports Foundation 109, 169
Hungarian Revolution 24, 40, 77, 116–117, 121, 127, 129–131, 132, 133–135, 136–139, 145, 148, 158, 203, 204, 209, 224
Hungary 90, 99, 117, 126, 159, 180, 192, 203

Iba, Hank 185–186
Igniting the Flame: America's First Olympic Team 18
Interagency Committee on International Athletics 42
International Cultural Exchange and Trade Fair Act of 1956 38
International Olympic Committee (IOC) 3, 4, 5, 7, 8, 10, 13, 14, 16–18, 19, 20–22, 23, 41, 51, 52, 54, 57, 58, 72–73, 74, 75, 76–77, 78, 83, 86–93, 95–98, 99–100, 102, 106, 108, 109–110, 115, 116, 117, 118, 119, 122–128, 132–134, 140, 145, 147–151, 152–156, 158, 165–167, 175, 177–180, 184, 187, 189, 191, 197–205, 208–210, 213–214, 215, 216, 217–220, 222, 223, 225, 226; Executive Committee 13, 97, 108, 123, 217
Israel 131, 211, 217, 219, 223, 225–226
Izvestia 81, 110

Jackson, C.D. 137
Jaffee, Irving 156
Japan 7, 74, 78, 83, 91, 143, 166, 188, 217, 220
Johnson, Lyndon B. 33, 40, 45–47, 70, 166, 168, 169, 174, 181–184, 190, 191–193, 194, 195–197, 208
Johnson, Rafer 158, 162

Kazansky, Igor 204
Kennan, George 79
Kennedy, John F. 8, 9, 25–26, 35, 36, 41–45, 46, 47–48, 62, 86, 144, 150, 156, 163, 165, 167–169, *168*, 170–174, 175, 180, 182, 186, 188, 191, 193, 194, 195, 196–197, 198
Kennedy, Robert F. 25, 171, 182–184, 186, 191, 198, 224

Keys, Barbara 5, 6, 15, 26
Khrushchev, Nikita 49, 50, 59, 70–71, 120, 121, 129–130, 141–144, 147–148, 157, *159*, 161, 167, 169–170, 174, 175, 188, 191, 193
Killanin, Lord 10, 99, 212, 213–214, 216, 218–220
Killy, Jean-Claude 204
Kiselyov, Roman 198
"Kitchen Debate" *143*, 144
Kobes, Frank J., Col. 39
Korean War 42–43, 96, 117, 131, 146
Korobkov, Gabriel 209
Kremlin 9, 27, 28, 33, 35, 39, 50, 51–52, 53–54, 55, 56, 59, 62, 65, 68, 71, 78, 79, 81, 96, 97, 100, 103, 109, 111, 120–121, 129, 130, 133, 135, 145–146, 158, 164, 169–170, 173, 181, 182, 187–188, 192, 203, 208, 209, 210, 218, 219, 221

Laguerre, Andre 137
Lake Placid 20, 32
League of Nations 19
Lenin, Vladimir 52
Lenin Stadium 40, 60, 66, 69, 149
Leningrad 60, 66
Lentz, Arthur 160, 162–163, 181–182
Levine, Irving 58, 68
Lewis, Jerry 103
Life 37
Lipsyte, Robert 196
"The Long Telegram" 79
Los Angeles 19, 32, 89, 111, 197, 220, 221
Luce, Henry 36–37, 38, 136–138, 155

MacArthur, Douglas 45
Main Street, USSR 58
Major League Baseball 32
Maraniss, David 7
March for Peace *193*
Marshall Plan *84*, 85
Martin, Dean 103
Master of Sports of the USSR 64
Mathias, Bob 114
Mayer, Otto 99–100, 108, 123–124, 149, 150, 178
McCarthy, Joseph 96, 107, 121, 145
McDougall, Walter 8, 145
"Miracle on Ice" 220
Molotov-Ribbontrop Pact 55
Morrow, Bobby 135
Moscow Dynamo 55–56, 66
Moscow World Youth Festival 149
Musel, Robert 88

Nadori, Laszlo 137
Nagy, Imry 40

Nasser, Gamal Abdel 131
National Aeronautics and Space Administration (NASA) 144, 161, 173
National Collegiate Athletic Association 27, 29, 33, 41, 44–45, 46, 62, 65, 66, 171
National Football League 33
National Security Council 131
Netherlands 132–133
New York Herald 30
New York Times 14, 56, 65, 81, 82, 91, 95, 98, 103, 104, 106, 107, 110, 112, 114, 147, 154, 157, 162, 171, 184, 185, 196, 207, 212, 218, 221
New Yorker 16
Newell, Pete 1, 21, 160
Nixon, Richard 10, 47, 121, 138, *143*, 144, 163, 191, 192, 194, 206
Norman, Pete *190*
North Atlantic Treaty Organization (NATO) 6, 41, 96, 123, 167, 175, 178–179, 199, 200, 201, 214, 217
North Korea 178, 211, 222
Norway 165, 204, 206
Nuclear Test Ban Treaty 169, 188, 193

Office of Policy Coordination 38
Olympic Day 119
Olympic Fund Telethon (1952) 103
Olympic Games: Summer—1896, 11, 12, 16, 18–19, 29–30, 50, 214; 1900, 18–19, 30, 50; 1904, 18–19, 50; 1908, 18–19, 50; 1912, 14, 19, 50, 51, 105; 1916, 19; 1920, 13, 19, 50, 77, 90, 93, 97; 1924, 19, 51; 1928, 13, 60, 77, 113; 1932, 19; 1936, 4, 5–6, 13, 14, 15, 17, 20, 54, 74, 90, 110, 115, 147, 204; 1940, 89; 1948, 7, 13, 20, 34, 58, 66, 73, 74–96, 101, 104, 108, 111–112, 113, 114, 116, 122, 128, 205, 213, 215, 224; 1952, 5, 7, 21, 22, 28, 50, 51, 56, 59, 62, 77, 86, 88, 93–94, 95–116, 117, 119, 120, 122, 187, 223, 224; 1956, 16, 38, 45, 56, 60, 61, 62, 64, 65, 109–110, 115, 116–139, 140, 141, 144, 148, 149–150, 152, 181, 185, 188, 204, 224; 1960, 1, 7, 25, 45, 65, 126, 129, 136, 139, 140–164, 165, 167, 171, 185, 186–187, 188, 189, 224; 1964, 25, 40, 45, 46, 57, 61, 141, 144, 164, 165–189, 196, 197, 198, 199, 202, 204; 1968, 3, 9, 10, 16, 20, 23–24, 40, *43*, 73, 174, 188, 189–212, 217, 226; 1972, 10, 199, 200, 201–202, 211, 212, 213, 214, 217–218, 226; 1976, 66, 218–219; 1980, 8, 32, 66, 100, 117, 194, 212, 215, 219–220; 1984, 21, 111, 215, 220–222; 1988, 222–223; 1992, 222, 223, 227; 1996, 227; 2016, 227; Winter—1932, 20, 32; 1948, 91; 1952, 102, 103; 1956, 125, 156–157; 1960, 2, 29, 41,

68, 72, 119, 139, 140, 147, 148, 149, 151–157, 175, 179, 180; 1964, 164, 166, 174, 175, 177, 180–181, 182, 186, 196, 205; 1968, 149, 180, 199, 201, 203, 204–205, 206; 1972, 217; 1976, 218–219; 1980, 220; 1992, 223; 1994, 222; 2006, 227; 2014, 227
Olympic medal count 6, 9, 23, 26, 30, 45, 59–60, 73, 86, 91, 95, 110, 112–113, 120, 122, 135–136, 141, 146, 156, 158, 161–162, 180, 182–183, 184, 185, 186–187, 188, 189, 196–197, 204, 205, 210, 220–221, 223, 225
Operation Nightingale 128
Orth, Franklin 184
Owens, Jesse 14, 74

Palestinian Liberation Organization (PLO) 10, 215, 217
People to People Sports Committee 38
Physical Culture and Sports 64
Physical Culture Council 53, 54
Physical Fitness Leadership Awards Program 46
Poland 79, 90, 99, 129–130, 192
The Politics of the Olympic Games 8
Pompidou, Georges 201
Povich, Shirley 34–35, 38, 78, 81, 83, 105–106, 186, 206
Power and Protest 10
Power, Politics, and the Games 7
Powers, Gary 142–43, 158
Prague Spring 21, 24, 47, 192–194, 203, 204, 207–208, 209, 228
Pravda 81, 105, 110, 162, 186
President's Advisory Council on Universal Training 34
President's Challenge 35, 44, 47, 144
President's Citizens Advisory Committee on the Fitness of American Youth 36
President's Council on Fitness 41, 43–44, 45, 163, 171, 196
President's Special International Program 119
"Progress Report from the President on Physical Fitness" 42
Princeton University 30
Prokopov, Vladimir 116–117
Propaganda 6, 9, 21, 27, 29, 37, 47, 53, 55, 58, 63, 67, 72, 73, 78, 81, 85, 95, 98, 101–100, 103, 107, 109, 118, 128, 132, 137–139, 144, 149, 160, 161–164, 171, 172–173, 174, 177, 184, 187, 188, 203, 209, 210, 217, 218
Public Law 159 103
Public Law 344 104
Putin, Vladimir 227

Radio Free Europe 131, 194, 218, 219
Reagan, Ronald 222

Red Army 58, 116, 117, 129–130, 192
Red Sport International 52
Reisler, Jim 18
Rhodesia 219
Riley, Jack 68, 156
Ritter von Halt, Karl 108–09, 124–125, 126, 151, 177
Rodis, Nicholas 182–183
Rogge, Jacques 119
Romanov, Alexi 109
Rome 1960 7
Roosevelt, Franklin 20, 32, 79, 121
Rudolph, Wilma 162
Russell, Bill 65, 135
Russia (pre–Soviet) 2, 50–51
Russian Revolution 2, 50, 79, 105
Russo-Japanese War 50
Ryan, Harold M. *43*

Salisbury, Harrison 114
Samaranch, Juan Antonio 216, 220–221, 222, 223
Sarantakes, Nicholas Evan 8
Schobel, Hans 125, 126, 150–151, 154, 198–200
Schwartz, Harry 98–99
Semenov, Vladimir *168*
Senate Joint Resolution 51 119
Senn, Albert 7, 8
Shakhlin, Boris 61
Sime, David 159
Sino-Soviet split 71, 170, 174
Sloane, Edward 29
Smith, Red 16, 180, 218
Smith, Tommie 24, 189, *190*, 208, 209
soccer 5, 26, 27, 29, 33, 49, 51, 53, 54, 55–56, 57, 59, 62, 63, 66, 67, 69–70, 73, 135, 162, 179, 183, 185, 196, 215
South Africa 202–203, 204, 208, 211, 219
Sovetsky Sport 54, 69, 70, 81, 106–107, 184
Soviet National Olympic Committee (NOC) 57, 88, 96, 100, 109, 111, 147, 150, 198, 202–204, 221
Soviet News Booklet 62
Soviet Socialist Republics 53, 60, 77, 126
Soviet Sports Ministry 27
space race 8–9, 25, 28, 42–43, 48, 71, 80, 82, 140, 144, 145–146, 161, 164, 167, 169, 173–174
Spain 97, 132–133, 200
Spartakiad 60–61, 62, 66, 70, 72, 182–183, 198
spectators 6, 7, 18, 19, 23, 26, 27, 29, 31–32, 33, 38, 39, 40, 41, 47, 48, 49, 53, 55, 61, 62, 63, 66, 69–70, 71, 80, 89, 103, 156, 163, 166, 172, 173, 205, 206, 213, 215, 216, 224, 227
Sport in the USSR 70, 198, 200, 202, 209

Sportintern 51, 52, 53, 60
Sports Illustrated 16, 25, 28, 36–38, 39, 40, 44, 47, 48, 61, 65, 70, 120–121, 133–134, 135, 136–139, 155, 161, 170–171, 172, 182, 198, 205–206, 215
"Sports of the Times" 81, 162
sports writing 10, 27, 28, 38, 48, 60, 64, 78, 80–83, 88, 98, 104, 106, 112, 113, 137, 154–156, 161, 163, 171, 172–173, 180, 183, 184, 186, 187, 195, 200, 201–202, 206–207, 208–209, 210–211, 213, 215, 218, 219, 220
Sputnik 144, 145, 161, 173, 174
Staebler, Neil *43*
Stalin, Joseph 3, 27, 29, 32, 33, 37, 49, 50–51, 52–53, 54, 55, 56, 58, 59, 60, 61, 71–72, 76, 78–79, 85, 86, 89, 96, 97–98, 101, 102, 103, 104, 105, 117, 119, 129, 141, 161
State Committee for Physical Culture and Sport 51, 52
Stull, Dorothy 38–39
Suez Canal 116, 117, 131–132
Suri, Jeremi 10
Susman, Warren 26
Sweden 41, 50, 91, 98, 156, 179
swimming 27, 63, 162, 186, 188, 196, 206, 224
Switzerland 19, 60, 132–133, 153, 157

Taiwan 147
Taylor, Maxwell 34
television 17, 23–24, 33, 47, 58, 78, 80–81, 103, 113, 120, 140, 164, 166, 189, 205–206, 213, 214, 215, 216, 218, 222, 226
tennis 27, 34–35, 55, 66
Ter-Ovanesyan, Igor 159
Thorpe, Jim 105
Tlatelolco Plaza 195
track and field 14, 23, 29, 39–40, 48, 53, 55, 60, 63, 64, 66, 67, 78, 89, 91, 105, 111, 112, 114, 120, 135, 149, 156, 157, 159, 162, 186, 187, 189, 190, 196, 197, 200, 206, 207, 208, 209, 210, 224
trade union 62–63
Truman, Harry S. 32, 33–34, 35, 36, 41, 43, 47, 56, 58, 78–79, 85–86, 96, 101–102, 104, 114–115, 118, 119, 144, 192, 197
Truman Doctrine 79, 194
Turkey 79
Turner, Gerald 135

U-2 incident 142–143, *142*, 144, 158, 159, 161, 197
Ukrainian Olympic Committee (UOC) 109, 117, 126–129, 150, 155
Ukrainian Soviet Socialist Republic 77, 93
Ukrainian World Committee for Sport Affairs 126

Ulbricht, Walter 158, 175
United Nations (UN) 77, 86, 87, 93, 116, 126–127, 130, 131, 132, 138, 161, 192
United States Congress 27, 35, 72, 103, 104, 121, 145, 164, 173
United States Department of State 15, 41, 42, 128, 148–149, 154, 155–156, 157, 179, 182, 197, 218, 221
United States Information Agency (USIA) 38, 118, 159, 160
United States Military Academy, West Point 34, 38–39, 103
United States National Security Administration 195
United States Olympic Association 7, 83, 85–86, 89, 102, 115, 118, 119, 120, 121, 136, 141, 154, 160, 216, 224
United States Olympic Committee 3, 9, 27, 32, 38, 46, 51, 57, 58, 66, 106, 107, 111, 126, 145, 171, 181, 184, 185, 208, 219
United States Olympic Development Committee 196
USA Hockey 148

Vietnam 33, 40, 43, 45, 46, 166, 169, 175, 191, 192, 192, 193, 197, 202–203, 208, 209, 210
volleyball 40, 183

Warsaw Pact 6, 35, 36, 148, 193
Washington Post 34, 81, 83, 90, 98, 105, 136, 158, 160, 187, 196, 204, 206, 220

water polo 116–117, 139, 224
West German National Olympic Committee (NOC) 77, 109, 151–153, 155, 177–178, 200, 201
West German Ski Association 153
Westerhoff, J.W. 200
White House 8, 9, 12, 19, 20, 22, 27, 28, 29, 32, 34, 36, 41, 42, 46, 47, 48, 63, 79, 82, 85, 100–101, 131, 136, 155, 164, 169, 171, 181, 184, 185, 192, 195, 196, 197, 208, 209, 210
Williamson, Samuel 106
Wilson, Kenneth 119, 171
Woolson, L. I. 121
Workers Olympics 52, 53, 54, 55, 60, 72
World Championships (basketball) 64, 65, 147, 160
World Tennis Association 34–35
World War I 13, 19, 31, 74, 77, 90
World War II 2, 3, 7, 13, 14, 20, 21, 27, 29, 32, 34, 36, 37, 39, 42, 43, 45, 47, 48, 50, 51, 53, 54, 55, 57, 59, 65, 66, 68, 69, 71, 74–75, 76–77, 83, 85, 86, 93, 108, 115, 130, 137, 143, 145, 166, 182, 225
Wrestling 40, 112, 135, 160

Yugoslavia 90, 99, 117

Zador, Ervin 116–117
Zapotek, Emil 112